SELDOM ASK, NEVER TELL

Oxford Studies in Anthropological Linguistics
William Bright, General Editor

Recent Volumes Published

6 Rosaleen Howard-Malverde (ed.): *Creating Context in Andean Cultures*

7 Charles L. Briggs (ed.): *Disorderly Discourse: Narrative, Conflict, and Inequality*

8 Anna Wierzbicka: *Understanding Cultures through Their Key Words: English, Russian, Polish, German, and Japanese*

9 Gerrit J. van Enk and Lourens de Vries: *The Korowai of Irian Jaya: Their Language in Its Cultural Context*

10 Peter Bakker: *A Language of Our Own: The Genesis of Michif, the Mixed Cree-French Language of the Canadian Métis*

11 Gunter Senft: *Referring to Space: Studies in Austronesian and Papuan Languages*

12 David McKnight: *People, Countries, and the Rainbow Serpent: Systems of Classification among the Lardil of Mornington Island*

13 Andrée Tabouret-Keller, Robert B. Le Page, Penelope Gardner-Chloros, and Gabrielle Varro (eds.): *Vernacular Literacy Revisited*

14 Steven Roger Fischer: *Rongorongo, the Easter Island Script: History, Traditions, Text*

15 Richard Feinberg: *Oral Traditions of Anuta: A Polynesian Outlier in the Solomon Islands*

16 Bambi Schieffelin, Kathryn A Woolard, and Paul Kroskrity (eds.): *Language Ideologies: Practice and Theory*

17 Susan U. Philips: *Ideology in the Language of Judges: How Judges Practice Law, Politics, and Courtroom Control*

18 Spike Gildea: *On Reconstructing Grammar: Comparative Cariban Morphosyntax*

19 Laine A. Berman: *Speaking through the Silence: Narratives, Social Conventions, and Power in Java*

20 Cecil H. Brown: *Lexical Acculturation in Native American Languages*

21 James M. Wilce: *Eloquence in Trouble: The Poetics and Politics of Complaint in Rural Bangladesh*

22 Peter Seitel: *The Powers of Genre: Interpreting Haya Oral Literature*

23 Elizabeth Keating: *Power Sharing: Language, Rank, Gender, and Social Space in Pohnpei, Micronesia*

24 Theodore B. Fernald and Paul Platero (eds.): *Athabaskan: Language and Linguistics*

25 Anita Puckett: *Seldom Ask, Never Tell: Labor and Discourse in Appalachia*

SELDOM ASK, NEVER TELL

LABOR AND DISCOURSE IN APPALACHIA

Anita Puckett

OXFORD
UNIVERSITY PRESS

2000

OXFORD
UNIVERSITY PRESS

Oxford New York
Athens Auckland Bangkok Bogotá Buenos Aires Calcutta
Cape Town Chennai Dar es Salaam Delhi Florence Hong Kong Istanbul
Karachi Kuala Lumpur Madrid Melbourne Mexico City Mumbai
Nairobi Paris São Paulo Shanghai Singapore Taipei Tokyo Toronto Warsaw

and associated companies in
Berlin Ibadan

Published by Oxford University Press, Inc.
198 Madison Avenue, New York, New York 10016

Library of Congress Cataloging-in-Publication Data
Puckett, Anita, 1949–
Seldom ask, never tell : labor and discourse in Appalachia /
Anita Puckett.
p. cm.—(Oxford studies in anthropological linguistics ; 25)
Includes bibliographical references and index.
ISBN 0-19-510277-0
1. Appalachian Region—Social conditions. 2. Appalachian Region—
Economic conditions. 3. Sociology, Urban—United States. I. Title. II. Series.
HN79.A127 .P83 2000
306'.0974—dc21 99-040241

9 8 7 6 5 4 3 2 1

Printed in the United States of America
on acid-free paper

For Ralph Clinton Puckett

PREFACE

This book is probative. Using information obtained through linguistic anthropological approaches to ethnographic fieldwork, it explores how ways of requesting in a rural coalfield Appalachian community construct a local socioeconomy. Responding to recent and theoretically reorienting advances in linguistic anthropology, it asserts necessary, irreducible relationships between verbal and material forms when people engage in socioeconomic behavior. To separate the material from the verbal in these instances of socioeconomic communication, to focus only upon how commodities, goods, and services are consumed, circulated, and produced, is either to dehumanize those individuals (or groups) who initiate or receive the result of such processes, or it is to impose the analyst's own conception of the motivating factors in such material transactions. To focus only on the verbal invites similar critiques of an analyst's imposition of his or her own system of meaning to socioeconomic communicative events. For socially involved, interacting individuals, socioeconomic communicative events reproduce or create behavior meaningful to them. How these meanings are "contextualized" in specific socioeconomic communications and "entextualized," or lifted from specific events so they can be talked about or "retextualized" in other verbal genres, could be the major goal of this work.

But this task is impossible, given the ascessibility of most coalfield Appalachian communities to new patterns of marketing commodities and services. Residents' own efforts to adapt or adjust to different job markets also preclude a totally closed, static system of language and socioeconomic relations. This book therefore focuses on how tropes, expressions, and other conventionalized verbal forms (metapragmatic designators) designate and interpret imperatives and other speech forms that effect a division of labor for the production, circulation, and consumption of resources in the rural eastern Kentucky community I have given the pseudonym of Ash Creek. These serve two contrasting major purposes: first, they provide a dynamic, interactive means for residents to negotiate how to categorize a specific socioeconomic communication. Second, they can be entextualized into more "textual" verbal practices such as humorous "tales" or sacred "prayers." These entextualizations connect the specific socioeconomic communications these expressions index to overtly political, moral, or religious verbal genres and construct a rich, complex, and constantly reassessed ideology of socioeconomic communication. To those who would appreciate either more detailed micro-analyses of specific communicative events than this work attempts or would prefer more careful analysis of performative verbal genres, my apologies. The focus of this work, however, precludes it.

However, the focus of this book is not only theoretical issues. I have life-long experiences with urban Appalachians who commonly call themselves "hillbillies," "country folks," or "briars." Their efforts at "makin a place" for themselves in the industrial cities of southwestern Ohio has been a deeply felt and sometimes very personal quest. Their frequently cited expression "ain't nobody tellin me what to do" has heartfelt meaning for them and for those in Ash Creek as well. Exploring this expression's contribution to the constitution of a local ideology of socioeconomic communication motivated my research.

When I have presented portions of this work publicly, one or more members of the audience commonly say, in reference to my examples and sometimes with agitation, "that's not just in Appalachia." Of course not. Linguistic anthropological research and the entextualization of the discursive interactions that constitute it into a published, publicly accessible forum not only shed light on theoretical understandings of a particular subject matter but also suggests interconnections to other fields, other approaches, and, in the case of linguistic anthropological ethnographic studies, speech-in-use in other communities and regions. In the case of Ash Creek and Appalachian communities similar to it, the social-historical context from which their present patterns emerge supports, rather than contradicts, full or partial overlap with language and socioeconomic relations in other communities and regions of the United States. This book does describe differences, sometimes significant differences, from those reported for more urban, professional language and socioeconomic relations. These differences do not preclude similarities. Perhaps these similarities are highly significant and can shed light on workplace and community language and socioeconomic contestations or conflict elsewhere.

To reach as broad an audience as possible, I have relegated many theoretical points and observations not critical to developing the basic argument to the endnotes, and have attempted to use technical jargon infrequently, only when necessary. The work does assume a stance toward language different from what many are accustomed to and therefore requires a certain amount of grounding in theoretical concepts. Many of the endnotes are glosses to explain how I am using some of these terms. Each chapter begins with one or more anecdotes based on my Ash Creek experiences. They are intended as framing devices in Goffman's (1967) sense of providing "footing" to the following discussion. They should not be viewed with the same linguistic rigor as the transcriptions of audiorecorded speech included in chapters for discussion.

Portions of chapter 3 appeared in two other works of mine (Puckett 1995; 1998). Some of the discussion and transcriptions concerning instructions in chapter 7 appeared previously in the 1998 work. Permission to reuse this material has been granted by the Center for Appalachian Studies and Services at East Tennessee State University and by SUNY Press.

I lived in Ash Creek from June 1985 to August 1987 and have returned frequently since then. From August 1987 to August 1993, I lived in areas adjacent to Ash Creek (except for one year) and could visit, telephone, or hear about residents regularly. Now I return when I can. I am deeply grateful to the people of Ash Creek who allowed me to enter their homes and their private lives to ask questions, tape talk, and generally to get in their way in order to write still another "book" about them. Their ability to see into my heart and beyond the goals of my study is something I treasure. In particular, I "owe" Bill, Sarah, Debbie, Linda, and Sandy (using pseudonyms that appear in the book and are annotated in Appendix A) a debt that can never be removed for their patience and kindness. They spent hundreds of hours working, listening, and talking with me. To Millie, I give thanks for being a sounding board who would listen and respond to my thoughts about community and language relations. To the administration and staff of the Environmental Center, my appreciation for allowing me to become your ethnographer-in-residence. To other members of Ash Creek who also tolerated so many questions, so much intrusion, thanks. For those who kindly gave me their love, I will gladly "do for" as best as I am able as long as I am able.

The research has generously been supported by several institutions that provided research grants. Loyal Jones and Berea College kindly awarded a Melon Foundation Appalachian Studies Fellowship. Other support was forthcoming from the National Science Foundation and a Virginia Polytechnic Institute and State University Arts and Sciences research travel grant. I am indebted to the faculty, staff, and students of Southeast Community College who provided professional and personal support for the writing of the dissertation portion of this project, allowed me to ask more questions and record their verbal interactions, and commented on local speech and economic patterns useful to this research.

This manuscript is indebted to the contribution of others who commented on it or took an active role in shaping its final form. I thank members of the anthropology and linguistics faculty of the University of Texas at Austin who shaped my thinking, encouraged my research, and commented so helpfully on this manuscript. These include, but are not limited to, Joel Sherzer, who convinced me it could be done and others that it had merit; Greg Urban whose theoretical insights provide a means for understanding how language-in-use "means"; Anthony Woodbury, whose linguistic abilities are beyond the exemplary; James Brow, who provided sound economic anthropological critiques; and Katie Stewart, who supported the last stages of the dissertation writing period. I am permanently indebted to Jane Hill for her input in writing this manuscript and continued support and to Shirley Brice Heath for her kind and useful evaluation of the manuscript, both as reviewers for Oxford University Press. Elizabeth Fine has been not only a supportive colleague in the pursuit of Appalachian Studies at Virginia Polytechnic Institute and State University but a serious and thoughtful critic as well.

Sincere thanks to Bill Bright, series editor, and Peter Ohlin, Oxford University Press editor, for their input into the preparation of this book. I could not have finished this manuscript without the tireless assistance of those friends and colleagues who assisted in manuscript preparation: Kathy Wager, Ben Logan, Mary Rhoades, and Anne Daugherty.

Finally, my heartfelt gratitude is extended to those family members who shaped my thinking about Appalachia or have continually supported me in my efforts to write about "the Mountains." This is especially true of my father, to whom this work is dedicated.

Blacksburg, Virginia A. P.
November 1999

CONTENTS

NOTE ON TRANSCRIPTION

Discourse transcribed for this work comes from approximately 180 hours of audiotaped speech occurring in routine, daily work and social conversational settings. As a generally spontaneous if not conversational set of data, it is most appropriately transcribed using methods developed in conversational analysis. I modified slightly the system developed by DuBois et al. (1993).

Ash Creek speech does conform, however, to features diagnostic of Appalachian English (Shopen and Williams 1980; C. Williams 1992; Wolfram and Christian 1976; Wolfram and Schilling-Estes 1998). Therefore, problems related to transcribing a highly stigmatized variety of American English also arose. The problems are complicated by the long-standing existence of both stylized and misleading orthographic representations in regional and local color fictional writing and popularized distortions of "hillbilly talk" found in pamphlets obtainable at roadside tourist stops or in newspaper cartoons. These preexisting orthographic distortions have their own well established semiotic meanings in popular culture that evoke highly negative images of lazy, poor, ignorant, and intellectually challenged individuals. Certain orthographic features of these representations such as the use of the apostrophe to indicate an alleged letter omission or certain spellings such as "yeller" for "yellow" can carry some of these negative significations with them when used in a rigorous transcription such as I attempted here.

Using a dual transcriptional system in which a close phonetic transcription is paired with a standardized English orthographic rendition is also unsuitable. Such dualities recreate a sense of "Other" with respect to Ash Creek speech. Ash Creek speech is a variety of American English, not a separate language. Many words are pronounced in ways conforming to national newscasters' pronunciations of Standard Broadcast American English. Using this type of transcriptional system would exaggerate linguistic differences for little scholarly purpose while reproducing a widely accepted and weakly substantiated sense of significant cultural differences.

I therefore chose to use standard American English orthography when it conformed to Ash Creek speech. Some dialectal variants, such as "holler," have accepted spellings in standard dictionaries or in the *Dictionary of American Regional English* (DARE). I used these spellings for variants if they are recorded in one of these authorized sources.

I did not transcribe individual phonetic idiosyncrasies, but I did transcribe phonemic differences between Standard Broadcast American English preferences as noted in authoritative dictionary notation. For example, I transcribe orthographic "get" as "gIt," using the /I/ as a phonological notation rather than "i" for its orthographic representation. In some cases, /I/ is transcribed as /ɛ/ to indicate variation in the pronunciation of this sound. This variation indexes either a gender difference in which women tend to use /ɛ/ more than men, or, in some cases, a register shift to more proper speech, also more common in women's speech than men's. The occasional substitution of phonetic nomenclature for alphabetic letters is done to avoid some of the semiotic baggage created by popularized orthographies mentioned before.

For similar reasons, I also omitted using an apostrophe at the end of present participles to indicate, as many put it, the loss of the final "g" in words such as "laughing," "crying," and "belonging" so that they are not transcribed as "laughin'," "cryin'," and "belongin'." In English speech, there is a phonemic difference between the velar /ng/ and the alveolar /n/. They are recognized as two different sounds. Ash Creek residents never use /ng/ to end present participles in everyday speech; there is no spoken variation between the two phonemes. Therefore, it is appropriate to transcribe present participles with only an /n/ and avoid the deficiency meanings associated with using the apostrophe to indicate "loss" of a letter or sound, which really is not a loss at all but a substitution.

Speech is transcribed in lines to capture intonational contours. As noted by DuBois et al. (1993) among others (e.g., Gumperz 1982; Hymes 1981; Sherzer 1987b; Woodbury 1987), speech among those accustomed to relying predominantly on oral communicative practices is organized in rhythm structures (contours) approximating poetic lines rather than in clauses or sentences. Ash Creek speakers conform to these expectations. Pauses at the end of lines vary for men and women. Men tend to take 3 to 6 second pauses; some take only 2 second pauses. Women take 1 to 3 with less than 1 common in some speakers. Certain nonstandard spellings were used to approximate the speed and rhythm of these contours. For example, I used "gonna" and "ɛm" for the standard orthographic "going to" and "him" when speakers' utterances approximated the pronounciation associated with these "allegro speech" representations. I did so to be more faithful to the intonation contours without sacrificing easy intelligibility—not, as Preston (1985:328) argues, to indicate slangy or not carefully monitored speech.

Notational features are oriented around intonations as well:

bold Text in bold indicates syntactic contructions pertinent to the focus of the chapter and to the immediate discussion.

—	A dash indicates that an intonational unit or word was truncated before completing its projected contour or sound unit. Generally, it means the speaker was interrupted or that there was no pause before another interlocutor spoke.
(4.0)	A number inside a single set of parentheses indicates the length of time, in seconds, between transcribed utterances. It is used when some type of interruption disrupts the flow of the speech segment under discussion.
((?1.0))	Indicates a period of unintelligible speech. The number indicates the number of seconds unintelligibility lasted.
((?lone?))	Indicates ambiguous or partially intelligible speech.
(*Setting*:)	Indicates annotation about components of the speech event such as setting, participants present, time, and location.
mine	Italics indicates a word or syllable emphasized more intensely than the intonation contour requires.
o:h	A colon indicates a lengthened sound segment, usually a vowel.
OH	Uppercase words indicate loudness or shouting.
[ ]	Single brackets below or beside a transcribed segment indicate intertextual annotation. Single brackets also indicate speech overlap to understandable segments of two speakers or multiple speakers talking at the same time.
.	A dot indicates a short pause of less than a normal line break similar to common recognition of comma placement.
. [or] ?	A period or question mark at the end of a line indicates the falling and rising pitch that corresponds to an indicative or interrogatory intonational phrasing.
Anita:	Every speaker has been given a pseudonym except for me (see Appendix A: Participants).
[100a:35 7/85]	A number sequence in brackets indicates audiotape reference notation: tape number, side, tape recorder counter number, and month/year of audio-recording.

The recorded tapes transcribed for this work were naturally occurring in work and other settings outside the home.

SELDOM ASK, NEVER TELL

1 INTRODUCTION

"I am just a simple man."

A foreman of a local work crew very rarely used any speech form but task-focused imperatives with his crew, in keeping with cultural rules of imperative uses. Once in midsummer, however, a worker indicated a "need" to take the weekend off and not cut grass because of an irritating skin ailment. The foreman suggested a solution involving wearing a different type of clothing and long sleeves; the worker indicated it was too hot. The foreman used a bald imperative construction: "You've got to work this weekend or I'll have to let you go." The worker resigned on the spot and was later reported by some to have harassed the foreman and sabotaged some equipment. [notes: 7/85]

A local man reported to me that an outsider visiting the Environmental Center had lobbied locals to put their land into a wildlife preserve; residents thought he was "orderin" them to give up their control over the use of their land; the outsider was warned by a neutral party, but felt that he was "right" and continued to talk about the project. His car was made inoperable, and he left the area soon after that. [notes: 8/85]

THESE ANECDOTES FROM COALFIELD APPALACHIA illustrate socioeconomic situations in which speakers of a highly stigmatized variety of American English contest, in fact, rebel against requests or demands from others to alter their control over two highly valued resources—labor and land. The examples seem to suggest that these individuals are easily upset or perhaps incapable of taking directives from anyone. Perhaps they are incapable of engaging in teamwork; perhaps they live by a "code" of violence in which human life is not valued; perhaps they are so "Other" that they cannot be assimilated into American capitalistic work procedures. Certainly these views have been applied to similar interactions involving Appalachian laborers. Such views have appeared in the popular press, in the offices and boardrooms of mining management, and in the entertainment media in an ongoing process of constructing Appalachian images.[1]

Perhaps a linguistic anthropological perspective has merit. These anecdotes are re-representations of fieldnotes of observed interactions recorded while I was living in a southeastern Kentucky community in the Appalachian coalfields I have given the pseudonym Ash Creek.[2] I found these contestations to be rare but strident in their aftermath because the nonlocal and local participants in them and the local residents hearing about them assessed them so differently. Perhaps they were interpreting the events from radically different perspectives. Perhaps certain verbal and nonverbal signs were functioning as contextualization cues to invoke different sets of presuppositions that participants "must rely on to . . . assess what is intended" (Gumperz 1992:230). Possibly these presuppositions were rooted in life trajectories in which request and demand contexts had been patterned differently, on occasion after occasion. Or these presuppositions may have reflected different semiotic experiences with the value of labor and of the goods or commodities that the utterance denoted or indexically referenced. Perhaps they were interpreting requests and demands by using processes not unlike those reported by linguistic anthropologists for other discursive practices among economically peripheral[3] regional or ethnic cultural groups in the United States (e.g., Basso 1979; Bauman 1986; Briggs 1988; Gumperz 1982; Heath 1983; Hill 1995; Philips 1993; see also Hill 1998 and Hill and Hill 1986 for a related Central Mexico discussion).

Perhaps, in both episodes, the verbal utterances sounded familiar to the participants and the grammatical forms were linguistically meaningful to them. Yet perhaps each reached a different conclusion about the event and the responses expected, based on interpretation of the contextual signs. What sounded like straightforward American English may not have been interpreted by each participant as the same English. Perhaps the Appalachian "native" was acting in socially responsible ways, or at least under culturally recognizable response patterns, given the interactional framework created by the sign functions within them. They were simply different from those of the speaker, leading to different outcomes. The locus of the labor problem may lie not solely in the character of the speakers but in the meanings assigned to the various elements in the communicative events. These constructed meanings may constitute different ideologies of socioeconomic communication that in turn implicate the construction of the cultural order.

Certainly such possibilities are not unheard of in linguistic anthropological circles and, in fact, have been a major contribution to the field since Hymes's (1972) reformulation of research from speaker-focused "competence" criteria to empirical, listener-focused "performance" representations as expressed in speaking events. Gumperz's (1982) ground-breaking examination showed how multiethnic participants in job interviews focused on different contextual variables (or "cues") and came to radically different interpretations of what the other was saying. Heath's (1982, 1983) ethnographic examination of "stories" and other narrative genres again showed how different components in Hymes's (1972, 1974a, 1974b) "speech events" affected the interpretation and social functions of them. The white community of Roadville in her South Carolina Piedmont work is, by some geographers' definitions, Appalachian (e.g., Raitz and Ulack 1984) and is therefore especially relevant to what I observed in Ash Creek. Much of her description of Roadville closely corresponds to Ash Creek, especially in terms of oral narrative structuring and community values for telling "true" stories.[4] Her scholarship points clearly to an active and educationally significant heteroglossia in Bakhtin's (1981) sense of multiple interpretations of speech that disrupt the dominant norms or at least call them into question. Both Gumperz and Heath make clear the disastrous effects of these different "interpretive schemes" (after Silverstein 1998:132) on simply gaining access to the resources and power that professional positions and educational success are perceived to offer to community residents.

Shifting the locus of analysis of contestative socioeconomic interactions to verbal and nonverbal interaction rather than issues of character provided a more objective, less culture-bound approach to my quest for answers to personal and professional questions related to why coalfield Appalachians are presumed, and I will argue erroneously presumed, to be so difficult to work with by many Americans. These presumptions have affected the incorporation of Appalachians into labor markets, have labeled them as psychologically distinct in their resistance to hierarchical corporate structures, and have created images of them as ready to destroy property with only slight provocation.[5]

This book is more than an attempt to shed light on Appalachian labor problems through analyses of verbal interactions under the powerful analytic tools currently offered by linguistic anthropology. A second thrust is theoretical. The ultimate goal is to contribute to linguistic anthropological knowledge of the *constitutive* role played by language-in-use in the construction and constitution of language and political economic relations. Irvine (1989), echoed in Friedrich (1989) and Gal (1989), noted that the copious body of scholarship on language and political economic relationships asserts that language's economic properties and meanings were only analogous to material ones. Therefore linguistic phenomena can be excluded from the economic realm. Central to the arguments offered in this book is Irvine's significant insight that language-in-use constructs contextual meanings that can, in turn, construct the semiotic valuation of both the division of labor and of material entities in multifunctional ways. Instead of simply being "like" some properties of material economic entities, language is an inseparable contextual force in constructing not just socioeconomic behavior, but socioeconomies. More generally, recent theoretical contributions have, in Duranti's word, "transformed" linguistic anthropology into a field in which practitioners use ethnographic methods of analysis, among others, to explore "communicative practices as *constitutive* of the culture of everyday life and [to] view . . . language as a powerful tool rather than a mirror of social realities established elsewhere" (1997:xv, italics mine). Speech-in-use is not only a set of transparent lenses that provide windows into cultural processes, practices, and meanings. Rather, it is recognized as multifunctional (Hymes 1972; Jakobson 1960; Silverstein 1976), multiplex in the sense of semiotically operating in multiple ways (Briggs 1988:80), yet evanescent substance out of which speakers construct the cultural order day after day, event after event, and utterance upon utterance.

In taking a stance in which Ash Creek communicative interactions are constitutive of a political economic order, I explore how verbal and material elements not only co-occur, but co-construct contextual, and therefore social, meanings in interactions. To focus this broad purpose, and to address the kinds of issues raised by the interactions noted at the beginning of this chapter, I explore the statement, "When someone asks (or demands) something, he or she *asks* for *some thing*." That is, I presume a culturally constructed self (or selves) engages in a type of interpersonal communicative interaction, which is also culturally constructed, to transfer the control or use of a material entity to control or use by another or to result in an exchange or in the performance of a task or labor activity by others. These material entities and labor are also culturally constructed.

Requests, demands, and ways of *seldom* asking and *never* telling (that is, commanding), offer interesting juxtapositions of verbal, interactional, and material interactions in Ash Creek. As Ervin-Tripp (1973 [1964]) first suggested and Irvine (1989:251) stated, "[W]ithin the linguistic system the study of directives (requests and commands) is especially relevant, because it concerns the verbal management of the flow of goods and services in an economy." When a person or persons require the acquisition or use of an entity or service, whether material or nonmaterial, and another person or persons control it in some form, then there must be some form of interaction between them to effect the transference (or nontransference) of it. The implications of this observation in the Ash Creek political-economic order become the guiding force for the content of subsequent chapters.

Requests as Political Economy

Briggs (1988:5) explained succinctly the relationship of linguistic anthropological theoretical scholarship to political economic theory: "Some ideas enter the intellectual landscape with great force, providing a common orientation for formerly disparate studies and motivating researchers to rethink old questions." Certainly this "rethinking" is causing a "Nekkar cube effect" in which "a switch in perception and perspective [allows] neglected, yet related, aspects of [various types of linguistic and cultural] phenomena to become newly visible" (Gal 1998:317). This burgeoning scholarship on linguistic ideologies provides a framework upon which to shape and reshape the significant developments in the ethnography of speaking traditions begun by Hymes (1964, 1972), Gumperz and Hymes (1972), and Bauman and Sherzer (1989 [1974]). Mertz (1998:151) suggests that "the study of linguistic ideology provides a much-needed bridge between linguistic and social theory because it relates the microculture of communicative action to political economic consideration of power and social inequality, confronting macrosocial constraints on language behavior."

The Ash Creek research leading to this writing has benefited from the explosion of these efforts. In 1985 my dissertation research applied ethnography of discourse approaches (after Sherzer 1987a) to construct a typology of verbal genres (for outstanding examples, see Briggs 1988; Gossen 1974; Sherzer 1983) of Ash Creek requesting practices. I used the concept of "ethnosemantic categories" in which "members of a community themselves categorize their own behavior" (Gumperz and Hymes 1972:106; see Frake 1972). I am now indebted to a number of recent works, especially Woolard's (1998) and Woolard and Schieffelin's (1994) remarkable synthesis of the theoretical implications of linguistic ideology as a guiding rubric for other theoretical works. Previously, I focused on microanalyses of verbal contexts to make relatively low-level inferences about the classification and function of requests and made *implications* about macroissues related to political economy. Now I am able to discuss ways of making *interconnections* among various discursive practices to constitute a political economy. For this reason, in this discussion I focus on how verbal and nonverbal communicative processes organize a division of labor and circulate commodities, goods, and services within Ash Creek. As relevant and pertinent as political economic theory may be to certain points of this discussion, I want to describe how the communications themselves, particularly verbal ones, create an arpeggio of meanings up and down the hierarchy of interlocking communicative constructions constituting political economic relations.

Some of the works in linguistic anthropology that have led to these current developments have refuted the Saussuerean dichotomy between material and verbal signs. These arguments demonstrate that speech-in-use can assume material properties and circulate as a "valued" resource (Gal 1989, 1998; Irvine 1989; Silverstein 1984) or become one of multiple sign modes within communicative events, including material ones. It can also intersect with other co-occurring nonverbal signs in communicative contexts in its constructions of complex heteroglossic significations,[6] which participants can draw on to construct a plurality of interpretations (Hanks 1990, 1992, 1996b; Haviland 1996a, 1996b). This scholarship allows me to consider "the utterance," or a minimal discursive unit spoken by an addresser in a labor exchange,[7] as one form of communication that can be compared to (but is not isomorphic with) other semiotic systems, including material ones, in a requesting event. Within Ash Creek, this distinction is critical, perhaps true of requests in labor situations universally (Ervin-Tripp 1973, 1976; Ervin-Tripp et al. 1987; Irvine 1989). Speech while one is engaged in choreographing manual activity is often minimal, structurally elliptic,[8] and in paradigmatic substitution with gestural or material exchanges. It is not organized in patterns consistent with conversation, although Ash Creek requests are often embedded within conversational exchanges. They exhibit their own interactional patterns.

In addition, incorporation of a Peircian semiotic framework to capture the nature of relationships between verbal or material signs and the kinds of meanings they signify has yielded extremely powerful reformulations of problems basic to the study of language, language-in-use, and the meanings of material entities circulating as components of a cultural order.[9] Central to most of this scholarship has been an elaboration and application of Peirce's semiotics, particularly of his formulation of the indexical sign. Indexes are "multidimensional" (Hanks 1996b:181) and exhibit spatial or temporal co-presence between the sign token and its meaning (Silverstein 1976). Parmentier (1994:17) further defines indexes as signs whose "grounds involve actual connection" or what some have considered "conventional" associations between sign and contextual meaning (see also Irvine 1998 and Lee 1997).

Indexical signs are now recognized as the semiotic glue that binds communicative activity to what Ochs (1992:341) has called "stances, social acts, [and] social activities" constructed in interactional contexts. These contextualized, or "pragmatic" meanings (after Levinson 1983), become the bricolage that metapragmatic communication glosses, comments upon, or directs interpretation of in complex ways within specific communicative events.

Metapragmatic forms can, in turn, function pragmatically and be interpreted by other metapragmatic discursive representations in an ordered but reflexive hierarchy of indexicality. Reflexivity between pragmatic and metapragmatic significations is constantly being reconstructed in communicative interactions. This total process (not the totality of the discursive forms) constitutes macrolevel understandings, explanations, or interpretations of portions of the cultural order, such as political economic ones (see Silverstein [1976, 1985, 1993, 1996a, 1998] for theoretically rigorous and expansive discussions of this process).

Far more than just unidirectional signs pointing to a single element in the context, or what Silverstein (1996a:269) considers "billiard ball" sociological models of indexicality,[10] indexical signs can also be embedded so that various components of the sound shape (phonological, morphological, phrasal, clausal, or rhetorical) can all function as co-occurring indexes (Duranti 1994; Irvine 1990). Indexical signs can be multifunctional, so one token can index a number of different meanings simultaneously (Briggs 1988), and they can assume myriad other relations currently being recognized. Verbal indexical signs can function both inside the discursive representation (e.g., anaphora, verbs of speaking, co-reference, and subject-verb agreement) and, under certain conditions, can be referential forms that index certain encoded properties of nonlinguistic context (such as, first- and second-person pronouns, relational deictics such as "this," "that," or "yonder," and plurality markers). They can be learned associations outside the grammatical plane (for example, the association of one's voice modulations as an index of affective states such as anger, pleasure, or fear).[11] Material signs can assume equally complex Peircian indexical significations, especially as semiotically validated by verbal genres or narrative discourse (Mertz and Parmentier 1985; Parmentier 1985, 1994; see also Gregory 1997:249–252). Parmentier's work, especially, reveals ways in which the meanings of material and verbal elements in communicative events resonate with each other and shape the cultural significance of socioeconomic actions.

Silverstein views these indexical sign functions as clustering into two contrasting modes: presuppositional and creative (or entailing) (1979, 1993, 1996a, 1998). Presuppositional indexical signs signal co-contextual sign "objects" as presumed simultaneous significations similar to the presumption that smoke indexes fire and vice versa and the deictic "that" presumably indexes some entity at a distance from the speaker. Gumperz's (1982) "contextualization cues" are often presuppostional in that speakers presume certain co-occurring relations between the way a verbal utterance is said and the role, status, or expectations of the person who said it. Tropes, aphorisms, greetings, leave-takings, and other "stylized" discursive forms common to conversation, and that punctuate many Ash Creek linguistic-economic events, are recognized as deeply sedimented[12] presuppositional indexes, subject to transgenerational meanings that can share in the burden of transmitting ideologies across lifetimes.

Creative indexes, on the other hand, function as novel indexical signs in a discursive context. Use of terms of address (*Mr.* + last name, *Mrs.* + last name, first name, and so forth)[13] to create interpersonal power symmetries or asymmetries among specific participants in a verbal exchange is one example. Ash Creek residents depend extensively on creative indexical significations to "cue" how they will construct or respond to direct requests and demands in a near-constant process of assessing relationships with each other and with nonlocals. Creative indexes also provide the semiotic means for linking or entailing one request event to another and then to those metapragmatic forms that classify different types of discursive practice, creating the hierarchy of interconnections among communicative patterns.

These developments, in concert with developments in economic anthropology and social theory, have led to an explosion of theoretical and descriptive works that reconsider and reformulate the relationship of language to economic and political arenas and to social theory in powerful, substantive, and extremely provocative ways.[14] Linguistic anthropological works are indebted to Silverstein's formulation of "linguistic ideology," a "set of beliefs about language articulated by the users as a rationalization or justification of perceived language structure and use" (1979:193). Arriving at clear and rigorous theoretical formulations and analytical approaches to detail how a given linguistic ideology is constituted is an ongoing scholarly process.[15] We know that indexical uses of language in context constitute a set of pragmatic patterns that are explained, justified, legitimized, or interpreted by discursive practices that function metapragmatically to give abstract or ideological meaning to them. These can become instances of other indexical significations that are also the subject of metapragmatic discursive forms. All instances can be reflexive. Interconnectivity among discursive practices is maintained through a hierarchical ordering of indexical sign functions from those closest to everyday interactions to those most removed from them.

Ideologies of socioeconomic communication are constituted from this dynamic, emergent, ongoing process of everyday and ritualized speech-in-use. Having this framework for talking about these interrelations, as they apply to the ways users of particular sets of communicative practices interpret them, provides a substantive step forward for talking about talk (or communication) without infusing a proscriptive theoretical model of language and political economic relations a priori in what Moerman (1988:5) sees as "the ethnographer's usual practice of selecting bits of the native world as illustrations for pre-existing theories." It is impossible for me to completely avoid all critiques of "ethnographic ventriloquism" in which the writer tries "to speak not just *about* another form of life but to speak from within it" (Geertz 1988:144; see Fine 1999 for its Appalachian implications). It is much easier to write about how *Ash Creek* residents interpret and construct a relationship between requesting patterns and socioeconomy when the terminology is descriptive about the form and function of these relationships rather than evaluative about whether they support or reject a given model.

To this end, I would like to delineate certain presuppositions I have about Ash Creek "requesting patterns."

First, the term *requesting patterns* references Ash Creek behaviors that are not isogenic with Searle's (1969, 1976, 1991) classification of request and demands as "directives." As Rosaldo's (1982:203) ethnographic discussion made clear, and as Bauman and Briggs's (1990) and Silverstein's (1979) theoretical discussion illuminated, Searle's classification diminuates or dismisses how contextual and cultural (read: linguistic ideological) constraints can construct entirely different interpretations of speech acts than the propositional and denotative meanings of the linguistic structure alone would suggest. Much of Searle's speech act theory is also predicated on English grammatical relations.[16] Ash Creek residents speak a variety (or varieties) of English, but these critiques still apply. Many basic requesting patterns are different from, sometimes opposite, for most residents from those reported for other English-speaking areas of the United States not only in grammatical structure but also in the contextual meanings they index.[17]

Brown and Levinson's (1987 [1978]) seminal work on the relationship between politeness criteria and request choice, Gumperz's (1982, 1996) careful attention to how co-occurring contextual "cues" assign meaning to requests, and Ervin-Tripp's (1976, 1996), Ervin-Tripp, O'Connor, and Rosenberg's (1984), and Gordon and Ervin-Tripp's (1984) ground-breaking scholarship on request and context relations are progenitors whose legacy informs much of this book's content. I have, however, reapplied this work to the theoretical approach I have detailed.

Second, my work asserts that requesting patterns constitute their own repertoire of communicative, but not necessarily verbal, forms even when embedded in other practices such as conversation. Ash Creek residents may make a salient request through nonverbal means. Language status is frequently diminuated in favor of nonverbal communicative modes, including the physical actions that indicate communication of or compliance to a request. Many of these physical actions are economic exchanges wherein goods or commodities move from one human owner, user, or possessor to another. Therefore, speech, when it is used, can often be equated with nonverbal semiotic modes, resulting in different hierarchies of structure and functions that characterize more fully developed discursive forms such as those found in routine conversation and most certainly in ritualized speech genres. Discursive forms that reveal overt power, authority, or political relations are often absent in favor of highly routine, often preconscious acts involving expected circulations of commodities, goods, or services. Because this study emphasizes a description of these interconnecting patterns in Ash Creek requesting events, I have abandoned Gal's (1989) and Irvine's (1989) formulation of these language and material relations as *political economy* in favor of *socioeconomy*, which backgrounds political authority and foregrounds resource circulation in social interaction.[18] Clearly, this usage of socioeconomy has implications to and interconnections with political economy and should be considered a subfield rather than an alternative to it.

Third, the conflation of verbal and nonverbal semiotic modes co-occurring in requesting contexts meant that I must, at least temporarily, expand Silverstein's definitions (1976, 1979, 1996a; 1998) of "pragmatics" and "metapragmatics" to include at least the possibility of other nondiscursive systems for creating meaning as co-present in a requesting event.

Finally, I assert that Ash Creek requesting patterns have empirical, sensorially accessible representations manifested in instances of communicative interactions. The verbal portions can be, and in some occasions were, audiorecorded for computerized transmutation from analogic sound to visual sonograms or digitalized speech segments. The oral productions of sound, the gestural and physical actions, and the physical objects that Ash Creek residents emitted, produced, or manipulated were accessible to the senses, "in the world," as Urban (1996b:xiii) says. They were accessible to any organism or device capable of processing sound, visual, and tactile phenomena in some fashion. Residents interpret these phenomena, however, in ways that they find meaningful, ways that may or may not conform to my initial interpretations or to the interpretations of the nonlocals represented in the anecdotes opening this chapter. It is to the credit of the metalingual function of language that residents can and did comment on how to interpret requesting events, sometimes at length. As a speaker of English and someone who grew up in the presence of familial and local speakers of urban Appalachian English, I found this metalingual discourse meaningful even when the communicative event precipitating it was confusing. We could talk to each other and the talk led to further talk, to further engagement in requesting events, and to some mutual understanding about how to interpret these events, at least at the level of indexical (and contextual) significations.[19] Communicative misfires, requesting contestations, and metapragmatic commentary "correcting" my behavior decreased as time went on, a tribute, I would argue, to the anthropological application of the ethnographic method in which I lived and engaged in community political economic life for a substantial length of time.

Ethnographer-in-Residence

When I planned to conduct fieldwork in Ash Creek in 1985, I could not think of its residents as "Other." How could they be? I confronted problems similar to those that late-nineteenth- and early-twentieth-century Kentucky Bluegrass local color writers—James Lane Allen and John Fox, Jr., for example—confronted. Whereas many wrote about Appalachians as if they were neobarbarians (Toynbee 1935), racially distinct populations (Harney 1995 [1873]), or as representatives of an inferior class (Murfree 1884), Allen and Fox could not. For they, like me, were kin to many of these people or had their own ancestral settlement history in this region.

I grew up in Dayton, Ohio, an industrial city that, among so many others, has attracted hundreds of thousands of Appalachian migrants, including my own family members, from the coalfields and oil fields of the Allegheny Plateau region of Ohio, Kentucky, West Virginia, and southwestern Virginia to work in its auto factories and other businesses. For me, paternal relatives, friends, and citizens were a significant Appalachian cultural factor from birth. Family mythic narratives, kinship talk, and animated, often divisive arguments over the merits of Eastern Kentucky led to a moral imperative: hate or love hillbillies, which you no longer are, but do not judge them as inferior.[20]

I came to Ash Creek through the recommendation and assistance of a former professor, who contacted the director of what I call the Environmental Center for possible temporary residence.[21] I did not want to just arrive "out in the county," looking for a nonexistent place to rent or finding myself either very alone "up a holler,"[22] or unwittingly incorporated into active local power disputes that would keep me from talking to people openly. I did not want to move to my father's family's homeplace and step into 200 years worth of contested relations and personal histories about which I had little local knowledge or too much emotional bias. I did not want to live "in town" where more urban patterns of cross-cultural and cross-linguistic heterogeneity would affect requesting patterns.[23] Nor did I want to commute from town to "out in the county" so that I was denied the ongoing flow of events around the clock yet granted the nighttime convenience of easily accessible grocery stores. I wanted to live in an area that was removed enough from the social complexities of urban life so that residents' daily interactions were mostly with each other and generally predictable and so that I could generalize my findings to the community as a whole. I also wanted an area that was not so isolated from the patterns of commerce in town that their interactive patterns were atypical of rural, non–coal camp communities in the region. I wanted my research findings to be applicable to other communities similar to it.

The Environmental Center was a good location to begin. It had been one of the more than 70 settlement schools started in coalfield Appalachia early in the twentieth century and was a county school for many years before state consolidation efforts closed it in the early 1970s. It then became a place where nonlocal students and elderhostelers could come, stay, and participate in nature walks and workshops. Programs for local adults and children have steadily increased since I first arrived in 1985. Maintenance, office, and kitchen staff are local residents and many have worked there for decades. A few live on campus. Most are accustomed to having nonlocals ask them questions about the area. I joined a long list of scholars who have stayed at the center to do some type of folkloric, sociohistorical, or sociological research. I stayed, however, longer than the others and did things others did not. When at the Environmental Center, I spent most of my time with the maintenance and kitchen staff and donated labor in exchange for talk. I washed dishes in the kitchen, swept floors and dusted, and was a fill-in receptionist at the local clinic. I taught extension classes for the county community college at the center, and, for a brief period, I worked in the office—I became the ethnographer-in-residence.

I quickly realized my moral imperative toward hillbillies as a patronizing stance. I could share life experiences with many local residents. From my second day there, I began networking away from the Center, wanting to know how people not affiliated with it talked, made requests, and obtained goods and services. Center staff knew local people, reckoned kinship with most of them, and kept up with local gossip well. They helped me to meet people and told me about local businesses and certain strategies for "gettin along" (see the "Note on Transcription" for transcription of spoken forms). I learned early that one Ash Creek woman had graduated from my high school a few years earlier than I had. I learned that Sandy and her family (see Appendix A) had lived in the Dayton area for several years before moving back to Ash Creek. So had many others, or they had children living in southwestern Ohio, or they lived in or knew Lexington, Kentucky, where I had also lived, worked, and gone to college. One was from my father's home county. We could "place" each other (chapter 3) even without the known kinship ties so very important to the region.[24] I was not that different from them nor they from me.

I was not a native anthropologist in classic colonialist uses of the term (see Narayen 1993 for a discussion), for my urban background and educational experiences meant I did not have mastery over many of the speaking practices and genres used by Ash Creek residents. I was not as experientially familiar with the natural world in which they oriented themselves as well. I came from liturgical, denominational Christian religious traditions rather than the fundamentalist or Pentecostal independent church traditions represented in Ash Creek. Nor did I have a lifetime of interactions with other residents, their homeplaces, and the geographical places in which 180 years of living had created mythic narratives of ancestral life events, often humorous supernatural stories, and deeply sedimented semiotic significations. A few residents made clear that I could never know because "you're not from here."

But neither was I totally unfamiliar with local interactional norms. Phrases, intonations, gestures, and ways of talking about most things were familiar. One day, when visiting Kaziah with other center teaching staff to make crafts, I found myself measuring how much to cut a short piece of corn shuck by marking my thumb rather than using literate measures of measuring such as inches. It was spontaneous, and I surprised myself by doing it. Kaziah nodded and said "yeah" without hesitation; I later discovered it was the appropriate way to measure small distances. I must have learned it as a child in the company of relatives, but I do not remember. Many other interactions similar to this one happened and still happen. I am no longer surprised. They made integration into Ash Creek easier. After an event in town one evening, I mentioned to Bill that I had been treated like a local by the people organizing the event. "Why yeah," he said, "you act just like ɛm." Visitors passing through sometimes treated me as if I were local; I did not dispel their presumptions unless asked.

Yet these details facilitating successful interaction did not reduce my ethnographic needs to become part of the community while maintaining some objectivity toward it. Rather, as Narayen (1993) has argued so well, I have found myself "enacting hybridity" in which distinctions between anthropological insiders and outsiders (as opposed to Ash Creek formulations) "is secondary to the need for dismantling objective distance to acknowledge our shared presence in the cultural worlds that we describe." To this end, the transcriptions that form the heart of the following chapters generally include me in some form of interaction with other Ash Creek residents. They situate me in relation to others, creating a re-representation of the fieldwork process and my often subjective and involved role in it.

My daily routine became exactly that, a routine. My initial research plan, like Graham's (1996:5), was to record naturally occurring speech. In my case, I wanted to record as many requesting events as possible, with special attention to the use of imperatives or other "order" structures. I became a cyborg, a human with a SONY Walkman or small, hand-held tape recorder attached. Some people noticed, many did not; most did not pay much attention to it. Most recordings are from Environmental Center settings because its history and formal institutional structure permitted the director to suggest that staff allow it and for them to recognize to some degree why I needed to do it. Others are from public events or group events. In a few cases, I asked forgiveness after the event rather than permission before it. Permission was given orally. Written consent would have been nearly impossible to obtain due to the indexical meanings signified by written, seemingly legal documents. For many, it would have indexed me as someone from an organization (government, media, education) who was out to trick them, as had happened so many times before.

I visited the center kitchen daily, usually in the afternoons and evenings. The staff of two to four cooks prepared full evening meals when groups were present, which was on most weeks and weekends. Afternoons were spent in evening meal preparation and in casual talk while working. At this time, and with the director's permission, kitchen space was relatively open to visits from family members, visitors, and other staff who had reasons to interrupt or join in the flow of postlunch cleanup or dinner preparation.[25] It was a good time to record because the workload was lighter and participants simply forgot the recorder was on as they engaged in friendly conversation. Evenings, when I did after-dinner dishwashing, were usually very busy times as cooks wanted to clean up and go home. Talk was very focused on the tasks at hand and characteristic of other situations I observed in which labor had priority over phatic communication. At night I would visit with Bill, the night watchman, for an hour or so to whittle and talk quietly and conversationally. He regularly instructed center visitors in "woodcarvin" as well, if they wished to stay up until midnight, and members of his family would often drop by. Center activities including playground events, folkloric events, community meetings, and staff daily work interactions were not closed to me but were constrained by workers' needs to get the job done and the various responses of participants to my presence.

Ash Creek residents had no particular interest in knowing how to pronounce "anthropology," a polysyllabic word of Greek origins that did not conform either to the stress or syllabification rules of Appalachian English nor in what it represented as a discipline. "Linguistic anthropology" and "ethnography" only confounded the problem. My erstwhile profession had no local value, but my presence did. W. Rodman's (1991:432) conclusion ("We are not just observers observed; we are interpreters interpreted") applied from the first day I arrived and has not ceased. Residents associated me with the Environmental Center and inserted my name into local gossip and narratives that they circulated among themselves to have some interpretive control of the activities, behaviors, and events happening there. I found myself being talked about and my actions circulated in the market of Ash Creek women's (and sometimes men's) face-to-face and telephone recountings of ongoing community activities in the streams of talk that fills much of the day while doing other things. I was talked to concerning my expected role while there—what I should and should not be doing, who I should and should not be talking to, what I should put in my "book," how I should write it, or that I should not write it at all because I could never know enough about them. This talk was always framed in binary, oppositional ways. I was "one of us," I was "not from here"; I was too educated, I had common sense like the common person; I needed to have a man, I could get by without one. And so on. Somewhere in this stream of talk, I realized I needed an identity; I need to be "placed" in Ash Creek terms.

To establish an identity, I taught extension college classes first at the center and then at the local grade school several miles from Ash Creek. Here I met adult students, mostly women, who allowed me to record classes and a few other interactions. Many became friends and I visited with them from time to time. Teaching allowed me to assume the role of "teacher" in Ash Creek, a very helpful one because it "placed" me in a status in which my nonmarried state was validated. Many center teachers were single. All residents had some way to talk to me and to shape their conversations with me. What few problems arose while I lived in Ash Creek were products of my being a single, educated, infrequent churchgoer, rather than being an "anthropologist" doing research.

During the day, I would "visit," an activity still widely practiced in Ash Creek. Either alone or with someone, I would perhaps stop at the local diner when it was in business, stop by homes where I had been invited or knew I was welcome, or attend a community event such as a yard sale, gospel sing, public meeting on political matters, wedding, or funeral. In the late summer 1986 I moved from the Environmental Center to a rented house in Ash Creek. I then visited the center less and visited homes more. I attended local churches occasionally, but the need of independent Protestant churches to have a "community of saints" meant that my participant-observer role would have to be abandoned in favor of deep commitment to participation.[26] It was easier not to attend regularly, a mistake I now regret. Yet, by the summer of 1988, I had visited the homes of all but a few residents, knew most of them by name, had something of a grasp on the extended and well-reckoned kinship ties, and felt like a community member having something of a "place" (chapter 3). I return regularly.

Ash Creek residents vary in their willingness to engage in nonlocal activities, business interactions, and conversations with outsiders. With rare exceptions, however, none want their pictures taken or their behavior video-recorded by nonlocals. The War on Poverty period (approximately 1964–1974) was not only an era of nearly unrestrained federal spending in Appalachia, among other so-called "poverty" areas, but also a period of intense media coverage and political image making.[27] The volume of researchers and other nonlocals visiting Ash Creek and "wantin somethin" increased during this period. They took photographs, made film recordings, and audiotaped, often without permission. According to local narratives, Dorothy saw photos of her children in a major Kentucky newspaper taken by reporters at the end of a long, vigorous outdoor play period. They were portrayed as poverty-struck, underfed, and in need of government support. Dorothy sued for libel and won. Residents feel strongly that photographs are commonly used to spread "lies" about them.

Reluctance to grant permission to outsiders to photograph does not mean residents shun recording technology. Graham's (1996) experiences when collaborators wanted her to record valued verbal resources were not mine, but residents' desire to preserve and record events they value highly is similar. In Ash Creek, however, residents themselves own or borrow video recorders or cameras to record family events. Photographs of revered ancestors may circulate in limited circles of close family members and are often stored in protected, safe places. They are rarely shared with outsiders. Most feel that someone from outside will devalue these individuals through their talk about their dress, demeanor, or actions in these videos or photographs.

Therefore, the few photographs and slides I have are of scenery or a few willing locals in staged settings. But photographs also remove any anonymity of location. As beneficial as photos or videos would be to the discussion of the communicative exchanges presented in this work, I have included none.

Ash Creek

"Appalachia" is a construct, "invented," according to Batteau (1990:1), as a "creature of the urban imagination." It is a term used in various ways to apply to a region that roughly corresponds to the mountainous area of the eastern United States. According to the Appalachian Regional Commission's (ARC) very broad and politically manipulated regional definition, Appalachia includes portions of 12 states and all of West Virginia. It runs from New York to Mississippi and, in 1995, included approximately 22 million persons. Popular images of Appalachia that have circulated most broadly often focus on the bituminous coalfields as images of poverty. This area had a 1995 population of approximately 5 million (Appalachian Regional Commission 1996:1). It is difficult to make sweeping linguistic or cultural generalizations about populations of this magnitude, especially when population centers cluster variously as cities (e.g., Charleston, West Virginia), towns (e.g., Princeton, West Virginia), former coal camps (e.g., Cranks Creek, Kentucky), rural crossroads (e.g., Rose Hill, Virginia) or rural nonfarming or farming households along creek valleys or branch hollers. Ash Creek corresponds to the latter.

Isserman's (1996) data indicate that images of broad regional poverty are now mistaken; much of the region is growing economically at a pace significantly higher than that of the rest of the United States. Pockets of low growth and relatively high poverty continue to exist, however, in areas removed from interstates and major highway arteries or major cities such as Atlanta, Georgia, or Charlotte, North Carolina (see also Eller 1994). Ash Creek is in one such pocket.

"Ash Creek" is not simply a pseudonym for an existing, locally recognized community. It is instead a term for an area about 8 miles long primarily located in the narrow floodplain along what I have renamed "Ash Creek" and its tributaries, or "branches." Although residents talk about "the community," the physical arrangement of architecture reinforces a rural "homeplace" pattern common to the eastern Kentucky region since first settlement,[28] in which children build homes or place mobile homes next to an ancestral house, or homeplace (see the inset in figure 1.1 for an Ash Creek homeplace arrangement).[29] Generally parents or grandparents live in the homeplace. Who takes over homeplace occupancy upon the death of the parents is often contested although a child living on homeplace land and who has perhaps been a caregiver often has privilege. Not uncommonly, this will be the eldest male child.

I delimited the boundaries of Ash Creek on the basis of the closeness of or degree of networking among residents at the various homeplaces. Debbie's homeplace, for example, included her husband, two daughters' families, and her brother-in-law's family. Her other children's families lived in two other homeplaces, and her husband's first cousin's families constituted three other homeplaces. All interact with each other regularly. In this manner of delimiting kinship interconnections among homeplaces, I determined a boundary to the Ash Creek area that included approximately 350 people. With few exceptions, homeplaces have at least one garden of quarter- to full-acre size for producing at least corn, beans, onions, potatoes, tomatoes, and squash for homeplace use. With family graveyards also on the premises, residents have deeply felt "occupations of space" (after Stewart 1996a, 1996b) that transcend generations.

Residents continue to use proper names for areas where branches meet Ash Creek and local centers of public interaction arose (mom and pop stores, churches, perhaps a post office or small restaurant). Yet these are not incorporated and do not function any longer as recognized community centers, although a few residents talk about efforts in community development and growth in relation to these locales.[30] Therefore, I have labeled these centers as public spaces in figure 1.1. Many, however, look to the Environmental Center as their center for community life, a point of view not totally shared by the center board of trustees when I lived there.

Land ownership along the Ash Creek valley tends to be private in small acreage, allowing the homeplace arrangement to continue. Land ownership up the hollers and on the ridges tends to be corporate or governmental, owned by coal companies, timber industries, state forestry departments, or the Environmental Center. People living on corporate property rent, often at nominal fees, and use surface land for gardening and other subsistence needs. They do not create homeplace configurations of space because house building and improvements are controlled by the corporate owner, which, in general, does not want to pay additional property taxes for improved land.

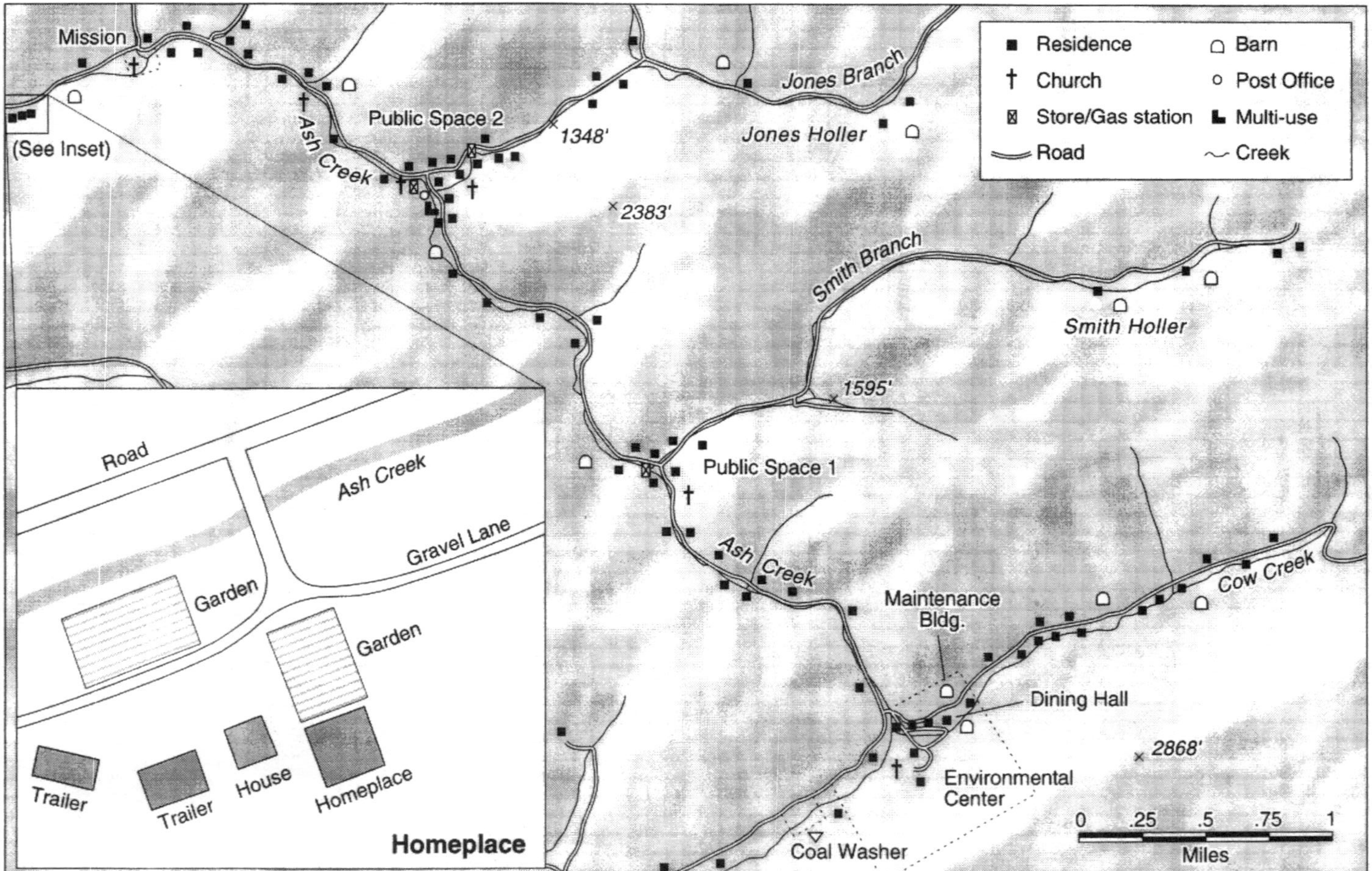

Figure 1.1. Map of Ash Creek

Ash Creek coal became a target of the coal mining industry in the 1960s, later than in other areas in the county. Many male residents were miners before this time and many currently work in the coal industry, but there are no mines under or in the community itself. Strip mining can be seen from the hill and ridge tops to the northwest and northeast, and some residents at the lower end of Ash Creek drive to picnic, hike, or ride four-wheelers and motorbikes at a large strip site (about 20 square miles) nearby. Well water problems are significant for many residents as wells are becoming polluted or full of unhealthy particulates from the ingress of mining activities. Ash Creek is too polluted to support fish.

Most Ash Creek men who are working regularly, and many are not, work as truckers in some capacity, hauling coal, gravel, or logs, or engaging in transcontinental overnight hauls.[31] Some run heavy equipment in coal mines, strip mines, or gravel quarries. Employment for nearly all involves jobs working with other kin or for other kin, even if it means commuting to some location outside of Ash Creek. Consequently, the kinds of "helpin out," (chapter 7) "takin care of," (chapter 6) and "doin for" (chapter 8) relations discussed in this book are extensions of community interactional patterns superimposed upon wage-labor contexts. Requesting patterns in corporate settings, described by researchers such as Ervin-Tripp (1976, 1982, 1996), Drew and Heritage (1992), and Weigel and Weigel (1985), are somewhat different in Ash Creek because corporate and formal institutional workplace practices are nugatory.[32]

The population pyramid of Ash Creek is more of a pillar, with a higher percentage of the population older than 50, reflecting extensive migration of young adults to find work. Most men in this group received some type of workers' compensation or health disability transfer payment. Many of all ages engaged in nonreportable cash labor, ginseng harvesting, or illegal activity such as marijuana growing, so Internal Revenue Service income data were unreliable. Table 1.1 captures socioeconomic data for that portion of Ash Creek for which I had detailed information.

As this table shows, gender roles are very well defined and women are expected to be married and have children. Men are expected to produce needed commodities and services, which generally means earning money through paid labor. Some women work in door-to-door or cottage industries such as selling Amway products, making crafts, or providing at-home child care. A few work full time as grade school teachers, teacher's aides, nurses, or office staff. The overall economic profile is rather bleak, with real unemployment at about 35% and annual income averaging slightly less than $15,000 per family in 1986. With low property taxes and a homeplace settlement pattern, with alternative subsistence means such as hunting and garden growing, and with alternative sources of unreported income, the picture is slightly less bleak, however, than this table suggests. Networks of individuals, generally kin, who can assist in meeting basic needs are important to ease the economic burden on all.

Ash Creek residents claim to be white, allegedly of Scots-Irish ancestry, and many admit, often proudly, to having a Cherokee ancestry.[33] With one exception (a Korean wife of a nonlocal man who stayed only two years), residents report that

Table 1.1. Ash Creek Demographic Data

	No.	*%*
Households (N = 54)[1]		
HOUSE TYPE		
Frame	34	63
Ranch	3	6
Mobile Home	13	24
Other	4	7
UTILITIES		
Electricity	52	95
Telephone	46	85
NUMBER OF OCCUPANTS		
1	7	13
2	22	41
3–4	21	39
> 4	4	7
OWNERSHIP		
Own home and land	23	43
Own home, no rent	11	20
Rent	20	37
REPORTED HOUSEHOLD INCOME		
< $15,000	25	46
$15–30,000	24	45
> $30,000	5	9
Men (N = 46)		
AGE		
18–35	8	17
35–55	30	65
> 55	8	17
MARITAL STATUS		
Never married	4	9
Married	40	87
Widowed	1	2
Divorced	1	2
OCCUPATIONS (FOR THOSE > 18)		
Heavy equipment operator	2	4
Truck hauling	6	13
Mining/Logging	5	11
Part-time labor	2	4
Professional	8	17
Unemployed (Welfare)	2	4
Disabled	5	11
Retired	9	20
Other[2]	7	15

	No.	%
EDUCATIONAL LEVEL		
< 8th grade	20	43
8th grade	7	15
9–12 grade	12	26
College	7	15
Women (N = 50)		
AGE		
18–35	18	36
35–55	17	34
> 55	15	30
MARITAL STATUS		
Never married	4	8
Married	36	72
Widowed	8	16
Divorced	2	4
OCCUPATIONS (FOR THOSE > 18)		
Homemaker	17	34
Part-time at-home work	5	10
Full-time	10	20
Part-time	4	8
Teaching/Nursing	10	20
Storekeeper	4	8
EDUCATIONAL LEVEL		
< 8th grade	12	24
8th grade	8	16
9–12 grade	17	34
College	13	26
NUMBER OF CHILDREN		
0	7	14
1–2	12	24
3–4	22	44
> 4	9	18

1. Includes 7 homes at the Environmental Center. 1986 data.
2. Includes Environmental Center labor.

no African Americans or speakers of non-English languages have ever lived in Ash Creek except as visitors to the Environmental Center. Daily activities are highly routine and circumscribed, especially for women. For most residents, variation in daily life comes not necessarily from going someplace different or engaging in significantly new activities but in changes in the states of interactions with each other. Pranks, practical jokes, work play, and "gɛttin one over on somebody" are very well-developed interactional patterns. Church life (or at least a Christian religious orientation) is very important to nearly all women and a majority of men, permeating every aspect of daily life. The transformational state created by being baptized and, for Pentecostals, speaking in tongues, mark major status changes for individuals and their role in community life and are the substance of much serious conversation, especially for women. Yet like most Ash Creek residents, by the time I moved "over the mountain" to town in 1987, I could, with a certain amount of predictability, say where a number of Ash Creek residents were and what they were doing at a particular time during the day. This level of predictability made this study possible because it allows me to generalize about pragmatic and metapragmatic patterns with a level of certainty not possible when people engage in more frequent and transitory interactions with strangers under more complex market patterns.

Ash Creek's communicative practices are often oriented (or thematically focused) around a number of discursive dualities. A person is a "saved Christian" or a "heathen"; a "man" or a "woman"; "married" or "not married"; "good" or "bad"; "rich" or "poor"; "a worker" or "sorry"; and so forth. Each of these binary oppositions is supported by discursive practices having highly moral themes that constitute ideologies of deontic language. As McCauley (1991) posits for all of coalfield Appalachia, residents interpret "heartfelt" expressions of religious conviction as more authentic than reasoned arguments of theological points from the "head." And, except for scripture as recorded in the King James Version of the Bible, written arguments, sources of information, or expositions are less worthy in a conversation than experiential knowledge about a subject. Also included among these binary deontic modes are representations of being "from here" or being an "outsider." Outsiders, who generally are researchers, policy makers, business representatives, and others coming to the area for professional reasons, and the educational levels they usually reveal by speech (Greco-latinate forms; reference to literate products such as policy statements, books, or contracts; and prosodic and grammatical differences from eastern Kentucky Appalachian English) represent a less moral world to residents, a world in which most inhabitants engage in what Ash Creek residents perceive as "sinful" conduct.[34] Therefore, the kinds of speech practices outsiders use and the grammatical structures from which they are constructed are often shunned by Ash Creek residents. So then are the people who speak them. Yet these outsiders are frequently employed by valued institutions such as the Environmental Center, a church's main headquarters, or a medical organization.[35] This book touches on the complexities these tensions create, but I note here that these boundaries between the two groups are well developed in discursive practices and in other semiotic systems of communication. Reproduction of the communicative systems that construct these differences is central to the continuation of the Ash Creek linguistic-economic system because they constitute barriers to the ebb and flow of certain commodities and services in and out of the area and the ideologies of political economic language that empower them.

The speech structures of most Ash Creek residents are consistent with the phonological, lexical, and grammatical patterns reported for Appalachian English (Blanton 1989; Carver 1987; Christian 1978; C. Williams 1992; Wolfram and

Christian 1976; Wolfram and Schilling-Estes 1998; see also McMillan and Montgomery 1989). Ash Creek falls within Carver's (1987:165–167) Upper South Layer of American English dialects. Its speech is therefore evaluated by many Americans as highly stigmatized and associated with backward, rustic, and uneducated people (see Blanton 1985 for a discussion of Appalachian English and Preston 1996 for how it patterns with respect to attitudes toward Southern speech). Ash Creek residents rarely label their speech "Appalachian," although they are very cognizant that it is "different" from more "proper" speech spoken by more educated people, usually outsiders. Instead, they refer to their speech patterns as "country," "hillbilly," or "mountain." Television has had little impact on speech patterns, even among the younger members. Direct television reception is impossible because the hilly topography breaks up signals; a cable or satellite system is mandatory for reception. Part of Ash Creek is served by an improvised local system that receives only four channels. Many programs reference situations or objects unfamiliar and therefore unimportant to residents (e.g., office buildings, subways, or Middle Eastern cuisine). They also use speech patterns residents find difficult to follow. Although I encountered no home without a television, if residents watched television at all, most women watched only soap operas, which are highly affective and have easy to follow plots, and most men watched only action shows or wrestling, which also require little attention to speech. Children watched cartoons. Action videos were very popular for similar reasons.

Oral secular performative genres such as storytelling, riddles, and ballads are currently vestigial in the verbal repertoire, even though this area was a major collection center for early Appalachian folk ballad collection. I attribute this loss to many factors, the Environmental Center's contribution to the missionary and folk life movement of the 1930s among them (Whisnant 1983). Older residents discuss how center teaching staff emphasized replacing traditional genres deemed unworthy with acceptable literate and audio-recorded folk forms from other cultural traditions. This practice constituted a hegemonic process supporting what Gal and Irvine (1995) call "erasure." The playing of secular folk or country music on porches or in homes is also rare, presumably for similar reasons. Tape players, radios, and a few compact disk players do, however, provide residents with an ample selection of country music. A few residents make regular trips to Dollywood or other tourist areas to attend famous country music performers' concerts.

Subsequent Chapters

The remaining chapters of this book are organized around how the various metapragmatic descriptors for requesting events construct Ash Creek interpretations of actual instances of requests. Consequently, each chapter discusses these relations as expressed in transcriptions of audio-recorded speech. These transcriptions are not to be viewed as textual artifacts but as printed entextualizations of transitory, highly evanescent utterances. To assist in recreating these instances of speech, I have adopted the transcriptional conventions of conversational analysts, specifically that of Du Bois et al. (1993), modifying it only slightly to accommodate the slightly different needs of these representations (see the "Note on Transcription"). As with any conventional notational system, the specificity of the notations aid in recreating how the transcription was originally uttered.

The audiotapes from which the transcriptions come do not represent all Ash Creek requesting discourse patterns but represent verbal exchange contexts for which I had permission to record. Given the routinized activities of most Ash Creek residents, it was possible for me to listen to requesting discourse throughout the community and by most speakers. The benefit of an ethnographic approach is that I had time and opportunity to listen over and over again to similar types of requests in different contexts, even when I could not record. I can therefore comment upon the transcribed segments using my exposure to other, nonrecorded requesting contexts and to the elicited responses residents gave me about them.

Chapter 2 addresses how Ash Creek speech constructs value, in the sense of assigning worth to an economic item. Although speech offers many ways to do this, the chapter focuses on constraints on the use of attributive possessive constructions. Contextual constraints on what can be possessed under what grammatical and contextual conditions reveal a major means by which residents transform commodities to personal goods and vice versa. Attributive possessives also construct networks of individuals, usually local and kin, upon whom they rely for socioeconomic exchanges and with whom they "belong." They also reveal how residents use a grammatical resource to construct cultural meanings about objects and labor.

Contextually sensitive scholarship on requests indicates clearly that requests are very sensitive indicators of social or political relationships among the participants (e.g., Blum-Kulka, House, and Kasper 1989a; Brown and Levinson 1987 [1978]; Ervin-Tripp 1976; Irvine 1980, 1989; Rosaldo 1982). Chapter 3 discusses how Ash Creek requests index "rights," "place," and "claims" relationships among participants and economic entities to construct appropriate linguistic-economic participant frameworks. The goal of this chapter is to describe how the creation of specific "rights," "place, and "claims" relations by a particular requesting event constructs appropriate or inappropriate socioeconomic relationships among residents and nonresidents.

Residents of every community must have appropriate ways to acquire or divest themselves of valued goods or labor. There must be a set of requesting patterns that facilitate this circulation of economic entities. Chapter 4 discusses the most common requesting patterns used by Ash Creek residents to accomplish this process at the level of utterance within a requesting exchange. Because imperative utterances are limited to very specific contextual configurations, they are not common requesting forms except in a few types of situations. Therefore, they are not discussed in this chapter.

Chapter 5 examines how these nonimperative patterns are organized into larger nonimperative communicative practices, specifically into what Ash Creek metapragmatic discursive forms refer to as "takin care of," "makin a deal," and "tradin." The kinds of linguistic-economic communication these designators index are generally nonlocal and outside the community. They are the major means by which commodities enter the local economy and goods and labor leave it, either becoming commodities or remaining as noncommodities. This chapter discusses how the continued reproduction of them, especially "takin care of" relations, undercuts and devalues business needs to make a profit, driving many attempts at business development into bankruptcy.

Chapter 6 discusses what kinds of utterances can receive "order" status in Ash Creek. "Orders" are highly salient requesting forms that usually result in noncompliance or, occasionally, physical violence. Centered around imperative forms or indicatives and interrogatives having imperative intonation and contextualization, "orders" form the core of Ash Creek linguistic-economic communication. This chapter presents their general grammatical expression and then discusses how stylized uses in routinized contexts or narrative entextualization change the pragmatic functions of "orders" to other functions.

Despite the highly negative evaluation residents give "orders," imperatives occur very commonly in Ash Creek with no recognition by residents that they are "orders." Chapter 7 addresses these appropriate uses in task contexts in which participants are indexed as co-equals. Residents interpret such contexts as "helpin out" somebody. This chapter concludes by discussing how "helpin out" communicative practices and the metapragmatic discourse that interprets the significance of them function to reproduce a local organization of labor that contradicts or is partially syncretic with wage-labor and capitalistic commoditization of labor expectations.

Chapter 8 discusses how "orders" index cultural unequals in the local socioeconomy. Appropriate "orders" are common in community "belongin" networks. "Orders" index a requestor who is in a dependent situation with the requestee for the performance of service or procurement of a good. Development of these "doin for" relations is critical for the continued cooperative success of the local socioeconomy and for the reproduction of an ideology of socioeconomic communication. Strongly developed "doin for" relations construct one dominant mode of expressing "love" in Ash Creek. When imperatives and other "order" discursive forms cannot index appropriate participant frames, "orders" evoke highly negative affective relations. Residents often choose to respond to inappropriate "orders" by agentless communications such as "messages" and "presents." Harm to highly valued goods or persons can result.

Chapter 9 returns to issues raised in chapter 1 to suggest how Ash Creek requesting patterns construct language and socioeconomic relations and constitute an ideology of socioeconomic communication. It discusses the implications of the arguments raised in the book for understanding language and economic relations in rural Appalachia. This chapter then suggests ways for developing what Silverstein introduces as an "empirical" element to postmodernism" (1998:138) in which the ways in which communication, particularly verbal communication, constitutes macrosocial structurings from the language users' own systems of interpreting them. It ends by suggesting that socioeconomic theories be reassessed according to results of studies into the constitution of ideologies of political economic language.

2 POSSESSIVE CONSTRUCTIONS AND LINGUISTIC-ECONOMICS

"Whose girl are you?"

A heated debate in the community over the "rights" of an elderly couple, former administrative staff of the Environmental Center, to continue living at the center includes extended discussions by the descendants of the original donor of the center's land about "their" center. [notes 5/86]

A man's dog is poisoned by some unidentified agent for some reason that can only be speculated upon by the dog's owner. [notes 3/86]

A conversation with Tom about beans while in what he calls "his garden" and his wife Mary calls "the garden" includes him saying "them's hers," pointing to a bushel of picked green beans. "Hers" references Mary, who has not been mentioned previously in the conversation. [notes 8/85]

SOCIOECONOMIES REQUIRE CULTURALLY BASED EXPRESSIONS of ownership, control, or possession of valued entities, whether by individuals, corporations, supernatural powers, or some other cultural category, in order to direct the ebb and flow of resources within a cultural arena.[1] As studies in nonmonetary exchange have demonstrated, any given set of cultural practices will emphasize one or several of these types of possession over the full range of possibilities. Recent anthropological scholarship in exchange systems details clear linkages between culturally constructed concepts of ownership and patterns in the distribution of resources.[2]

Furthermore, recent scholarship applying Peircian semiotics has taken the give-and-take focus of these exchange *transactions* into dynamic, evolving relations of sociomaterial *interactions*.[3] Under this type of reanalysis, the purpose of an exchange event can be explored constitutively, as a choice in constructing social selves in immediate relations to other social selves and material entities in an exchange event.

This focus on sociomaterial interactions has two applications to this discussion. First, it permits an analysis of how speech and nonverbal communications co-construct meanings with exchange entities within communicative events. The basic components of communicative events articulated by Hymes (1964, 1972) and developed under the ethnography of speaking scholarship can now include valued economic entities and the meanings they signify as one of several factors creating context. Second, this reorientation toward material exchange allows application of certain concepts and approaches developed in conversational analysis to these socioeconomic events. In particular, turn-takings can be both verbal, silent, gestural, and material. Adjacency pairs can consist of a verbal turn followed by a nonverbal prestation.[4] With this methodological and theoretical shift, *how* speech behavior constructs culturally valid conditions of "possession" becomes accessible to investigation. This refocusing has revealed new domains for scholarly exploration in which the verbal and the material representations within a common instance of social interaction can be simultaneously examined under a common theoretical framework.

In addition, recent linguistic scholarship on possessive constructions reassesses the presumed locative functions of genitives in terms of both semantics and pragmatics.[5] Languages having what are commonly called alienable ("my money") and inalienable ("my foot" or "his mother") possessive markers in their grammar have been reassessed. The semantic meanings of these constructions have led to questioning inalienable constructions as capturing metonymic or synecdochic distinctions. Instead, some favor simple physical contiguity relations between possessed nouns and possessors. It is not that one's foot is part of the whole body, but a part always in close proximity to the rest of the self.[6]

In addition, recent analyses of these types of languages and also of ergative languages, which also mark alienability, have led to serious reconsiderations of the pragmatic and semantic roles of possessives. Careful and nuanced analyses of relationships between possessor, entity possessed, and other interlocutors in the utterance event reveal the complex interpersonal relationships encoded in genitive utterances. Taylor (1989, 1996), for example, argues that grammatical categories of possession involve a constellation of properties such as the possessed noun references a specific concrete thing and that only the possessor has the right to use the possessed entity unless the possessor grants permission to someone else. Duranti and Ochs observe that genitive constructions encode nine semantic roles such as benefactive, agent, actor, experiencer, and patient. They note that "absolutive NP [noun phrase] in a two-constituent utterance is often heavy, loaded with information concerning human participant and the actions, states, and locations that bind them" (1996:187). These revelations have opened up the very nature of what constitutes "ownership" or "possession" in linguistic terms. They reveal ways to examine naturally occurring possessive constructions as a linguistic source to understand how speakers construct valuation of cultural entities within a broadly conceived concept of ownership or use. It is because of this new area of linguisitic scholarship that this discussion of the actual use of Ash Creek English possessives can occur.

In general accord with nonfictional accounts about the Appalachian region,[7] individual-focused forms and expressions of ownership and possession are a central, organizing force that motivates and directs a number of culture-specific socioeconomic processes within Ash Creek. From the first day of my living in Ash Creek, I regularly and frequently engaged in or overheard conversations that contained emphasized possessive constructions using phrases such as "that's *his*," "where's *Amy's* apron?" or "why's *Bill's* truck there?" I soon found myself paying careful attention to the physical proximity of animate and inanimate things in relation to individuals in order to evaluate the activities and character of other residents. Trucks, for example, became associated with specific men (or a few women), cars with women (or a few men) as complex signs concerning who the drivers were, what they were doing, and why they were doing it. When one local woman allowed me to drive her sedan one afternoon, others commented on how significant it was that she trusted me enough to let me drive "*her* car."

Individual claims to various tangible and intangible entities are readily acknowledged by residents, are routinely given greater value than any corporate or governmental rights, and can become frequent conversational topics as residents assess or assert the proprietary rights and correctness of individuals' claims on valued items. These linguistically based processes of valuation connect individuals to complex socioeconomic patterns of prestations, exchanges, and productions of goods and services that bind individuals into networks of ownership and usufruct. They unite constructs of individual selves into a constantly recreated matrix of socioeconomic acts.

These identity constructs should not and must not be viewed, however, as only and primarily ego-focused in the sense of an autonomous, autogenous self who acts as a distinct agent apart from the social world. Nor should they be viewed as merging identities into a diffuse socioeconomic world around them. Such a formulation would support a dichotomous view of individuals in relation to a material world, as summarized by Parmentier:

> If in the West the self, whether as "ego" or "personality," is considered to be entirely personal, for tribal peoples the self is the product of social mediations involving other people and objects of exchange. Conversely, social conventions such as language and morality are differentially evaluated. In tribal societies they are thought to be "discovered" within the person . . . , whereas in the West the individual's task is to become socialized into conventional norms existing outside the person. (1994:109)[8]

For Ash Creek patterns, these dichotomies do not hold. If forced to apply, they would recreate the kinds of popular bipolar classification of rural Appalachian communities into an "other America," which is "tribal" and not part of the West. Or they would create a nontribal but deficient model of what happens in "the West."[9] Instead, these interactive patterns create situated identities constructed within

$$\Big[[\text{+human NP's}]_{DET}\text{N}\Big]_{NP} \text{ or } [\text{-3rd person Poss Pro N}]_{NP}$$

[Bills's son] or [my car]

Figure 2.1. Attributive possessive constructions

networks of valued potable entities, geographic space, and other valued human beings. These identities instead resonate with Urban and Lee's (1989:15–26) understanding of Wolf's constructions of "selfobject" in which "the important point is that the sense of self is not necessarily associated just with the limits of the body, as in Mauss's formulation of the universal of self awareness . . . the feeling of selfhood may depend upon the involvement of the individual with other objects" (1989:2–3). It is in the dynamic, intersubjectivity of self and objects with respect to other selves that Ash Creek residents construct their relationships to resources.

In verbally assessing or asserting such relations, discourse patterns, socioeconomic activities, and individual identity domains merge to create or recreate a culturally legitimated community economy. When one individual "says" a certain patch of trees belongs to him and another individual "says" it does not, and when residents dispute this matter among themselves (courts being a last resort) to determine who has the "right" to log it, the very process of talking creates alliances among residents about who is a proper owner and shapes the relationship of these individuals to each other and to the community. This process, in turn, constructs cultural identities.[10]

From an empirical perspective, verbal expression of ownership or possession in such discourse involves English semantic and pragmatic constructions that permeate the full range of the Ash Creek verbal repertoire.[11] The most overt grammatical constructions encoding possession, however, and ones that unambiguously signify some type of ownership relation, are attributive possessive constructions of the form depicted in figure 2.1:

They can also be predicative possessive pronouns (such as "mine," "ours," "his," "hers," "theirs," and rarely, "our-n," "your-n," "his-n," "her-n," and "their-n"[12]).

These constructions contain the dual ability to denotatively or indexically reference a specific possessor and an entity possessed. Residents know that "Bill's truck" references a local man named "Bill" as well as the "truck" that he drives or is known to be in some proximate relationship to him. The construction simultaneously encodes a grammatical relationship of Bill possessing the truck. The possessive construction therefore presupposes referential significations usually known to all interlocutors (figure 2.2). The referential certainty captured by these constructions in Ash Creek everyday discourse cannot be overstressed. The entities referenced in these constructions are concretely and empirically real. For example:

(2.1) Debbie: Her mother . always uh . she uh . ((1.0)) wondered if she was practicin the pianer [94b:215 8/86]

Dillon: Is these Sheryl's keys? [94b:222 8/86]

These very typical examples taken from routine conversational discourse contain one possessive construction each, "Her mother" and "Sheryl's keys." In each case, the possessor lexemes ("her" and "Sheryl") reference known individuals currently living in the community, while the possessed nouns ("mother" and "keys") also reference known and tangibly accessible if not actually co-present entities. Such communicative constraints on Ash Creek possessive constructions are normative. Nearly all quotidian discourse among residents is about events, personalities, activities, things, and behaviors empirically accessible to interlocutors at the time of utterance or accessible at some previous time. This linguistic process therefore links the material domains of Ash Creek to given individuals through a grammatical relation,[13] providing a linguistic window into the structuring of Ash Creek's patterns of possession and therefore into the structuring of the local economy.

If what each individual possessed were idiosyncratic and not subject to the imposition of semiotic processes other than those encoded in the grammar, then such a window would be of minimal cultural value because each resident would possess only what was allowable under grammatical constraints.[14] It is not, however. Simply put, as revealed by patterned variation in discourse, who can possess what under what conditions is neither random nor entirely subject to the strategic uses of a given speaker in a specific speech situation. Rather, the way possessive construction is contextualized in a speech event creates or recreates presupposed indexical meanings that bond two entities in appropriate relationships. In terms of grammatical intersections with socioeconomic processes, these bonding relations are most apparent in constructions in which the possessed noun is either +human or +concrete object, which is true of most usages, conforming to the syntactic formulation given before.

"Belongin" Possessive Patterns

It is perhaps in the contextualization of possessive constructions as greetings that the cultural significance of [+human N] possessed noun constructions are most salient. As would be expected in a highly face-to-face interactional society, Ash Creek residents rely extensively on expanded verbal greetings to frame and begin interactions.[15] When two individuals meet who are significantly different in age,

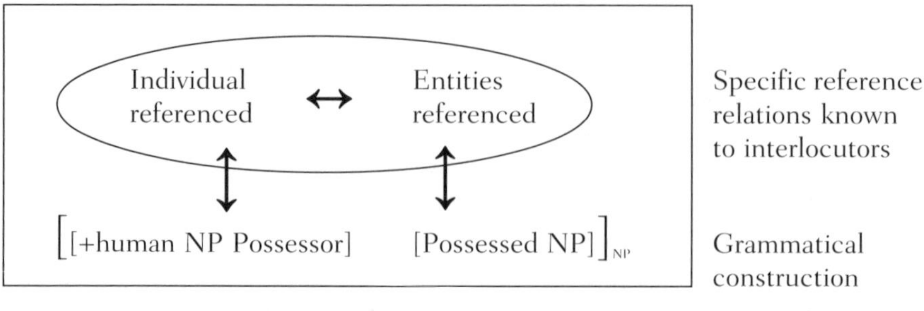

Figure 2.2. Possessive reference relations in Ash Creek conversational speech events (community residents as participants)

and the older one is uncertain of the younger's identity but other cues indicate local residence (facial features, clothing, or setting), he or she will demand early in the greeting sequence, "Whose [boy/girl] are you?" The respondent is expected to reply with the name of the parent matching the sex of the questioner. For example, an acceptable response might be "Joe Smith's boy" (boy to older man) or "Sarah Smith's boy" (boy to older woman) or with some more expanded utterance such as "I be Joe Smith's wife. He's Bill Smith's son." Failure to respond with a familiar name as a possessor nominal truncates the potential interaction because kinship relations cannot then be discussed and assessed. Such a termination often leaves the younger interlocutor with the "gates"[16] to community membership and its economy closed.

Ash Creek residents discuss such obligatory relations as "[Name] belongs to [Family Last Name (or) Individual's Full Name]." For example, a common form of question about an unfamiliar person is "Who does he belong to?" and a common indicative type is, for example, "Jane belongs to those Smiths up Spruce Holler." If individuals who do not have such kinship relations are to be community participants, they must instead "belong" to a formal institution, such as the Environmental Center, a church mission, or a medical clinic, or they must acquire a fictive kin categorization. Only then will they have a status in community terms, a "place" where they "belong," and the capability to participate in greeting contexts. The following scenario provides an example:

> After meeting a new person through a mutual work relationship or through someone else's introduction, a local resident who is in community "belongin" networks and who is preferably of the same gender as the nonlocal assumes the responsibility of introducing the newcomer to local residents by announcing, after an appropriate greeting sequence between the residents, that "This is Susie, the nurse at the clinic," "I'd like for you to meet Joe, he works at the School," or "Do you know Brother Bill, he's staying at the mission."

Direct greeting exchanges then take place between the new person and the local resident. Instead of greeting behavior such as "Who's boy are you," the nonlocal may hear questions such as "Are you with Brother Tom's church?" Further conversation can continue as the local individual relates his or her own experiences to that institution, or to those of someone who is part of that institution. The outsider may begin developing low-level community relations with this individual, including socioeconomic activity.

If the institution or profession to which the individual "belongs" does not have a recognized identity or an instrumental function for local speakers, such conversation cannot continue because common relational experiences do not exist. For example, if a computer programmer does not allow someone to introduce him or her and instead introduces him or herself directly as a "programmer" working for an architectural firm in Lexington, the greeting sequence is likely to end with silence. Nonlocals must either reframe themselves into a community-recognized "belongin" status, such as a husband who is interested in hunting, a wife who likes crafting, or a Christian interested in church matters, or expect to be denied even marginal "belongin" interactions.[17]

When fictive relations can develop, nonlocals become "like a [Kin Term]" and are said to "belong to" or "be tight with" a given family or "set." Individuals who don't "belong" either receive no greetings because their presence is not recognized, receive only highly elliptic local service encounter discourse in making a purchase or asking for a service, or receive a truncated or misfired version of the greeting forms as residents realize they "don't belong." Outsiders receiving such behavior frequently reported to me that they thought local people were rude or that they wondered what happened to mountain hospitality. Prolonged interactions of this type generally resulted in the outsider leaving the community.

Possessive constructions of this "belongin" type are of course not restricted to specific greeting structures, but frequently appear in other, less conventionalized, conversational Ash Creek speaking practices:[18]

(2.2)	Debbie:	My children got it in high school.	[95a:348 7/86]
	Debbie:	My Suzie's not here."	[95a:348 7/86]
	Linda:	My dad, I'd say. he'd play triple handed.[19] [about playing spoons as a musical instrument)	[95b:66 7/86]
	Karen:	Called my aunt . they said I might get to talk to her today.	[95b:421 7/86]
	Man:	He'd gIt his daughter an ol ((2.0)). an then they'd gIt these phone calls.	[96b:360 3/86]
	Debbie:	You should see my grandson if you think her legs are long.	[97a:139 6/86]

These constructions create relations between two lexemes that reference individuals whom speakers presume other interlocutors know. Therefore, one goal function[20] of possessive constructions is to assert publicly an acknowledged "belongin" relationship. Whether novel or repetitive, the utterance of these constructions reveals members of a resident's core network of individuals on whom certain culturally valued socioeconomic expectations can be placed.

As these conversational segments make clear, the strongly preferred form shown in figure 2.3 constrains such "belongin" relations to individuals known to be in real or fictive kinship categories with each other.[21] This grammatical relation of proper name plus kin term merges the cultural category of kinship with the grammatical category of possession and is consistent with much cultural anthropological discussion about community and family.[22] Yet +human possessed nouns are not

[[proper name +'s] / [poss pro]] + [kinship term]

Figure 2.3. "Belongin" relations possessive constructions

only kin terms, neither are they fixed, mechanical constructions, as a discussion of Ash Creek kinship terminology could suggest.

Instead, segment (2.3) makes clear that kinship relations are not coterminous with "belongin" ones:

(2.3) Sarah: Sally Jo is her teacher. [97a:602 6/86]

Teachers of Ash Creek students are often also kin to many in the community, but nonlocal teachers can also assume "belongin" network status through their school and community activities. Residents may then talk about the teacher as someone who is "like a mother to Julie" (speaker's daughter) or "acts like a sister to the children."

It becomes possible through these types of possessive constructions to extend community membership criteria revealed in the more stylized greeting possessive patterns to the full range of possible culturally acknowledged real, fictive, and extended kin relations in Ash Creek.[23] Consequently "belongin" networks are not static matrices predicated only on natal or consanquinial ascribed statuses, but are constructed networks of trusted individuals whom residents call upon to meet various needs, including socioeconomic ones.

As grammatical units within clause or phrase structures, possessive constructions also participate fully within the semantic plane of discourse. The individuals referenced by the possessed lexemes can be assigned attributes, behaviors, values, and qualities that contribute to the maintenance, creation, or destruction of a personal or family "name" or reputation through discourse structuring. The possessor referenced within the possessive construction gains or loses symbolic capital[24] from these semantic processes according to the meaning and value given the utterance containing the possessive. The segments in (2.2) and (2.3) are, in general, mildly positive and are, at the minimum, culturally appropriate and "name" maintaining. Playing spoons, for example, is considered a somewhat frivolous, but acceptable activity. Segment (2.4), on the other hand, is possibly negative, depending on how the respondent structures her answers:

(2.4) Millie: Your daddy's the cause of them not gIttin along better? [97a:314 6/86]

The possessor therefore (the person indexically referenced by "your") becomes linked with the cultural assessment of a kinsperson ("daddy") through "belongin" relations expressed possessively in Ash Creek discourse.

Most Ash Creek residents recognize and trace close and distant kinship relations among each other. Therefore, these constructions have the actual or potential power to strengthen or destroy interpersonal relations, including socioeconomic ones:

(2.5) Two workmen within a work crew of local men talked at length about the failings of a particular local woman in highly negative terms. Finally, after about five minutes of negative gossip about her, a young male worker quietly, using statement intonation patterns, said that this woman was

> his aunt. Verbal silence ensued, and the men talked later at length about not *knowin* she was his aunt, expressing concern that there would be negative sanctions against them not so much from the young worker as from the family of the aunt. [notes 6/86]
>
> A middle-aged, single woman who has lived away from Ash Creek for several years took her car to a local dealership in town for air conditioner freon and servicing. A charge of $45 was levied for the "checking" of the air conditioning system and injection of freon. Her father called the dealership asking about the charge, indicating it was high. The service representative reportedly said, "I didn't know she was *your* daughter," and sent a refund of $34 to her. [notes 7/87]

The young worker did not resign as a result of this first conversation, allegedly because "jobs are too hard to get," but conversational faux pas such as this one create at least differential access to favors and services according to who "belongs" to whom, as evidenced in the second example. From statements such as "We don't mess with none of them kind of people," and "They ain't none of ours," authentically uttered "belongin" possessive constructions reproduce or create networks among specific sets of residents. Kin-oriented, these networks provide the interactional matrices in which specific socioeconomic activities occur, activities that transform the market meanings of K-mart commodities and cable company services into Ash Creek valuations.

They also reveal a linguistic-based source for understanding the construction of interpersonal networks.[25] Those who cannot authentically use "belongin" possessives in Ash Creek discourse are excluded not only from successful completion of stylized greetings but also from much culturally valued conversational discourse in community settings. For without such grammatical privileges, an individual has no "name" and no culturally recognized process for assessing his or her reputation or for assignation to specific network membership. Degrees of trust and accountability in trade or reciprocity transactions cannot be readily assigned. Even after a person has resided in the area for several years, elements of skepticism are likely to remain. One outsider of 18 years who had not been assigned an appropriate fictive status reported a conversation to me in which someone had made comments to him about not being part of the community. In response to his questioning of this evaluation, the resident said, "Don't you know who you are?" The outsider and I agreed that she meant, "Don't you know you don't yet 'belong'?"

Possession, Gender, and Decommoditization

"Belongin" possessive constructions represent of course only one set of possible possessive relations within Ash Creek discourse. Among other possible relations, attributive possessives also express reference relations between individuals and nonhuman entities. They therefore have the potential to create close personal ties to the nonhuman world. As with +human possessed nouns, these constructions reference tangible or concrete entities known or potentially accessible to Ash Creek residents. Again, contextual and grammatical constraints direct syntactic ordering and paradigmatic substitution of possessor or possessed nominals into certain preferred constructions. These preferences guide how commodities are transformed into goods and "property."[26]

Whereas "belongin" possessives reference networking relations among persons, material possessives signify the control and use of valued items by members within these networks. The semantic and pragmatic constraints on these constructions create cultural preferences concerning who can possess what under what conditions that give meaning and direction to the acquisition and circulation of valued entities. However, these constraints are not based on sharp dualities between commodities and goods or gifts and commodities. Rather, they conform to Appadurai's (1986) insight that assignment of value varies within "realms of circulation" rather than being homogeneous within a sphere of exchange. They also support Kopytof's (1986) observation that "things" both come into and go out of commodity valuation across socioeconomic situations. These are constraints upon the linguistic system rather than parameters, constraints that provide direction and range to what lexemes can be possessed and what contextual conditions are appropriate for application of possessive rules. In turn, these constraints provide direction and flow to the construction of the socioeconomic system, affecting what goods and services are readily accepted, weakly accepted, or rejected.

Within the linguistic system itself, grammatical constraints on lexeme selection are an element in determining the discourse shape of Ash Creek material possessives. Most Ash Creek residents prefer a mono- or disyllabic lexicon, which is weakly represented by medieval and postmedieval Greco-Latinate borrowings. Unless part of a borrowed lexicon or representative of style shifts into a Standard Written American English variety, Greco-Latinate nouns, which are major constituents of many other varieties of American English, rarely occur as possessives.[27] Nor are they recognized as appropriate Ash Creek utterances if they do occur.[28] Consequently, many abstract nouns in Standard Written American English that reference qualities, mental or cognitive states, or moral attributes are very rare in Ash Creek discourse. Constructions such as

*her perception

*his moral dilemma

*Joe's belligerence

are excluded from routine, daily conversational discourse. The predominantly Anglo-Saxon–based nouns of Ash Creek tend to be concrete in reference, reinforcing reference to tangible material items in possessive constructions. In the overwhelming number of uses, they also reference entities that interlocutors have personally experienced in the community, county, or regional cities. When potentially abstract nouns do occur, they are usually defined in terms of concrete reference, mitigating potential abstraction: "God's deliverance," for example, will denote an empirical, observed divine intervention to "save" someone or call on a common memory about such an observed event.

Possessive tokens occurring in conversational discourse incorporate this preferred lexicon according to pragmatically and semantically based discourse processes. These processes also create or reproduce indexical relations between possessive constructions and their discursive and situational contexts. These contextualization processes in turn constrain what sets of lexemes can be paired to construct culturally acceptable possessive constructions. Dominant among these constraints are the type of co-occurring nonverbal activities that motivate the utterances in which possessives occur. When individuals are in the act of performing or completing a task, speakers will possess nouns referencing items and actions necessary for them to perform or complete that task:

(2.6) (*Setting: Kitchen at Environmental Center during day work shift; food preparation in progress; lunch bell has been rung for serving lunch. Participants: Sarah, Sandy, Debbie, and I.*)

Sarah: Where is **our milk** we got yesterday.
Is it here in **the refrigerator**?

Sandy: Yeah . that's it.
What's there's right there.

Sarah: Did you get it?
Is that **yours** Debbie?

Debbie: Yeah . I already got one out

Sarah: Oh . ok. [laughing sounds] ((?1.5?))

Sandy: [laughing sounds]

No . but they lacked but what little what was *in* there that one this mornin

You got **cream** with it?

Sarah: Uh-huh.

Edna: Did you gIt **my butter** yesterday Sandy?

Sandy: Uh-huh.
It's right there in **the refrigerator**.

Edna: O:k.

Sandy: An you got **a dime** back out a **your five-dollar bill**.

[98b:134 7/86]

"Our milk," "yours," "my butter," and "your five-dollar bill" represent possessives constructed under such constraints. Motivating possession of "milk," "yours," "butter," and "five-dollar bill" is the ability of the possessor to use or employ the referent to complete some task co-occurring at the time of utterance or at the time referenced by the utterance. "Our milk" indicates that the cooks, as a group, will serve the milk shortly with a meal they have prepared; "yours" and "my butter" imply that the women will use the milk and butter in cooking or as a spread at this meal; and, in this discursive context, "your five dollar bill" indicates that Edna's own money was used ("traded" in Ash Creek usage) the morning before to purchase butter from the center vendor for home use. Contrast phrases, "the refrigerator," "cream," and "a dime," further exemplify these use relations.[29] The absence of a possessor in these constructions is due to one of two possible relations. First, "the refrigerator" references an object used collectively by not only the cooks in the room but the other shift of cooks, the center staff, and, from time to time, guests. Collective use rights mean that an entity cannot be possessed to perform an individual or group task by those performing the task, in this case, the cooks. Second, "cream" is a more abstract noun, although it still references actual individual servings of coffee creamer stored in the refrigerator. It is not being used for this lunch, so the noun is not possessed. Like "our milk," however, it will be when the cooks talk about it in relation to preparing or serving a meal. Similarly, Edna "got a dime back" in change. She is not using this coin for a purchase or some other task, so it, too, is not needed yet. It is, however, "hers" to use as she sees fit when a "need" occurs. Nouns referencing items used in a task become possessed when the items they reference in the present, past, or future are being used to complete the task, unless they reference a collectively owned good.

Likewise, possessives in (2.7) also reflect the task-focused constraint for generating possessive constructions in male discourse:

(2.7) (*Setting: Night woodcarving session with Bill, the woodcarver. Participants: Bill, older visiting woman from North, young outsider man temporarily working in the area, and I.*)

[Sanding is going on in background.]

Bill: I like to carve things that you can [use an]

Woman: [yeah]

Bill: Not jIst sit and look at.

Woman: Yeah.

Bill: ((?2.5?))

Woman: ((?2.5?))

Woman: Around Brasstown

Outsider: [chuckles] or use it an look at it in between times

Anita: [chuckles]

[Woman talking to Bill in background ((?4.0?))]

Bill: They do a lot around Brasstown

Woman: Yeah . that's where I got this a . this a . little piece.

Bill: I think that's where Elizabeth Jones learnt to do **her woodcarvin.**

Woman: Really . at Brasstown?

Bill: But she won't tell ya that . but that's where she went.

Woman: Oh. They have some good carvers down there.

Bill: Yeah . they do . they do have some—

Woman:	—But I don't think they do uh . much with things like this [laugh aspirations] [I'm with you I like]
Bill:	[unintelligible overlap]
Woman:	things that are useful.
Bill:	Yeah . ((?2.0?)) Let me see here . its gIttin . almost
Woman:	Too thick.
Bill:	No . its not gIttin too thick
	It's gIttin where you can use **the finer sandpaper** on this ((?2.0?))
	[watch]
Woman:	[oh]
Bill:	**Your rough sandpaper** up. Do it like—
Woman:	—O:h—
Bill:	—This ya see It don't believe Now when you do **the edge** *this* way, you do it very lightly—
Woman:	—eah—
Bill:	—in order to—
Woman:	—ea—
Bill:	—gIt a smooth finish.
Woman:	And I look at this here It's not . see that. An . an I got a work on that.
Bill:	Now stay . that'll come right out with **your sandpaper** if you do it
	((?smoothly?)) [102b:225 9/85]

The possessive pronoun "her" in "her woodcarvin" is a more abstract usage, modifying a gerund. It encompasses the activity of woodcarving, the tasks included within it, and the products it produces. Therefore, the possessive still references a set of tasks, so it is appropriate. "Your" in the phrases "your rough sandpaper" and "your sandpaper" again assigns possession to a specific piece of equipment used in the process. Both "the edge" and "the finer sandpaper" reference entities that neither Bill nor the woman is modifying or using at that moment. Therefore, the objects are not possessed. These examples reflect typical conversational usages[30] and a highly productive process.

The grammatical process of possessing nouns in co-occurring task contexts binds things to individual or collective selves. This process decommoditizies referenced entities by removing them from the domain of markets where they could be exchanged. A possessed –human lexeme within an utterance references an entity that is not available for gift-giving, trade, or sale—at least at the time of speaking. The entity is instead bound to an individual or sets of individuals who are doing something with it or to it at the time. This proximity to a self or selves creates a visual image of an individual unified with whatever he or she is using at the time and an image of objects that are extensions of those who are using it.

This process becomes further enriched and deepened when only singular possessive pronouns are considered. Tasks are routinely, and often strictly, organized in terms of gender, so singular possessive constructions of the task-linked type regularly reference entities within either women's or men's domains. In addition, residents tend to perform the same types of tasks over and over on a daily or weekly basis. Therefore, certain subsets of possessive constructions become regularized. Bill always uses certain kinds of tools and supplies when he carves, which is five to seven days a week. Sarah always uses pot holders when opening the center oven, which she does five to seven days a week.

As a result of this regularization of possessive constructions in routine task contexts, constructions referencing entities most central to valued gender roles become extended to contexts outside those that originally generated them. Constructions referencing items of lesser value or those that are gender-neutral (e.g., junk mail, pencils, or matches) show high variability in whether they are possessed at all in any context. If they are, they conform to task-oriented contextual constraints. Rarely are they extended outside the task context where the entity referenced is used.[31]

Segment (2.8) represents typical speech of two women talking, in this case, Susie and I. Susie shifts to a slightly more "proper" style to accommodate the "proper" speech bias she presumes I have (e.g., use of "vehicle" and slight phonological shifts not transcribed):

(2.8) (*Setting: Susie and I are talking in a local diner. Susie, who is the diner waitress, is explaining her troubles in getting her young son to his babysitter for the day.*)

Susie: I was tryin to catch **Diane Rogers** [a local school teacher] . an I didn't have **a vehicle**

So I went out to **Mary's** [Diane's mother's local store] an I had **two bags** an there was no way I could make it down the road with **Billy** [her young son] . **the bags**, an **my pocketbook** too

So **Thomas** [Diane's husband] brought me down here

An I called **Mable** [babysitter, kin by marriage] an ((?offered?)) **her vehicle** to this guy. **Penny** [Billy's sister] had **the duster**

Had to have **Billy's** [Susie's husband] **car**

An **Sally** [in-law] took **Cary's** [in-law] **car** into town to have it worked on.

She was without **a vehicle**.

I couldn't get **Sue** [sister in the church]

So I called **Liz** [sister] . an I said "Pick **Billy** up here an take him to **Mable's** for me. [61b:24 5/86]

The problem described is presented as a woman's problem, told by that woman to a woman. Susie was trying to get her young son to a babysitter so she can arrive at work on time when she doesn't have access to a car. The text references this woman's concerns through narrative chronology. Ride after ride eluded her until she phoned her sister, one person in the speaker's "belongin" network who would not have an excuse of sufficient merit to refuse her.

Possessive constructions within the discourse context establish use relations between automobiles and Ash Creek women. They clearly convey an interpretation that one aspect of "belongin" networks is to provide services for its members and clearly convey an interpretation that women have access to and use of cars (not trucks).[32] One possessive construction, "my pocketbook," bonds Susie to a woman's item. "Pocketbooks," which almost all women have, are likely to be possessed whenever they are referenced under the possessive extension pattern. Similarly, "Mary's," ("Mary's place" in more complete phrasal form), "her vehicle," "Billy's car," "Cary's car," and "Mable's" are also extended possessive constructions. They reference human-nonhuman entity relationships used for tasks in so many contexts and so often that they have become regularized to nearly all contexts in which speakers reference them, regardless of whether the utterance references a task or not.

Other phrases, "two bags," "the bags," "a vehicle," and "the duster" also conform to the task-oriented possessive constraints. The "bags" are not being used to complete a task here; Susie is acting as a transporter from the store to the diner where she waitresses. The "a vehicle" phrase references something Sally does not have, so it is not being used. The phrase "the duster" is a token of a regularized gendered process for core, highly valued items. "The duster" is Billy's car, so, even if Penny is driving it, it remains "his" and she cannot possess it. This regularized genderization of vehicles is discussed more fully below.

The use of proper names (or nicknames for men)[33] rather than kin terms in such task-focused narratives is routine in Ash Creek and has, as one major explanation, the need for specific reference. Kin terms (such as "sister-in-law") can be ambiguous or vague or cumbersome to utter. In contexts such as this one in which "belongin" relations are mitigated to focus on the speaker's difficulties rather than the individuals in her network, proper names create a third-person objectification that distances Susie from these subjective relations even though she is drawing on them to solve her transporation problem. Therefore, Susie does not possess the proper name as her mother did in (2.2) when referencing her.[34] Proper names place Susie within a sociocentric matrix of Ash Creek life rather than an egocentric world of herself in relation to her kindred.

For listeners who can physically access the entities referenced by the possessive constructions, the conversational segment assumes a symbolic richness as memories associated with these women, their lives, and their vehicles, and their relationship to both interlocutors can become interpreters for further conversational discourse. The simple recounting of an event therefore becomes a thick text[35] for both reproducing and creating women's place in community life and, in the telling, creating expectations of women's activity domains. These processes in turn implicate these women's socioeconomic domains. Possessive constructions ground these domains through productive, regularized grammatical processes.

Similarly, narrative segment (2.9) presents a daily life problem from a male speaker:

(2.9) (*Setting: Woodcarving session at maintenance building of the Environmental Center. Participants: Bill and I.*)

[Sawing in progress.]

Bill: Well I had a close call tonight.

Anita: Ya did.

Bill: Yeah.

Anita: How so?

Bill: Comin to work.
I tol Sam [his son] ((?2.0?)) he said "naw
It'l go around there"

Anita: Go around where?

Bill: Where you turn off the hi:ll down here and turn into **the campus**
The way it slopes down there

That truck [I said "wont turn around in there"]

Anita: [uh-huh]

Bill: He said "yes it will"
I turned in there an ((?it wouldn't cut?)) and I ski:dded.
An I put on **my brakes** an not have **low gear**.
An uh the back end was doin all right an uh [clears throat]

Anita: [coughs]

Bill: I couldn't control it I mean it was bein—

Anita: —Where'd you end up?

Bill: Right at the edge of **that bank** there with **my nose** that far right down

[gestures toward creek] in **the creek**

[both laugh]

Sam had to gɛt out and push it back in to **the road**

[both laugh]

Anita: He was with ya?

Bill: Yeah [continues to emit tense laughter] [103b:080 1/86]

Bill explains a difficulty he had earlier in the evening driving a truck legally owned by the Environmental Center. As in (2.8), this narrative is also self-directed, focusing on Bill's action. This text contains only two possessives, "my brakes" and "my nose." In each case, Bill has done something to the referent of the possessed noun to change its previous position. This manipulation of an object to alter its position and control the truck constitutes a task. Therefore, as in (2.8), these possessives create a semantic relationship between the man speaking and items within his activity spheres. These spheres are described within the clause in which the possessive is embedded and reference the tasks performed. These are engaging brakes and driving the "nose" (a metaphoric usage) of the truck off the road.

"Low gear" is not possessed because Bill is not using it. "Truck" is not possessed as this discussion would suggest it should be, most transparently because the deictic "that" before a noun excludes possessive pronoun use in English. In addition, center trucks are collective nouns, like refrigerators, and, while other workers may possess "truck" when using one, Bill acknowledges the collective sense of the word here. "The campus," "that bank," "the creek," and "the road" reference geographical places that are part of the center. Nouns referencing geographical places, including personal property, are rarely possessed unless the utterance references the perceived owner under conditions of core, central value discussed below. In this case, Bill treats the nouns as collective, referencing public locations. The functions of the possessives in this text are similar to those in (2.8), where possessives index gender domains of activity for the interlocutors.

Speakers in each example also present themselves as agents willing to perform a job or task but unable to complete it due to the actions of some human or nonhuman other. Segment (2.9) focuses on the truck's actions, which Bill wanted to control but could not. Yet the narrative attributes this incapacity not to Bill's ignorance or stupidity but to the result of following the suggestions of his son, a fully justifiable mistake in Ash Creek family dynamics. A strategic goal of this text therefore differs from (2.8) in that it is intended to enhance Bill's skills for me, a female listener, while, at the same time, explain why the accident should not be seen as a self-deprecating event. By truthfully shifting the burden of the driving error to the youthful son, who does not have the experience of the father, both goals are achieved. Such conversational "work talk" frequently occurs between a man and a woman. Accounts of these types of events among only men tend to omit such causal detail.[36]

Segment (2.10) represents a more stylized narrative genre in which verbal elements are selected according to criteria necessary to develop a humorous or didactic "tale." Consequently, its functions in the conversation are different, with different speech goals achieved by Bill and different discourse functions foregrounded. Contrasting grammatical units in which some nouns are possessed and in which some are not reflect these different goals and, at the same time, express the underlying discourse rules of socioeconomic genderization of tasks and resources.

It contains two conversational anecdotes, each clearly possessing the narrative structure of a "story":[37]

(2.10) (*Setting: Conversational segment between Bill and me during carving session. Participants: Bill and I.*)

Bill: He was makin **this moonshine** an he had **Billie** [his son] watchin for **the revenue men**.

And uh

He was singin **this little song** call uh

"You got shoe:s an I got shoe:s an were gon a walk all over **God's heaven**" ur somethin like that [or]

Anita: [uh-huh]

Bill: Uh . somethin like that

And uh

So Billie got sort a . relaxed an wasn't payin no attention to what he was doin an was leanin againt **a tree** an sort a dozed off an big ol racket down **the hill** and sees **these revenue men** right on im an

So he jumps up

An runs out there an **his dad's** singin **this song** an all an he said "Well you might as well gIt ready

[clears throat]

Anita: [light laugh]

Bill: If you're not gon a walk all over God's heaven . you're gon a walk all over **the Hazard jail house**."

[both laugh]

Bill: So they arrested him an took em both to **jail**. [laughs]
But he'd make **that whiskey**
An hide it in **his bee gums**.
So if somebody wanted to buy **whiskey** off a him
He'd say "I'll be back in a few minutes"
An he'd go out to **his bee gums**
An what . the way he did that was
Ya see . ya have the sections on **the bee gums**
An he'd seal one section off
Of each **hive**
An—

Anita: —Uh-huh—

Bill: —He'd sit **the quart jars** down in there an everybody thought well . he's got a

Fine crop a bees out there

But most of it was **moonshine**.

[both chuckle] [113b:003 10/85]

As a representation of a culturally recognized verbal genre, details and events referenced through discourse are selected to create a desired story structure. It entextualizes actual events presumed to have actually occurred at an earlier time under a guiding set of rhetorical conventions. These conventions foreground intradiscourse coherence features and mute contextualization of possessives into a co-occurring task activity.[38] Grammatical elements, including possessives, become more stylized and conventional. Spontaneous constructions are generally omitted because they could distract from the intended overall effect of the tale. Contrasts between possessed and nonpossessed nouns in this example can therefore be assumed to capture significant cultural meanings rather than be potentially idiosyncratic to the speaker's personal style or to the pragmatic needs of a specific communicative event.

The first anecdote relates a moonshine-making occasion, an activity almost always performed by males and a source of cash income for them.[39] Irony is created through the singing of a religious song while making illegal whiskey. This irony is made salient by the possessive "God's heaven," a presumed real place over which God has proprietary rights and in which making alcohol is strictly prohibited in the Protestant fundamentalist or Pentecostal traditions of the community. The son, Billie, is the focal agent of the story, and the father remains nameless. The possessive "his dad" in the middle of the tale makes clear why Billie would not run from the revenuers. As a co-worker in an economic task involving participants in close "belongin" relations, he is expected to warn the father. Parallelism in the punch line contrasts a holy place with a very profane one, making clear not only that the man was caught in an illegal act but also that the act was highly sinful, thereby adding a didactic element to the narrative.

The second anecdote, also about moonshine and about the same father, uses a task-focused possessive in "his bee gums." It captures the task-focused use of possessives and the gendering of valued items. Bee gums are linked to male beekeeping activities and they are storage facilities for both bees and moonshine. They are not commodities. Equally important, however, are other items involved in the man's beekeeping and whiskey production and selling activities that are not possessed. "Whiskey," "moonshine," "quart jars," and "each hive" are not possessed, even though they are items involved in the tasks of moonshine making and honey production. In not showing possession, these constructions form an obvious contrast set with "his bee gum." If one function of possession is to show bonding of possessed lexemes to possessors as extensions of self (or vice versa), then nonpossessed constructions of the same lexemes must not be in such relations and capable of full alienation from the possessor. Certainly this anecdotal narrative supports this assertion: moonshine is to be sold ("if somebody wanted to buy whiskey") and it is packaged in quart jars, which are sold along with the whiskey. Beehives are harvested for their honey, which is also sold. Selling is by definition a fully alienating economic activity.

Other nouns that could be possessed and are not include "a tree," "the hill," and "the Hazard jail house." These constructions again reference geographical locations and are to be treated as collective, public entities as in (2.9). The phrases "this moonshine," "these revenue men," "this song, "and "that whiskey" contain deictic pronouns being used as adjectives to modify nouns central to the plot of the narrative. They therefore have a dual function here to focus listeners' attention to key narrative elements and to distance the audience from the entities referenced: it was not my moonshine, nor Bill's, but someone else's moonshine that plays a role in this story.

Within the context of a narrative, these contrast sets make clear the discourse patterns that create marketable versus nonmarketable relationships among things and individuals. Possessive constuctions capture nonmarketability of entities referenced by creating a given individual's personal identity in relation to these referenced things. Possessed entities become, at least temporarily, appropriated to one's physical being. In a narrative contextualization when the use of possessives becomes stylized and the tale itself circulates among community residents, these constructions also bond grammatical relations to cultural interpretations of identity. Stories such as this one function metapragmatically to interconnect spontaneous use of possessive constructions in routine daily tasks with narrative retextualizations (or entextualizations). These narratives then circulate as semi-autonomous texts within the community discursive repertoire. As texts, they can be further interpreted, commented on, and used to provide interpretations of how commodities become goods and what this process means to Ash Creek residents.

Underlying use of task-focused possessives in Ash Creek discourse, then, is a grammatical pattern that approaches rule status, as figure 2.4 shows.

As residents perform tasks or activities that require repetitive use of the same resources, discourse that references these resources will reflect possessive use according to the grammatical patterns captured in this rule. Inalienable relationships will become well developed through grammatical, discursive, and activity intersections so that actual conditions of expected, presupposed bonding to self will apply. The entities closely associated with a given individual become cultural extensions of self and, as some residents express it, "as if it's part of me." Phrases such as "my pocketbook" (2.8), "God's heaven" (2.10) and "his bee gums" (2.10)

$$NP_1 \begin{bmatrix} \text{+concrete noun} \\ \text{+task use} \\ \text{+gender appropriate} \\ \text{–alienable} \end{bmatrix} \longrightarrow$$

$$\left[\left[NP_2 \quad \text{Poss} \begin{bmatrix} \text{+human} \\ \text{+gender} \end{bmatrix} \right]_{Det} \quad NP_1 \right]_{NP}$$

Figure 2.4. Possessive constructions with task-activity discourse

accrue deeply symbolic and highly affective significations as interlocutors' associations with the individual (or divinity) possessing the entity are indexed through the possessive. As these ownership relations become expected and presupposed, alienability becomes either inconceivable or a matter of question. Pocketbooks are replaceable, but Susie's purse is part of her and evokes memories of shared interactions and common experiences while creating new ones; it becomes unspeakable to assume that Heaven could be alienated by the divinity; and the man's bee gums sit there for year after year as he alone uses them for multiple personal purposes. They become identified with him and the stories, recollections, and anecdotes about them become stories, recollections, and anecdotes about him as well.

Under these conditions, the task-oriented constraint on possessive use is neutralized and certain core nouns are regularly possessed across discursive contexts. Certain nouns referencing a subset of a particular individual's inventory of things are always possessed, except under a few clearly recognizable discursive conditions: first, whether the entity is a +male or +female item; and, second, whether it is being separated from its possessor for sale, trade, gift, or some other alienating activity.

The nouns that are regularly possessed may be idiosyncratic to a given individual (e.g., "his apple trees," "his bee gums," or "her wooden thimbles") or generalized, applying to most or all community members of a given gender (e.g., "his truck," "her kitchen," or "her car"). Idiosyncratic uses contribute to the construction of an individualized self within a sphere of these generalized activities. Generalized constructions express cultural norms concerning expectations of what each gender should own or have use of and create strong expectations of how men and women should construct their identity in the community. Much conversational discourse functions metadiscursively to reinforce these norms.

Generalized possessed nouns having cultural validity center around central and highly valued activities of men and women that nearly all Ash Creek men and women do. They tend to express identity relations with items related to the sociohistorical dominance of mountain hunting and farming subsistence patterns within Ash Creek. These ownership relations approach the kind of obligatory construction found in the use of body part lexemes such as "his head," or "her foot," or kin terms such as "his daddy" or "her mom." Unlike body part or kinship term possessives, however, the set of possible possessed nouns is not finite, but open, subject to family and community expansion according to regularization in the performance of new or existing community-sanctioned activities. For example, utterance of the tokens "his horse" or "her rug beater," reportedly common in the early part of this century, are much less common now than are "his truck" or "her vacuum."

At the center of +male regularized ownership possessives are nouns referencing culturally valued male items that residents perceive to be absolutely necessary to daily life. These include trucks, firearms, hunting dogs, "cash money," and items related to the maintenance or use of them. Lexemes referencing these kinds of items must be possessed unless they are being alienated for some purpose or being used by a member of the opposite gender. Usage conforms to the following paradigm using "truck" as an example:[40]

(2.11) (M Speaker = male speaker; F Speaker = female speaker)
(2.11.1) M speaker: I drove his truck [friend's].
(2.11.2) M speaker: I drove my truck.
(2.11.3) M Speaker: I drove the truck.
(2.11.4) M Speaker: *I drove her truck.
(2.11.5) F Speaker: I drove his truck [husband's].
(2.11.6) F Speaker: *I drove my truck [husband owns it, she is driving it].
(2.11.7) M Speaker: I drove my truck [wife owns it, he is driving it].
(2.11.8) F Speaker: I drove the truck [husband's].

In each case, variation in the modifier for "truck" is culturally significant with economic implications. Examples (2.11.1) and (2.11.2) are routine, expected uses occurring frequently in everyday conversational discourse. "Truck" references a male item that is generally used and owned by men. Example (2.11.2) implies that the truck is either owned by the speaker or it is owned by someone else and he was using it to perform a task. Such ambiquity is usually resolved by the discourse context. Example (2.11.3) is even more ambiguous but implies that the truck is alienable, either because it is to be sold, given away, or trashed; because it belongs to a corporation, as in the woodcarver's usage in segment (2.9); or because it belongs to a woman in his family—a highly unlikely occurrence. Example (2.11.4) represents the unlikelihood of this possibility. Although not ungrammatical, it is a marked usage uncharacteristic of Ash Creek "truck" sense relations with respect to gendered possession of vehicles. Example (2.11.5) maintains the male gendering of truck, although a female speaker claims to have driven one. This usage is rare, but if a woman has a "need" and no man will drive the truck for her, then she is assumed to have no choice but to drive one. Example (2.11.6) suggests a more egalitarian family power dynamics, also highly unlikely. For a woman to apply the task-focused possessive constraint and say "my truck" when it is commonly used by and probably titled to her husband is an irregular and marked usage. Such a usage can evoke metapragmatic discourse in which women are typed as having more "say." Example (2.11.7) maintains concordance among these sense relations, however. The male speaker is both using the truck and is an appropriate possessor, even though legal title for the vehicle belongs to his wife, a highly unlikely condition. The absence of a possessor in example (2.11.8) need not signify alienability when uttered by a female speaker, although a +male possessor would be preferred. It simply signifies the woman's acknowledgment that she drove a vehicle not part of her domain of gendered entities.

Similar rules apply for +female lexemes referencing resources central to women's core domains (children, scripture and church, homes and the kitchens within them, and cars):

(2.12)
(2.12.1) W Speaker: Jim [son] took my car to be fixed.
(2.12.2) W Speaker: Jim took the car to be fixed.

(2.12.3) W Speaker: *Jim took Bill's [husband's] car to be fixed.

(2.12.4) W Speaker: Jim took her car to be fixed.

(2.12.5) M Speaker: Jim [son] took my car to be fixed.

(2.12.6) M Speaker: Jim took the car to be fixed.

(2.12.7) M Speaker: Jim took Sarah's [wife's] car to be fixed.

(2.12.8) M Speaker: Jim took her car to be fixed.

In these examples, similar constraints apply as in (2.11) except that +female is the preferred possessor marking. It is unusual for a +male possessor to be used with "car." Unlike (2.11), +male possessors can co-occur with "car" (2.12.5) when referentially accurate; it is normative, however, for women to drive cars and for men to drive trucks.

This variation does not apply to nouns such as "kitchen," which reference women's core task areas. Example sentences of the form: *"I went to my kitchen" (male speaker) are inappropriate, and appropriate sentences such as "I went to the kitchen" (male speaker) imply a condition of only neutralizing gender, not that the kitchen is for sale. Whether +concrete nouns referencing these core resource domains are possessed or not depends on what type of core resource domain the noun references. Nouns referencing core women's domains receive only +female possessors; nouns referencing core male domains receive only +male possessors. The presence of gender-marked possessors also link culturally recognized male resources to men and bond culturally recognized women's resources to women. Open and productive, these possessive processes nevertheless are constrained by what is culturally appropriate for a man "to do" and for a woman "to do" and to which resources they should have access to in order to do them.

These processes of singular possession in Ash Creek conversational discourse assume a more complex semiotic structuring when plural possessives are considered. Uniting a set of individuals in a common "belongin" relation with specific task-focused uses, these constructions bond a *group* of human referents to resources. The use of plural possessor forms therefore creates a grammatical construction that indexically or denotatively references those complex personal and communal associations members of the group have with others. At the same time, these constructions link this group to those meanings applicable to the entity possessed. For constructions constrained by a task context, as in "our milk" in segment (2.6), such complex relations are relatively straightforward. "Our" references only the group of three cooks preparing to serve (who are in a "belongin" relationship with each other) and "milk," a food commodity to be consumed by guests. In other discourse contexts, however, these relationships assume much more encompassing associations, providing justification for organized action:

(2.13) (*Setting: Community meeting to discuss plans for Environmental Center programs. Participants: About 35 community members, men and women plus Environmental Center staff. Sally, a local teacher, is speaking.*)

Sally: I really think it's time that we do something.
We got unwelcome here on this campus.
We been . the gates have been shut.
We've been asked to leave.
I've been asked why I was out here.
An all I said was I decided to take a walk . what are you doin.
I mean you ask me what I'm doin . I'm gon a ask you what you're doin.
Uh . **this is ours**.
An if we let it go.
An let them ya know take it an do what they want with it
This is it.
This is the turning point.
We grab hold . we ((?1.0?)) a rope
We grab hold an hang on or we forget it. [93b: 158 6/86]

In this brief segment from a lengthy meeting discussing perceived problems at the Environmental Center, Sally attempts to mobilize the audience into community action. The embedded "this is ours" possessive becomes a rallying point for justifying action. "Ours" references not only the people present, who are all kin, but also all others in the community who have a "belongin" network potential with Sally and the other heirs of the ancestor who donated a parcel of land to create the center. With such a large and multigenerational group referenced, "ours" assumes poetic if not mythic elements, transforming the text into a mythopoetic plane of oral and published "stories" about the founder, his family, the original builders and administrators of the center when it was a boarding school, the shared experiences of those who worked as help at the school or actually attended it, and the memories associated with such "stories"—some or all of which are known to the members of the audience.[41] "This" in the text functions anaphorically to reference "campus" and deictically (as the meeting is on the campus) to index the material array of land and property in the participants' view. As all present had either attended school there, worked there, or had parents who had labored to build buildings or landscape grounds there, "this" also functions symbolically to associate the myriad of tasks and activities forming a composite of memories for the participants. It unifies present activities to past ones and creates a diachronic and historical dimension to one instance of a linguistic token. Implied in this plural possessive construction is plural ownership through doing, through activities and tasks, rather than through legal deed or corporate goals. As used here, possession is neutralized for gender but not for a task orientation. Nor is the possessed noun alienable.

Sally uses plural possessive pronouns to evoke memories of the center and of those mythopoetic verbal genres that interpret and give symbolic and affective meaning to these memories. When residents talk about their homeplaces (chapter 3), their ancestral land, and their ancestors, similar symbolic dimensions are both created and reproduced. The phrase "it's ours" can be highly significant in Ash Creek discourse.

As an overt grammatical category, "belongin" possessive constructions in Ash Creek conversational discourse define a set of potential economic partners. These networks in turn construct preferred patterns for the acquisition, circulation, consumption, and destruction of commodities, decommoditized entities, and noncommodities within the community of Ash Creek. In addition, possessed +concrete nouns are routinely constructed under task-oriented contextual constraints and represent a context-dependent bonding of self to things through the performance of a physical activity. In situations of repetitive use and routinization of the contextual pattern to possess such nouns, regularized possessive constructions construct symbolic meanings that have deep affective significance among members of the possessor's "belongin" network. For core nonhuman resources central to the construction of a gendered social self within Ash Creek, possession of nouns that reference these resources is obligatory in all conversational discourse, except under certain pragmatic conditions involving degenderization or alienability. By linking resources to selves, these obligatory grammatical constructions also personalize economic activities. Possessives create extensions of persons through bonding highly valued entities to selves in a decommoditization process. One outcome of these possessive processes is a set of linguistically based patterns of resource valuation that can support capitalistic commodity-based systems but more commonly works either against it or in syncretic symbiosis with it. General requesting patterns and "order" discourse elaborate on these processes to dynamic, diachronic, and agentive socioeconomic patterns.

3 PARTICIPANT FRAMEWORKS INDEXED BY REQUESTING DISCOURSE

"That's not right."

A local man "drops by" a trailer I'm renting while the landlord is repairing some wiring. After a greeting, the landlord asks the visitor if he "needs" something, to which the visitor replies, "No, I just stopped by to see if you needed some help." After about 15 minutes of conversation about various noncontroversial topics as well as commentary about the cause and best remedies for the task at hand, the visitor asks if the landlord "happens" to own any metric-gauged rachets. The landlord replies, "Yeah, do ya need to borrer them?" "Yeah, thanks." The landlord hands him the box of rachets that have been sitting on top of the dryer the whole time. [notes 8/90]

As I visited a local store one afternoon, a woman stopped by with some items to be delivered to the clerk's sister-in-law. After a greeting and some brief conversation, the patron indicated that she "needs" to get these items to Mable [the clerk's sister-in-law]. The clerk replied, "I don't care to git it to her." [notes 9/85]

ASH CREEK RESIDENTS COMMUNICATE REQUESTS[1] through a repertoire of various verbal, nonverbal, and, very rarely, literate requesting practices. This repertoire contains discourse tokens that are highly conventional in form and appear in routine interactions, not only in interactions with "belongin" network members but also with others in the immediate area and in town. Commonly, verbal forms are single words, short phrases, or abbreviated versions of longer, more formal requesting sequences. Verbal requesting discourse uses deictics, personal pronouns, and concrete nouns as presuppositional and creative indexes to reproduce culturally significant meanings about socioeconomic relationships. Requests are rarely imperatives, although they can have directive force similar to imperatives and can obligate the requestee to comply under certain contextual constraints.[2] Many requests are not direct requests at all, but involve extremely indirect and subtle contextual cues to get the requestee to volunteer to meet a "want" or "need." Most requests accomplish several socioeconomic functions. They enhance or diminish the interpersonal strength of "belongin" networks; they reproduce, create, or conflict with a culturally validated division of labor; they change or maintain the existing status of an entity that has economic value; or they reproduce or change who has access to what valued resources. This chapter focuses on how specific alignments of participants and entities construct basic participant frameworks[3] that reflexively index the kinds of requests that can occur to accomplish these functions.

Through its conventional and nearly invariant structurings, requesting discourse effectively enables residents to circulate culturally valued economic entities on a daily, repetitive basis. Because of the frequency and conventionality of requests, expected or presupposed indexical sign features are strongly reinforced with each utterance. Certain conventional forms acquire a concretion of these indexical significations to the extent that most if not all semantic meanings lie buried under densely packed laminae of presuppositional indexical meanings. The continual reinforcement of these indexes also permits participants to assign complex symbolic meanings to these practical and routine interactions by enveloping them in characterizations, multiple memories, and behavioral expectations about their relations with others in their "belongin" networks.

These indexical relationships between requesting form and participant framework bind the importance and value of entities indexed, the situational appropriateness of who is making a request of whom, the cultural value of the socioeconomic activity requested, and the prestige of the code-type itself into speech act representations that reproduce deeply valued norms regarding socioeconomic relationships. These forms become verbal representations of the state of the socioeconomic relationship as participants assess or reassess it at the moment of utterance. A conventional "can I hɛp ya?" when spoken in culturally appropriate participant frameworks can and frequently does become a meaningful instantiation of an entire set of developed, expanded, or potential socioeconomic relationships. I will discuss the constraints on these frameworks that make them culturally appropriate in order to delimit the contexts in which various types of requesting discourse can occur. I focus on how residents talk about and classify or interpret the participant frameworks in which requests occur.

Personal Pronouns and "Want" and "Need" Constraints

Studies of personal pronouns in interactional contexts have revealed their complexity when contextualized in verbal exchanges. At the very least, they index status relationships and construct social and sociopolitical relationships among interlocutors.[4] It has also become commonplace in the philosophical and linguistic study of pragmatics to assign significance to pronominal shifts in the cultural construction of self.[5] In the Peircian semiotic frame guiding this discussion, the functional roles of personal pronominal shifts assume an additional dimension—

that of personal pronouns as signs in relation to other communicative signs having socioeconomic value in a requesting event. I do not separate interpronominal relations (e.g., "I" in relation to "we" in relation to "you" in relation to third-person forms) from nonhuman objects in discussions of the construction of self in discourse. Rather, I incorporate these nonhuman objects into such discussions. Urban and Lee argue that "the semiotic point of view suggests that the self may be a precipitate of the dialogue with other selves, conceived as second persons" (1989:5). Here, I argue that the self is a precipitate not only of the dialogue with other selves but also with other nonhuman entities having cultural value that are referenced and often physically co-present in a socioeconomic communicative event.

Within the linguistic-economic system of Ash Creek, interlocutors' use of personal pronouns in requesting events is critical to defining the nature of the socioeconomic relationship with others. Nonimperative requesting forms necessarily rely on the indexical functions of English personal pronouns to anchor requesting discourse in the immediate social interactional context.[6] Shifts in person construct closeness or distance among interacting selves and the entities requested. Singular first-person "I" when used with a second-person "you" creates an unambiguous, direct, and subjective relationship among two or more individuals and things within that immediate context. Use of a third-person "he" or "she" to refer to the requestor or requestee creates an ambiguous, indirect, and objective relationship that mitigates or removes obligations to comply and distances participants from the socioeconomic items signified by the utterance.[7] These forms can then create a specific, instantive requesting relationship between or among interlocutors and items that minimize or maximize interlocutors' obligations to acknowledge or fulfill the request. Despite a fixed choice of formal requesting options, the requestor can select from a few personal pronoun choices to construct a unique requesting relationship with a requestee in each requesting discourse event.

In general, Ash Creek personal pronoun usages conform to those reported for English in terms of genderization, intimacy, conversational or narrative cohesion, and levels of formality.[8] Any differences are highly significant for understanding and participating in the Ash Creek socioeconomic system. Residents are conscious of them and possess a metapragmatic and metalingual discourse about them.[9] This discourse reveals that residents impose a second-order classification on categories of person and plurality above what is encoded in the grammar.

When first-person singular "I" appears as a clausal subject, it is clearly distinguished as substantively different from other personal pronoun uses.[10] "I" usages often represent a distinction between a requesting *individual*, who is ego-focused, and any other possible requester configuration. Asserting one's self through the singular "I" foregrounds a specific single subject in a requesting sequence and necessarily separates the indexed individual from others present. There is always the potential that residents will interpret this pronoun as indexing social superiority or distance from others as it simultaneously indexes the person referenced. An "I" form may therefore disengage the speaker from potential relations with others present. Directing pronominal choice away from first-person singular neutralizes the inherent egocentricity of any request and shifts requesting discourse to what Hanks (1990) develops as the sociocentricity of deictic reference in which the *interactional* component of an exchange is foregrounded at the expense of focusing on a particular person.

For Ash Creek residents, the use of first-person pronouns in requests also reveals complex negotiations between two types of egos. The first is the assertion of a subjective, personally assertive, "wantin" self who is negotiating control relations over others by distancing himself or herself from another or a group. "Wantin" selves assert their own desires, impluses, or expectations with little or no consideration for others. In contrast, a "needin" self asserts personal recognition of a laboring, personally devaluating individual who assumes a social stance in concert with other laboring selves or with those who will benefit from his or her labor.[11] "Wantin" selves foreground an egocentric relationship with others; "needin" selves foreground a sociocentric one. Sociocentric selves do things that benefit others or fulfill cultural expectations of how individuals should interact with others. Residents interpret "I need a couch" (woman's usage) or "I need a boat" (man's usage) as very different types of statements from "I want a couch" or "I want a boat" on the basis of distinctions in types of egos. The former foregrounds an instrumental use for the item to accomplish some task necessary for the requestor and others in their networks. The latter foregrounds personal desire with implications that the requestor wants the item for personal prestige or superiority.

The terms "want" and "need" and their lexical or grammatical variants interconnect with fully developed metapragmatic discursive usages that provide insight into how to interpret "want" and "need" requests. The terms themselves are often inserted into conversations through stylized phrases, or "expressions," that justify, explain, or simply classify an individual's motivation or strategy for social action. "He wants somethin" or "she's awantin her way" are commonly heard formulae that stand in stark contrast with "she needs some help" or "he's aneedin him a new truck." Furthermore, nearly any visit to mothers' homes, the county Wal-Mart, or a town grocery store provides occasions for overhearing mothers correcting or questioning their children's speech by saying, "Do you want it or need it?" Many children quickly learn that an utterance conforming to a "want" request is of lesser cultural value and is likely not to be granted.

The entire requesting discourse system consists of routinized requesting patterns in which speakers manipulate personal pronouns within these two core dimensions. Whether explicitly stated or not, residents classify requests into these two categories. A subset of the "wantin" forms becomes embellished in Ash Creek political discourse practices in which "order" constructions and other bald statements of control or power are expected and dominate. "Need" requesting discourse forms become linguistic prestations of a socioeconomic self who participates in the task-focused social domains of Ash Creek productive, distributive, and consumptive activities. Therefore, the full range of "need" requesting discourse patterns are pertinent to this discussion, rather than "want" forms that directly address overt political or control issues. Of course, interacting individuals frequently conflate these two dimensions within a given conversation, and issues of control or power are inherent in nearly any socioeconomic activity.[12] Yet speakers frequently recognize different goals and purposes in "wantin" requesting discourse than in "needin" discourse.[13] It is these culturally recognized differences in functions rather than formal features that allow me to distinguish between these two requesting discourse domains.

"Need" requesting forms reproduce or create complex triadic reflexive indexical relations among request interlocutors, entity requested, and utterance formal features to create appropriate participant frameworks. The formal features of an utterance index these relations by expected contextual associations rather than by properties of the grammatical elements. Certain formal features such as the clause "if you don't care to" or the verbal phrases "let's" or "we need" presuppositionally index a range of appropriate or acceptable interlocutor relations in which a given speaker can appropriately utter one of these clauses or phrases to the other. These forms also simultaneously index appropriate domains of entities that appropriate participants can request given these interlocutor relations. Culturally appropriate requests must honor these complex, reflexive, and intersecting meaning constraints if speakers are to be successfully included in the community socioeconomy.

These presuppositional relations are signified by preferred word order patterns. These relations change as residents negotiate relationships over time. Yet most requestors are known to each other and make requests of each other over and over again, often for the same things or types of things, directing the requesting system toward routinization. Repeated processes of negotiation therefore tightly constrain flexibility in the system by regularities of use that transcend generations and bring the full force of cultural approbation or condemnation to them. Even minor attempts at changing these indexes can be catastrophic. A man, for example, may attempt to create presuppositional indexes with his wife to request the use of her kitchen so he can prepare a meal. Family, kin, or others overhearing the request are likely to engage in teasing, gossip, or other forms of negative evaluation that may force the man to change his behavior and retire this type of request. He may be teased about these efforts for years. For those interacting extensively or entirely within the well-defined "belongin" networks of most Ash Creek residents, such constraints are not trivial, driving the direction and scope of the local socioeconomic system.

Within these presuppositional structures, first- and second-person pronominal forms construct instantative, contextually creative indexes to create immediate relationships between specific speech event interlocutors. For example, the stylized polite asking form "if you don't care to [*predicate specifying entity requested*]" indexically presupposes certain basic relationships among interlocutors that permit the requestor to make a direct request of someone. The pronoun "you" embedded within it indexes a specific person addressed in the specific instance of asking. This customization of the requesting form to a particular participant framework reproduces preexisting relations among interlocutors or provides a means for extending normative requesting patterns to new participant frameworks.

Furthermore, the entities referenced or indexed by the request predicate may also be creative, chosen by speakers for a specific request under specific "need" parameters at a particular time. This level of interactive creativity within a requesting exchange introduces a means for reassessing the status of a requesting relationship. Requesting relationships can be created, reaffirmed, or redefined, or old ones can be broken depending on how the residents interpret the creative indexical sign properties with respect to expected presuppositional indexical patterns.

"Rights," "Place," and "Claims" Relations

Within the Ash Creek verbal repertoire exist numerous tropes and formulaic expressions that contribute to popular conceptions of Southern Mountain speech as "colorful."[14] Their very regularity, conventionality, and level of predictability within what residents call "just talkin" impose a socially agreed upon order to residents' memories of and associations with Ash Creek individuals and things. When someone says someone is "stubborn as a mule," then an individual's behavior becomes one of all behaviors that residents can compare to a mule's stubbornness, and the behavior ceases to be an eccentric or highly individualized subjective occurrence.

Many of these "sayins" also fulfill metapragmatic functions as commentary upon socioeconomic communication. These expressions constitute sets of interpretive schemes[15] that, in turn, reveal facets of an ideology of linguistic-economics in the community. For example, when a wife utters the very common expression, "He [her husband] loves me, he does for me," then she is not only referring to a set of actions performed by her husband but also to a set of presupposed indexical meanings associated with this type of saying. These meanings will vary somewhat from person to person but will encompass a set of shared expectations about what socioeconomic actions men, as loving spouses, should "do" for their wives.

For requesting discourse, three core domains emerge, converging around the terms "rights," "place," and "claims." These lexemes are embedded in a broad set of sayings, conversational topical themes, and religious discourse genres that are central to communicative life and ultimately reveal the metapragmatic interconnections among discursive practices and events that constitute Ash Creek ideologies of linguistic-economy. They invariably refer to human actions or characteristics and therefore commonly comment on the state, value, or appropriateness of socioeconomic activity. For example, when someone commits an unacceptable act, or is talked about as having done so, residents frequently gloss such actions with "that's not right"; if someone performs an action not in keeping with his or her expected roles, a speaker may say, "that's not her place" or some variant; and when individuals condemn or praise a person, usually kin, for some action or character trait, someone may say "we don't claim that one" or, conversely, "we claim her." The relationship of individuals to "rights," "claims," and "place" criteria is constantly reasserted or renegotiated in daily interactions. This renegotiation is central to the construction and continuation of appropriate requesting participant frameworks.

The participant frameworks indexed by discourse containing these metapragmatic designators organize socioeconomic behavior according to a set of interactional roles and appropriate behaviors within these roles. People in Ash Creek have culturally acknowledged "rights" to do certain activities. A primary requirement of a requesting pattern is that the participant framework in which it occurs and that it presuppositionally indexes must create the possibility of "right" behavior by the participants. The requesting pattern must also reflexively index appropriate "place" relations between interlocutors who, with co-occurring or co-referenced entities, constitute the participant framework. Finally, the participant framework must also index some type of "claims" upon other participants and the requested entities.

Most basically, to engage in requesting discourse within socioeconomic transactions, a resident must have the "right" to both make the request and to ask for whatever entity the request entails. As used in Ash Creek speaking practices, "rights" encompass actions that must be moral as determined not only by law, but by God as interpreted in Protestant fundamentalist or Pentecostal beliefs.[16] The semantic meanings of "rights" is nearly identical to what Heath reported for Roadville, a South Carolina Piedmont white community: "The grandparents and parents of the present generation of parents in Roadville often speak of what they did in their childrearing practices by asserting it was 'right.' The rightness of their behaviors and beliefs is, in their minds, in line with their religious teachings and the precepts of the Bible" (1983:138–139). In Ash Creek, however, current parents still talk about "rights" with this level of religious approbation.

"Rights" are not granted on the basis of education, professional qualifications, law or statute, or perceived social class but are predicated on what actions are appropriate within gender, age, religious status categories, or other "kinds of people" criteria.[17] These various "kinds of people" criteria can intersect and conflict in a specific requesting instance, but residents negotiate how to prioritize them through metapragmatic discourse exchanged with members of their "belongin" networks. Stratification of individuals into ranked categories may, in a given instance, conform to other variables that demographers have used to define class membership (income level, educational level, or source of income), but these indicators do not motivate most Ash Creek residents to assign value to what is "right." Religious discursive practices mediated by conversational metapragmatic discourse do.[18]

Individuals engage in labor or economic exchanges according to their "rights,"[19] and what is right is a frequent topic for preaching, testifying, witnessing, and praying within religious settings. Men can hunt in the woods, for example, because it is a man's God-given right; women can demand that visitors eat a meal in their homes because it is a woman's God-given right; and older women can command labor from sons and grandsons because scripture verifies that age has its privileges. These activity domains are predictably rooted in culturally embellished attention to certain life cycle functions and in the subsistence agricultural patterns practiced at all homeplaces until well into the twentieth century. Women's "rights" revolve around childbearing and rearing, literacy, gardening, domestic activities compatible with if not actually supportive of self-sufficient household life, and areas related to moral or religious behavior. Men's "rights" center around nondomestic subsistence or wage labor activities (e.g., logging, coal mining, cash cropping, fishing, or hunting), politics and other matters related to the exercise of personal authority or control, and extra-community cash-money or barter transactions. When someone violates basic "rights" activity patterns, such as when a woman "works like a man," then "it's not right" and sanction, at least as gossip, is likely to follow.

Configurations of men and women's "rights" valued by Ash Creek residents are dynamically reproduced in daily interactions among individuals. The composition of a given individual's corpus of what is "right" may indeed be constructed differently than another's, but speech, particularly speech on or about moral or spiritual topics, functions in part to offer consensus about core, basic, and commonly agreed upon legitimate domains of behavior. Preachers, who have been called and who have "rights" to the major power status in Ash Creek, have a central role in contributing to the construction of "rights."[20] Their moral and spiritual calling imposes a second-order ranking on their more basic roles based on gender.[21]

Even when consensus confirms that individuals are within their "rights," they must conform to their "place" within family or community social organizational structure. "Place" is an extremely complex multivocal construct in Ash Creek discourse practices. The word "place" in Ash Creek speech has an overlapping but still different definition than it does in scholarly geographical and cultural discussions in which issues related to more abstract relations involving region, space, locale, and identification are explored for theoretical or analytical purposes.[22] Ash Creek meanings exhibit dual, interconnecting levels of usage. As reported for many rural Southern Appalachian communities,[23] "place" assigns an individual to a geographical locale such as specific holler, creek, or incorporated town (as in, for example, "up Laurel Holler"). Denotational reference to these geographical locales evokes its own indexical relationships. Specific hollers, community material lore, valleys, towns, and other places of human occupation have histories and community narratives about them. Discourse that includes reference to these locales will index these memories, signaling presuppositional indexes about any new human referent living in such a place. When one Ash Creek resident says to another that someone has moved into Jones Holler, the interlocutors will be able to immediately assess where the resident is living, what his or her daily life at home will be like, and probable reasons why the person chose to move there. These reasons are often based on "belongin" obligations (or "claims").

The last names of the residents who live in these places also evoke narratives and historical descriptions that have become associated with them often because families have lived on the same land for generations. Anyone familiar with rural Appalachian communities or older Appalachians has encountered discourse about a particular family's "homeplace," or physical location (which may or may not include an extant house) from which a family claimes to have originated. And they have listened to the myriad narratives and mythologies about these homeplaces and their ancestral or current residents as discursive practices which empower descendants in cultural life, not at the margins, but in the center of it.[24] Ash Creek is no exception and residents talk extensively about where homeplaces are, where they were, and what has happened to them. For some, births, burials, marriages, funerals, gardens, and the full complement of daily life activities are still centered at the "homeplace" because it still exists, although it may have been remodeled or redesigned. Others build new homes or locate mobile homes near decaying "homeplace" houses just to be near the "homeplace" or on "homeplace" land. Still others are left with only "stories," material remembrances, or photographs. Grandchildren or great-grandchildren presented with family land may have demolished the family "homeplace" to erect more modern structures but still keep the land and many of the narratives that transform it into a mythic plane. A "homeplace" grants residents community identities within the matrix of Ash Creek social relations, and grounds them in cultural time and space as autochthonous. Those with kinship ties to multiple family "homeplaces" are in particularly strategic positions to negotiate socioeconomic and sociopolitical relations in the community, county, or region because they have access to discourse appropriate to a number of family identities and multiple "belongin" networks.

On the other hand, previous generations may have lost or sold land to logging corporations, mining companies, or the Environmental Center. Those without ownership or use rights to real "homeplaces" or "homeplace" land are disenfranchised or marginal, subject to the discountability or social rejection discussed by Batteau (1983b) as applying to "just renters."

The meanings of "homeplace" center the discursive uses of "place" itself in a specific locale so that residents can talk about the holler, branch, mountain, or "place" from which someone comes. Such assignment of "place" then opens up discourse about that locale within the narrative representations of families and community history. "Homeplace" meanings also serve to distinguish individuals who have fully legitimate membership in community life from those who never can. For if a person must assert, as I did, that a family's homeplace was lost when grandparents migrated to urban centers, or that this "homeplace" is in another county some distance away, then the fixing of a given self in time and space is tenuous, predicated on the knowledge of a few who may know the "place" from which this outsider comes. Ash Creek usages of geographical "place" meanings are therefore well developed and particularly rich. They contrast with reported uses of "place" by many coal camp residents, for whom "homeplace" is meaningless or ungrounded in a real locale because they have lost any physical ties to a specific homeplace.[25]

A more dominant meaning of "place" that restricts and redefines this primary geographical one refers to an individual's position within a complex set of relationships with others, generally kin in a "belongin" network. In this sense, "place" is negotiated, asserted, and developed over a lifetime of community life with others rather than assigned statically on the basis of discursive practices involving a specific space. Negotiated "place" relations are often also linked to physical placement of a person in relation to others. A woman's "place" with respect to her husband is to be at home while he is out providing for her and his children. An elderly woman's "place" at a family reunion picnic is at the head of the table while a young newly married daughter-in-law sits on the side, away from her mother-in-law. Therefore, "place" relations resonate with Duranti's description of place within Samoan ceremonial greetings (1992) in which an individual negotiates status and authority through placement of his body within a ceremonial greeting space and through the greeting discourse such placement evokes. Ash Creek uses, however, extend to all culturally recognized spaces and settings[26] and involve the activity of placing each other in requesting participant frameworks in relation to each other's entire social and socioeconomic network. They therefore overlap with the functions of "placing" Kingsolver describes for an east-central Kentucky county:

> Rather than shifting always between *fixed* roles and statuses, I believe Greenway Countians, when "placing," are crafting social structure in each interaction in order to establish, disrupt, or maintain relatedness and, among other things, access to decision-making and resources considered vital. (1992:131; italics in original)

The "crafting" of "place" in Ash Creek is also an ongoing interactional process but is not identical to that in Greenway County. The kind of openness in place negotiations suggested by Kingsolver is less developed in Ash Creek. It is instead rooted in the primary, geographical definition that limits and directs placing structures. I quickly learned, for example, that even when I was within my "rights" as a woman to do household tasks for one ailing older woman or to offer automobile transportation to another younger woman, for some it was not my "place" to do so, whereas for others who were less "placed" geographically in community life, such offers were welcome. Likewise, even if a resident has the "right" to show someone how to do a task, it must be his or her "place" in relation to the other to perform the demonstration. Once a set of "place" relations are created through negotiated relations with others over time, residents have relatively little power to change how a known other "places" them, for most of their social interactions are with a finite set of known, local, and familiar "belongin" network members. Exceptions are culturally recognized epiphanies such as a religious conversion experience in which a public, much discussed change in personal identity is acknowledged and incorporated into daily interactions. As a result of these known communicative structurings, "place" relations among interlocutors create participant frameworks that have encompassing indexical significations within requesting discourse events.

To develop reciprocal or trade relations, however, individuals must have "claims" on each other, meaning they must be in an active, ongoing, face-to-face and personal relationship with someone who meets "rights" and "place" criteria and who can be expected to fulfill each other's "needs" to some degree. Family members in belonging networks can "claim" time, labor, goods, and information from each other simply because they have the "right" to do so, it is within their "place" to do so, and they are in regular contact with members so they can exercise "claims" relations over them.

For close family members,[27] the exercise of "claims" relations usually requires members to transcend the immediate state of the interpersonal relationship even if it is being contested. Nuclear, affinal and natal family schedules, itineraries, or plans will be altered, often significantly and on very short notice, to address the need of a brother or sister in a crisis, such as a personal injury from a truck accident, an onset of the flu or other temporary illness, or a need for transportation because of a vehicle problem. In another example, members provide assistance to obtain a grandparent's christening dress for an infant niece or nephew scheduled that day or the next, regardless of the current condition of the "belongin" relationship with the parents. "Claims" relations demand immediate attention when made salient, with little to no tolerance for previous obligations or commitments. Students will miss classes, adults may miss work, and vacations may be canceled to meet "claims" obligations.

"Claims" relations rarely appear as overt referential statements within conversational discourse, or what most residents call "just talkin." Although talk about how individuals' actions conform to "rights" and "place" obligations is common, discourse that makes "claims" salient and a matter of discursive reference is not. Occasionally a speaker will assess one's character by saying, "I don't claim him," or some variant of that statement. These statements led me to ask about what such sentences meant and how people developed "claims" with each other. Commentary was extensive, effusive, and narrative-rich.[28] Clearly "claims" in Ash Creek denote actions related to reciprocity exchanges. It is, however, a metapragmatic designator that is rarely uttered. It is the component of participant frameworks most dependent on my own imposition of meaning on the sound representation and least represented in Ash Creek "sayins" or everyday discourse.

Although "claims" are rarely acknowledged publicly by the person obligated, much family conversational discourse involves discussions of "claims" violations by close relatives through tropes such as "it's not right." For close family members, "claims" criteria will apply regardless of a specific slight or violation until someone consciously ceases to "claim" another, a very rare and socially disruptive occurrence. It does happen, however, even between parents and children.[29]

More distant kin may or may not be "claimed" according to individual preferences or "needs." When affirmed and developed, an expanded network is created through negotiating such ties by both interlocutors. Men, for example, obtain different vehicles by "tradin" with a cousin who obtained it from a brother-in-law; a woman is given clothes for her newborn from a sister who got them from her sister-in-law's niece. Conversely, a man ignores potential "claims" relations with a first cousin, saying, "I don't want nothin to do with him."

Claims relations must be nurtured and reaffirmed on a regular, often time-consuming basis. When months go by without some form of exchange between those obligated, "claims" relations are likely to be dropped. Previously provided goods and services are offered no more. Participants avoid each other. "Claims" can be redeveloped, but suspicion always remains that the individual who has let the "claims" ball drop will do so again. One expression frequently spoken in a slightly humorous manner captures the obligatory nature of "claims": "What have you done for me—lately?"

Speaking practices that address the reckoning of kinship become critical discursive practices in determining how "claims" relations can develop, if at all, and in revealing the kind of "belongin" relations that underpin them. "Claims" relations are not begun without some preamble that "places" interlocutors in relation to each other. In this sense, "kinship talk" functions as socioeconomic sorting discourse among accepted community residents, categorizing individuals according to their ability to talk about natal or affinal ties among residents and those events, narratives, or actions that illuminate such ties. These, in turn, actualize or legitimize "claims" relations among a culturally appropriate set of individuals.

The following segments discussing kin relations in some fashion are what I call "kinship talk." In each segment I am an interlocutor. Each references kinship relations in ways significant to the other interlocutors, who already know most kin relations within the community. Residents correctly assumed that I was unfamiliar with the scope and complexity of these kin relations, so they often provided me with information about them. In the following segments they used discursive practices that shape the meanings given to these relations and that demonstrate *how* individuals talk about kin. In so doing, they also relayed information about what "claims" relations were possible. The discourse incorporated the neophyte, in this case, me, into the social network through a requisite reference to a kinsperson or other "belongin" network member whom we knew in common. Should the speaker not be able to make such a referential link with the addressee, kinship talk fails to create a culturally appropriate pragmatic relation between participants. "Claims" relations cannot be created.

Segment (3.1) offers an explanation as to why the speaker knows little about his grandparents and clarifies kinship relations to his grandparent generation so that I (or potentially any newcomer) can insert living residents into the community kinship lattices more accurately:

(3.1) (*Setting: Maintenance room at the center where Bill eats his supper and instructs in woodcarving around 10 P.M. Participants: Only Bill and I.*)

[both pounding and sawing noises in background as we are preparing wood for carving]

Bill: I think my [pounding noises] Grandpa uh Miller didn't want ((?2.0?))

[pounding noises]

He made . a lot a whiskey I think.

Anita: What was his first name again?

Bill: Paul was his name.

[pounding]

Tim was my . grandpa's ((?1.0?))) on my [pounding] father's side.

Anita: On your father's side?

Bill: Yeah.

But see my mother and Dorthy's mother is uh sisters.

Anita: Uh-huh. [81a:564 1/86]

Bill's last statement references Dorothy, a woman I knew and had been interacting with frequently. This reference linked what I knew about her and her family to his own kin network and included me into this larger meshing of relations. Such information facilitated an understanding of an individual's actions or behavior in the present and the development of "claims" individuals have placed on each other in the past. In this case, any reciprocity relations between Bill and Dorothy and, equally or more likely, between Bill and Dorothy's husband, can be explained in terms of "claims" developed between first cousins. In a community in which time itself is a significant variable in developing or truncating these "claims," such knowledge assumes far more than simply referential viability. It assumes mythic and legendary dimensions as well. The conversational narratives contextualizing such references into discourse displace specific individuals, both living and deceased, and their actions into a timeless dimension of family "stories" or "tales." It is this process of encrypting names of relatives with attributes, actions, and narratives that transforms them into unifying, symbolic forces that embellish their descendants with family identity.

Segment (3.2) is an example of such a contextualization:

(3.2) (*Setting: Maintenance building of center at night. Participants: Bill and I.*)

[sanding noises in background]

Bill: Martha Smith's husband's . dad
Anita: Ok.
Bill: An . they called im Marvin
And uh . they's all sittin around eatin their
Dinner . lunch . scuse me
An uh [chuckles]
Anita: [aspirated laugh]
Bill: But tuh—
Anita: —Ya know I'm gone a gIt you fɛr that (aspirated laugh)
Bill: They got into a conversation about ya know
All of what people like
An what people *didn't* like
An what people thought
An all this kin a stuff an the conversation kept goin on
An somebody uh . raised the issue "Well . I don't see why in the world"
Said "Everybody can't think like I think."
An uh . Marvin's wife was named *Ollie*.
And uh . he said "Well . I'm glad everybody don't think like I do."
An directly he said "Well . why Marvin?"
He said "Because everybody'd be wantin Ollie" [chuckles]

[83a:000 10/85]

The necessary referential link to individuals I know is "Martha Smith," an older Ash Creek woman. The anecdote is humorous and representative of Ash Creek conversational narrative structure. Similar to a parable in form, it also serves to situate Martha's father-in-law into the timeless dimension of Smith "doins," or expected behavior, reproducing a mythology that extols individuation of self within a small, kindred-based group of men who interact with each other often. As a reproduction of a cultural core value, the anecdote has a conversational function of informing me, the newcomer, about that matrix of relations surrounding Martha, which community members know or should know about. The implication of the narrative that monogamy is morally correct suggests that Marvin is a worthy man. This, in turn, implies that Martha's "set" of kin (those Smiths living in a known and lexically designated "place") can be called "good people."

Segment (3.3) is an example of the speaking practice of kinship reckoning, a type of kin talk overtly marked for gender. Among other forms of gender marking such as types of topics and paralinguistic features, kinship reckoning requires that the speaker link to other kin through his or her own gender; general preference is for women to link to other women and men to link to other men.

(3.3) (*Setting: Kitchen of Environmental Center during afternoon work shift. Evening meal preparation in progress. Participants: The cooks Sarah and Linda, the center staff member Karen, Karen's niece currently living in a town in an adjacent county, and I.*)

[Karen and her niece have just entered to use the phone in the back of the kitchen, and introductions are taking place.]

Karen: You all know Kris? You do don't ya?

Linda: Yeah . I do.
[background] conversational exchanges ((4.0))

Karen: This is Anita Puckett.
This is my niece Kris.

Kris: Hi . [I know you.]

Anita: [Hi.]
Yeah . where'd we meet?

Kris: Down at the store.
You came down lookin—

Anita: —Oh that's *ri:ght*.
Was your hair different?

Kris: Yeah . I . I haven't done a thing to it today.
I jIst washed it an Mother stopped by an gIt me and away we went.

Sarah: I bet you know . uh . Red . don't ya?

Kris: Red who?

Sarah: Red Lead. [polite laugh] Melvin Thomas.
He's my brother.
Kris: Yeah . is that right?
Sarah: Uh-huh.
Over here we know em by Red Lead.
Kris: Lives up Elm Branch.
Sarah: Yeah . uh-huh . married Samantha.
Kris: I've known im forever.

[Conversational interlude as I describe where the phone is located: Karen asks Linda about her mom's health; Kris talks about "needin" a car—this becomes a volunteering discourse section—I inject a comment about my vehicle woes; Kris and Karen leave, a loaner car having been found.]

Linda: That's Herman Smith's girl . that's Mable Jones' girl. ((?2.0?))
Yeah . that's Karen's brother's girl.
Sarah: Uh-huh.
Where'd she live at now . Nonesuch?
Linda: No . she married Ralph Thompson brother to them other fellers . Loyal . an Fred an all them.
Anita: She lives in Homestead.
She's got a store there . right?
Linda: No . she did have.
She ain't never . she lives over in Ashwood. [24a:350; 10/86]

This form of discourse contains at least two major segments: first is the introduction of Kris, an interlocutor, into a conversational segment that is then followed by discussion of how that person is related to one of the participants or to some commonly known kin group.

In this example, the act of introducing Kris ("You all know Kris?") is a prestation of a valued person into the setting of women participants. "Knowing" her depends on placing her into the community matrix of kin, which Sarah does by asking if she "knows" a man (Sarah's brother) who is addressed by a two-morpheme, rhyming nickname. Kris apparently does not know him well enough to "place" his nickname but does recognize his legal name. She uses a formulaic hyperbole, "I've known im forever," legitimating her "belongin" criteria for group membership in Red Lead's locale. After Kris and Karen leave, Linda further "places" her into a specific kinship network using links through women ("Mable Jones' girl" and "Karen's brother's girl") as well as men ("Herman Smith's girl" and "married Ralph Thompson brother to them other fellers"). She also situates her in a real, known geographical place, thus opening up "rights" to construct "claims" relationships, should there be a "need" to do so.

For those, such as nonlocals, who cannot be referenced legitimately through such kinship discourse, fictive "belongin" "rights," "place," and "claims" criteria are established through involvement in church affairs in which an individual can assert saved or born-again status. When such identities are recognized by church members, the new individual can be addressed or referenced as "sister" or "brother,"[30] which are appropriate to any member of the community known to be a practicing, saved Christian. Once established, similar claims are placed on such individuals as would be levied upon a biological brother or sister, with an added spiritual dimension. Since most churches have extended family members as parishioners, such congregational expectations tend to overlap with already existing familial claims. For nonlocals, however, these claims become appropriate means for integrating into the reciprocal Ash Creek socioeconomic system. For not only can "belongin" possessives apply, but also "rights" and "place" criteria as well, giving an outside woman or man an opportunity to engage in the full range of Ash Creek cultural life as either a male or female participant.

Similar fictive criteria can be assigned to valued professional statuses, assuming they also meet "rights" criteria. These are very limited in Ash Creek.[31] teachers (usually female), nurses (always female), and medical doctors (usually male). Nonlocal women can also be "placed" by marrying an Ash Creek man. A nonlocal man marrying an Ash Creek woman is less likely to develop strong "place" relations in Ash Creek strictly on the basis of marriage.

For nonlocal, non–church-going men, "claims" relations can be developed to a limited degree through willing participation in community-valued male task activities, whether automobile repair or coal hauling. In exercising appropriate requesting patterns, such individuals become a "buddy" and can participate fully in task-centered male activities. These claims, however, are work- and labor-focused so that the structuring of "place" presuppositional indexes exclude them from the types of "belongin" matrices fictively recreated in religious extensions of the terms "sister" or "brother." They are, however, a significant set of interactional processes by which non-Christian men, but rarely women, can be incorporated into community life, functioning as a significant opportunity for the genderization of labor.

It is through "claims" and "claims" processes that goods and services circulate in the local, community economy generally among members of a "belongin" network; it is through "having claims" on someone that communicative patterns of requesting or obtaining such goods or services operate. It is through the well-developed speaking practice of kinship reckoning and other, less structured uses of kinship discourse that such patterns are given cultural approbation.

All requests must index appropriate participant frameworks that reproduce or create appropriate "rights," "place," and "claims" relations. Requesting discourse patterns construct intersections of these three basic interpersonal relationships that create or reproduce specific participant configurations. The interactional meanings indexed by these configurations are the major constitutive force in generating the local socioeconomy.

4 "VOLUNTEERINS," DIRECT "ASKINS," AND OPTIONAL USES OF NONIMPERATIVE REQUESTING DISCOURSE

"You shouldn't have to ask for that."

I am talking with a temporary staff person at the Environmental Center about differences in the ways local people speak. The staff person mentions going to a local mom-and-pop store and asking for something only to have the clerk respond "I don't care to." The clerk's positive intonation patterns confused the negative meaning the staff person wanted to assign to the utterance, leading him to question what the phrase actually means. [notes 10/85]

I mention to Debbie that I need to mow the grass at the house I am renting but that the landlord does not have a mower for me to use. She immediately "volunteers" her husband's mower if I come over and pick it up. I do, but when I return it, I find myself "shamed" by her praise over how much I had mowed in so short a time—a clear exaggeration. I do not borrow the mower again. [notes 6/86)

An Ash Creek woman's son has been targeted as a young man with artistic talent by a local teacher. She tells his mother that she "wants" him to apply to an art school in Pittsburgh. His mother mention's the teacher's conversation to me. I respond with enthusiastic endorsement and suggest that she obtain some brochures and other information about the school. The mother quickly responds negatively saying that she can't tell him what to do; he has to make up his own mind about attending. [notes 10/87]

ROUTINE WAYS OF MAKING and interpreting "need" requests in Ash Creek differ, sometimes significantly, from patterns reported for more urban, formal institutional or corporate settings.[1] Similarly, patterns of who can ask something of whom may also vary according to the specific configuration of "rights," "place," and "claims" relations and how a particular individual interprets communicative indexes constructing them. These variations in the form and functions of requesting patterns suggest that they also constitute different linguistic-economic processes.

This chapter focuses on how the most common ways of making (or not making) requests construct divisions of labor and facilitate the circulation of commodities, goods, and services in Ash Creek. These patterns are strongly developed and, in most cases, create requesting contexts in which the requestor does not make a direct request—rather, the requestee offers or volunteers to do or provide something. I organized these common patterns into optional uses of requesting discourse, "volunteerin" discourse, and direct "askin" discourse.

"You Shouldn't Have to Ask": Optional Uses of Requesting Discourse

When individuals create a requesting participant framework in which their copresence presuppositionally indexes appropriate and developed "rights," "claims," and "place" criteria, then a requestor has full cultural approbation for obtaining a valued item from another or others within a common "belongin" network, as long as the acquisition of the requested item does not violate these "rights," "place," and "claims" relations. In appropriate cases, the normative, or expected, pattern of exchange is for the requestor to simply take the item (whether it is material or intangible) without any verbal requesting discourse. Or the requestee may give the item or perform a service, again without a verbal exchange. Of course, such nonverbal action may be accompanied by extensive "just talkin" (conversation) on other matters while the exchange is being executed. Planning or discussion about the exchange may have taken place earlier as narratives or informative discourse under "need" categorizations. For example, days or weeks after a conversational exchange about how a son "needs" a chain saw to cut down some trees, the son borrows a chain saw from his father by simply taking the tool from the shed. On another occasion, a sister announces to her sister-in-law that she "needs" her vacuum cleaner as an aside within an animated exchange of "just talkin" and simply takes it on her way out unless stopped by the sister-in-law. When picking up her own daughter at an after-school event, a woman drives her niece home from school because the niece "needs a ride"; and women relatives bring gifts of food to the bereaved family at a wake seemingly without any discussion whatsoever, while male relatives dig the grave, monitor parking, or, possibly, act as ushers.[2]

Well developed in scope and complexity, these nonverbal actions within the highly developed exchange system based on "claims" in Ash Creek daily life assume a communicative priority over verbal ones and assert a metacommunicative message about the strength and quality of dyadic social relationships: the more frequently silent acquisitions are made and labor performed without contestation, the more binding the relationship.[3] A person in such a relationship "shouldn't have to ask for nothin."

When such alignment of requesting relations exists, sometimes an explanation is necessary, especially when the "right" to take the item is not certain or problematic. These explanations will be a single, simple, declarative or interrogative utterance spoken with declarative intonation. These declaratives generally reference the co-occurring action, telling the requestee how the requestor interprets the act he or she is performing. They therefore exhibit what Urban (1993) defines as a "signaling function," implying they contribute to the meaning of the communication of which they are a part as it is being communicated. Their explanatory value enhances "claims" relations by giving the requestee (or possessor of the item) an opportunity to respond that the co-occurring action is or is not acceptable to the possessor at that time. They also allow the requestee to validate that the action is "right" and that he or she is in his or her "place." Usually the subject of these declaratives is a first-person pronoun ("I" or "we") that indexes the speaker. The pronominal subject anchors the declarative to the speaker and to the action he or she is performing. It contextualizes the utterance to the co-occurring nonverbal communicative act.

In the following five segments, (4.1)–(4.5), the verbal construction co-occurs with the action it references, indexing deeply sedimented "rights," "place," and "claims" relations:

(4.1) (*Setting: Environmental Center kitchen at end of first shift; second shift cooking staff arrived one half hour earlier.*)

Sarah: Well . we're goin. See you girls later. [34b:664 12/85]

Segment (4.1) has the explicit ends function of a leave-taking. The plural pronominal subject ("we're") indexes Sarah and the other cooks leaving with her. It is a woman's core "right" to labor in a kitchen, so it is "right" for a woman to utter a clear leave-taking that describes their departure when leaving a kitchen. The use of "girls" also reproduces this "right" by referencing the other women who are now in the kitchen, first by their "place" by virtue of a woman's "right" and second by their hired position as cooks.[4] Sarah is the head cook and she has kinship ties to the other women working in the kitchen whom she is addressing. Therefore, the workplace "belongin" network created by these workers is also a subset of a community "belongin" network that exists apart from the work setting. Over decades, Sarah has negotiated her "place" in this "belongin" network as work organizer, menu planner, and inventory and kitchen manager at the center. It is therefore her "place" to refer to the change of shift with this inclusive ("we're") leave-taking. She reasserts the "claims" relations developed among these women with "See you girls later," which foregrounds the cyclical, reoccurring nature of the labor obligations they have created among themselves through working together in this "place." On the other hand, men who came into this kitchen for whatever reason would either leave without any verbal leave-taking or use a more concise form such as "see you later," uttered softly or as they actually opened the door. It was often impossible to hear these utterances if spoken at all or to know whom among the group of male and female workers the ambiguous "you" indexed.

Segment (4.2) represents a teenage boy's glossing of a routine activity, performed regularly in this kitchen at this time (paying for the soda pop as he takes it by putting money in a jar):

(4.2) (*Setting: Environmental Center kitchen during the afternoon. Food preparation in progress.*)

Boy (female worker's son): I'm gIttin me a pop.

[as he obtains a soft drink from the refrigerator] [100a:72 6/86]

The action referenced is within his "rights" because children generally have full access to whatever kitchen food items are available in any household. It is also his "place" as the son of a co-worker at the center to treat the kitchen as an extension of his home kitchen with certain modifications such as paying for the soft drink. In addition, any child has "claims" on an adult woman to have her provide core women's resources, including food. By glossing the action with words, he is developing "claims" with the kitchen help. He has developed a debt, albeit a small one, with them unless they respond to his statement negatively so that he cannot obtain the drink. After several occasions of this type of requesting pattern, the cooks were able to ask him "to do" things for them such as fetching or carrying items or taking messages to someone with expectations that he would comply. The young man "owed" the cooks by virtue of their "claims" on him and his debt to them.

Segment (4.3) informs others about where Sarah is going and why she is leaving the kitchen setting:

(4.3) (*Setting: Environmental Center kitchen during food preparation period. Participants: Sarah, Linda, Sandy, and myself*)

Sarah: I'm goin downstairs and gIt us some good. [108b:295 7/86]

The "I'm goin downstairs" clause refers to what Sarah is actually doing as she is talking. "GIt us some good" frames the activity as one "needed" by all, thereby centering it in the sociocentric area of group cooperative interaction. In doing so, Sarah is recreating "claims" relations with the other cooks so they will perform services for her that she may need done at some future time. It also indexes the "rights" and "place" of this cook to perform this action and reproduces them as she performs the nonverbal activity itself.

The fourth declarative, segment (4.4), is a contestative declarative utterance that violates these "rights," "place," and "claims" indexes. All three female cooks are watching hot food cool while waiting for Johnny, who is paying for the meal, to announce it so serving can begin.

(4.4) (*Setting: Dining hall at Environmental Center at night. A special event hosted at and catered by the center is in progress. Cooks have been waiting to serve for several minutes. Cooks are waiting behind serving line.*)

Debbie: JOHNNY, WE'RE READY TO SERVE.

[No verbal or nonverbal response comes from Johnny. He addresses the group shortly, calling for grace, which he gives. After grace, with no prompting from him, guests line up to be served.] [100b:425 6/1986]

As a verbal gloss on what the cooks are doing at the time it is uttered, this declarative (and its first-person plural pronominal subject) clearly indexes the cooks' "rights" as women to control food preparation, distribution, and consumption. Johnny and his guests are in the cooks' "place," that is, the dining hall where food is served, so the utterance also reproduces their "place" as hired food preparers to serve it. Any potential authority privileges that Johnny may have as a male caterer and dinner organizer are called into question by these presuppositional indexical "place" and "rights" relations. "Claims" relations between the cooks and Johnny are also weak because there are none. The cooks are in only a temporary, wage-labor relationship with him. He is not acknowledged kin and not a member of the cooks' "belongin" networks, although he is from a nearby area in the county and they are familiar with his "name." Under such problematic "claims" conditions, the preferred requesting form from Debbie would be either a "volunteerin" pattern or a direct "askin" pattern. In this situation, Debbie's declarative falsely indexes "claims" between requestor and requestee. It therefore foregrounds that "claims" do not apply. Johnny is "wrong" and out of "place." He should not expect and did not receive any pro-offerings of extra labor or services, common when "claims" are developed and rare when the relationship is entirely based on wage-labor.[5]

In segment (4.5), Edna uses an interrogative form to refer to her putting her own quarter in a hat:

(4.5) (*Setting: Environmental Center kitchen during meal preparation. Participants: Sarah, Linda, Sandy, Edna* [*a temporary helper*], *and I.*)

Edna: Did you say put a quarter in?

[puts quarter into a jar as she speaks.]

Sandy: Uh-huh.

[Edna puts quarter into a jar for betting pool on exact date of delivery for an expectant woman in the community, not a member of the staff. Proceeds were to go to the expectant mother.] [6b:120 1/86]

With this utterance and its accompanying action, personal "claims" are clearly being affirmed by Edna's giving money voluntarily for a betting pool, an activity the cooks agreed to do as a gift to a member of their community "belongin" network. Such an activity, which is outside of usual tasks performed in the kitchen, is not related to Edna's "place" obligations as a wage-laboring cook at the Environmental Center but to her "place" among others in her more encompassing "belongin" network. The embedded clause "put a quarter in" is an imperative. In situations such as this one when "claims" relations are clear and being reproduced, the controlling and directive force of such constructions is mitigated, especially when embedded in another clause so it becomes reported speech.[6] Rather than an "order" indexing "wants," it is a "need" construction requesting others to do an activity Sandy cannot do entirely herself.

Segment (4.6) is not part of the metapragmatic speaking practices that gloss socioeconomic activities but is included for contrast purposes as a representation of a set of larger conversational discourse patterns:

(4.6) (*Setting: Environmental Center kitchen during food preparation. Participants: Sarah, Sandy, Linda, Edna* [*a temporary helper*], *and I.*)

Sarah (to kitchen staff): So whoever finds out about it first is supposed to call the others.

[Request is for future information about the upcoming birth mentioned in (4.5).] [6b:199 1/86]

Sarah attempts to commit a third-person subject "whoever" to the action of notifying others about the upcoming birth. This formulation simultaneously describes a future act, that of notification, and attempts to commit one of the group to perform this action at some later time. This utterance entextualizes declarative patterns that contextualize socioeconomic acquisitions into a mandative subjunctive. The embedded declarative has not lost its "rights," "place," and "claims" indexes, however, in this entextualization. Under "claims" relations, a person who obtained this information and did not pass it on would be jeopardizing her "claims" status with the other women if they found out. Privacy is very hard to obtain in Ash Creek, so it is likely they would not comply. Exceptions would be a serious "claims" activity such as an illness for a close family member. Much conversation consists of such reference to obligations, intents, clarifications, and needs through the use of clause structures similar to segment (4.6) or reported speech that incorporates patterns similar to (4.2)–(4.5) as direct or indirect quotations. Focusing primarily on topics of tasks, behaviors, or moral obligations, these conversational patterns create interconnecting metapragmatic discourse that interprets or evaluates the "rightness" or "place" of people's actions at a plane more removed from the actual context of socioeconomic activity. At the same time, these conversational patterns index other actual contexts in which these optional declarative utterances occur, providing a means for interpreting them.

In general, patterns of daily socioeconomic activity within the Ash Creek area are highly predictable for a given individual (for a detailed description, see "Summary of Daily Activities," Appendix B). Therefore, "claims" on one another are created through the repetition of similar types of services or prestations, exchanges, and borrowings often of the same items with or from the same individual or "belongin" network members. Individuals come to depend on one another for meeting their daily life needs. Therefore, these distributional and exchange patterns become highly routinized, especially in terms of what residents come to expect they can or should obtain from whom and where, creating socioeconomic grooves into which labor, exchanges, and goods are channeled.

"Let It Be Known": "Volunteerin" Patterns in Requesting Discourse

At certain stages in church services, at public meetings, or at other events when a leader has the floor, he or she may call for members of the audience to comment on a policy or make a "need" salient, using the expression "just let it be known." If residents uptake[7] on the referential meaning of the expression, they are likely to state a problem or "need," often in a narrative. The leader may then offer to help or call on others present to pray or perform some efficacious task. In doing so, the group uses "volunteerin" requesting discourse patterns, a phrase I adopted based on residents' use of it.

When "rights" and "place" contextual meanings are appropriate, but "claims" presuppositional indexes are unclear or not established, some verbal form of communicating a request becomes not only appropriate, but necessary. Participants in an exchange do not know what the others "need." The ability of language to specify the nature and type of service or item needed assumes a paramount function in a situation of uncertainty. Preferably, the item or service should be offered by the person having the resources rather than actually requested by the one who does not. This cultural preference shifts the burden of defining the parameters and content of the request from the requestor to the requestee. It also inverts request control and compliance relations to the requestee. It frees the requestor from shame or humiliation and burdens the requestee with the likelihood of condemnation or embarrassment if the request is not granted.[8]

Among the most developed preferences is the requestor's use of a conversational narrative, often lengthy, that presents a problematic condition. A potential requestee should respond to the conditions in the "story" by volunteering to help. For example, the lawn mower synopsis at the beginning of this chapter resulted from my conversational narrative about how much trouble I was having mowing my grass. Without being aware of it (until much later in my fieldwork), I had used requesting narrative discourse with the local woman. She responded to the narrative with a volunteering of her husband's mower. At the time, I was surprised and pleased at her kindness; she was responding to what she understood to be a request.

Other modes of circumventing a direct request include the use of a "broker" or intermediary who intercedes for the requester and presents a third-person narrative detailing a problem. Often requestors will refer obliquely to a request through questions, statements, or by proximity—simply positioning oneself physically in the presence of someone who can fulfill certain requesting "needs." Requestors may also use silence and noncommunication, often over long periods (perhaps years) to coax or "shame" the presenter into a "voluntary" pro-offering of a service or item. The saying "you shouldn't have to ask for that" is a culturally meaningful epithet, capturing core cultural norms about exchange participant frameworks, frameworks that often contradict more professional, corporate models of American English discourse interactional patterns, which encourage development of direct request forms.[9]

Even when "right" and in their "place" (in community terms), outsiders who encounter this system experience major conversational disjunctions or miscommunications. Many locals seem unwilling to ask for anything, whether for the office hours of the Environmental Center, assistance in filling out forms, health care information or assistance, or information about educational curricula or governmental programs for them. Conversely, local residents frequently comment on how these outsiders don't want to "help us" or "think they are better than we are":

(4.7) Outsiders who were acting as servers at the food line at the Environmental Center stood patiently in line waiting for local youth to ask them for a drink preference, Coke, Mellow Yellow, milk, etc. The teenagers stood in front of the drinks for about thirty seconds before a worker finally asked, "What drink would you like?" [notes 6/85]

In discussing enrollment in a local community college extension class, a local woman said to me that she simply didn't know classes were being offered. I mentioned that the county newspaper had printed announcements and schedules. This evoked the response that she didn't get the paper and no one had made the effort to tell her; she had children and couldn't get out much. I offered to bring her schedules in the future. [notes 10/86]

Routinely, local women or men enter the office of the Environmental Center for some purpose. The expected pattern is for them to simply stand near the main door until someone notices them and asks them how they can be helped. If no one offers, they eventually leave. A few younger women, on the other hand, may utter a referential declarative such as "I'm waitin," move into a position more obvious to the secretarial help, or begin a conversation with a woman clerk after several minutes. A few exceptions of course exist among these younger women, usually among those who have lived "up North" and returned to Ash Creek, but the preferred pattern is to wait until acknowledged. [summation of notes, fall 1985–summer 1987)[10]

All residents, whether male or female, expect the requestee to initiate the requesting interaction. Should a "volunteerin"[11] utterance not be offered by the requestee, the requestor has the option of leaving without having been compromised or "shamed" by rejection. Conversely, once a "volunteerin" participant structure has been created, it is very inappropriate for the requestee to deny volunteering compliance to the implied request. Residents are extremely aware of the indexical meanings created by the co-presence of individuals within these problematic "claims" categories and in some cases will engage in complex avoidance techniques:

(4.8) For those women receiving government aid to dependent children, the completion of Department of Human Services certification and recommendation forms is a requisite for receiving benefits. One local woman, who regularly acted as recommender for several others who were in her "belongin" relations, reported that when she saw X coming, she was never at home because it meant she was going to be asked to either fill out a form or exchange food stamps for cash, something she didn't want or need to do. [notes 5/86]

Denying the requestor would have been impossible, as "talk" would have ensued and "belongin" networks jeopardized. Other strategies requestees use to avoid the onus of "volunteerin" include taking different roads to reach a desired destination and timing necessary or fabricated departures in order to miss requestors who might stop by "the house," who might be at the local store or post office to meet them, or who might wait by the side of the road where they could flag the requestee down under some other pretext. In some cases, people have avoided certain local stores, have changed churches, or even, in one case, have moved away from the community area entirely to avoid certain requestees.

"Volunteerin" discourse as used here represents a common set of conversational structures that generally have socioeconomic ramifications for obtaining goods and services under the problematic "claims" conditions I discussed above. As conversational structures, they conform to various expandable and reducible turn-taking patterns common to any verbal interaction.

The six stages depicted in figure 4.1 represent fully developed "volunteerin" exchanges. Truncation of all but the requestee's "volunteerin" core of these patterns regularly occurs when the requestee knows the requestor well enough or uses other contextual cues to discern a probable "need." The requestee may also desire to control the direction and scope of the goods or services volunteered by preventing full development of the narrative of the problem. Otherwise, the

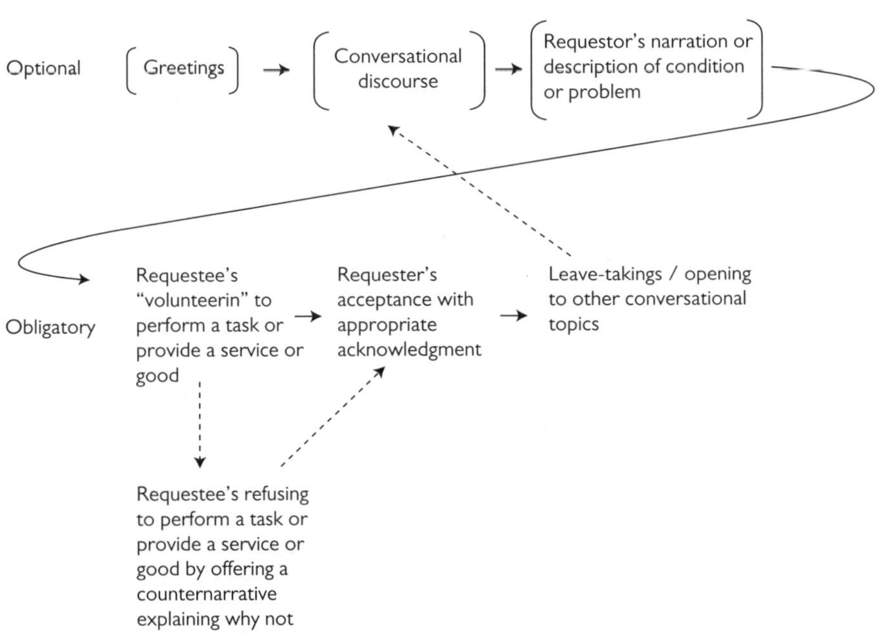

Figure 4.1 "Volunteerin" conversational patterns

requestee complies with the request then or later, depending on the type of labor, good, or commodity requested, the nature of its relationship to the requestee (e.g., whether it is possessed property or an alienable commodity), and the "rights," "place," and "claims" relations among the participants.

In more fully developed volunteering sequences, it is up to the requestee to take the conversational initiative by volunteering during or after the presentation of a "need" narrative or description:

(4.9) (*Setting: Community college extension class I am teaching during class break, all women; those talking are married with children. Example represents a brief segment from an extended conversation.*)

[Discussion revolves around whether Student 2, who is traveling to the University of Kentucky Medical Center in Lexington to be with a sick father, will go to the university library and get some books for other students while she is there. She will not but offers to go to the community college book store on the other side of the county.]

Student 1: I've got to go to the libary an gIt me some more books.

Student 2: What day do ya want a go.
I can't before Friday. [Students 1 and 2 are cousins.]

Student 1: No . you cant go tomorrer either . can ya?

Student 2: No::

Student 3: She can go Thursday. [Student 3 is a sister to student 2.]

Student 1: She'll be gone.

Student 3: I mean Lexington.

Student 4: You can go to the UK library Thursday. [Student 4 is a cousin to Student 2 and knows about Student 1's upcoming trip.]

Student 2: I ain't goin to the UK library Thursday.
I don't know where it's at.

Student 4: Well call up Susie [Susie is niece of Student 3 who attends the University of Kentucky in Lexington.]
((?She'll tell ya?))

Student 2: I ain't gonna do it
I got my th . thoughts on other things as fɛr as gIttin out a that place.

Student 4: Well excuse us . fɛr livin.

Student 2: You ((?welcome?))
I'm goin to the bookstore tomorrer
Can I gIt you anythin?

Student 3: Not much you can buy me ((?unless you buy?)) ((?2.0?))
[112b:325 9/86]

Segment (4.9) is a complex representation of a "volunteerin." Student 2 receives strong suggestions through indirect imperative syntax ("you can . . .") from her classmates (and kin) to get books from the University of Kentucky library, suggestions that she rejects. This rejection is followed by her "volunteerin" to buy things at the community college bookstore, which she is visiting the next day. Although this "volunteerin" could be interpreted as a strategic use to mitigate the rejection of the other students' bald, on-record suggestions to visit the University of Kentucky library, it also observes rules of use regarding "volunteerin" discourse. Embedded in previous conversational discourse not transcribed here was a reference to problems students were having obtaining material for and writing on topics for a final library term paper. These discussions established a narrative frame for presenting a problem common to most members of the class. The clause "I've got to go to the library and gIt me some more books" summarizes the previous loosely structured and interactionally constructed narrative and makes the problem clear. Student 2 volunteered to address that problem by "gIttin anythin" for them toward the end of the segment. As most could not afford or would not spend money to buy anything unnecessary for a class, such a "volunteerin" presumed minimal effort on the speaker's part, and the phrasing of the "volunteerin" did not commit her to "buy" anything for them using her own or their money. She artfully met her volunteering obligations without risking a potential commitment in time and money.

Segments (4.10) and (4.11) represent "volunteerin" contexts in which the requestee offers use of resources or labor unavailable to the requestor because of gendered division of access and control of them:

(4.10) (*Setting: Environmental Center kitchen; cooks are cleaning up after a meal. Participants: Sarah, Debbie, Karen and her niece Kris, who have entered the kitchen to use its telephone, and I. Conversation in progress.* [*See segment* (3.3) *for conversational exchanges surrounding this one.*])

Kris: Karen [woman on phone]

If they can't that's ok

I'll ((?2.0?)) gɛt a car.

Anita: What is it you need?

Kris: My car tore up an my husband's in the hospital an I got a go pick Im up

So I got a borrer a car

Ur either go get

I was gonna borrer Alice's but she ain't got hers it's in the shop.

Anita: Yeah . I got one

Got a truck out there but I gotta gIt out a here in a minute and use it

And I got another one

But you wouldn't want a use it
It's not workin . it's in the shop.
Kris: Yeah . everybody's is in the shop
[aspirated light laughter from both]
Karen: **He said come on . he'll take ya.**
Kris: Oh . ok.
Karen: I figured he would.
Kris: Ok. [24a:377 10/86]

(4.11) (*Setting: Bake sale table outside voting location during voting hours on election day. Four local women sitting at table. I knew two of them, Mable and Becky, who are sisters.*)
[woman voter to women at table after brief greetings]
Voter: **My husband said to give you this.**
Sorry it can't be more . but that's all he had.
[hands a handful of change to woman at table]
[Women at table thank her as she enters the voting place.] [notes 11/85]

In (4.10), Kris "needed" a vehicle for a very highly valued reason, to transport her husband home from the local hospital. Kris lived some distance away and had not developed strong "claims" relations in this community, so Karen acted as an intermediary to make a telephone request of a common male relative. In this segment, Kris repeats the problem to me after I asked for clarification. Kris and I are not in any form of "claims" or "place" relation, nor would it have been "right" for her to ask a near stranger for anything, so she did not use "volunteerin" discourse with me. Karen, however, did use normative "volunteerin" discourse patterning to the male caller. Having found a male relative to volunteer both a vehicle and himself as driver (a male-preferred role), Karen returned to the kitchen, informed Kris of the results of the transaction, and both of them left to meet the man who was to pick them up.

Segment (4.11) reflects a more complex expression of gendered control of resources in "volunteerin" discourse. The woman, having seen the table of bake sale goods, proceeded to talk to the women minding the table about their health and the purpose for the bake sale. This conversation established a problem through narrative structuring. She then took out her wallet and checked for change, giving all the coins she had to the women at the table. She bought nothing. She framed her donation in terms of her husband's wishes rather than her own, creating a context in which she deferred the use of the money to a man.[12] With some exceptions (such as money made from crafts or part-time work), the earning and spending of money is within the domain of men, who may choose to give some to their wives, as alleged here. "Volunteerin" constructions often require the shifting of agency from the presenter to an individual not present who has the gendered "right" to possess, control, or offer the good or service.

Finally, segment (4.12) represents an artful and highly indirect example of volunteering discourse:

(4.12) (*Setting: Homemakers' meeting in Environmental Center community room, about 12 local women plus a few young children, ages 4 to 8, and I. All are kin but three—including me—who are affiliated with the center in some way. We are making some craft from preshaped wooden figures.*)

Mable (local woman with high prestige and a "good name"): HEY BECKY.

[loudly to her sister, all overhear]

Becky: What?

Mable: **Uh**

I thought

And we could pay a dollar dues each . each month.

Becky: Six dollars?

Mable: Yeah . uh-huh . yeah.

[to six-year-old nephew] **Jimmy . we need to give you**

Get you a dollar here

You got a dollar?

Becky: **Get you a dollar.**

[By addressing the nephew and getting him a dollar out of her purse, Mable circumvents any discussion of the matter by the group; willingly or unwillingly, we voluntarily pay a dollar at the end of the meeting.]

[50a:210 6/86]

Mable and Becky had stated to me earlier that getting women to pay dues had been a problem. The topic has been raised in previous meetings with no dues offered. Therefore, Mable's strategy was predicated on a previously stated problem. Mable states the problem of paying dues in terms of a "need" to pay one dollar each month. She then redirects the "need" to making sure her young nephew (approximately six years old) has dues to contribute. This action successfully removes any possibility of the other women not paying dues. No one wished to be "shamed" by not doing what this small boy did, which was to hand the dollar back to his aunt as a dues payment at the end of the meeting (although he probably didn't know what "dues" were). The increase in dues becomes a fait accompli, and we all "volunteer" through prestations of a dollar accompanied by declarative glosses such as "here's my dues." Mable elicited full compliance through verbal means.

These segments represent common examples of "volunteerin" conversational discourse in which compliance was granted. Nevertheless, after a problem narrative, the requestee can also reject the implied request by not volunteering to do anything. A phatic "well" or "is that so?" or some nonverbal gesture such as eye contact must be made as a politeness device. These discourse markers[13] also function as noncommittal responses to the request embedded in the narrative. Whereas "well" often means "yes," it also functions as a backchanneling utterance, simply acknowledging that the speaker has heard what the other interlocutor said. Another response is for the requestee to offer another narrative that explains why he or she cannot meet the "need" described in the requestor's narrative. This strategy then shifts the burden of "volunteerin" from the original requestee to the original requestor, turning the tables. The "volunteerin" cycle can begin anew. These turn-taking options save face without forcing a requestee to comply.

Regardless of the discursive complexity surrounding a "volunteerin" exchange, requestees commonly use two highly conventionalized verbal constructions, both clausal, when volunteering compliance. As conventional, routine forms, these constructions are nearly invariant presuppositional indexes of specific "rights," "place," and "claims" configurations in participant frameworks.

In accord with most "volunteerin" constructions, these conventional clauses require a first-person pronominal subject that both indexes the requestee and acts as a subject referencing the predicate. This dual functionality commits the requestee to an action specified by the utterance. When the "volunteerin" is clearly performable by the requestee, when "rights" and "place" criteria are unclear but not inappropriate on the part of both participants, and when "claims" for the specific type of request are weakly developed,[14] the preferred form a requestee uses in response to a posed problem is "I don't care to [*reference to task/request*]."

As Ash Creek referential meaning is the opposite of the urban, professional American English meaning, this conventional "volunteerin" form also performs a gate-keeping function by confusing nonlocals who have not mastered its local uses:[15]

(4.13) (*Setting: Maintenance building of Environmental Center late night during Bill's supper break. Participants: Bill and I.*

[Conversational segments are interspersed with long pauses as each of us works on our carving. I have been eliciting comments from Bill about the ways people talk.]

Bill: Yeah, people that come in here gIts confused about the way we talk.

Heather [his daughter] asked Abe [Heather's husband] one time to do something

An he said "We:ll . I don't care if I do."

An she said somethin like "Well . what does that mean?" [chuckles]

That means—

Anita: —Ye:s.

Bill: "Yeah . I will."

She said "Well . I just wanted to be sure" [chuckles]

[86a:30 2/86]

Because "I don't care to" configures problematic "claims" participant frameworks, it is one of the first requesting discourse patterns an outsider will encounter in community socioeconomic interactions:

(4.14) (*Setting: Local mom-and-pop store, during open hours. Participants: Loretta, who is daughter of owner minding the counter, and I. This event occurred early in my stay in Ash Creek before I was aware of how kinship relations affected which local store a person patronized.*)

Environmental Center staff have given me a package to deliver to a local woman, Mable, by leaving it "at the store." Knowing only that Mable's mother-in-law owns a store, I have stopped by to drop it off. I indicate that this is to be given to Mable, and the clerk looks confused. I ask if she will see her soon. "Yeah, on Saturday." I ask again if it would be possible to give it to her. Clerk responds, "I don't care to," with clear eye contact. I offer her the package, which she takes, and Mable eventually receives it. [Confusion occurs over why that store was selected; Mable's mother also owns a store a few miles away, and, as I found out later, that's the store that the package should have been delivered to.] [notes 8/85]

Offered in response to a requestor stating a problem in narrative form or posing a requesting question, the "I don't care to" "volunteerin" discourse form is strongly preferred in most situations in which "something unusual" is "needed," as presented in segment (4.15):

(4.15) (*Setting: Local medical clinic during working hours. Participants: clinic nurse practitioner* [*Millie*], *who manages the clinic, receptionist* [*Joan*], *and I. I am waiting for Millie to be free for a casual conversation.*)

Millie has been talking to Joan about her "need" to be gone on Thursday and Friday to attend a statewide continuing education workshop series in Lexington. She mentions that the health care provider organization stated that the clinic could be open during these days to schedule appointments and take calls. Joan then responds "I don't care to work Thursday." [notes 3/92]

However, when "rights" and "place" criteria are clearly indexed, a requestee may reconfigure "volunteerin" verbal exchanges so that he or she anticipates a "volunteerin" sequence. The requestee does not wait for the narrative portion of the sequence but offers to meet the anticipated "need," using "let" constructions, a question form, or perhaps a declarative.[16] Although very common in all culturally appropriate requesting contexts, "let" constructions are the preferred verb (i.e., the more normative or appropriate) under conditions in which "claims" are being developed or are somewhat problematic. Under such conditions, the politeness implication of "let" is preferred.[17]

"Let" implies permission with a deleted "you" subject and mitigates the unilateral ends function of direct imperatives to demand compliance from the addressee. "Let" constructions also maintain "volunteerin" requirements that the burden of acknowledging and then completing the requested act is still on the speaker, not on the one spoken to. This syntactic shift maintains the highly preferred cultural practice of a requestee's volunteering to complete a task or to initiate an exchange of a valued entity.

The transcribed utterances in (4.16) function as metapragmatic glosses of simultaneous action and are very similar in speech act function to optional declarative forms exemplified in (4.1)–(4.5).

(4.16) (*Setting: Center kitchen, Sarah to other cooks*)

Let me check an see fore we go down" (to the basement) [112a:067 12/85]

(*Setting: Center kitchen, male maintenance worker to cooks.*)

Let me take the trash out here. [34b:392 12/85]

(*Setting: Center kitchen, Sarah to me in response to my showing her a recipe in a magazine.*)

Let me gIt my glasses. [73a:101 7/86]

(*Setting: Woodcarving sessions at maintenance building of center; Bill to nonlocal visitor.*)

Here . Nancy . let me show you what I did after you left Saturday [101a:050 8/85]

In addition, the /let me/ construction exemplified here foregrounds a request for permission from the addressee through the "let" form itself. It therefore incorporates an overt politeness dimension as the speaker begins an action.[18] The use of these constructions constitutes a "volunteerin" because the speaker assumes responsibility to perform a task or activity in response to a "need" posed by or shared with other participants. In these examples, the "need" is presented nonverbally through the speaker's interpretation of the ongoing sequence of daily activities. In other situations, others may have introduced some conversational topic that shapes a communicative context into which a /let/ construction can be introduced.

The requestee's performance of the action glossed by the "let" utterance also marks creation, enhancement, or reproduction of "claims" relations because the speaker is doing something ostensibly for another or others. This action must, of course, reference activities suitable to the speaker's gendered "rights" and "place."

In addition to the previous functions, segment (4.17) also signifies authority relations through the postposing of the tag question "we can use that some day, can't we?"

(4.17) (*Setting: Center kitchen, Sarah to Linda. Sarah is examining an old pot they found in cleaning.*)

Let me look.

We can use that some day . can't we? [111a:105 7/86]

"We can use that some day" asserts that the utensil being examined has a potential use, yet the tag question hedges this assertion.[19] Uses of tag questions to mitigate assertions are very rare in Ash Creek women's speech. They tend to occur among women who are nonlocal or have lived in urban areas or work in jobs where they frequently interact with urban tourists or visitors. This tag, then, marks Sarah as talking "proper" (i.e., as talking more like the outsider women who visit the Environmental Center or who have been administrators of it). It sets Sarah apart from the other cooks as having a different social ranking. Likewise, /can/ in the statement portion reinforces this "proper" usage, since use of a double modal, /might could/, would be more representative of Appalachian English[20] and accord with the speech of the other cooks. Here, Sarah is asserting her "place" as head cook.

Segment (4.18) is a stylized conversational marker and, despite the syntax, not a demand nor a "volunteerin" form:

(4.18) (*Setting: Center kitchen, Sarah to me at the beginning of a conversational turn*)

Let me tell you [60a:299 7/86]

It opens an expressive discourse segment in which a speaker, in this case, Sarah, "speaks her mind" about some matter. As with many "volunteerin" forms, extensive repetition across speech events creates stylized uses so that conversational functions take precedence over the propositional meaning of the clause.[21] Such functions mitigate their requesting force.

Segment (4.19), on the other hand, represents an utterance of "let" volunteering discourse ending a conversational narrative in which Linda related an incident with her son-in-law. Therefore, pragmatic constraints affecting the construction of segments (4.16)–(4.17) do not apply:

(4.19) (*Setting: Center kitchen, Linda to other cooks and myself. This utterance concludes an anecdotal conversational narrative.*)

I let him borrer my car . didn't want him to. [109b:044 7/86]

The effect of "claims" criteria to mitigate a control or authority function of "let" is very apparent in this utterance. Linda "let" him use her car, although she didn't desire to do so, revealing a significant pragmatic meaning of volunteering discourse. To volunteer is an obligation under recognized "rights," "place," and "claims" criteria and need not signify volition in response to a "needs" request.

"Let" constructions can be deeply embedded as residents attempt to comply with "rights" requirements. Women will use "volunteerin" discourse patterning with women in their "belongin" network to ask them to act as intermediaries for access to male goods or service resources. They will attempt to elicit "volunteerins" from the wives, mothers, or other close female "belongin" network members who have developed rights and place relations with the men controlling the desired goods or services.

(4.20) (*Setting: Parking lot outside the post office.*)

Susie and another local woman, both mothers, were discussing the "need" of one's husband to borrow a motorized tool possessed by the other's husband. After following the general volunteering pattern, the requestee

> volunteered: "Let me let him [her husband] let Billy [Susie's husband] use it." [notes 8/85]

Under close family "claims" relations, a woman can often volunteer to "ask" her husband to agree to do something for someone in the wife's "belongin" network, as made clear here. Men also engage in similar multilayered and cross-gendered requesting patterns.

Therefore, "let" constructions can also permit the requestee to commit someone who is not present and has different "rights" domains to fulfill a request at a later date. Such a commitment requires that both the requestee and the referenced individual be in a well-developed "claims" relationship so that the commitment is met. In actual Ash Creek relationships, such "claims" obligations are often problematic. Volunteering one's spouse to do something for someone else does not carry the performative force of a promise.[22] It does, however, reproduce "rights" and "place" relations among those participants who created the "volunteerin" frame in the first place.

These embedded volunteering constructions represent an intersection of not only "volunteerin" discourse forms, "claims" processes, and socioeconomic distribution activities but also control relations based on status and prestige. Interlocutors assume the power to make commitments of others' resources and time. Should follow-through occur, and it may not, the person committing another's goods or labor enhances his or her own "name" as someone who can "get things done" and who is a "good neighbor" or "true family." "Claims" are also enhanced.

These embedded constructions also make clear cultural boundaries concerning the distributional spheres of economic goods and services. Such commitments of others occurs only when the requestee is unable or inappropriate to fulfill the terms of the "volunteerin." The previous encounter constructs a "volunteerin" structure for two men to exchange certain power tools, objects not usually possessed or used by women. It therefore reveals the distinct separation of men's domains from women's. The men do not interact directly in this case because they are not in a "belongin" relation, and "claims" between them are weak, a situation not true of the women.

These embedded forms are relatively rare and less preferred by residents because they reveal asymmetrical control over economic domains in Ash Creek. They overtly reference acts culturally acceptable for each gender and age to perform, and, most importantly, they commit those not present to future activities. Committing others to any act is almost always problematic. Few residents placed in a situation of volunteering another wish to risk the potential "shame" associated with the possible noncompliance that may result. Most will chose to use a non-"volunteerin" strategy to deflect the request.

Occasionally, the powerful ability of "volunteerin" patterns to index the current status of "rights," "place," and "claims" among participants in face-to-face situations must be neutralized. The kinds of participant frames face-to-face interactions create may force the receiver of the good or service to be overly indebted to the "volunteerin" giver. The receiver may not be able to reciprocate at an equal or greater level. Or perhaps the giver is actually a group of individuals who do not want to "shame" or embarrass the receiver through the size of the gift. Under such circumstances, those "volunteerin" strive to deny agency. Anonymous deeds are done when the receiver (and his close family members) are not around. Gifts are sent through the mail, left on a porch, a truck seat, or in a shed. Of course, the giver is often known to the receiver through such factors as passersby noticing who makes the prestation, by the type and quality of food offered, by the nature of the Christmas gift selected, or by the type of tool offered. The result is that only semi-autonomy is created by such efforts. Ultimately given cultural value through residents' use of commentary and conversational discourse that explains, assesses, and evaluates the nature and purpose of such gifts, these gift givings create highly affective meanings in situations of use. Many residents discuss such acts as "showing we care," where "we" refers to those in tight or loose "belongin" relations with the receiver.

"I Need Some Gravels": "Askins" and Direct Requests

Certain communicative contexts exclude the possibility of "volunteerin" discursive practices or make them a less desirable option. It may be necessary for a requestor to ask for something directly. Ash Creek residents make a clear distinction between "askin" and "tellin" someone what to do, using such expressions as "Are you askin me or tellin me?" and "Ain't nobody tellin me what to do." Nevertheless, in most communicative contexts, the transparency of "askin" discourse demands as much compliance on the part of the requestee as does "tellin" someone what to do. "Tellin" discourse includes imperatives and other forms of "order" discourse, asserts the requestor's control over the listener's behavior, often involves "want" requests or demands, and may evoke hostility or violence if improperly used. On the other hand, "askin" discourse is also problematic in terms of personal obligations. It obligates the requester to the requestee if the requestee fulfills the request or can create ill feelings and grudges if he or she does not. When granted, and "askins" usually are, "they" create debt and asymmetrical control relations between interlocutors.[23] Consequently, "askin" discourse can detract or weaken "claims" relations, rather than enhancing them, and, over time, may jeopardize social relations in general.

Yet in many situations, "askin" discourse becomes the most appropriate means for requesting the procurement of a good, commodity, or labor. Participants who are close members of a "belongin" network in which "doin for" relations apply (see chapter 8) can use direct "askin" discourse frequently and across contexts. They are not the focus of this discussion here. Participant frameworks that are *not* "belongin" ones and that reflexively index "askin" contexts are.

For those not in "belongin" relations, certain contexts[24] create participant frameworks that requestors recognize as legitimating the "right" to ask directly. These requesting contexts tend to occur in settings in which commodities or commoditized services are provided. These commodities and services can be based on employer-employee relations in which the requestor is working for the requestee for wages or wage equivalents. They can also be contexts in which the requestees are business proprietors or employees, public service providers, ministers, postsecondary educational institutions, medical providers, and county political officeholders acting in a professional, work-related, or political capacity.

These potential requestees may also be in a real or potential "belongin" network with the requestor. If "belongin" relations can apply or be developed, one or both of the participants may reconstruct "askin" contexts as "doin for" relations with the stronger and more binding "claims" obligations than these non-"belongin" relations demand. Therefore, direct requesting contexts often conflate non-"belongin" and "belongin" discursive patterns as interlocutors negotiate how to frame the requesting interaction. For a direct request to be possible, the requestor "needs" access to or the benefits of something the requestee controls or has power over.

Among "askin" contextual features are those that index age, gender, setting (e.g., local mom-and-pop store or the chain grocery store in town), dress (e.g., long dresses and no jewelry or wedding ring for Pentecostal women or fashionable suit and tie with watch and wedding bands for some professional men), representations of literate practices (brochures, books, posters, Bibles, or no reading material), verbal register of requestee ("proper," nonlocal speech or local "country" speech), and other nonverbal situational components (e.g., gestures, eye contact, or body proxemics), which possible requestors interpret to assign sharply defined and asymmetrical "place" relations among interlocutors.[25] If Christian status, political roles, and family or personal "name" are also known, requestors will assign a social ranking as a "kind of person" to the requestee that allows further specification of "place" relationships.

Assignment of "rights" to ask are likely to be equally defined, but "claims" are problematic to construct or enhance. If the person making the request is local, he or she is also likely to take stock of the noncommodity valuation of the goods or services to the owner or provider of the resources. These valuations are likely to be verbally expressed through the applicability or nonapplicability of regularized possessive constructions such as "my homeplace" or "my truck," as discussed in chapter 2.

Requestors' assessment of the specific configuration of these "rights" and "place" criteria permits them to justify making a direct request for an item or service. This assessment is also subject to recognition that the request is perceived as meeting a "need" of the requestor and that it is within the scope of culturally recognized responsibilities of the requestee (i.e., that it is "right"). When all such constraints align, the requestor is said "to ask" for something, and compliance is fully expected, as with "volunteerin" patterns. A summary of these criteria is presented in table 4.1.

"Askin" relations are significant not only in those parameters presented in this table that detail who *can* ask what of whom but also in the type and direction of power relations created by the direct request. These acceptable patterns, unless modified for strategic purposes in a specific "askin" context, require those with less control of the resources under consideration to make a request of those in a privileged ranking with respect to these resources, and not vice versa. The very

Table 4.1. Non-"Belongin" Direct "Askin" Relations

Requestors	*Requestees*	*Constraints*
Acceptable Patterns		
Male[1]	Professional	Requestees are professional men or skilled male workers acting in professional capacity or able to use their influence, such as doctors, lawyers, ministers, or coal operators.
	Preachers	Requestees are "called" preachers (if a saved and practicing Christian) for matters related to faith or in the name of the church.
	Politicians	Requestees are considered politicians with whom a "takin care of" relationship has been constructed: county judges, state representatives, U.S. representatives, etc.
	Women	Requestees are women who are co-present with men who can be asked to do a woman's task, such as bring food or drink, fetch or hand a tool or implement, clean up a mess.
Female[2]	Professional	Requestees are men or women working as professionals in areas related to child care or children's health: doctors, paramedics, babysitters, child care providers, etc.
	Professional women	Requestees are professional women or skilled female workers acting in professional capacity or able to use their influence: nurses, teachers, or welfare workers.
	Preachers	Requestees are "called" preachers (if acting in a religious role as interpreter of "what's right").[3]
	Men	Requestees are men who are in a woman's activity domain to perform a male task: lifting or moving a heavy object, disking or plowing a garden, assembling a mechanical toy, etc.
Unacceptable Patterns		
Any person acting in a professional role or representing a formal institution	Any adult male	—
	Any adult woman	Acceptable if a *man* asks a woman for something in his "core rights," e.g., find her husband so he can talk to him.

1. Condition: Requestee must personally know or be known by reputation to requestor.

2. Condition: Any request concerning a woman's own children's behavior or well-being can be made to anyone. Otherwise, requestee should be known by reputation or "name."

3. Condition: Requestor should be a saved Christian.

act of asking reproduces or creates these relations of control through an acknowledgment that the requestee has something of value the requestor needs.

These normal asymmetrical relations express two types of ranking. The first, more basic one is a biblically supported ordering of genders and types of relationship to God. The second is an expression of patron-client relations consciously recognized by residents as representations of different "kinds of people" who "get things done." In the former, direct request privileges are predicated on perceived cosmological status categories, discussed and recognized as differences that occur between men and women because it's "just the way God wanted it to be." Exercising these types of privileges through "askin" discursive practices does occur but is less frequent than are the more common "volunteerin" discourse. In the second type of ranking, power and control relations directly apply. Residents recognize that people differ in their access to services, goods, wealth, or power. They commonly use "askin" discourse to reproduce these power differentials. They directly ask the person in charge of county roads to put new gravel on a back road; they directly ask Millie to obtain prescription medications; or they directly ask a teacher for assistance in reading a legal document. The two types of ranking can and often are conflated: for example, residents may directly ask a preacher who owns a truck hauling company to pray for them while also directly asking him for a job driving a truck. In both spheres of ranking, the requestor fully expects compliance by the requestee when he or she directly asks for something.[26]

Conversely, Ash Creek patterns do not mandate that residents comply with direct requests from professionals or officials in formal institutional statuses simply on the basis of their professional position or training. Having a "title," the term many Ash Creek residents use to refer to professional qualifications, does not mean the professional has the "right" to "ask" residents to do something. Professional qualifications and employment in a position validated by these qualifications do not give the professional the "right" to ask clients or patrons directly in and of themselves.[27] If the requestee does not recognize a "need" when asked to do something by a professional acting in a professional capacity, then compliance is not to be expected simply on the basis of professional knowledge or official position. The preferred direction for direct "askin" discourse is from the have-not to the one who has; professional requests usually violate this pattern.[28] Therefore, residents often record such discourse as "orders," that is, as a "wantin" demand for behavior modification. Most residents shun being "told what to do."

(4.21) A newly hired nurse practitioner at a regional health care facility frequented by many Ash Creek residents told her male patient to take off his pants for a rectal exam. He refused, left the clinic, and didn't come back.

Medical practitioners regularly ask patients to return for annual check ups, to lose weight or begin a light exercise program, or follow directions on prescription labels, with little or no compliance. Patients' failing to follow instructions, requests, or directions are frequent topics of conversation among local medical practitioners.

> Teachers (K–12 and community college) who are not from the area frequently comment on the lack of "respect" given to them by students as requests for schoolwork or class attendance are ignored, especially by male students to female instructors. [all from notes 85–88]

The result of the request norms captured by (4.21) for those in professional fields is an inevitable frustration on the part of many outsiders, who cannot understand why conversational misfires, lack of clientele, or blatant noncompliance to seemingly simple requests result from "simply doing my job." Until fictive "belongin" relations are established, so that "rights," "place," and "claims" relations and processes expected in "belongin" networks can apply, such institutional interfacing appears very problematic. For these reasons, local institutions prefer to employ personnel who have been reared locally or at least in the immediate region, regardless of the locale of their training. These local individuals tend to stay longer and are reported to have better rapport with clients and cause fewer administrative problems.

When "askin" forms occur, they are frequently interrogatives uttered with question intonation or are unambiguous indicative "askin" forms uttered with a flat, declarative pattern, often without the standard American politeness marker such as "please," which Ash Creek residents consider "proper," not "country." When the request is a salient, marked speech act, strong preference is given to using one of two direct request forms: "I need [*predicate referencing desired service or item*]" or an "if you don't care to" clause, which is either at the beginning or end of the "askin" sequence. The "I need" forms are straightforward English independent clauses. Residents use them when the "right" to make the direct request is very clearly indexed by the participant framework. For example, a man who has supported a given political official in his successful campaign may ask directly for some products of political patronage such as "I need some gravels for my road" or "I need my social security disability." "If you don't care to" constructions are more marked for politeness and require a modal in the main clause, imperatives being considered unacceptable. They are used when "rights" and "place" are more problematic.[29]

(4.22) (*Hypothetical nonlocal man to female proprietor in Ash Creek mom-and-pop store*[30])

(4.22.1) If you don't care to, Sue, would you fix me a sandwich.

(4.22.2) Would you fix me a sandwich, Sue, if you don't care to.

(4.22.3) *Fix me a sandwich, Sue, if you don't care to.

(4.22.4) *If you don't care to, Sue, fix me a sandwich.[31]

If the patron is not part of a "belongin" network so that "claims" are not well developed and "rights" are unclear, then the patron must ask directly for the item, commonly by using an "if you don't care to" form. The paradigm in (4.22) reveals the preferred syntactic ordering of these types of "askins" within an appropriate context. It can be "right" to ask a woman to prepare food in a food setting that is "hers," especially if the product is being paid for as a monetary exchange rather than as a "claims" transaction. It is her "place" (in both Ash Creek senses of the word) to prepare it. Yet the store setting mitigates the requestor's "right" to ask because it creates possibilities for multiple "rights" and "place" indexical relations. For example, the proprietor may assess the store setting as an index of commerce over that of a woman's control of food preparation and distribution. She may therefore value the selling of store commodities more highly than taking the time to actually prepare a single sandwich. Consequently, an "if you don't care to" clause is required.

It would be inappropriate for the patron to use embedded imperatives as in (4.22.3) and (4.22.4). They would be interpreted as "orders." The shopkeeper would probably comply and fix the sandwich but may talk about feeling "put out" later. Of course these "rights" and "place" indexical relations can be manipulated for strategic uses but only in so far as appropriate presuppositional indexical relations among participant frameworks are maintained. Direct requests must meet culturally validated conditions for their use if compliance is to be expected.[32]

Segments (4.23)–(4.24) conform to non-"belongin" "rights" and "place" "askin" relations. These segments use question forms, common when asymmetrical "place" relations in terms of control over resources are clear and compliance fully expected:

(4.23) (*local woman at craft booth asking female salesperson*)

Do you have a red one of these that you could sell me?

[30a:217 8/85]

(4.24) (*man at food booth to female salesperson*)

Sue . will you kindly give me one a these? [30a:280 8/85]

Segments (4.23) and (4.24) are service encounters between a craft booth patron and a crafter. As a possible selling transaction ("tradin" in Ash Creek speech), "rights" and "place" criteria apply, and "claims" are either irrelevant or of lesser importance than the value of the exchange itself. As selling of a good is presumed to be a willing act on the part of the seller, question "askin" forms are fully appropriate. Segment (4.23) also requests specific information about a particular color, a function performed easily by this type of interrogative structuring. Segment (4.24) reveals the basic, primary importance of "claims" relations as the man asks Sue to "give" him one of the items, not "sell" him one. He does, however, pay for the ice cream sandwich, revealing the lesser value of "claims" in this type of participant framework.

Segments (4.25) and (4.26) use "need" constructions and represent more problematic "place" relations:

(4.25) (*Setting: Environmental Center community meeting to discuss problems between the center administration and local residents. Participants: About 40 local residents and center staff.*)

Sally: We need someone who will . uh . also

The board member said . to gIt the other board members' attention

Is to send the other board member a copy of these.

[21b:009 6/86]

(4.26) (*Setting: Community college extension class at Environmental Center before class begins. Participants: An adult woman student and myself.*)

Student: Nita I need fɛr you to . look at that an see if it's all right fɛr me to turn it in to you. [1a:615 2/1986]

Segment (4.25) is from a lengthy community meeting concerning Environmental Center policy. Sally is asking other community members to volunteer to make copies of petition letters and mail them to the various members of the center board of trustees. As literacy and secretarial work is within a woman's domain, she has a "right" to ask women, but not men. Nor is it her "place" to ask anyone to do writing activities. She therefore hedges, shifting burden of the request to a quotative ("the board member said") reportedly uttered by a board member with whom she has spoken. An initial request is reformed into reported speech allegedly uttered by someone whose "place" relations are secure.

Segment (4.26) is a transparent example of "need" as an "askin" form. The student is performing the task of writing an essay and "needs" assistance in completing it. "Place" and "rights" relations are clear, but "claims" relations between us are nonexistent at this point. The student recognizes that my complying to her request is potentially problematic because instructors may not wish to examine a presubmitted essay. Yet it is a fully developed, salient "askin" form that situates the request as a sociocentric task and mitigates any possibility of my denying the request. I felt I could not refuse her and I did not. As familiarity developed between this student and me, "want" forms replaced these early "need" constructions (e.g., "Nita, I want you to look at this"). She restructured our student-pupil relationship into one of my assisting her in getting her desires fulfilled.

On the other hand, segment (4.27) is a nonrequesting subjunctive use of "need," included here as an example of a group-oriented task use of "need" in Ash Creek discourse:

(4.27) (*Setting: Environmental Center community meeting to discuss problems between the center administration and local residents. Participants: About 40 local residents and center staff. Same event as in* (4.26)

Man: That's it right there.
We need ta a find out what we can offer
An what we can teach
An what we've got
Ur see wha what we can gIt involved in now
Ur gIt involved in. [21a:719 6/1986]

This segment has as one of its goals to organize community members into a task-focused cooperative effort to achieve a set of investigative purposes. This segment also reproduces the consciously recognized distinction between social selves who "need" and individualized selves who "want." Here, the speaker is attempting to form a coalition of residents to investigate a center problem in response to a need.

Segment (4.28) exemplifies the formal, polite form "if you don't care to":

(4.28) (*Setting: Environmental Center kitchen during food preparation. Participants: Second-shift cooks and I.*)

Debbie: Nita . if you don't care to
Would you bring me a pIncil from over there? [notes 8/85]

In addition to indexing weak "claims" relations, it marks formality and distances interlocutors from each other. These forms are appropriate only in situations in which "rights" and "place" relations are most problematic or weakly formed. Here a straightforward request to provide a pencil is framed by a formal request form, marking the event as one in which Debbie is unsure of her "rights" or "place" to ask me, a near stranger at that time, for *any* entity. A man in this situation would create different "rights" and "place" relations. He would not "need" to employ such a formal "askin" form and, indeed, in a similar context, did not. He used an imperative: "GIt me a pIncil."

The last segment (4.29) presents transparent "askin" indexical relations through use of formulaic expressions characteristic of the oral genre of prayer:

(4.29) (*Setting: Funeral for local man. Participants: About 60 local residents, two preachers, and myself.*)

Preacher: Lord **we ask you** now. in this tryin time
To bless Billie . his family . each one Lord that is so very low
That your spirit would be upon them
That you would comfort them Lord and lift them up to your everlasting arms
We ask you father to touch the hearts
That maybe . ((?and watch out . an shout out?)) the fact that Jesus loves and cares for each one of us
And maybe even as they climb through the valley of the shadow of death
They'll gIt a glimpse of that light
Of that light that's shining for each one of us
Which is the Son of God.
Help us Lord . today.
Keep us strong.
We ask these things in Jesus name.
Amen. [66b:315 8/86]

Complex in form and meanings, the "askin" functions are unambiguous and direct through use of the performative verb /ask/. The imperatives "Help us Lord" and "Keep us strong" are reassigned appropriate "order" status by the following line, "We ask these things," in keeping with "doin for" discursive practices discussed in chapter 8. These "askin" relations, removed from quotidian, secular "askins," are embedded in a sacred verbal genre, public prayer. They therefore assume more stylized, conventionalized meanings characteristic of ritualized speech.[33] These meanings, expressed in generically defined discursive rhetorical and syntactic arrangements, function metapragmatically to provide interpretation for how "askins" relations should function. As a church leader, the man praying is in presumed grace and has both the cultural "right" and "place" to ask the divinity for assistance. "Place" relations are sharply defined and God has control over highly valued resources. Presumed to be divinely created, these relations are considered binding for both the requestor and the requestee. A direct request must be granted.

Inasmuch as they are presumed to be predicated on such theological concepts as "sanctification" and "love," they fall into a spiritual "belongin" relation unlike those represented in segments (4.23)–(4.28) in which "claims" are problematic or nonexistent. It therefore is an example of a "doin for" relationship. It is included here as a metapragmatic representation of a fully appropriate "askin" formulation to demonstrate how significant direct "askins" are to the constitution of an ideology of requesting communication. The very use of /ask/ rather than a synonym or a more oblique direct requesting pattern reveals the significance of direct "askin" discourse in Ash Creek life. A direct "askin" is a human-to-human reconstruction of a human-to-God relationship. For a requestor to ask someone directly for something or to do something presuppositionally indexes mandatory or near-mandatory compliance, regardless of the status of "claims" relations. Most Ash Creek residents use them with care.

These non-"belongin" requesting discourse constructions of optional, volunteering, or direct "askin" forms represent ways Ash Creek residents construct socioeconomic relations among people whose responses are less predictable or familiar than those in close "belongin" relations. Many of these relations are different in form, function, and meaning from what most Ash Creek residents are accustomed to when requesting locally among "belongin" network members. To outside merchants, economic developers, and political policy makers, these seemingly straightforward English requesting patterns construct a set of conventional requests that are very familiar to them. Yet the indexical meanings specific participant frameworks create are often different from if not actually the opposite of the textual and contextual meanings outsiders assign to these requests. Use of these patterns therefore commonly creates disjunctive socioeconomic relations, especially when used with those "outsiders" unfamiliar with them.

Nonimperative requesting patterns both inside and outside of "belongin" networks are of course culturally elaborated on and combined into culturally recognized speaking practices with greater scope, more involved discursive representations, and more complex semiotic significations. Integration, from extensive to full exists between speakers' use of these practices and socioeconomic activities or processes. Possibile miscommunication with those not familiar with the speaking practices that incorporate these nonimperative requesting patterns in Ash Creek increases significantly at the more encompassing level of speaking practices. The complexity in the nature and scope of socioeconomic disjunctions also increases.

5 NONIMPERATIVE REQUESTING PRACTICES: "TAKIN CARE OF," "TRADIN," AND "MAKIN A DEAL"

"Can I hep ya?"

I took my Volkswagen beetle to a car repair establishment in another part of the county. After discussion of the problem, the mechanic said, "We'll take care of you." [notes 10/87]

As I was making my usual visits to local stores and the center one summer day, I noted that Don was not at Marylin's [his wife's] store. Becky told me he was out "tradin" for a truck. We subsequently discussed how car "tradin" was better done by men—they got a better deal with the dealerships. [notes 8/86]

A local man who sells satellite dish equipment made an oral agreement with another man in the area for several thousand dollars' worth of products. The purchaser made only a down payment and refused to pay the rest. The seller sought the purchaser out and they allegedly exchanged heated words. The seller reportedly said to Bill, "We made a deal—he's goin to pay one way or the other." [notes 11/86]

ASH CREEK'S NONIMPERATIVE OPTIONAL, "VOLUNTEERIN," and direct "askin" forms are usually embedded within speaking practices that vary from complex but open-ended forms of talk such as "just talkin" to more circumscribed, readily recognizable verbal exchanges such as "tradin." These practices reconstitute the indexical significations of these nonimperative requesting patterns in themselves by constraining and shaping their meanings in the emergent discursive, grammatical, and social interactional context interlocutors create. They therefore function pragmatically to effect transparent economic transactions, maintain or create basic political-economic relations among interlocutors, and, in many cases, reproduce structures of institutionalized power.[1] They also function metapragmatically to direct how requests should be interpreted, evaluated, and placed as constitutive elements within the Ash Creek ideology of socioeconomic communication.

Nonimperative requests that have transparent socioeconomic functions are most commonly found within three communicative practices. These practices include both material and verbal exchanges in various combinations. Residents describe these practices using clauses such as "Bill's takin care of Bob," "they made a deal," or "we traded for some plunder at the flea market." The fullest discourse structurings appear in the practice of "takin care of" someone.

"Takin Care Of" Requesting Patterns

When individuals, usually (but not always) men, are in a business or overtly political interaction, one participant (or a small group of two or three having common interests) will be in a lesser-valued position in terms of access to power and resources and may "need" or "want" to make a request of the one controlling these resources. The one in the higher-valued position will "want" and "need" the other to validate his continued control over these resources. The one in the higher-valued position is usually a single individual whose greater access to or control of certain types of resources gives him the "right" to "take care of" other(s). It is his "place" to do so. In most cases, he has acquired this resource access and control through "claims" relationships created in "belongin" networks or has developed fictive claims-like criteria through repeatedly providing such goods and services to the public. A county supervisor controls road improvement funds by virtue of having been elected. He was elected, however, because he had strong enough "belongin" or "claims" relations with others in the county to garner a plurality of votes. Similarly, an Ash Creek man owns a small trucking company and has control over several trucking jobs. He began the company using family funds he had "claim" to through "belongin" network "claims" configurations. Therefore, the majority of those who "take care of" others are also deeply committed to maintaining and enhancing "claims" relations.

The person in a position to "take care of" others assumes a patronage role with those who make requests of him. Once a "takin care of" interaction has successfully occurred, both participants expect that the beneficiary of the transaction will be indebted to the benefactor in ways that create loyalty, gratitude, or political fidelity. The benefactor is also obligated to continue to provide future commodities or services over which he (or she) has control as long as the beneficiary recognizes his fidelity through actions such as political support or continued business. The ongoing maintenance of these obligations is reaffirmed in various communicative practices that often embed requests within them. Requests therefore assume additional configurations of pragmatic and metapragmatic meanings when contextualized as "takin care of" requesting communication.

"Takin care of" relations are one of the few ways commodities from local, regional, and global markets enter and leave the Ash Creek community. Benefactors control businesses and institutions responsible for making regional, national, and global markets accessible to Ash Creek residents. They also control access to local jobs that these markets generate and most means for getting the very few local commodities Ash Creek residents may produce to these markets.[2] The benefactors in these relationships can have enormous local political-economic power through their access to highly valued commodities (such as political appointments, educational positions, legal land ownership, or state or county funds). They can conflate "wants" and "needs" in the exercise of it.

Reproducing these relations in communicative events constructs a local economic praxis that can contradict the goals and functions of formal institutions and businesses. Some business owners find themselves providing commodities or services in ways that hinder their ability to break even or actually make a profit because they must "take care of" their constituency even if it means extending credit or hiring less qualified personnel. Some individuals use dual methods of accounting to satisfy both local and governmental requirements, one formal using standard accounting procedures and the other informal in accord with Ash Creek "takin care of" expectations. Political patronage can result in hiring of less-skilled applicants for political positions, use of higher-priced vendors for purchases, or use of governmental equipment for private ends. These obligatory relations are so strong that they construct a transcounty political economy, which forms the basis for the entrenched political institutions that have traditionally determined who would benefit from educational and economic development in the local area.[3] This is a local political economy that cannot continue without a steady flow of outside commodities and capital to sustain it.

"Takin care of" discourse practices are often much less overtly political, however, as they occur simply in situations in which someone has control over resources another may "need" rather than "want" regularly. In these cases, "needs" take precedence over "wants," although assertions of individual desires are often a component of the specific encounter. They can, however, have enormous economic impact on local businesses and services.

Interpersonal and economic tensions between differences in capitalistic and "takin care of" functions can result in significant commitments of personal time to maintain both systems or can lead to financial ruin. In addition, once a "takin care of" relation has been started, a patron's refusal to continue the relationship because of money owed or moral problems with the beneficiary's expectations of service can lead to grudges, gossip, and other discursive practices expressing conflict[4] with the organization. For example, Millie, the nurse practitioner managing the Ash Creek medical clinic, spends extra time talking with a client who brought her garden produce or a handmade wood placard as a prestation to acknowledge the "takin care of" relationship she has with him for medical care, while, at the same time, working overtime to file Medicaid, Medicare, or insurance claims for partial monetary reimbursement for his care. Millie has more fresh corn or home-canned food than she can use. She freezes or cans it if she has time, which she rarely has, or gives some of it away to visitors and other outsiders, like me. The co-payment due by the client may or may not ever be paid. If it is not, she or Joan spend more time processing the paperwork for nonpayment.[5] The client returns regularly under "takin care of" expectations so that "takin care of" "claims" relations are further developed. Millie receives after-hour calls or clinic visits from this same individual and is asked to assist in filing for a black lung[6] or other disability claims. He expects a physical exam report that will aid his disability claim, regardless of his actual medical condition. She abides by her medical code of ethics and does not support his claim. Millie's medical organization receives no copayments and writes off the loss to its trust created for such purposes. The client is declared ineligible for black lung disability insurance and switches clinics, while maligning Millie in the community. This pattern becomes one of theme and variation involving several clients. This clinic ceased operations in 1992.

Millie, on the other hand, has expectations that a client sees her only for medical care. Nevertheless, she finds her time off often consumed by free consultations in homes or drop-by visits of people "needin" or "wantin" something, despite the fact that her professional advice may not be taken. Loyalty from residents toward her medical "place" in the community is strengthened. She is usually exhausted.

Service encounters with proprietors operating locally owned businesses are often in situations in which interlocutors interpret specific configurations of "volunteerin" discourse as representations of "takin care of" communicative practices. These "takin care of" interactions occur not only in Ash Creek but also in many locally owned town businesses that residents also frequent. These service encounter patterns differ markedly from those imposed upon their employees by national chain stores such as Wal-Mart, Kmart, and McDonald's.[7] For locally owned town and Ash Creek businesses, highly truncated volunteering forms become "takin care of" extensions of gender-based "rights," and "place," relations also characteristic of "doin for" (chapter 8) requesting patterns. In these service contexts, however, construction of acceptable "claims" relations is constrained by both "rights" appropriate to a given gender and by the "need" of a client to exchange money or ask for credit and the "need" of the proprietor to at least break even. Nevertheless, the reciprocal obligations of "claims" relations do apply as most clients "trade" for groceries, gasoline, and other domestic goods under expectations that the proprietor will obtain goods that they frequently use and will extend credit on an "as needed" basis. The proprietor, who is usually a woman in Ash Creek, expects customer loyalty and payment in return.

Most of the patrons of a particular Ash Creek store or business are in a "belongin" relationship with the proprietor and are likely to be kin. Therefore, the requesting patterns used in such "takin care of" exchanges often blend with "doin for" ones and are in large part very similar to the types of interactions between mothers, fathers, and other family members within households. Whether a given interaction is framed as a non-"belongin" network "takin care of" practice or as a family-focused "doin for" communicative exchange then becomes a matter of negotiated individual relationships rather than situational ones predicated on the asymmetrical relationships indexed by the store setting.

These relational choices can conflate the public versus home distinction and can further complicate the ability of the establishment to do business beyond problems raised by "takin care of" relations alone. For example, some patrons, often kin, can tie up space and store resources by extending their visits to watch the store's television, engage in long conversational sessions either inside the store or outside on chairs or benches, or prepare food in store kitchen areas. "Claims" may broaden to incorporate more and more of these family interactional patterns, leaving proprietors, who regularly extend credit to customers, in a position of denying the "takin care of" relation for a "doin for" one that abrogates patrons from paying their account.

The existence of "doin for" relationships should not suggest that those in "takin care of" relations always pay off their accounts as well. Yet in "takin care of" situations, payment of debt is at least expected by both parties. Nevertheless, the "claims" relations created in either framing regularly dominate commodity exchange criteria, creating a precarious cash flow problem for most businesses and causing store after store to eventually go out of business or use other resources or business strategies to absorb unpaid debt.[8] Only in institutions monitored nonlocally, such as the Environmental Center, are such culturally normative "belongin" "claims" processes somewhat mitigated so that expectations of paying debt are salient to all parties.[9]

Within these local service encounters, the elliptic volunteering "Can I hɛp ya?" is one of several stylized service encounter openings that begins an interaction. When uttered by a proprietor or manager in a business setting, residents interpret it as indexically framing what will follow as a probable "takin care of" relationship. It may or may not begin a longer, more elaborate "volunteerin" pattern. It will result in at least a service encounter.

Segment (5.1) represents a stylized form, which is one service opening among several within Don's repertoire and which evolved as an opening between him and me over time because I visited this store frequently:

(5.1) (*Setting: Local mom-and-pop store. I have just entered. Don is standing behind the counter.*)

Don: "What can I *do* for *you* today?" [notes 86–88]

Don admitted this opening was an adaptation of a more urban service verbal pattern he had heard when visiting Lexington. It is a question-type volunteering form uttered shortly after a brief conversational or greeting segment, framing and opening a service encounter. The "volunteerin" structuring, using an interrogative with a first-person "I" subject offering to "do" something, presuppositionally indexes Don's "right" to offer goods and services available in the store. Don is retired from a coal-hauling trucking company he owned and is "helpin Marilyn out." Marilyn has managed the store for approximately 40 years. That a man known to most residents utters this "volunteerin" interrogative creates an indexical relation to those male domains of "takin care of" activities he is known to provide. These include pumping gasoline for women, making small adjustments in costs of items (a soda pop may be given away, a candy bar may have its price reduced by a nickel), or taking out heavy bags of groceries to vehicles for women. When his elderly wife opens up a service encounter, on the other hand, with a more conventional "can I hɛp ya?" similar indexical relations to her domains of "takin care of" activities are created. Patrons expect her to direct them to various food items, to respond to a question about whether a given item is inventoried, to tally a purchase, or to prepare a bill on account. Like most Ash Creek men, Don does not do accounts or most other writing activities.

Segment (5.2) is a complex service encounter because the waitress's ability to complete a food order is constantly being diverted by other patrons' conversations with her or by children's activities:

(5.2) (*Setting: Local cafe, several patrons have already been served as I enter with two nonlocals who are teaching staff at the Environmental Center, a husband and wife with their two-year-old daughter. Susie is the waitress that day.*)

Susie: Hi

Let me clear the table.

Oh . thank you [to current patron who hands Susie some dirty dishes]

How's Barbara? [to couple's two-year-old child]

Father: How's Barbara? [echoes Susie's greeting to child]

[Child nods in acknowledgment; father attends to its needs; from time to time she screams out.]

Susie: Oh:

[resumes conversation briefly with other patrons as she continues to clean table (7.0)]

Sue called an said ((?4.0?))

No . sit . sit here.

They . they'll be ((?going?)). [to us]

Mother: Oh . there's Anita [to daughter]

Oh . I see.

Susie: [resumes conversation with other patrons; we seat ourselves and engage in conversation with one current patron; children become active and talk or scream, multiple conversations; leave-taking from one woman patron (3 minutes)]

Anita . you want a grilled ham and cheese?

Anita: Nuh-uh. ((?5.0?))

I don't like to eat that much.

Susie: **Now . we have some a**

Chili

Homemade chili.

It's— [to couple]

Anita: —That's good too—

Susie: —delicious.

We got onion rings.

[semi-intelligible discussion among mother, father, and me about what to order (16.0)]

Susie: **We have good cheese sandwiches too.**

Father: Cheeseburger.

Susie: Ok. [92b:650 5/86]

A "let" construction opens the encounter with the new customers, creating normative indexical "rights" and "place" relations under conditions of minimal "claims," and provides Susie with footing to develop a "takin care of" verbal exchange in this public setting. Although Susie uses "want" verbal constructions, the restaurant situation presupposes the underlying "need" condition that lunch was a necessary meal. Subsequent verbal and nonverbal activity creates an informal context in which both the patrons and the waitress are co-participants in the service encounter. The aside conversations also merge "takin care of" relations with family-appropriate "doin for" relations. In fact, all but two of the other customers already in the restaurant are close kin to the waitress; the other two are sisters in the church. All but one are engaging in similar conversational and food-related distributional patterns similar to those I encountered in their homes.

Our orders are negotiated rather than placed through discussions about what is good and what I want. Susie uses questions ("Anita . you want a grilled ham and cheese?") and declaratives ("We got onion rings") to construct her role as a volunteer in the service process appropriate to "takin care of" structuring. In keeping with "takin care of" practices, Susie "wants" and "needs" to make sure we get the order we "want" or "need."

As a female food server, she has the "right" to extend her woman's home role as a cook and food preparer to her "place" as a waitress in the restaurant. She therefore can rightfully also extend her use of "volunteerin" discourse to the patrons in a restaurant setting. The use of an imperative ("No . sit . sit here"), however, indexes her gendered "right" as director of a food preparation activity and is appropriate to family-focused "doin for" practices. This construction conflates her "takin care of" role with a "doin for" one as it functions to index control over the activity.

In segment (5.3), the receptionist frames the "takin care of" volunteering with a stylized question form ("can I help you"),[10] and the client responds with information:

(5.3) (*Setting: Local medical clinic. Participants: Joan, female client with young son, and I. A few clients are waiting to be examined.*)

Joan: **Hi**

Can I help you?

Client: Yeah . he cut his head yesterday.

Joan: Ok.

Client: An I think it's infected.

Joan: How deep is it?
Client: Uh
I can't tell.
It's got a big blood clot inside of it.
Joan: Done it yesterday?
Client: Uh-huh.
They went to the cave yesterday.
Joan: What's his name?
Client: Jim—.
Joan: —Smith.
[turns rolladex for chart number; initiates a brief question/answer sequence concerning child's medical history]
Let me go ahead and fix his chart and I'll tell Millie.
Go ahead an have ya a seat. [10a:500 10/86]

In keeping with verbal medical questioning schema this receptionist has been both formally and informally trained to perform, information is obtained about the nature of the injury. When Joan determines that an office visit is in order, she uses a "let" form to indicate a change in action ("Let me go ahead and fix his chart") and a declarative (I'll tell Millie") to volunteer to notify Millie. The imperative "Go ahead and have ya a seat" is a routinized closing for Joan in the clinic setting and represents an extension of a woman's "right" to direct placement of visitors within her domestic domain under a situation of "need." In this case, it has become a conventional utterance for this receptionist through repetition of the "need" to do so over time. As a result, it lacks the "doin for" gestural and affective features of the waitress's imperative in segment (5.2).[11] No confusion with "doin for" discourse is represented in this verbal exchange. The client takes her son and sits without verbal comment.

Segment (5.4) is an example of an exchange between two service providers: Susie, a waitress, and man who is a dairy product vendor from the county seat.

(5.4) (*Setting: Local cafe in afternoon. Participants: Susie, dairy products vendor from the county seat, and I.*)
Vendor: Hey Sue.
Susie: Hey Sam.
Vendor: Everybody doin all right?
Susie: Uh-oh
Bernie's not here . bud.
Vendor: Sue . I
Well . I don't have any anyway.
I'll—

Susie: —Well . good—
Vendor: **[have some Monday] if they [need it]**
Susie: [(Laughs) Well good] [well listen . that's great.]
He's started buildin on his . his house [an uh]
Vendor: [yeah]
Susie: He **let me come in**
But I heard him tell you to come back an I know he didn't say anything.
Vendor: Yeah.
Susie: **He wasn't goin to order anything else was he Bill?**
[You]—
Vendor: [I might]
Susie: **—might ought to bring some little things of milk.**
Vendor: **Little creamers?**
You need them?
Susie: Yeah
Vendor: **Today?** . Monday?
Susie: No: . yeah
You might already have ɛm with you Monday.
Vendor: Ok.
Susie: Do you have ɛm every time?
Vendor: Yeah.
Susie: Ok.
Vendor: Yeah . yeah.
Ya know it's jIst . a rare thing ya know that I run out of Im.
Susie: Ok . good Sam. Thank ya.
Vendor: Have a good weekend.
Susie: Ok.
[Door slams.] [61b:103; 5/86]

In this case, Susie truncates the potential "takin care of" "volunteerin" sequence by the vendor through a declarative, "Sam's not here . bud." Considered rude and like an outsider's speech, this denial of his "place" to make service offers is further reinforced through overlaps and waitress interruptions throughout the verbal exchange. The declarative "You might ought to bring some little things of milk" is a clear directive, mitigated from being an imperative only by the double modal phrase "might ought to." Again, Susie is asserting "doin for" control relations over "her" claimed food preparation space rather than permitting the vendor to develop indebtedness and fictive claims characteristic of "takin care of" relations among unrelated cultural unequals. The vendor is not a member of the community, but from town, and needs the business to help ensure his job. The waitress asserts control over the situation so that she is not obligated to the vendor, an assertion difficult to make with "belongin" network members. He acknowledges this strategic use of requesting discourse by yielding turns when interrupted, a strategy that could also be in deference to her gender except that, when "right" and in their "place," men seldom use such politeness. The exchange ends a potential requesting misfire appropriately with Susie offering a polite closing: "thank ya" and "have a good weekend."

Appropriate use of these verbal exchanges facilitates the exchange and flow of commodities, goods and services within the county and region, not just within Ash Creek. Local merchants and service providers (not national chains) recognize the cultural importance of replicating these requesting processes:

(5.5) (*Setting: Woodcarving session, Bill and I are "just talkin." Current topic is the reputation of grocery store in town, which is not a chain but owned by someone who lives in the county seat.*)

Bill: They uh . they made a . mistake there one time
In cashin my check
((?70 some dollars too much?))
I'd already walked away from the winda an was countin it ((?2.0?))
Walked back up there an I said uh "**Can I see that check?**"
She said "Is there somethin wrong?"
I said "Well . I'm not sure ((?2.0?))
She said "**Let's see.**"
She found the check ya know I'd give her an I looked at it.
She'd given me seventy some dollars too much change
An I jIst pushed the money back in to her and I said
"**Count that money**" an ((?1.0?)) she said ((?1.5?))
An I said "I figured you did" [chuckles]
An uh
When I came around to check out my wife an sister was with me at the that time
An I was out doin my shoppin . in ((?.5?)) an I came up to cash
Cashier's at the check out counter.
She was around there to check me out.
She'd been workin in the office.
She ((?said?)) "Ya know
I thought I'd come over here an check ya out and talk to ya

That's straightened out everything with the check and gIttin your money back"

And uh

I said "It was the only thing to do."

"Yeah . I know . but" she ((?said?)) "How many people ur gonna *do* that!"

[chuckles]

An uh I asked her

I said . "Well, would that a come out a your pocket?

If they had found out about it."

She said . "No.

But it would a looked bad."

Come up that much short.

Anita: Um-huh . yeah.

That's a good one.

Bill: Yeah.

An uh

Any time I went in to the store to do my shoppin

If she was in the office

She would . would always wait on me or if I needed my check cashin ((?1.0?))

She would usually holler out

An say uh

She knew my name an would always speak to me.

[103b:402 1/86]

Once Bill had rectified a calculation error with the clerk, "takin care of" relations applied between the female clerk and him. As these relations were developed and continued over time, they created fictive "claims" relations; she was "takin care of" him when he came to that grocery store.

When individuals are cultural unequals and not in "belongin" networks, developing "claims," or relations of indebtedness, through various uses of "takin care of" "volunteerin" discourse patterns, is a socioeconomic requisite for Ash Creek residents. These relations permit residents to interface with nonlocal economic and political economic institutions and exchange systems, albeit through a set of communicative patterns that can undercut the profits of these same institutions and systems. With perhaps the exception of one household,[12] Ash Creek residents all depend on regional, national, and international markets to at least a limited extent and the local and regional businesses that provide the products and services these markets offer. The Ash Creek linguistic-economic system cannot function without these "takin care of" patterns.

"Volunteerin" discourse within "takin care of" practices becomes a mode for developing the highly preferential dyadic exchange patterns in which the "claims" relations they index are clearly a complex form of reciprocity. The obligatory nature of these exchange patterns frequently take precedence over the monetary exchange value of a given good or service. Such encompassing and widely applied systems of "takin care of" relations foster construction of a de-commoditizing system in which nonmonetary items such as community information through gossip or "just talkin" can also be included.[13] These relationships become statements of negotiated power indexed through appropriate use of "takin care of" nonimperative requesting discourse that replicates resource control disparities time and time again by gendered selves.

Benefactors who honor their "takin care of" relations develop a "name" for themselves. Utterance of the epithet "you can count on [Personal Name]" becomes a trope encapsulating those processes which construct the matrix of the exchange system. To be "counted on" in Ash Creek terms is to meet one of a finite set of criteria for continued membership in community life.

"Tradin" and "Makin a Deal"

Items or services obtained through market means routinely enter or leave the Ash Creek socioeconomic system, frequently, of course, through the exchange of cash. Barter is also extensive. With only a few exceptions, credit cards or even checks are rarely used by Ash Creek residents for exchanges. Money orders are the preferred means of mail order purchase or payment. Market items support the existing community socioeconomic system or expand it, according to perceived needs of residents, which are overwhelmingly predicated upon culturally normative domains of appropriate socioeconomic activity. Residents often travel to town or to local or regional flea markets; occasionally visit regional cities such as Lexington, Kingsport, or Knoxville; or, in the case of many men, meet in back yards, garages, or other informal settings to exchange cars or trucks, game chickens, weapons, hunting dogs, bootlegged alcohol or moonshine, or other items having commodity value. These exchanges frequently involve clear bartering activities. The haggling or "makin a deal" over the cost of a car results in an exchange, for example, of a 1980 Ford 150 truck for two older Chevrolet sedans plus or minus some cash.[14] Many men spend a great amount of time engaging in "makin a deal," obviously relishing the social and negotiating components of the conversational discourse surrounding such actions.[15]

Residents, especially those in their later thirties or older, that is, those approaching or having reached grandparent status, assume that the word "money" means only cash tender and is only one of several valued means of exchange for an item or service, although a very highly regarded one. It is a means for obtaining something of value that can then be incorporated into the local "claims"-based economy of "belongin" networks or used to meet purely personal "wants."

Money is not a source of capital for investment. Some residents do have savings accounts that earn interest, a very few (approximately 10 nuclear families) have checking accounts, and only one household in Ash Creek engages in any significant investment activities, treating money as capital.[16] Consequently, the metapragmatic designator of "tradin" to refer to any encounter that involves the exchange of commodity items, money included, is an appropriate lexeme for most Ash Creek residents.[17] To "trade," however, does not necessarily mean to talk, and verbal requesting patterns that co-occur with "tradin" are, for the most part, truncations of either "takin care of" requesting patterns or impositions of regional or national commodity market patterns learned by employees of chain store businesses. Use of the former frames the exchange as a "claims" or fictive "claims" encounter, while use of the latter constitutes a commodity-based service encounter similar to one in urban businesses of the same chain.

As activities with a dominant economic function, "tradin" must necessarily involve using linguistic-economic patterns that have the capacity to transcend Ash Creek itself and integrate with regional or national patterns. These articulations are especially evident in national or regional chain stores such as Kmart, Wal-Mart, Kroger's, and McDonald's.[18] Younger residents frequently shop at these establishments and say that doing so allows them to be in touch with what others their age are doing everywhere. The service encounters of chain stores and restaurants provide models for economic interactions in large cities, giving many younger residents an added confidence to migrate to urban centers to find employment. Many older or adult male residents shun chain businesses, preferring instead to trade at older, locally owned businesses where such functional and efficient service encounters using bar code scanners or drive-through windows do not confuse them and where "takin care of" "volunteerin" constructions and the fictive "claims" relations they create can apply.[19] The result is a system of purchasing that exhibits strongly patterned variation according to age and gender, with women, regardless of age, being more likely to try a chain store. An older woman is more likely to experiment if she is accompanied by a younger female relative. Ash Creek residents are keenly aware of the different semiotic systems presented by each linguistic-economic system, talking frequently about changes in town and whether they're good or bad for the county. Noting such factors as failure to provide adequate "service" or non-Christian managers, many residents, especially grandparents (older than 35), often express desires not to shop or to shop only occasionally at these franchised stores.

At backyard "tradin" exchanges for men, at yard sales, bake sales, and church rummage sales for women, and at flea markets for everyone, however, residents of all ages view themselves as participating and involved agents in a market setting. Yard sales and other community-located take-as-it-comes informal exchanges are often social events, dominated by "belongin" relations as local participants look for something they can actually use or something they can just purchase to make a donation to the organizer of the event. These are usually women's events. Frequently the profits are not used for personal gain but for funding school or church events. Yard sales are very rarely advertised in the county newspaper, although handmade signs at local businesses, churches, and schools may appear. Often, yard sale traders are in the "belongin" network of the host and have either contributed items to the sale or have previously given some sale items to the host as gifts. Talk among women at these events may include a humorous discussion of how the buyer is finally acquiring her sister's sweater that she always wanted or how she no longer wanted the clearly used hand-held electric mixer her mother had given the host for the host's birthday. These events reproduce "claims" relations; close "belongin" network members must at least make a visit to the event as a show of support.

All physically able adult residents within Ash Creek visit flea markets.[20] Most will drive as far as 60 or 70 miles to "trade" at a "good one," and a few residents scour the region weekly or biweekly in search of bargains or memorabilia. One retired couple pursues flea market "tradin" avidly as an avocation. At flea markets residents are in no way bound by "claims" relations. The devotee's focus is on establishing larger social networks of exchange partners; the occasional trader's goal is to simply obtain a useful item at a reasonable price.[21] In both cases, traders are asserting themselves as individuals outside of the constraints of community "claims" relations in ways that do not directly challenge the significations created in Ash Creek requesting discourse.

Ash Creek traders are also exercising a well-developed community norm of "savin," that is, of being judicious in the use of personal economic resources by obtaining items perceived as bargains, whether they actually are or not. Unlike expensive minimally functional items from commercial businesses such as artistic paintings, gold or mahogany picture frames, or ornate gas-burning outside grills, flea market items can be publicly displayed at home. Their flea market status ensures residents of not giving in to displays of "worldliness" or putting themselves above other community residents or family and being subject to the highly negative label of being "above their raisin."[22] After all, these goods came from a flea market.[23]

Exchange discourse at flea markets constitutes a distinct discursive practice and may not occur at all as buyers simply take an item, look at a pricing label, and hand over cash. They or the seller may be talking conversationally to someone else as they do so. When requesting discourse does occur, it is characteristically an optional requesting pattern, perhaps a truncated "volunteerin" pattern, or, occasionally, a direct "askin." First-person pronouns are often omitted and the discourse may be subclausal in syntax. A preliminary period of "just talkin" is often engaged in and is perhaps the sole outcome of the encounter. For actual exchanges, discourse becomes highly utilitarian, with speech act functions assuming the direct and unambiguous intent characteristic of trade:[24]

(5.6) (*Setting: Requesting segments obtained at area flea market frequently visited by Ash Creek residents; vendors are either under shelters or out in the open, and potential customers mill around from table to table, sometimes stopping for conversation or to examine a good or ware. Participants: Vendors are not from Ash Creek; patrons are local or regional. Millie and I are together; M Vendor = male vendor; W Vendor = female vendor.*)

(5.6.1) Woman: You don't have any green peppers . do ya.

M Vendor: Uh-Uh. [Woman walks on without comment.]

[120a:149 10/1988]

(5.6.2) W Vendor: Those are five for a dollar.

[Millie and I are examining placards and humorous buttons.]

[47a:40 10/1988]

The utilitarian forms that dominate these verbal exchanges in segments (5.6.1) and (5.6.2) can, in some cases, be abandoned altogether as buyers simply examine the price tag on an item and hand over cash money for the purchase. In this type of setting, "tradin" is clearly dominated by the utilitarian and economic function of the physical act of the exchange. In each of these segments, requesting discourse forms, uttered without politeness markers and usually for information about a good or its price, refocus the participant relations from a personal pro-offering of a good or service to the mutual performance of a task, that of potentially exchanging items of value in a market setting. The community identity or cultural value of the selves participating in the transaction are devalued and the merit of the exchange itself enhanced as knowledge of the buyer's or seller's "belongin" networks are of no or marginal importance. On the other hand, the worth of the interactors as traders can be enhanced through sharp trading, exchange of pertinent and humorous narratives, or displays of knowledge about the production or history of a product.[25] Consequently, presuppositional indexes assume different configurations from those characteristic of "takin care of" structuring.

The extensive reliance on interrogative "askin" forms indexes "rights" of the participants to exchange goods under common interpretive structures of appropriate exchanging behavior by each: interrogatives will be answered, a "fair" price will be asked in relation to the cost of the good to the seller, and, if a purchase is made, "cash money" will be the mode of exchange. "Place" and "claims" relations are irrelevant, so other nonimperative requesting forms are inappropriate or used strategically for a desired effect.

The tag "do ya" ending segment (5.6.1) marks a style shift to more "proper" forms but does not violate flea market norms of requesting discourse. Similarly, segment (5.6.2) simply states the cost of an item being examined by a potential buyer, an anticipated response to an interrogative. In both examples, no greetings have been given, no narrative of a problem has been offered, and no anticipation on the part of the buyer that the vendor will volunteer the possession or use of a good free of charge is indexed. The clear interrogative structuring in (5.6.1) indexes her "right" to ask; the seller answers with a two-syllable vocable indicating "no." Segment (5.6.2) anticipates this "right" to ask when the seller offers a verbal response to a silent examination of goods. The absence of any other conversational structuring fails to recreate indexical functions to "place" or "claims" participant relations.

Segment (5.7) represents a more fully developed exchange sequence:

(5.7) (*Setting: Male food vendor selling green beans and other produce at a flea market.*)

M Vendor: What? I ain't got a bushel for sale over there.
Millie: That looks good.
Anita: Yeah.
M Vendor: I make more money by the pound cause I'm down to one bushel a day.
Millie: **What's this?**
M Vendor: Homemade chowchow.
Millie: Homemade chowchow.
How much is it?
M Vendor: **I gIt a dollar an a half a quart . seventy five a pint.**
Millie: Humm.
M Vendor: There's sauerkraut
Hurt your feelings to eat that.
[polite laugh from two women]
It [((?is rea:l goo:d?))]
Millie: [((?I could get a pint?))] of it
Anita: Why don't you get a pint?
M Vendor: That's the last pint.
Millie: **Yeah . I'll take a pint.**
Anita: That's a little one.
[referencing baskets of tomatoes Millie is now looking at]
Millie: How much uh are the baskets?
M Vendor: **Big baskets ((?we're askin for is five?))**
Millie: Ok.
M Vendor: These big fancy baskets cost us almost three a piece.
Millie: Uh-huh . uh-huh.
Let me take just this right now.
M Vendor: All right.
Give me a quarter here . honey.
Millie: **How much is cushaws?**
M Vendor: **Two apiece.**
Millie: Thank you. [leaves] [47a:005 10/1988]

Interrogatives request information and index the "right" to ask a seller about his or her goods. Responses are subclausal ("Homemade chowchow") to conversational ("There's sauerkraut / Hurt your feelings to eat that"), with a referential focus on the good under discussion and minimal use of requesting discourse formal patterns. Referentially denotative discourse describing the product dominates.

This reduction of requesting discourse to subclausal forms means that first-person pronominals, as in "I need" are either absent or used infrequently. Their absence weakens creative indexes to the buyer and seller and therefore results in the abrogation of potential "place" and "claims" relations. Millie shifts to a "let" construction rather than a flea market–preferred indicative such as "I'll take this right now" as she hands over the money. This construction shifts and reframes the exchange into a requesting sequence that indexes "rights" and "place" and admits "claims" indexical relations as a possibility. But none is created by other communicative signs in the exchange. The vendor applies his own and reframes the exchange to what would be a male-female "doin for" structuring in Ash Creek and uses an imperative followed by a +female term of address ("Give me a quarter here . honey").[26] In these domains, imperatives from either party are appropriate within his or her resource domain. In this case, the vendor indexes his "right" and "place" to control the acquisition and dispensation of money. More consistent with flea market discourse would have been "this takes a quarter," "a quarter, then," or "twenty-five cents (if you don't care to)." With the following interrogative ("How much is cushaws?"), the woman again asserts flea market exchange structuring, the vendor responds appropriately, and the encounter soon ends.

Segment (5.8) begins after a man has asked a vendor for information about assembling a complex tool unassembled on the vendor's table. The vendor offers to show how it is put together and what it does:

(5.8) (*Setting: Flea market. Male vendor is selling handtools.*)

M Vendor:	**You want me to put ɛm together?** [tool parts]
Man 1:	Yeah.
M Vendor:	Huh?
Man 1:	Yeah . I could ((?unintelligible overlap (2.0)?)).
	What I need, then—
M Vendor:	—Could you do it Sarah?
Man 1:	No
	((?I can handle it?)).
	I never tried.
M Vendor:	Hu:h?
	I ((?1.5?))
	Some people say they're easier to carry that way
	But they . that's why I don't put em together.
	I don't ((?believe I can?)) myself.
	I might could put the big ones together

See those ol big uns right there
They come o:ff just like this when you gIt Im.
They come oh in about how many pieces . Bill?

Man 2: **What a ya gIt out a these?** [asking about baseball card storage cases]

M Vendor: How many ya want?

Man 2: I don't know.

M Vendor: Buddy . *I* give four dollars . you want some for three?
Thirty-two hundred cards is what that'll hold.
It'll hold . it'll the same as what . these right here

[Exchange becomes unintelligible due to overlap; Man 1 attempts to "make a deal" in which vendor keeps half and he buys half; not agreed to by vendor.] [47a:85 10/1988]

The vendor frames this interaction as a task-focused "helpin out" (chapter 7) verbal exchange when he uses an interrogative ("You want me to put ɛm together?") to obtain consent that he should attempt the task. This segment captures "want" and "need" distinctions clearly. The vendor's "want" offers to meet the potential buyer's personal wishes; the vendor's "need" is for assistance in terms of parts to put the tool together so that it will function for a potential group.

A second man reframes the interaction into a typical flea market exchange pattern, using an interrogative to obtain cost information about baseball card storage boxes. The first item is dropped temporarily as a conversational topic to accommodate this "tradin" exchange. Later reintroduced, this matter becomes the subject of "makin a deal," or negotiating a price.

In this exchange and to a lesser degree in segment (5.3), the fluid structuring of flea market discourse is evident. Participants negotiate transitory relationships with each other based on economic exchanges within the socioeconomic arena of the marketplace.

Participants interacting in "tradin" contexts frequently value appropriate "tradin" discourse at or below that of silent material exchanges. Nonverbal actions are substitutable paradigms for certain verbal behavior patterns and vice versa. "Makin a deal" communications, however, elevate verbal interaction to one of its most complex representations. Entirely within the domain of male verbal practices,[27] "makin a deal" provides a discourse intersection between personal, economic, and political sectors of control. Men use it to engage in negotiated, often highly face-threatening verbal exchanges to construct a transaction that blatantly asserts personal control or power and usually involves an exchange of entities having high commodity value. Embellished and fully representative "makin a deal" discursive practices were therefore not available for audiotape recording.[28]

"Makin a deal" constructs a contractual relation. A man who breaks a "deal" invites assault, personal property damage, or slander, affecting his "name." The outcome of such discourse should therefore be terms acceptable to both parties, although one may talk about how he was cheated or led into a "bad deal" later.

Either lengthy or abbreviated, these verbal exchanges allow men who are not kin or for whom "belongin" relations are not acknowledged to reach an agreement about some expensive economic or serious political-economic matter, whether the negotiated cost of a vehicle, the manner in which a contractor is to complete a construction job, or acceptable contractual arrangements for votes between a local politician and his constituents.

Deals cannot be made without the appropriate use of "makin a deal" discourse, and "makin a deal" discourse must involve verbal turn-takings that negotiate conditions and terms of agreement. The following two examples meet these criteria but are diminutive representations that could be taperecorded. Bill, the teller of them, wanted to evoke humor over a well-known "savin" resident's greed and a young man's conflation of animal and machine price values:

(5.9) (*Setting: Woodcarving session in maintenance building of the Environmental Center. Participants: Bill and I.*)

Bill: I told ya about . Abe [Bill's son-in-law] goin down there to buy hay last year?

Did I tell ya about that?

Anita: I don't recall

You . start over an see if I don't remember.

Bill: Uh . he said he'd run out a hay an he hated to run all the way to Lenoir to gIt him hay.

He told Heather [Bill's daughter] "I bet Tom's got plenty a hay down there

He'll probably sell me a bale or two."

Heather said . "Yeah . he has."

Abe said he run down there an said . him and Heather

An Heather went up there an sees he was layin on the couch.

Heather said she asked him

"Tom . we'd like to buy a bale a hay . if you could spare us a little until such time we can gIt some hay."

He said . "Well, now . I don't know."

"Or a couple a bales if you can afford it . or spare it."

He said . "Well I don't know . I might run short."

She said Mary [Tom's wife] was standin there listenin

Anita: Uh-huh.

Bill: She said . "Well . if you can't spare it then

I guess we'll have to go all the way to Lenoir an gIt us some hay."

She said Mary said . **"Tom, gIt up from there an gIt them some hay."**

[Both laugh.]

An uh . said Tom got up real slow ya know an come down there an he said "I'll let ya have two bales."

An Abe said he didn't have nothin but a twenty dollar bill . ya know

An he was gonna sell ɛm . for two dollars a bale.

He got ɛm for a dollar an a half a bale.

He said . uh . he handed the twenty dollar bill

An . Tom said . "I 'ain't got no ch[ange to]." [laughs]

Anita: [change]

I knew this one was coming

Bill: Yeah

Uh . an uh he said . "Well . you can uh

You can jIst keep the twenty dollars an when you gIt change

You can jIst give me the rest of it back."

Tom kept hold of that money ya know an ((?directly the man?)) said

"**Well . why don't you just take it all in hay**."

[Both laugh.]

An Bill said . said he was just like a little boy

Once he got aholt of it he didn't wanna [((?let it go?))]

Anita: [let it go]

[Both laugh.]

Bill: Said he had plenty a hay to spare. [104a:250 1/1986]

(5.10) (*Setting: Woodcarving session in maintenance building at Environmental Center. Participants: Bill and I.*)

Bill: Did I ever tell ya that one where he was tryin to sell Jamie a pony?

Anita: No:

Bill: No?

They's a in . I think about fifth grade at that time

Fourth or fifth

Anita: Yea:h

Bill: An uh

We lived at Blue Place [home, part of Environmental Center campus]

An Tommy Lee called . Jamie one evenin an I heard ((?them talkin?)) on the phone

An they

I could tell they was negotiatin some kind of price

An uh . an Jamie said "Seventy-five dollars."

An . he kept talkin.

He said . "That's high."

Then I heared him say . "Well, you shouldn't charge the same price ya paid for it because it's been *used*." [laughs]

I couldn't ((?get over that?))

He didn't wanna buy it.

He didn't wanna give the same price cause the pony's been used. [92a:675 5/86]

Segments (5.9) and (5.10) contain reported speech in which the speaker was not a participant in the "makin a deal" event. The exact phrasing of the original speech is therefore not available and the text has been reconfigured to meet Ash Creek oral narrative conventions.[29] At the same time, Bill and many older Ash Creek residents are extremely capable of reproducing speech very close to the way it was spoken to them. There is a high probability that the speech he reports in these retellings is more closely consistent with what he heard than I would remember and that the original teller of segment (5.9) also reported accurately what was said.

In both segments (5.9) and (5.10) participants negotiate value using money as a means of barter to exchange needed or wanted items. In segment (5.9), the seller can negotiate value; in segment (5.10), the buyer attempts to establish a price, but an unrealistic one. Such an exchange can be viewed as a "makin a deal" socialization example in which two children practice how to negotiate. Events reported through dialogue in segment (5.9) present a "need" situation, evoking direct "askin" structuring. In the winter months, hay is mandatory if livestock are to survive. Abe had two horses and Tom two draft animals that he still used occasionally for plowing instead of his tractor. Abe's wife Heather was a frequent visitor to Tom and Mary's house and had developed strong "rights," and "place" relations with them, especially with Mary, much her senior, a highly respected woman in the community and a distant relative. Heather is therefore much more comfortable in talking with Tom, a farmer, than is Abe, who commutes two hours to work and is rarely home during the daylight hours. As Bill's daughter, Heather is a close member of his "belongin" network, and this story is more likely to be recounted by him in conversation as well.

Heather frames a direct request with "we'd like to buy," marking her younger, more urban-experienced and college-educated background with the more "proper" "like" and "buy" forms rather than the more "country" "need" and "trade" tokens. As a direct "askin," this example indexes strong "rights" and "place" relations and reproduces them through the process of recreating these presuppositional indexical relations. Dialogic pronominals "we," "you," and "I" constitute creative indexes, linking participants in a common negotiation for a specific trade. The request for a bale of hay, selling in town for around $2.00, is minimal for this well-stocked farmer. When Tom hedges, suggesting noncompliance, Heather counters with a "need" declarative, indicating that a 50-mile round trip taking them out of the holler by a dirt road would be their only other choice if their animals were not to go hungry. The inconvenience Tom's prospective noncompliance suggests is extremely disproportionate to the nature of the request, jeopardizing the strength of the relationship between the couples. Mary recognizes this disparity and utters a "doin for" imperative, "Tom, gIt up from there and gIt them some hay," reproducing close "claims" relations between them, developed over more than 50 years of marriage. Tom's reluctance in procuring the hay evaporates with the large payment, and the deal is renegotiated, as Tom's personal desire or "want" for money exceeds his "need" for surplus hay. He utters a declarative request form, and Abe and Heather obtain ample hay. "Deals" are negotiated and evolve over the course of the verbal exchanges; both sides expect and demand a substantive exchange in which they receive something they each value, creating a sociocentric arena for an economic transaction.

Normative use of "makin a deal" discourse circulates economic or political-economic items within the community and within political-economic networks that necessarily expand to areas outside Ash Creek itself. Such discourse transforms goods from commodities into prestations of a male-gendered socioeconomic self who negotiates with others to address each other's respective needs. At the nexus of culturally valued socioeconomic processes, "makin a deal" discourse is hegemonic, constructing asymmetrical relations of political-economic power. Central to these verbal processes is reproduction of presuppositional indexical relations of "rights" and "place" that permit construction of participant structures that can make "deals." These practices simultaneously construct creative indexical relations that bind interacting participants in a specific contractual relationship for valued and agreed-upon services or goods.

Men who have a good "name" in Ash Creek, whether community residents or simply residents of the area, are skilled at making deals, for making successful deals creates or reproduces a man's personal value through "name" enhancement. Women and less skilled men in belonging relations with such men recognize this fact as many actively pursue viable, vital "place" and "claims" relations with them. As one resident said about this process, "If you have a good name, you can get anything you need."

Patterned variation in the use of nonimperative requesting discourse also constructs socioeconomic exchanges through its semantic ability to reference and its pragmatic ability to index core, critical "rights" and "place" relations in community life. By facilitating the construction and recreation of "claims" relations, "takin care of," "tradin," and "makin a deal" discursive practices become the semiotic means by which material items and behavior are given culturally validated political-economic meanings. Nonverbal exchanges intersect with these patterns, assuming communicative meanings specific to themselves, but meanings ultimately dependent on the discourse that glossed, commented, or co-occurred with them in the ongoing, routinized, and substantive meaningful behavior that constitutes Ash Creek cultural life.

These linguistically mediated processes, ongoing, negotiated, and regionally recognized,[30] construct an ideology of political economics that can vest significant power and control over the daily lives of residents in the personalities of a very few men. These processes in turn reproduce irresolvable tensions between the local political-economic order that values, first, interpersonal claims relationships and a formal institutional capitalistic model that values, first, productivity and job or career professionalism.

6 NONREQUESTING USES OF IMPERATIVES

"Did I tell you about the time . . . ?"

One afternoon early in my fieldwork, Cindy and I parted company after I had assisted her in some errands involving her children. As she turned to leave, she said, "Come to supper." I responded, "I can't. Not tonight." She looked at Anne and said, "Does she think I'm really askin her to supper?" [notes 7/85]

As I leave one woman's home, again early in my fieldwork, I offer a necessary "reason" for leaving that involves commitments to others or a "need." She responds with "Stay now, you stay." Understanding this utterance as an "order," I sit down. She looks surprised. Talk lags. I soon take an exit again. This time I leave. [notes 7/85]

PIVOTAL TO ALL OF ASH CREEK requesting discourse is a system of acceptable uses of imperatives, or other unambiguous directives having imperative functions, to demand compliance of listeners. Except under certain very specific and highly restricted contextual constraints, Ash Creek residents will recognize such imperative forms as "orders." "Orders" are a speaker's blatant assertions of control over another individual and are invariably interpreted negatively—with sometimes highly negative responses involving violence. Residents have well-developed metapragmatic discourse about the use of "orders," which, in turn, constructs a well-developed ideology of "order" language. At the same time, Ash Creek English does not exclude the imperative mood from its grammar. Imperative constructions can be, under certain contextual constraints, very common. This chapter explores the usage patterns that lead to this apparent contradiction as they relate to the reproduction or transformation of the community socioeconomy. It first discusses formal constraints on normative imperative syntax and then considers nonrequesting uses of "orders" in reported speech and oral narratives.

Like other forms of requesting discourse, imperatives index participant frameworks that construct specific instances of socioeconomic activity. In this case, they direct an addressee's economic behavior or activity by voicing the addresser's conscious "wants" or "needs." Highly conventional uses also function pragmatically to contextualize propositional content so deeply that the referential meaning of the imperative is either inconsequential or is interpreted as its opposite. Any "order" function is lost. However, unlike other requesting discourse, "order" imperatives can also suddenly and intensely terminate economic relationships and the interpersonal relationships to commodities, goods, and services that other types of requesting discourse can create or reproduce. They can create interpersonal and intracommunity conflict. In this sense this type of speech act constitutes "the process of *differentiating* an Other from a Self [which] is often deemed to be more crucial to the creation of both identities and communities than the presence of a shared cognitive substratum" (Briggs 1996a:5).

As a result of this saliency of command function, imperative constructions can function as independent discourse units more so than any other forms of requesting discourse, except for, perhaps, direct "askin" forms. They therefore assume an independent ideological dimension as residents verbally classify them, often quickly, into acceptable uses in which they become forms of asking (not "orders") or into unacceptable "order" status. "Orders" within Ash Creek call into question, attempt to redefine, or disregard "rights," "place," and, especially, "claims" relations. Because they can be socially disruptive, residents shun their use and express their negative evaluations through well-developed metacommentary about them. Consequently, discourse forms-in-use that Ash Creek residents classify as "orders" are readily recognized in verbal interactions; they are talked about frequently, often epithetically with the phrases "ain't nobody telling me what to do," or "ain't no man telling me what to do," or "ain't no woman gonna tell me what to do." Furthermore, mothers consciously instruct children to ask, never "order" (or "tell") someone what to do, reinforcing the strong negative value given order discourse.

Residents can also discuss this type of discourse out of context, as a distinct, recognizable speaking practice, so that conversation often includes a well-developed metapragmatic discourse for interpreting them. This metapragmatic discourse is so well developed, in fact, that it assumes the functions of an ideology of authority embedded within a task-focused culture. Consequently, acceptable uses of imperatives or other "order" forms become culturally valued utterances about appropriate relations of authority or power as well as ways of demanding some socioeconomic activity.

Unlike "volunteerins" or direct "askin" forms of requesting, which are frequently embedded within "takin care of" or "makin a deal" practices, "orders" are tightly bounded in formal configuration and referential possibilities. They always reveal or index asymmetrical or disparate relationships among interlocutors. The requestor's "want" or "need" is transparent to the requestee. "Orders also reveal what are acceptable or unacceptable behaviors through requestee compliance or noncompliance. "Order" discourse therefore constitutes an empirical, observable system in which linguistic and political-economic intersections are transparent and recognizable. Consequently, appropriate uses reproduce culturally sanctioned power or control relationships over valued resources, and inappropriate ones reveal disjunctions in the linguistic-economic system that are highly meaningful to residents. "Orders" in situations of use therefore represent the core of the requesting system of Ash Creek. To understand the use of the "order" discourse system is to understand the socioeconomic and political economic system as well.

"Order" Discourse Formal Structure

Because "order" discourse is readily elicited and identified, it is one discourse easily explored through conversational feedback and formal or informal elicitation. As determined by these techniques and through observation, discourse that precipitated an "order" lexical label corresponded to imperatives, or interrogatives or declaratives uttered in imperative intonational contours.[1] As utterances recognized as tokens indicative of a speech act type, the following examples are culturally meaningful as well as grammatically representative:[2]

(6.1)

(6.1.1) Behave. [mother to young child at regional hospital waiting room] [notes: 8/87]

(6.1.2) Move your car. [local man to me] [notes 11/86]

(6.1.3) You mow the grass. [foreman to maintenance worker at Environmental Center] [notes 8/85]

(6.1.4) Take your son to the emergency room. [Millie to local mother] [notes 12/86]

(6.1.5) Don't sit there. [elicited; homemaker to visitor] [notes 4/87]

(6.1.6) Don't. [many instances, usually parents to children]

(6.1.7) Let (or leave) Susie alone. [elicited; mother to child] [notes 6/86]

In each case, the segment is in clausal form, the primary grammatical characteristic of "orders." In each utterance, the segment contains a surface or deleted but understood "you" singular that functions as a deictic, creatively indexing the other interlocutor co-present in the speech situation. In each case, the verb form denotes a behavior (or cessation of an activity) that the speaker "wants" or "needs" performed, terminated, or modified. It may be transitive or intransitive.

In segments (6.1.1)–(6.1.7), "order" forms express conservative criteria for imperative construction in English: "you" subject deletion and a tenseless verb form expressing imperative mood in simple, monoclausal constructions.[3] The form/function relationship between the imperative grammatical structure of these instances and their command function is transparent and unmitigated, clearly recognized and identified by residents.

Segments (6.2.1)–(6.2.3) illustrate more indirect order forms in which verbal imperatives are mitigated through some modifying phrases or clause:

(6.2)

(6.2.1) If you don't care to, gɛt me some beans. [elicited] [notes 4/87]

(6.2.2) Gɛt me some beans . if you don't care to. [elicited] [notes 4/87]

(6.2.3) You ought to clean off the table. [older woman, outsider, to Debbie in Environmental Center dining hall] [notes 8/86]

In segments (6.2.1) and (6.2.2), the requesting "if you don't care to" preposes or postposes the imperative and constitutes an outsider's usage. "If you don't care to" is rarely used by residents in conjunction with an imperative because it conflates a conventional direct "askin" request form (chapter 4) with an "order" form. As an improper construction in which an "order" and an "askin" are mixed, most respondents indicated that this form "wasn't right" although outsiders and some speakers, usually men, were observed to embed imperatives in this fashion as if to weaken or mitigate an otherwise transparent "order." Their usage was similar to "proper" English use of "please." Segment (6.2.3) is a clear deontic construction, expressing obligation through the modal "ought," as well as demanding compliance. The speaker did not receive compliance and Debbie commented on her behavior: "Who does she think she is? I oughta do this and I oughta do that. Ain't nobody tellin me what to do."

Absent from this category are forms such as the following:

*Please get me some beans from the garden.

*Do get me some beans from the garden.

Both constructions are considered "proper talk," and "please" is a stereotype sometimes used in what residents consider formal settings (public offices and businesses) or with those considered "educated."[4]

Segments (6.3.1)–(6.3.5) represent possible "orders," depending on the participant framework created by the interlocutors and by the intonation contours with which the speaker utters the command:

(6.3)

(6.3.1) You need to go to church. [elicited; Christian to younger woman] [notes 1/87]

(6.3.2) You should pray about that. [Debbie to temporary cook who is nonkin] [notes 8/85]

(6.3.3) You're bein aggravatin [Debbie to me for asking too many questions in a direct "askin" manner] [notes 8/85]

(6.3.4) What are you doin? [mother to adult daughter] [notes 8/85]

(6.3.5) When are you gonna fix supper? [elicited] [notes 4/87]

All of these examples were uttered flatly, yet emphatically. Their directive goals function was always clear to the addressee. Paralinguistic features also assist in disambiguating these forms: these include focused eye contact, as well as an increased intensity and volume relative to the speaker's conversational style.

Based on these types of examples, "order" discourse centers around, but is not limited to, the use of imperative sentence types in which the speaker is modifying or directing the behavior of the addressee. If residents' own commentaries were considered alone, all imperative uses would appear to be "orders" and subject to noncompliance. Yet, within many observed speech events, "order" forms occurred but were not interpreted as "orders." That is, residents uttered imperative sentences, generally expected some form of compliance, yet addressees did not recognize the discourse as anything approaching an "order." Some were stylized forms, highly predictable at certain stages in social interaction; others also lacked "order" intonation or paralinguistic features and were clearly constituents of other speaking practices, such as instructions; others did indeed appear to meet basic formal criteria for "order" lexical labeling. In addition, outsiders, like me, frequently responded to these forms in situations of use as "orders," whereas Ash Creek residents did not.

Clearly, patterned pragmatic constraints were operating to construct communicative event relations that changed the functions and metapragmatic designation of such imperatives. Clearly, the contextualized meanings of such verbal exchanges were taking precedence over the semantic meaning of the utterance. Clearly, the empirical data contradicted the reported uses, suggesting that these pragmatic constraints are so culturally significant that they neutralize one of the most salient and negatively valued speech acts in the Ash Creek communicative repertoire. Clearly, these constraints had established such strong indexical relationships that they contributed to the construction of an overall Ash Creek system of imperatives-in-use as well. To understand the cultural and linguistic-economic rules of use for "orders," then, requires an understanding of the use of imperative constructions in Ash Creek. To understand the use of imperatives in Ash Creek requires a complete discussion of those discourse practices in which imperatives can occur.

Stylized Uses of Imperatives

Much imperative discourse is highly stylized,[5] consistent in grammatical form and intonational contouring, and predictable in its structural placement in verbal interactions among speakers or in speech situations. Because these forms are so predictable and discourse position so patterned, their primary function is to frame the verbal interaction or discourse topic rather than assert a semantic-referential proposition or a transparent directive function.[6]

Certain forms of greeting segments, leave-takings, and conversational or topic openings or closings are especially controlled by such imperative uses. In beginning an appropriate verbal interaction between acceptable interlocutors, the one who has the "right" either by status criteria (generally age, gender, or religious position) and is in his or her physical "place," where a core resource is controlled or managed, is likely to open with one of the following:

(6.4)

(6.4.1) Come on in/Come in. [Speaker inside home, other occupied establishment, or a vehicle; door need not be shut and other participants may or may not have signaled a desire to interact by a knock or other form of greeting.]

(6.4.2) Come over here a minute/Come here. [Other greetings may be optional.]

(6.4.3) Take you a seat/Sit down/Sit a minute/Sit a spell. [Speaker already in his or her physical "place" such as a home or office. Other participants may or may not have greeted.]

(6.4.4) Get you some coffee/get you a pop/get you some supper/grab you something to eat. [once a visitor has entered a home]

As with other culturally recognized "order" usages, these forms also demand compliance,[7] but residents do not assign them "order" classification or respond to them as "orders." Their position at the start or beginning of communicative interaction and the indicative intonation pattern that accompanies them mitigates their potential "order" status. Their goals function is to begin an interaction by establishing expected physical and spatial relationships among interlocutors. The one uttering the opening will be in control of these arrangements.[8]

Leave-takings where one or more participants leave the interactional setting, removing themselves from real or potential continuation of communicative exchanges, may also contain stylized imperative forms if the leave-taker is not a close family member in the speaker's "belongin" network. For close family members, interlocutors may simply state an assertion such as "I'm goin to Mom's," utter a "bye" or "see ya" as they depart, or, frequently, just leave the interactional arena when their perceived contribution to a conversation or nonverbal activity is not required. Others are likely to receive one of the following, depending on setting and type of relationship between the participants:

(6.5)

(6.5.1) Come see us. [Speaker not at home; expectations are that future reciprocal exchanges are possible between interlocutors.]

(6.5.2) Come to supper/come home with me. [Speaker not at home; addressee in a positive, familiar relationship with speaker; usually spoken by a married, established woman who has a home and family.]

(6.5.3) Stay now/You stay. [Speaker at home; addressee in a positive relationship with speaker; may be uttered by either male or female head of household.]

Leave-takings present a transparent argument for the importance of contextualization in changing denotative referential meanings of an utterance: "come see us" is pro forma and, within a specific interaction, can mean not to come back; "come to supper" is not an invitation to a meal but a statement that continuing a relationship is possible; and "you stay" signifies agreement by home residents that visitors should leave.[9] In these cases, compliance with the pragmatic meaning of the utterance is also expected, but the intended dominant meaning is opposite or nearly opposite the surface referential meaning.

Other uses of stylized forms are less standardized in terms of their pragmatic meanings or expected participant structuring, but I discuss them here because they constitute a collection of possible expressions that affect the rhetorical dimension of conversational discourse. Older accounts of Appalachian English would categorize these forms as stock phrases, idioms, expressions, or sayings.[10] Many of these structures are idiomatic, learned in family settings or within family interactions, and are generally shared by members of the same gender, creating complex social and discourse relationships in which particular forms can communicate symbolically and indexically such culturally meaningful dimensions as personal or family name or reputation, historical or mythic identity, or genderization of self.

As discourse units, these forms also signify conversational segment openings or closings, forcing a change in speech event topics. They are in this sense especially complex discourse features because they function within a specific conversation in creative ways while simultaneously communicating context-free cultural interpretations conveyed as formulaic forms. Compliance with these imperatives is often not expected as their major functions are intratextual, creating cohesion through discursive co-referential relationships[11] or through simply framing a discourse segment. The discourse function of "you" in such instances therefore assumes a primary rhetorical and referential function inside the text,[12] while the extratextual deictic function that dominates in "order" discourse is secondary or not present.

In segments (6.6)–(6.8), the highlighted imperative constructions are specific instances of these complex polysemous and multifunctional meanings. However, with respect to those features that distinguish them from "orders," they also reveal certain generalities that apply to most "sayins" (Ash Creek usage) incorporated into narratives and other verbal genres.

The imperative "and you'll li::ke it" in segment (6.6) is a well-known "sayin," rather than an "order":

(6.6) (*Setting: Environmental Center kitchen; afternoon food preparation tasks are in progress; male maintenance workers are installing a ceiling fan casing so sounds of pounding in background add to the usual noise of the air circulation fan; I have just entered with audiorecorder on. Participants: Sarah and Linda, Dillon* [*Sarah's husband*], *another maintenance worker, and I. Conversation is about some personnel problems the center is having.*)

Dillon: We're about to have a fireside chat.

Anita: Are they still living up there?
Or they up at Monday House?

Sarah: The president used to address us . on the
You know on the condition of ((?1.5?)) ((?just?)) like Brown—
[Brown is center director.]

Anita: Yeah yeah ((?yeah?))
Sarah: —is gonna do us
He's gonna sit that ((?2.0?)) [pounding noises] and then we're ((?gonna go along with it?))
Anita: Well . um
Dillon: **And you'll li::ke it—**
Sarah: —an you'll [like it]
Anita: [like] it [chuckles]
[Others smile.] [76a:6/86]

"Sayins" in Ash Creek are subject to their own metalingual and metapragmatic discursive practices. Interlocutors' recognition of this one ("and you'll like it") as an independent and stylized verbal entity is evidenced by all interlocutors' overlapping with Dillon to complete it. This particular one is linked to the type of authoritative discourse used by a drill sergeant. Its use is therefore an instance of style switching to a well-known, stereotypic segment of authoritative discourse characteristic of 1940s American military speaking practices experienced by Dillon. As semantically constrained by the co-text "fireside chat" and "the president used to address us," both allusions to President Franklin Roosevelt's radio broadcasts in the early 1940s when Dillon was a young man, the "sayin" reframes the discourse segment into a metaphor for an authoritative, if not military, verbal event in which an individual (the president, by implication, Franklin Roosevelt, who is like Mr. Brown, the Environmental Center Director,) will exercise power unilaterally over others.

At the same time, the pragmatic meaning of "and you'll li:ke it" is not completely overridden by intratextual referential significations. The "order" grammatical structure of the expression simultaneously functions to address the kitchen audience about the situation at hand. The pronouns in "we're about to have," "—is gonna do us," and "we're gonna go along with it" anchor the narrative analogy into the immediate context, relating it directly to the other interlocutors and to the center events discussed just before this segment. The "you" in the saying "and you'll li::ke it" then assumes a dual signaling function, completing the narrative and coding how the workers will respond to new directives from the center director.

Therefore, its possible range of referential meanings as a "sayin" is reinterpreted ("recontextualized" after Bauman and Briggs 1990) by the surrounding discursive text to direct the immediate audience in how to understand the current crisis in center management. The embedded "sayin" tells the workers that they will go along with whatever the director does because they, like soldiers, have no choice.[13] It implies obligatory compliance.

The absurdity of being given an order to "like" or "dislike" something reproduces the negative value given superior power positions by Ash Creek residents. By virtue of its culturally recognized value as a "sayin," the form "and you'll li::ke it" expresses a different configuration of communicative functions than do Ash Creek "orders." Instead, it is redefined as having semantic and rhetorical functions first within the text of the discourse alone, then to the audience hearing it. It is a representation of the metapragmatic functions of discourse to constitute the Ash Creek ideology of authoritative language.

The imperative "you can bring it by" in segment (6.7), on the other hand, is not a "sayin," but a complex representation of both conversational discourse structures and cultural rules of interpretation:

(6.7) (*Setting: Local medical clinic; Edward is discussing payment of his account by the insurance company; conversation in progress. Participants: Joan, Edward, a nonlocal older man of some reputation who has lived in Ash Creek for at least 35 years, and I.*)

Edward: But
To make a long story short
We found out eventually
Paid ɛm
And a—
Joan: —Sent it to the [wro::]—
Edward: [mis] takenly sent—
Joan: —it to the [wro:]
Edward: [the ac]count to Lexington instead of to [Louisville]
Joan: [Louisville].
See I didn't know they [had different places]
Edward: [I talk I talked] I talked to Lexington
Woman: I gotta go [voice from back of clinic]
Edward: And Lexington said
"We don't have that ((?name?)) on our list we don't have Dr. ((??)) *on*"
Joan: *Huh*
Probably sent it to the wrong place.
Edward: That's what it turned out to be
Larryville helped— [Larryville is psuedonym for a small town in the area where clinic's central office is.]
Joan: —Uh-huh
Edward: To figure that out.
Now the this other that came
Joan: Yeah

Edward: Two months ago.
I think I put it aside to bring up here the next time I was coming
Oh . but then *I think* that
Something then came through from Blue Cross
So I . we had to—
Joan: —you they paid that [day]
Edward: [we] were paid for Dr. Smith
For this and this
I'll
Joan: Uh-hum
Edward: Have to [((?.5?))]
Joan: [Ok] well
Sometime when you're up **you can bring it by.**
[10b:217 10/86]

As a closing to a conversational segment, the imperative ends previous discourse by asserting future action. In this case, Joan is terminating the detailed descriptive discourse referencing Edward's medical insurance payment difficulties. She takes advantage of a pause to insert a closing sequence ("Ok well") and then provides closure with the imperative. Unlike the "sayin" imperative in segment (6.6), the "you" pronoun is indeed deictic, indexing the patient, and the utterance is clearly directed to Edward as co-interlocutor. As mitigated by the indefinite "sometime" and the modal "can," the construction nevertheless lacks the transparent ends functions of direct "orders" to evoke immediate compliance. This non-"order" framing creates a structure in which the deictic value of "you" is not clearly dominant over an intratextual referential function of "you," which characterized the "sayin" imperative in (6.6). Furthermore, the entire imperative form in (6.7) is not a speech act in itself but is a necessary structural component of the verbal interactional sequence conforming to English conversational closings and turn-taking rules.[14]

These conversational semantic and pragmatic functions are insufficient factors, however, for all Ash Creek residents to unambiguously dismiss this construction as a non-"order." The mitigating elements that shift it toward "askin" discourse patterns are minimal within the Ash Creek system, and individuals' sensitivity to "order" use is fully developed. Instead, two other presuppositional indexical functions determine non-"order" classification for such usages. The first is a complex one related to the socioeconomic system of "rights," "place," and "claims" and links closely to the use of appropriate "order" discourse usages by women. It is Joan's "right" to request or even demand that patients bring billing materials or other necessary materials for the processing of a claim to her at the clinic, not because of her position as receptionist within the medical services provider hierarchy but because it's her "place" within the moral order to do so. Healing is within the domain of women; the receptionist is a woman laboring in a healing setting; therefore, she can request or demand items or services that facilitate that process. Furthermore, reading and writing activities are within women's domain as well.[15] Therefore, the imperative indexes that she can exercise "rights" to obtain such materials from two gendered domains of resources.

The second interpretive structure involves constructions of cultural concepts of self and personal identity. This non-"order" imperative form, coming at the end of a potential request sequence, is Joan's verbal way of acknowledging her obligations when a client asks directly or requests using a "volunteerin" framework to adjust, investigate, or initiate a medical claim or account. It is therefore stylized in the sense that it is one of her idioms, one member of numerous stock forms within her workplace discourse repertoire, and one familiar to her and her coworkers. Frequent patients, such as Edward, also recognize these forms as characteristic of her speaking style. The imperative becomes an index to Joan's way of "volunteerin" to do the tasks her position requires.

As a representation of Joan's individual speaking style, it is also an example of what Ash Creek residents term "learnin" someone. To "learn" individuals is to know their expressions, gestures, behavior, and speech patterns so that an accurate interpretation of their "ways" is possible, social interaction predictable, and a consistent assessment of their personality valid.[16] Individuals, particularly in family interactional settings, will assimilate the ways of those who are admired or in a superior generation and of the same gender, including idiomatic discourse and "sayins." Through these processes of imitation, patterns of how individuals interact and communicate with others become more predictable, even across generations. Some patterns can assume an historical and mythic sense through their seeming permanence over time.[17] Although the imperative construction in this example is at this point simply one token of the young receptionist's ways of talking, it is an index to the metapragmatic discourse that interprets this process. Its potential "order" classification is therefore neutralized not only by discourse textual features but also by a culturally based semiotic system that provides an interpretive framework for disambiguation and assignation of meaning.

Stylized imperative segment (6.8) contains three imperative constructions, only two of which meet the criteria for stylized usage so that they are predictable in both form and function:

(6.8) (*Setting: Environmental Center kitchen; meal being prepared; background noises of pots and pans being handled and food chopped; conversation in progress as workers discuss their workload; Sarah's voice is agitated, with tensing of vocal cords, rapid speech, and above normal volume. Participants: Sarah, Debbie, Linda, Sandy, and I.*)

Sarah: **Well let me tell you somethin** they're not goin to

Linda: ((?3.0?))

Sarah: Come back here and do what we do [fər]
Sandy: [that's] what I was gonna
[((?3.0?))]
Debbie: [law ((?2.0?))]
Sandy: [((?2.0?))]
Sarah: They make fun a you.
Debbie: Why I don't ((?.5?))((?working with her?))
Sarah: I don't care
I do enough work for two or three.
Linda: We know. [Phone rings; I leave kitchen to answer it.]
Sarah: I . I ((?had a problem?)) trying to get to church here a while ago all day long
And *it's* been been like that for the last . month but I—
Linda: —Yeah . yeah ((?.5?))—
Sarah: —enjoy my job
Sandy: Well it helps
I enjoy workin cause I . a body *needs* to
Anita: *Sandy* . it's fər you. [I return from back room as I talk.]
Linda: *Me*?
Anita: No . Sandy . Sandra.
Sandy: **Wait just a second** [leaves room to answer phone]
Sarah: Yeah . I'd like the one that would have studied that.
I'd caused her to work [((?2.0?))]
Debbie: [((?2.0?))] jIst . you know
Sarah: And have to do what we do
Fər a week.
Linda: ((?2.0?)) I would ((?think?)) that they'd do it volunteerly—
Sarah: —No
Pay ɛm $3.35 an hour jIst like we do it an **let them see what we do.** [60a:299 7/86]

The first "let me tell you something" is a recognized conversational mechanism for controlling a conversational turn and gaining the floor. In this segment, Sarah uses the imperative form to begin a unit of expressive discourse to convey her workload frustration. Paralinguistic features, including agitated facial expressions as well as quick hand gestures, support her more rapid and louder than usual speech. Clearly the imperative does not require compliance here, as others vie for turns, yielding the floor only when she literally outshouts and outtalks them.

This imperative form is highly predictable, appearing frequently in all Ash Creek conversations as one of a finite set of conversational structures that mark a clear call for the floor, unlike the usual careful turn-taking narrative conversational activity.

The second imperative discourse in this example, "wait jIst a second," is, in this instance, a conversational place holder to the others she has been talking to. Sandy has a necessary task to perform immediately, that of leaving the room to answer the phone. She requests that the others recognize this "need" and reincorporate her into the ongoing meal preparation after she returns. It also functions as a task-focused imperative in this instance in which a participant in an activity must alter her behavior, which in turn inconveniences others co-participating in the task. It represents one of the other major appropriate imperative use dimensions in Ash Creek. Therefore, unlike the other stylized forms mentioned, this one can also function as an "order" when uttered by Ash Creek residents under specific "rights" and "claims" situations, as discussed in chapters 7 and 8.

Stylized uses of discourse that exhibit "order" grammatical structure belong to a different set of imperative semantic and pragmatic functions and exhibit a different hierarchy of meaning relations than do true "orders." Nevertheless, within this hierarchy is the clear maintenance and use of imperatives, capable of signifying the functions of commands, albeit in a mitigated or transformed capacity. Since they maintain various aspects of imperative functions, they are therefore significant and powerful participants within the analytic domain of formulaic discourse while also fulfilling the extremely complex significations of formulae-in-use. They constitute a set of metapragmatic discourse practices that construct medial levels of removal from actual instances of linguistic-economic activity. They are members of what Silverstein (1996a:266) refers to as "the indexical order," which "shows us how to relate the *micro*-social to the *macro*-social frame of analysis of any sociolinguistic phenomenon." They are not "orders." Nevertheless, their use as various stylized or formulaic expressions reveals certain parameters affecting how the actual "order" system is constituted.

7 "HELPIN SOMEBODY OUT": IMPERATIVES IN TASK SITUATIONS

"Hey, Claude, hand me that rope."

I visited Cindy's place one afternoon, knowing that she was moving and that I was "needed" to help load the truck. Tom was there with his truck, helping to load and volunteering to drive his truck to the new place. Having greeted him, I asked what brought him here on a sunny afternoon. He replied, "Just hɛpin a neighbor out." [notes 7/86]

One summer afternoon, Susie related her daily activities to me as she usually did when we visited. In the narrative stream of events, she mentioned that she "swung by Mom's." She "needed help" with Matthew (a young grandson, not one of Susie's children). [notes 6/86]

CONTRARY TO POPULAR CULTURE STEREOTYPES, Ash Creek residents are generally laboring, or "doin somethin" during waking hours. Most children are socialized from five or six years old to activities that contribute to household maintenance. One's activities at any given time are likely to dominate "just talkin" exchanges. The metapragmatic functions created or reproduced in these conversations reassert a well-developed ideology of task-focused communication. A primitive component in constituting this ideology[1] is that "doin somethin" references a physical activity. The "sayin" "around here, honey, we work with our hands, not with our heads" describes one way individuals are likely to interpret and assign value to labor. Individuals are expected to be "keepin busy," even if it is simply turning the pages of a grocery store insert in a newspaper or waiting for hours to shoot unwanted groundhogs in a garden. This task-orientation is so well developed that performing some type of task often replaces other forms of recreational activity, such as reading or playing board games, which do not result in something "gIttin done."

Pervasive, encompassing, and open-ended, this orientation toward task-focused activity dominates Ash Creek social life and causes residents to interact in groups that produce a culturally valued product or end result that may involve the acquisition of wages or the production of commodities. For most Ash Creek adult residents, wage-paying laboring contexts are superimposed on the more encompassing and basic task-oriented patterns of work.[2]

One type of stylized conversational opening is "What are ya doin?" Residents often respond with detailed narratives of recent tasks or activities that are engaging and occasionally humorous.[3] Many residents do, of course, engage in activities such as watching television soap operas, watching action-oriented movies on a video-cassette recorder, or (for women) reading tabloid newspapers or mass market romance novels. Because such activities do not produce a culturally recognized end product, such as a paycheck or a clean kitchen floor, few, even those who engage in these activities, admit that such activities are appropriate behavior. It would not be wrong to argue that "doin" symbolizes an expansive set of interpretive schema that are constantly recombined in verbal practice to shape and provide meaning to those physical activities that constitute the nexus of Ash Creek daily life.

The tasks themselves are organized into three general types of participant frameworks: those performed by a single person, those performed by small groups of presumed cultural equals, and those performed by small groups of presumed cultural unequals. When the participant framework involves labor between cultural equals, the participants are usually of the same gender. Residents frequently gloss such activities as "helpin [name of person, group, or organization] out." When the task involves participant frameworks reproducing or creating cultural unequals within a person's "belongin" network, it usually involves both men and women. Often the presuppositional indexes of unequality are due not only to scriptural approbation for gender differences but also to practical reasons. Significant disparities in the skill and knowledge of how to do the task usually exist between men and women. Residents often gloss these occasions as "I'm doin for [name of person, group, or organization]."[4] In both types of tasks, participants perceive themselves as laboring for an individual or organization that "needs" the task performed.[5] This chapter focuses upon requesting discourse in "helpin out" contexts.

Ash Creek discourse encodes this task-focused orientation in a number of preferred grammatical constructions. A frequent usage is through gerunds rather than infinitives or nouns to reference speaking or laboring practices. A productive and generative system of task classification,[6] these /-ing/ (or /-in/ in Southern Mountain speech) nominalizations of present participles create sense relations of action-in-progress rather than of a static, bounded entity. In so doing, lexemes for both physical action and speaking practices merge into one large and expansive set of metapragmatic terms. This merging of verbal and nonverbal behavior under a common grammatical process in turn blurs the semantic boundaries between nonverbal and verbal behavior. A given clause can often insert either a present participle denoting a concrete entity or one that refers to a speaking practice:

(7.1)

Label	*Practice + example*
just talkin	to converse or engage in phatic verbal communication:
	We had us a good talkin-to.
	*He talked to us seriously.
workin	to perform a task, such as cleaning a graveyard, as a group:
	We had us a good workin last week.
	*We got together as a group to clean the cemetery.
prayin	to pray:
	They went to prayin.
	*They said their prayers.
huntin	to hunt:
	He went out huntin Friday.
	*He likes the thrill of the hunt.
gossipin	to gossip, or spread rumors about someone:
	They took to gossipin about Sue.
	*They enjoy spreading gossip.
studyin	to ponder, to think about a problem or matter;
	He took to studyin on that all last week.
	*He thought about that problem all last week.

These preferences for a particular type of grammatical construction create an open and productive set of metapragmatic designators for speaking and laboring practices. Speaking practices such as "prayin" are "doin" as much as "coal minin" or "sewin" is "doin," and "doin" something for a desired outcome is normative.

The use of requesting discourse practices appropriate to laboring situations constructed another component in an ideology of task-focused communication. Dyadic or group labor requires coordination of interpersonal actions and circulation of tools, supplies, and equipment. This coordination can rarely be done without some verbal requests to specifically communicate various participants' needs at a particular moment. In general, Ash Creek residents prefer the dominant requesting pattern of having the requestor volunteer what is needed. In "helpin out" contexts, however, activities have very specific goals to complete such tasks as load a truck, roof a house, lay a water line, or prepare a large meal. These tasks are therefore often performed under rapid or closely coordinated team action that cannot tolerate lengthy or embellished "volunteerin" discourse with its characteristic narrative component. "Helpin out" requesting discourse repertoire requires more directness through the use of first-person plural "askin" forms and the use of imperatives to make one's "needs" known quickly and effectively. Cooperative, non-"order" "let's," "let us," or modal ("we could"/"we might could") constructions are common first-person plural forms, whereas non-"order" imperatives are crucial to the production and reproduction of these speaking practices.

"Let's" Constructions and Other Nonimperative Task-Focused Discourse

Most cooperative tasks are gender-specific, requiring requesting patterns that recreate or maintain expected symmetrical power or control relations among participants. These requesting discourse practices preserve gendered "rights" and "place" relations and either create or maintain culturally appropriate "claims" relations. Such affirmation of power egalitarianism among participants requires the use of requesting discourse forms that direct others' behavior without threatening face[7] or "shamin" the participants.

First-person plural pronouns in /let's/ and /we could/ or /we might could/ constructions coordinate and direct activity without creating culturally recognized indexes of authority or power.[8] Pronominal /we/ + modal and /let/ + /(u)s/ in main clasuses index all participants in the co-occurring activity referenced by the predicate. These plural pronouns create a group of individuals all contributing to the completion of a given task. They also include the speaker as a co-participant with others in the activity, mitigating, but not abrogating, potential activity-control implications.

Similarly, permission implications of "let" and subjunctive functions of modals such as "could" weaken any implications of authority inherent in the utterance. They also redirect the transparent goal of the utterance to direct the labor of others from a speaker "wantin" compliance to a plurality of interlocutors agreeing that there is a "need" to do it. Despite mitigations, however, control and authority implications remain. The participant frameworks created by doing the task must index a speaker who is within his "rights" and "place" to use such discourse if compliance is not to be questioned:

(7.2)

(7.2.1) Let us pray. [Preacher at church service; "proper" speech register of "let us" characteristic of religious discourse based on diction levels in King James Bible.] [24a:058 10/86]

(7.2.2) Let's . let's us three go upstairs an I can tell some jokes. [18-year-old boy in joke-telling session with younger siblings and researcher; hypercorrective example in which the youngest member of the group attempts to enhance his "place" by inserting an inappropriate "let's us" as an index of propriety and status.] [51b:287 6/85]

(7.2.3) Can you sit down a few minutes? Let's sit down. [Sarah to Sandy in Environmental Center kitchen; the two women are working together to prepare fresh vegetables for a meal; this is an appropriate usage in which Sarah meets "rights," "place," and "claims" criteria to direct the physical location and position to do the task.] [68b:165 9/86]

(7.2.4) Come on Pedro . let's go gIt a load a boxes. [teenage male mover to other teenage male mover; no compliance—considered joking in response to overhearing an exchange between two other men] [50b:013 6/86]

(7.2.5) Let's see . mostly I guess . insurance. [Joan to me in giving instructions; stylized usage of "let's see" in which she frames the topic to be discussed and "shown" to me] [10a:320 10/86]

Each of the examples in (7.2) reveals ways in which first-person plural requesting forms construct co-equal relations in task-focused participant frameworks. Segments (7.2.1)–(7.2.4) represent clauses that reference participants completing either a co-occurring action or one that happens as a turn-taking in response to the "let's" construction—praying, changing locations in a house, sitting down, and obtaining moving boxes. Participants are all involved in performing the same action referenced by the "let's" construction or, in the case of (7.2.2) and (7.2.4), all addressees ignored the speaker. The "let's" construction fails to index appropriate participant frameworks so noncompliance follows.[9] The stylized usage in (7.2.5) ("let's see") frames how participants are to interpret the subsequent clause that references the beginning of a new task, that of filing insurance claims.

The "let's" in each segment conforms to a conventional requesting pattern, so conventional in fact that it presuppositionally indexes "rights," "place," and actual or potential "claims" relationships among interlocutors. The use of this stylized, deeply presuppositional nonimperative requesting form referencing co-occurring or subsequent action constitutes the basic nonimperative "helpin out" task-focused requesting pattern. These indexical relationships are reflexive, however. When the participant framework indexed does not conform to the empirical relations among co-present interlocutors, then noncompliance is likely, as in (7.2.2) and (7.2.4). Noncompliance can be contestative or even hostile if the task-framework indexed is one involving highly valued resources. The mitigating of authority of "let's" constructions becomes extremely important when such violations occur. Therefore, most residents, both men and women, prefer "let's" constructions over imperatives in task-focused "helpin out" contexts.

Conversational patterns incorporate the equality norms indexed by these cooperative "let's" requesting forms further and also reveal how such inclusive requesting forms can communicate authority relations:

(7.3) (*Setting: Local medical clinic. Joan is instructing me in how to do her job so I can be her replacement when she takes off work.*)

Anita: Now . how do you look up your charts now?

Joan: **Ok . let's do that now.**

[She takes a chart from the wall file.] [10b:580 8/86]

In (7.3), Joan responds to my question with a "let's" construction, refocusing the request for information to one of action in keeping with preferred task-focused uses of "let's." The participant framework indexed by the "let's" is appropriate. Joan is the instructor in this exchange, so she has the "right" and is in her "place" to control the direction and flow of the task, which she does throughout the instructional sequence. In this segment, the clause "let's do that now" frames the impending action, introducing the new task through the referential power of the discourse, in this instance through a deictic /that/. This culturally sanctioned privilege assigns Joan symbolic capital[10] with regard to her control and domination over culturally valued knowledge and her ability to perform the tasks associated with it.

Segments (7.4) and (7.5) represent misuses of cooperative task-focused discourse. Both are discourse segments from a lengthy community meeting discussing current problems at the Environmental Center, which many of them attended when it was a local school:

(7.4) (*Setting: Community meeting about Environmental Center events: Participants: About 45 local residents, center director, one outsider, and I.*)

Man: **Let's . let's gIt this first mission accomplished first.**
All this other stuff is good and well . but **look at this person first.**
[21b:017 6/86]

(7.5) (*Segment for the same meeting as in* (7.4), *about* 5 *minutes later.*)

Doris: Well . if we're gonna dig *this* deep
An if we're gon . if we're gonna gIt everythin *stirred* up
I think that the majority of the people here have questions concerning federal and state monies that have been
Given to the school
But yet no buildins you don't see any improvements whatsoever
An if we're gonna go that far
Let's just dig deep an get through all of it.

Sally: **Let's make us some committees to do this.**
But right now . **I want these letters that you all can gIt εm**
So I can gIt εm this evenin. [93a:342 6/86]

In Segment (7.4), the male speaker is addressing three women who have called for investigations into a number of areas of concern. One dominant goal of the utterance is to refocus discussion to the primary purpose for calling the meeting, which is to understand why the former director and his wife were allegedly being required to move from their house at the center. He is within his "rights" as a man to correct these women by refocusing the topic of discussion, but the grammatical form of his "let's" request is inconsistent with appropriate "let's" "helpin out" cooperative discourse. The predicate offers no clearly recognized culturally acknowledged physical *task* to which participants can respond. Consequently, the glossing function of "let's" constructions to label an activity is not fulfilled with "gIt this first mission accomplished first." Instead, it functions as an embedded imperative, rather than as an example of cooperative discourse. In the next line, he uses a clear imperative "look at this person first" as well. Yet the participant frameworks that permit the use of imperatives do not apply in this public meeting because none are actively cooperating physically to do a task. These constructions can be reinterpreted as "orders." Not only is compliance not granted, but no verbal acknowledgement of his utterance was given.

Segment (7.5) reveals similar lack of conjunction between the referential content of the utterance and a co-occurring task. Furthermore, attributive possessive constraints and genderization of tasks place money decisions within +male resource domains. Doris had no clear "right" to lead an investigation into money matters (although she could be a participant). She was therefore also out of "place" in her attempted role as investigation organizer. No support was offered; and rather than accumulate any symbolic capital which would enhance her "name," she risked having her reputation called into question as someone who didn't "know what she was doin."

Sally's call for the formation of committees in (7.5) also does meet task-oriented requirements through its call for specific, cooperative action. Committees cannot be "made" like pies or cakes; someone has to take charge and organize them. Therefore, the task is not one of co-equality. Furthermore, Sally's use of a "let's" construction pushes but does not exceed her "rights" and "place" as a female schoolteacher to organize tasks involving writing activities. She was able to form some ad hoc committees to address residents' concerns.[11] Her "want" demand, however, was not supported by most attendees. They either could not write well enough to comply or were not close members of her "belongin" network in which "doin for" relations permit certain types of "want" constructions. She did not receive compliance; letters were not forthcoming except from her and two other women in her close "belongin" network.

The pragmatic functions of nonimperative task-focused requesting discourse establish contexts that shape how cooperative labor is to be performed and valued in Ash Creek daily life. These types of request both initiate and reference the expected action requested and index appropriate "rights," "place," and, possibly, "claims" relations. When appropriately used, they contribute to a speaker's symbolic capital in cultural terms. They also reveal how authority and control are culturally manifested. Those having the "right" and who are in their "place" can control the direction and flow of cooperative labor. These interlocutors may have institutional authority as work supervisors, foremen, or managers. These functions are further developed in normative uses of imperatives in task-focused requesting discourse.

Task-Focused Imperatives

Task-focused imperatives are the most expansive and generative domain of all acceptable imperative contexts within Ash Creek. The dominant function of imperatives in task-focused events is overwhelmingly utilitarian, facilitating or effecting completion of a task or directing labor or work.[12] Addressee responses to such uses are therefore not usually verbal (except in rare instances of clarification), but laborial, in which the addressee complies through an action. This merging of communicative modes creates a conflation of semiotic systems in which physical actions, gesture, or kinesics, the transference of tools, or the manipulation of motorized equipment validates imperative directive force as a meaningful response within a single task event.[13] The communicative exchange becomes one in which verbal turn-taking functions must be semiotically comparable to, if not replaceable with, nonverbal ones.

The cultural conventions and individual choices concerning which communicative mode and form to use create laboring events that often value nonverbal communication more highly than verbal communications. Discourse in general, and imperatives in particular, often become a communicative choice of last resort. The result is that speech itself is subordinate to the efficacy and meanings of nonverbal action. These are contexts in which Hymes's (1972:39–40) formulation of a "communicative event" as a multichanneled, multi-instrumental exchange of meanings has more efficacy than do the concepts "verbal practice" or "speaking event" with their implied primacy of linguistic forms.

When imperatives do occur, they are often truncated, reduced to just a core verb or a core verb, a dative, and a deictic predicate (e.g., "move" or "hand me that"). The verbs commonly used are often from a finite subset of all possible verbs. The routinization of verb choices reduces the possibility of miscommunication among participants in performing a task.

When more fully expanded, these imperative clauses usually contain a number of deictics or other referential indexes that bind the utterance to the immediate event so complexly that the denotational function of the clause is diminuated. Possessive pronouns participate in this extensive contextualization process to create participant frames that include noncommodity valuation of material items used. Clauses such as "hand me my hammer" or "put our chicken here" bind participants into an identity framework involving "rights" to use (or possess) "things." The task becomes fully sociocentric, and individual egos are merged into a common task-focused frame. The result is that the directive functions encoded in the grammar that would allow some residents to interpret imperatives as "orders" are reconfigured.

Men generally have knowledge in common about how to construct and perform within male task-focused frames, and women generally share knowledge about how to organize and perform within women's task frames considered central to family and community life. Some are better at these tasks than others, but residents generally assess the quality of others' work from the perspective of someone who can also perform the task. Migration of young adults to towns and cities for work and a reorientation of younger residents toward extensive dependence on consumer markets have altered the configuration of this common knowledge base, but a basic "right" still exists to know how to do what other community members of the same gender do and is reproduced through metacommentary about others' activities. Reproduction of this "right" through the metapragmatic functions of more textualized discursive practices such as "just talkin" and "preachin" results in the construction of socioeconomic filters that permit new skills and knowledge to be embraced, rejected, or partially incorporated by residents.

In general, task-directing imperatives in laboring contexts are appropriate *only* in situations in which participants are cooperating to produce a specified product, material item, or piece of work. There must be a perceived, readily acknowledged sense of teamwork or joint effort to obtain or create something "needed" in cultural terms. Consequently, any trading, political negotiation resulting in "deals," or other activity that would benefit a given party's "wants" at the expense of another excludes appropriate uses of task-focused imperatives.[14]

In addition, the metapragmatic and pragmatic patterns of meaning that constrain and define appropriate speech situations for these imperatives also constrain and define the participant frameworks and activity situations that they index. Unlike other discourse practices occurring within these task or labor situations such as "just talkin," "gIttin one over on somebody," or "bull shittin," task-focused imperative discourse can be used only in two types of task situations and by certain participants in specific types of relationships with each other.

The first type of task situations are those in which a knowledge or skill disparity (but not a discontinuity) exists among the participants in performing the task at hand, as in the following:

(7.6) (*Setting: Inside large U-Haul moving truck; moving and loading of house hold goods into U-Haul for an outsider family who had resigned from the Environmental Center and was moving out of state. Participants: Two high-school-age young men—one local, Carol's son (calling himself "Clyde"), the other from the next county, Cindy's son (calling himself "Pedro")—Devon, who was moving, and I. Pedro and Clyde are being paid a minimal amount for their labor.*)

Clyde: Come here . Pedro
Let's hoist this thing up here.
Pedro: Now what a we into Clyde
What a we into?
Clyde: We into putting this right up here.
Pedro: Oh . ok.
Devon: On its side.
Pedro: **Wait a minute.**
Devon: On the side of the truck.
Clyde: How ((?many?))
Pedro: **Wheel this dude around.**
Clyde: ((?2.0?)) that un right there—
Pedro: —Now wait a minute.
What is this right here? [50a:16 6/86]

In this segment, Devon's "place" as an outsider excludes him from integrated participation in the local "belongin," networks. He and his wife did not attempt to construct fictive "belongin" relations with community members during their year at the Environmental Center. Therefore, they had not developed "claims" strong enough to compel any men to "volunteer" to help them load. They were obligated to hire these two young men who were interested in earning some money. Neither of these teenagers knew each other, and both were children of women who worked at the Environmental Center with Dillon. In keeping with the requirement for knowledge and skill egalitarianism indexed by task-focused discourse, each young man presumed the other knew how to load furniture. Yet, in this instance of minimal shared work experience, labor had to be orchestrated through imperatives because each teenager could not anticipate fully what the other was going to do. Such usages included the formulaic action slot-holder "wait a minute" as well as spontaneous formulations, often containing wordplay, necessary for this specific task. The full power of imperatives to quickly and unambiguously direct another's action was needed to reference the action intended by the speaker.

Ash Creek residents recognize frequent use of imperatives in these task contexts as a presuppositional index of inexperience or unfamiliarity with either the task or the other participants. Loading trucks for moving is considered a common, simple task. Even though use of so many imperatives was not inappropriate, it was devalued. Experienced teams, who are frequently related men in a "belongin" network, do not "need" them as much as they "just know what to do." Such silence[15] mitigates any knowledge or skill disparity among the laborers and reproduces highly valued presuppositional indexes of skill. It also circumvents the powerful and explicit referential functions of imperatives to demand compliance or to require refocusing of mental attention away from the task at hand simply to listen. Therefore, the nonverbal modes of communication arising from the labor behavior itself assume a prioritized ranking in selection of communicative channels. Speech always assumes a lower ranking in the hierarchy of communicative systems when performing tasks.

Such valuation of nonverbal communication in tasks promotes development of gestural and nonverbal communicative practices that become their own expanded semiotic systems with culturally significant symbolic meanings and contributions to the construction of an ideology of task communication. Lack of talk while performing tasks indexes participants' skills and knowledge; men who don't talk while working are considered "good workers" and, by implication, "good men." These significant symbolic meanings associated with taciturnity are frequently extended to other situations unrelated to tasks, resulting in presentations of minimally expressive male identities that in turn have community value.[16]

A second type of task situation allowing the use of task-focused imperatives is that in which the task is necessarily complex. In such cases, imperatives facilitate labor under two basic conditions. First is the use of imperatives when a participant cannot access a tool or item necessary to complete the task from his or her position. Similar to dinner table imperatives such as "pass the salt,"[17] these imperatives are appropriate as long as participants recognize the inaccessibility condition as valid. A second use of imperatives occurs when directions are given by a person whose "place" it is to coordinate and direct the labor of those performing subtasks who need or directly ask for instruction. This second constraint applying to complex tasks results in the use of imperatives even with highly skilled and practiced work crews:

(7.7) (*Setting: Recently cleared area uphill and away from the main campus of the Environmental Center. Participants: a hired work crew of five men, Environmental Center staff, and I.*)

A heavy and very large water storage tank "needed" to be moved from its position by the side of a creek to a position uphill, on the slope of a hill where a trench had been dug and lined with gravel in which to seat the tank. Two pieces of heavy equipment ("dozers"), each manned, framed the ends of the tank that was now resting on a jerry-rigged flat bed. The work team on loan from a county construction company was familiar with the equipment and each other and worked silently for minutes as they negotiated the move up the slope. A company supervisor, noted for his skill and experience, used hand signals, whistles, and occasional imperatives to coordinate the movements of the two bulldozers. Imperatives consisted of such phrases as "Move to your right two feet, Bill," Slow down, Joe," and "Easy." [notes 8/85]

Verbal imperatives were clearly needed to direct work because of their referential capacity to specify action accurately (for example, "two feet") and to evoke compliance through an auditory channel when the addressee cannot see the speaker. Here, the task is so complex that one individual cannot access all the required stimuli and contextual information to do their subtask without the assistance of others. The imperatives become directions in which one person, in this case, a foreman, uses them to direct actions when he cannot do them himself.

Segment (7.8), on the other hand, is an expanded, more contestative example of direction discourse:

(7.8) (*Setting: U-Haul truck being loaded by Pedro and Clyde, for Devon, a nonlocal center staff member who is moving away from Ash Creek. I am also present.*)

Clyde: Where do you want that?

Devon: **Right there.** [gestures toward a spot in the truck where a lamp has been placed]

Clyde: You'd be crazy to put it on that.

Pedro: Hey.

Devon: I don't know.

Put it on top a somethin.

Clyde: You don't wanna put it on top a this *lamp*. [50b:89 6/86]

Clyde opens the exchange about where to load a full-size mattress with a question. An elliptic imperative "right there" accompanied by a hand gesture toward the lamp area is offered by Devon in response. Clyde then contested his directive using a potential insult containing a second-person pronoun. Devon responded with another, hedged imperative, "put it on top a somethin," turning decision-making obligations over to the young movers. It was visually transparent that placing the mattress where the owner first indicated would potentially damage a lamp, yet use of the potential insult by the teenager not only violated politeness criteria but, more germane to Ash Creek usages, violated turn-taking patterns of direction discourse.[18] First, Clyde asked for direction through a question; Devon responded with an elliptic imperative. Clyde did not respond appropriately by complying with physical labor but countered with an imperative. In order to meet appropriate participant-structuring criteria, Clyde should have either done what Devon directed (put the mattress on top of the lamp) or used direct "askin" discourse for clarification. His assertion of his own knowledge superiority ("You'd be crazy to put it on that") inverts participant egalitarian roles. It would have been received less tolerably by many local Ash Creek residents than it was by Devon. Many would have understood this utterance as an "order."

Direction imperatives cannot be understood as a transparent index of the addresser's authority if the participant framework meets the "place" and "rights" relations indexed by them as well. If the participant framework does not conform to these relations, then these "rights" and "place" pragmatic constraints are nonbinding. Imperative forms appropriate within one participant framework can be inappropriate in another even when uttered in the same setting:

(7.9) While working in the Environmental Center kitchen one afternoon, Debbie entered the dining area to sweep, a routine task performed by whoever was "free" to do it. A guest lingering in the dining area told her she "ought to wipe the tables." Debbie entered the kitchen area angry, saying the woman "had no right to tell me what to do." She did not wipe the tables. [notes 8/85]

The female guest had no "right" to exercise control over dining area space because no possessive construction constraints applied to make it "hers" (it was not her resource, at least to Debbie), so she had no "right" to direct Debbie. No "place" relations existed that would have permitted her to direct Debbie's activities. Nor was the guest a participant in a table-cleaning task with Debbie. The deontic implications of "ought to" within the embedded imperative construction further emphasizes the obligatory compliance force of the demand, making the violation of indexical relations even more salient. The imperative was interpreted as an "order" by Debbie, and noncompliance as well as nonacceptance was the outcome. Sarah could have "told" Debbie to clean the tables in the same way and received less anger. She does not, however, preferring to use direct "askin" forms such as "We need to wipe the tables off."

These pragmatic constraints on imperative usage, predicated on indexes to socioeconomic criteria for constructing relationships, are significant ones, and frequently lead to misconceptions of labor relations in wage-labor settings by outsiders or those not familiar with Ash Creek rules of use.[19] There must be a task at hand to perform, and the "rights" and "place" of the imperative user with respect to resources, labor, and relationship to the other participants in a setting must be appropriately indexed through the communicative exchange.[20] When these criteria are met, the imperative becomes a pragmatic index of an individual's control over task events and a means for asserting self within a task-egalitarian set of lattices in a task-focused culture.

Consequently, task-focused imperative discourse shapes and is shaped by the kinds and dimensions of activities, tasks, labor, and participant relations that can and cannot be integrated into Ash Creek linguistic-economic life. These interactive processes create a dynamic system that, when controlled for gender and end product production, varies along at least two dimensions: task complexity and disparity among skill and abilities of participants, captured in figure 7.1. Where these two dimensions intersect is flexible and subject to individual or small-group negotiation. Most Ash Creek "helpin out" situations involve people who are in a common "belongin" network, even when "helpin out" situations are for wages. They are accustomed to working with each other and have developed common nonverbal communication systems. Therefore, the intersections tend to be when task complexity is very high, as in segment (7.7), and when common knowledge and skill levels are very low, as in segment (7.6). The latter is rare among adults in Ash Creek, especially among men. The "shame" and threats to personal identity revealed by the "need" to use frequent imperatives to coordinate the labor of those unfamiliar with how to do something are too high.

Intersections of shared knowledge and task complexity create appropriate opportunities for the use of task-focused imperatives. Exactly where these intersections occur along the two dimensions vary from participant framework to participant framework and may be influenced by gender—women tend to use more verbal cues than men.

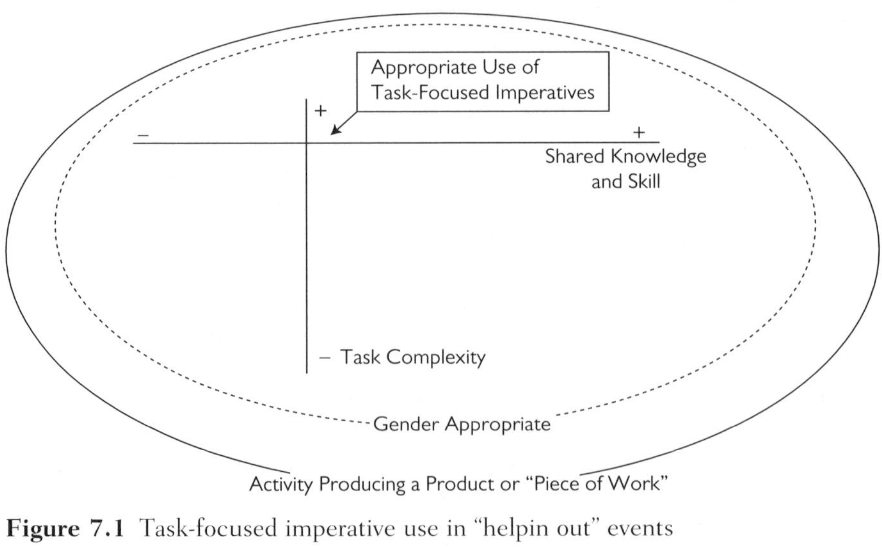

Figure 7.1 Task-focused imperative use in "helpin out" events

Deixis, reference, and other modes of signaling indexicality anchor task-focused imperative discourse so completely to the event structure that it often lacks the kinds of internal discursive cohesion or conversational structurings that characterize nonrequesting imperative speaking practices (chapter 6). Instead, coherence in "helpin out" imperative discourse is created by insertion of speech in the sequencing of physical maneuvers needed to complete the task. Utterances either gloss (denotatively or deicticly reference) what is co-occurring as action or they direct who should do what to perform the next sequence. Imperatives tend to do the latter.

Because similar sets of tasks tend to be completed by similar groups of individuals, certain generalizations emerge from the repeated sequencing of these indexical meanings. These generalizations make it possible to construct open and permeable types of "helpin out" contexts. Ash Creek residents generally recognize two differences in the usages of task-directing imperatives when "helpin out." A person is either just "helpin somebody out" or is "showin" him or her "how to do somethin."

"Helpin Somebody Out"

Canning, gardening, cleaning, hunting, mining, and other gerunds in the generative system of terms that designate culturally recognized laboring activities determine the tasks at hand for which task-directing imperatives can serve a socioeconomic purpose. Of course, tasks can be embedded within one another and dominant ones subordinated in the course of labor activities, but Ash Creek participants will generally recognize communicative reframings of task types and shift interactional structures accordingly. These types of metapragmatic terms reference activity lattices in which task-directing imperatives can appropriately occur, and, conversely, task-directing imperatives-in-use index the kinds of task structures that are culturally acceptable. Since this system of terms is expandable and generative, it is impossible to give a finite list of these lattices. It is possible, however, to describe activity conditions that must exist in order for task-directing imperatives in "helpin somebody out" contexts to be appropriately functional.

Participants in "helpin somebody out" activities must be in a type of relationship in which "claims" can be reproduced or created. "Claims" cannot be neutralized as they are in "tradin" contexts. Either "belongin" or established "takin care of" relations permit "claims" relations. A wage-labor relationship with the person "needin" a task completed does not negate the "claims" relationship requirement. Therefore, "helpin somebody out" wage-labor relationships must also conform to the more abstract requirements of "takin care of" or "belongin" relationships.

Ash Creek men may say, for example, that they "work for the center" but will also say, "I'm helpin Frank out" (the center director) as they perform a particular job. The ramifications of this "claims" requirement is encompassing. When "helpin somebody out" task-directing imperatives are used, they index that the participants are in some culturally normative form of socioeconomic relationship that creates or enhances "claims." This in turn means that the reproduction of successful "claims" relations when "helpin somebody out" indexes that either a "takin care of" or a "belongin" relation is also in effect at some level of intensity. If imperatives are replaced by other forms of requesting discourse in a "helpin somebody out" task, and the immediate need for cooperative labor would otherwise require them (see figure 7.1), then "claims" relationships are weak or nonexistent.[21]

Second, the task or subtask when "helpin somebody out" must require plural cooperative effort, not just a pooling of work with each member of the group doing identical or very similar labor. As exemplified in (7.6) and (7.7), cooperative effort demands that the task be too expansive, difficult, or complex for one individual to accomplish alone.

This requirement is a significant one, for most Ash Creek tasks can be completed individually but not necessarily alone. From "prayin" in church to "breakin beans" on the front porch for women, and from "deer huntin" to "coal truck drivin" for men, individuals often come together as separate units combining similar labor as a pooling of labor to complete one larger task, each having various degrees of knowledge and skill, but all possessing some facility in all subtasks making up the activity event. Consequently, individuals seldom labor as specialists who possess expertise and knowledge that others in the group do not share, nor do they recognize a multitiered hierarchy of authority as necessary to produce a common end product. Therefore, justification for the use of task-directing imperatives is inappropriate unless cooperative effort is required because of one individual's physical inability to complete a task alone, as in loading heavy household furniture or building a house. Otherwise, the use of imperatives would constitute a marked form and be notable to all participants, and potentially reinterpreted as "orders."

A third requirement of the imperative-permitting task is that the activity lattice must not deny one participant access to task knowledge possessed by the other participants, whether by observation, experience, or practice. This requirement creates expectations of task egalitarianism in which all are potentially equally able to assist in completing the task. Skills and knowledge that individualize people, separating them from others in terms of their knowledge schema, cannot be appropriately integrated into these types of laboring situations. Therefore, except in terms of presumed gender differences, the coordination of different kinds of professional knowledge and skill that characterize most formal institutions is foreign and anathematic to most Ash Creek residents. Imperative discourse that indexes or references such knowledge does not appear except as verbal misfires, usually by outsiders:

(7.10) (*Setting: Community meeting to discuss problems with bad well water allegedly due to underground coal mining; a representative of a Kentucky grass-roots lobbying group was invited to attend by a local woman and me. Originally intended as a small meeting among the three of us, news of the meeting became public knowledge and 14 men and women attended. Since the meeting was held at a local church, the minister of this church introduced the lobbyist but had no clear understanding of his purpose, creating speculation as to why this man was speaking. To avoid assertions of power or authority, I did not clarify the situation, nor did the other woman involved in supporting the event.*)

[The lobbyist has dominated the discussion with presentations of how other groups have become involved in solving local issues and how communities can organize themselves, obtain political clout, and solve problems.]

Lobbyist: The other thing, I . I think that's a good idea
I think if you al . uh . in a week . ur ur two weeks .
Ur whatever you all wanna do
Uhm . follow up some of these leads
Some of these ideas
Maybe you can contact Hal Rogers
You know . contact the . the .
I'm I'm sorry I've forgotten his name again
The fellow the . who does the filters [Bill]

Man 1: [Bill] Smith

Lobbyist: Smith?
Uhm . ya know
Contact those people an see if you get any kind a, any kind of information
Uhm . I'd be . I could make a couple a calls I'd be willin to call some a those some a those folks
The hydrologist that has worked with other groups in the KFTC [Kentuckians for the Commonwealth] in the past
An see if any of them have any ideas or just if they're interested.
I don't . I don't necessarily have enough information to get . much . response
out of ɛm but just see if they're interested ya know in doin somethin
Uhm
An then . uh . the other thing for you all to be thinkin about is
If you all want
If you all want to organize
Your group and if you want a work . through or with the Kentucky Fair Tax Coalition
An that basically would just
That would mean . havin some of *my* time to to assist in the organizin

An any other resources that the organization has access to those groups that have worked . on water problems before.

Whatever.

Uhm . an you all can think about that ya know I don't need to know that or anything like that tonight.

But . if KFTC if that steering committee asks me ta . to work with you all an . an provide some resources

They would hope that you all would become members of KFTC

An in turn . work on some of the things KFTC works on.

An . again . that's jIst . you can think about that

But I . I would recommend *if* that's the direction you want a go in tryin to form a group an

An deal with it in that way

That . when you call another meeting

Or you have another meeting

An . put up posters . ya know

An notify people just by word . word a mouth

Is really the best way . ya know

An . how many of us are there tonight?

Fourteen?

Contact seventy families

That's only . that's only about four or five calls for everybody *here*

Somethin like that.

You can work it out ta, ta gIt word out to everybody . pretty . pretty good

Uhm . especially if everybody's concerned about it.

But I would recommend that . that . the next meeting you have be to . organize . your . community group . to deal with this water problem.

Ok?

So the people comin know . that that's what they're comin for

Is to get this community group together to talk about the water problem an to get the group together an decide where . where do we go from here.

Maybe that's what you all come for tonight I don't know

But I was jIst . I was tryin to feel out an see if

If . if we were all talkin about the same thing.

If we're all on the same track.

Man 2: We'd better have another meetin an thIn see how many gIts here.

Lobbyist: Uhm-hum.

Man 2: See what they say.

Fourteen can't do much can they.

Lobbyist: Well . fourteen can do a lot.

Fourteen can do a lot more n one.

I mean if two people are ready to organize . then that's a start.

An then they . the first thing they do is try n recruit more people.

You can uh . if you have jIst the same folks here next time

You can . form yourselves a group an then get out an say "Look

We need your help" . an do it

((?Saying?)) "Look . you got a water problem."

Talk to your neighbors that way.

Uhm . you don't have to wait until everybody in the community wants to be

Wants to be in a group

To form a group.

Form your group

Start workin on it

An as people want a . as people wanna help n wanna get involved . they will.

Keep it kind a open-ended.

But if . if that's the direction you wanna go in

Then . people who come to meetin know that's what they're comin for an ya

You all are workin on the same . on the same idea . ya know

An so . people who are not yet

People who are not yet interested in organizin or don . don't wanna organize yet

They don't have to come to the uh meetin

You see what kind of interest you have in that ((?realm?)).

Nancy: Well . I think the show we had tonight . I mean . that's . that's a start.

And uh.

Lobbyist: Yeah . I think you're right.

I definitely do.

When do you all want a try an meet again?

How soon do you want a try n do that?

Nancy: **Well . what a . what are we gonna say?**

Between now an the next meeting . does someone wanna

Joe said he'd try an contact that one guy

Shall we . do you think in that length of time we should try to contact?

Lobbyist: **I think it's worth makin some . some initial contacts.**

One thing about it is ya

I think you don't wanna gIt *too* far . until you kinda got ever . everybody's gotten together an you can share

You know . share ideas n . n everybody decide what's gonna happen . . .

[Lobbyist continues to stress working together as a group; at end of plea, man mentions coal companies not responding to requests for information about mining and topic shifts to discussion of what these companies are doing. Meeting ends with further discussion, primarily by women, of making posters and setting time for next meeting.] [74a:635 6/86]

Participants dismissed this lobbyist as someone who simply wanted contributors of money and labor for "his group."[22] No other follow-up or discussion of his suggestions occurred except in the form of a second, poorly attended water meeting approximately a month later, which was dominated by a local, politically active resident[23] who reframed the problem into a "takin care of us" event in which the "county" and "state" were planning a system for pumping treated water to the Ash Creek area from a lake over 60 miles away. The matter was dropped and no further meetings were held during my stay (for at least two years). No water line was laid either.

It is tempting for nonlocals to dismiss this event as a straightforward boundary-maintenance one in which an "outsider" is perceived as an intruder into community business, as an occasion in which residents demonstrate their inability to organize, or as a miscommunication couched in the lobbyist's use of a different and somewhat unfamiliar set of discourse and grammatical patterns. Residents "help out" nonlocals on a regular basis through wage-labor, however, and must interact with them in many governmental, medical, or financial encounters in towns or cities. Rather, the communicative event and this particular sequence failed to meet the three basic "helpin somebody out" task-oriented imperative requirements I discussed.

The participants at the meeting have no "claims" relations with the lobbyist and vice versa. The lobbyist had not employed any participants, so he has not developed any "takin care of" relations with residents. Nor had he developed any fictive "belongin" networks in this community (even though he lived "up a holler" at the margins of Ash Creek). Nor did he have a "place" in relation to the others attending the meeting, and his "right" to tell others, particularly men, what to do and how to organize is highly disputable, particularly with reference to biblical authority, the ultimate source for "rights" legitimization.

Rather, his request for KFTC membership if his group works with local people foregrounds his allegiance to a politically motivated formal organization, alienating the lobbyist from potential task-egalitarian inclusion in the immediate communicative event context. With this request for membership, this discourse segment meets "takin care of" requesting discourse functions characteristic of political discourse in which a politically influential individual recruits members into his power networks. But no "takin care of" participant framework exists. In order for participants to be willing to begin developing the "claims" relations such discursive practices create, they must perceive that the lobbyist has control over resources they "want" or "need" access to. They do not.

The lobbyist's volunteering of his time to "make a couple a calls" to the hydrologist or other KFTC consultants does not mitigate this attempt at political discourse structuring because of his reference to "other groups in the KFTC," suggesting political alliances. Finally, the allusion to telephoning U.S. Congressman Hal Rogers among others for any kind of information misrepresents the function of "takin care of" requesting communication. The dominant function of political "takin care of" relations is to allow those individuals with control over valued resources to instigate political action, not just to be asked for information. The event failed to frame an appropriate "helpin somebody out" task-oriented participant structure. The lobbyist presented discourse appropriate to established "takin care of" requesting events instead and then failed to create utterance functions normative for such discourse.

Community organizing is indeed a complex task. Yet discourse in (7.10) also does not specify the plural cooperative efforts needed to complete the task. The imperatives, for example "You can . form yourselves a group an then get out an say 'Look . We need your help'" and "Keep it kind a open-ended" fail to specify what residents are to do in this context or *how* to accomplish the suggested tasks in the future. Hedges such as "maybe you can contact Hal Rogers," "whatever you all wanna do," and "if you all want to organize" fail to define the parameters of the complex cooperative task that will result in obtaining a potable water supply. In the final exchange, "I think it's worth makin some some initial contacts" also fails to specify exactly what to "do" in Ash Creek task-oriented terms. The woman's response "Well . what a . what are we gonna say?" responds to this violation of speaking practice norms and represents a well-formed discourse example of task-redirection as she attempts to direct the lobbyist into task-oriented discourse patterns. No uptake follows as task-abstract references such as "share ideas" and "decide what's gonna happen" are offered in response. Task-cooperation becomes impossible.

Finally, (7.10) denies access to knowledge to the full range of participants. Despite hedges and deprecations of his own knowledge and expertise (e.g., "I don't. I don't necessarily have enough information to get . much . response out of ɛm but just see if they're interested ya know in doin somethin"), the lobbyist's repeated calls for obtaining information from experts communicates knowledge and skill differentials between the residents and the speaker. He has the knowledge to organize; he has done it before; residents have not. Mastery of Latinate forms such as "hydrologist" and more broadcast American English grammatical constructions further reinforce such knowledge disparity.

In contrast, Ash Creek residents do not routinely engage in "organizin," and a task matrix for this type of activity is not commonly known to event participants. Therefore, this speech event structure and the discourse used within it are open to metapragmatic reinterpretation by residents as a discursive practice with which they are familiar. Many glossed the event as one of "outsiders" attempting to "put us down," an interpretation that encourages the types of boundary-maintenance arguments that began discussion of this segment. From a discourse-centered perspective, however, communicative failure is less a problem in the lobbyist's character and more one of a violation of those pragmatic constraints and discourse rules of use that construct an ideology of task-focused communication.

Segment (7.11), however, represents a very common task-oriented discourse segment, one that conforms to task-oriented imperative constraints:

(7.11) (*Setting: Environmental Center kitchen during after-dinner cleanup period. Participants Debbie, Linda, a visiting student as helper, and I. I'm washing dishes.*)

Helper: It's hot.

Sarah: It's hot.

Sit that right back here.

Sit that here. [directing helper on where to put pots]

Let's see.

We'll just have to pour that un down the sink here.

[water turned on, pots moved; helper pours liquid down the sink]

I don't think that's good.

It's history.

Anita: Where do you want all these pots here Linda?

Don't ya think we oughta—

Linda: —Huh?—

Anita: —find somethin to do with these pots?

Sarah: Here . Nita put these ((?2.0?)) [pots bumping]

Anita: Hu:h?

Sarah: **GIt ya one of these kIttles here an put it in.**

[Pots continue to be washed and moved.] [60a:070 7/86]

In (7.11) Sarah directs the helper when she notices that the helper is attempting to find room for partially full serving dishes, while Linda instructs me in stacking washed pots and kettles. In the first case, nonverbal action prompts an imperative from Sarah who is within her "place" to "claim" control over space and material objects; in the second, my question is answered with imperatives by Linda, the woman in charge of second-shift duties as well as someone who knows the job and is within her "rights," and "place" to instruct a newcomer in what to do with washed pots. The first is a clear example of directions in that Sarah, the head cook, is not involved in the task; the second is an example of instructions in that Linda is also not involved in the task, but a knowledge disparity does exist between Linda and me as she instructs me on their "way of doin things." Such appropriate uses of directional imperatives recreates authority and control relations in task events, relations that must index culturally valued "rights" and "place" criteria as well.

Appropriate uses of imperatives in "helpin somebody out" contexts reproduce task-focused socioeconomic patterns through their pragmatic and semantic meanings. These uses create or reproduce an open and generative system of interrelationships among gender domains, plural cooperative effort "needs" and task-skill egalitarianism. New task-focused imperative uses are commonly introduced into the community system as residents incorporate new tasks meeting these requirements. Yet the system is selective. It admits only those activities that reproduce existing core components of gendered domains of task knowledge, skill egalitarianism, and product production. It also requires the reproduction of "rights" and "place" relations that are culturally appropriate and demands that "claims" can be developed or enhanced. A task must be too complex or too difficult in terms of physical labor for individuals to perform the task alone. Otherwise, residents will reframe the discourse into "doin for" relations. If the participant frameworks indexed by imperatives used in these situations are not appropriate, residents are likely to treat any imperatives as "orders."[24]

"Showin Somebody"

Ash Creek residents master most new tasks or skills by observation or practice, often listening to older family members or others tell "how they do it." Seldom does anyone instruct a new member of a work group using verbal communicative structures. Under strong assumptions that an adult man or woman should already know what is required, residents, especially men, prefer instead to simply do the activity while permitting the new person to observe or comment, or perhaps ask for clarification using narrative patterns to create analogies to other, similar tasks. For adult male work groups, which frequently work with heavy, motorized machinery, this "showin" rather than "tellin" is especially common and diffused throughout all male tasks.[25] For women, narrative descriptions of "how *I* do it" are common as well and are an expected component of adult married women's conversations. Consequently, a verbally distinct practice of "instructions" is nonexistent except among those few residents, generally women, who rely on written instructional genres such as recipes. Instead, people "help out" each other by "showin" someone how to do something, under well-developed conceptions of what constitutes learning and valued knowledge:

(7.12) (*Setting: Woodcarving session at Environmental Center maintenance building. Participants: Bill, a young woman college student visiting the center, and I. Bill is instructing visitor; instruction in progress.*)

Bill:	Ok now . if you *watch* people
	You can learn as much from watchin somebody do somethin as ya can
	From them tryin to show ya sometimes ya learn *more* from watchin
	Then ya then ya
Woman:	Uh-huh
Bill:	What ya can ((?from what he's sayin?))
	I can *watch* a person do somethin an pick it up just *real* quick
Woman:	Uh-huh
Bill:	Where I wouldn't be able to pick it up if he was tryin to tell me
	An tryin to *tell* me an
Woman:	Uh-huh
Bill:	Not *show* me at the same time
	Its harder to get
Anita:	*Uh-huh*
Bill:	But if ya can work him
	An tell him at the same time
	He can get it real quick.[26] [27b:90 8/85]

Residents regularly reconfirm this metapragmatic commentary about "showin somebody" when outsiders, like me, ask for verbal instructions on how to do something. We are told repeatedly, "I can't tell you; I can show you," or "I'd tell you if I could, but I need to show you." It is in the watching and the showing that valued and valuable knowledge is transmitted among Ash Creek residents, not by referential and directive functions of verbal instructions. Instead discourse co-occurring with and pragmatically indexed to an instructional event is primarily a metapragmatic gloss on the task itself, relying extensively on linguistic referential properties to specify steps and procedures and to label or classify the action at hand, or to narrate a set of procedures usually followed by the performer of the instructional activity.[27]

These constraints upon instructional norms create unavoidable tensions when residents encounter formal educational, corporate, or vocational training situations. There are only very limited culturally appropriate ways for adults to be verbally instructed by another; training sessions or work direction often rely on very differently constituted instructional discursive forms. Ash Creek residents often choose not to engage in them, do so contestively, or rely on instructors who use practices similar to those of Ash Creek.[28]

The power of discourse in the context of "showin" someone "how to do" something is pragmatically powerful as well. "Showin" discourse indexes the knowledge disparity between the addresser, who shows, and the addressee, who is shown. Consequently, showing someone how to do something, including both physical actions and showing discourse, necessarily reveals disjunctions in the system of knowledge egalitarianism. Variations and differences in the skills and abilities of participants is foregrounded within a context of meaningful action. One participant knows something the other does not, and the showing task situation communicates this overtly as one individual directs the other(s). Imperative forms assist significantly in signifying this disparity in that they give the addresser an especially powerful communicative mechanism to direct the specific actions of the addressee. Addressers recognize this directive function and frequently substitute "you need to . . ." constructions for clear command forms, mitigating the force of the imperative to that of an indicative with indicative intonation and a rhetorical, indefinite "you" as a subject.

Because of this potential power of imperatives to demand something and to index knowledge disparity, fully developed forms of "showin" discourse are rarely used among male interlocutors, seldom between women, and commonly between adults and children of the same gender. Seldom is "showin" discourse used among adult participants of different genders; exceptions are notable and constitute marked usages. Bill, for example, instructs men, women, teenagers, children, and researchers who are outsiders visiting the center. He's "helpin them out" because they generally "don't know how to do nothin." "Whittlin," as locals term his form of woodcarving, is generally a male activity picked up by men and boys through watching and practicing.[29]

In extended "showin" discourse of the type necessary for explaining a new task, imperative constructions always appear, despite some speakers' concern for using mitigation. The danger in uttering imperatives lies not only with the type of task being shown, but more primitively, with the kind of participant relationship indexed. Imperatives in "showin" discourse must index a limited set of participant status relations or frameworks, or they become "orders."

In general, only one group of relations exist in which such disparities are normative: adults with children or young adults. Indeed, most "showin" discourse is between adults and children, or between adults and those, such as some outsiders, who are willing to assume a child's role. Thus, "showin" discourse replicates or recreates asymmetric socioeconomic relationships predicated on age. Even so, few adults, including parents, spend much time showing children how to do something, relying instead on the high value given watching and self-instruction through practice. To augment such dominant practices, adults and parents will often use truncated or abbreviated showing communication forms, which are readily assimilated into ongoing task or conversational interaction:

(7.13) (*Setting: Homemakers' meeting at Environmental Center, about 15 women, all but four are "claimed" kin in a "belongin" network; Mable is addressing her six-year-old nephew who attended the meeting with his mother, Becky. He was the only young child. Four not in the others' "belongin" network include three center women staff and me.*)

Mable: Ok, uh . Johnny what ya need to do
Is turn it over
An trace it on these but I think its ((?runnin?)) that way
Can ya do it on yours back here an then trace it over.
It'll come off on this.
I'll give ya some trays with the i:ce an the milk
An the ((?parts?)) on the ((?bead?)) there.
You have to paint it on this side so you can turn it over.
Dark side first. [03b:068 3/87]

Mable then resumes conversation with other women at the meeting, occasionally supervising Johnny's actions with further abbreviated instructions or by showing him what to do. Her verbal instructions also function to guide some of the rest of us who are new to the task of decorating wooden craft figures without directly addressing us. I could learn without being "shamed." Such utterances, especially those using imperative forms, can be used strategically by adult speakers to create or make salient otherwise tacit or covert asymmetrical relationships among presumed co-equals. These intentional imperative uses can have potentially damaging socioeconomic effect because "claims" relationships both inside of and apart from wage-labor relationships will be threatened.

If the task dynamics permit participants to carry on conversation, some, primarily women, may introduce a narrative segment into the conversational structure to describe how they, or some skilled individual whom they know, has performed the task. They shape the narrative structure to foreground referenced action or technique to apply to immediate task context:

(7.14) (*Setting: Kitchen of Environmental Center; Sarah, Linda, and I are participants; meal preparation in progress; squash is in season and is to be a menu item. Discussions of the menu and the cooking of today's squash precede this segment.*)

Sarah: You know how Bernie used to do the squash . Linda.
He . he growed over an acre of squash like we fixed the other day
Ya know that big yeller

Now he'd buy it by the bushels an he . made . . ya know he put ɛm in a
In a big kIttle like *that* down there. [points to a kettle]
He'd fill it full a hot water
An he'd boil ɛm
An then . an then he'd drop the . the squash
Down in the . that boilin water
Get a sack . like an onion sack ur somethin

Linda: Uh-hum.

Sarah: An he'd take ɛm out like that. [demonstrates how he removed them]
An then it
He'd always cook it ((?weak?)) as a pea
It'd it'd just slice
He could ((?feed?)) it as a ((?baby food?)).

Linda: Huh

Sarah: Ah we'd
Then we'd bring it upstairs an **we'd put brown sugar and butter**
And uh . su . an a little cinnamon
Or somethin like that
An we'd put it in the *oven* an bake it
Until it got done an that *juice'd* run out of it.
Before that ((?did it?)) . we'd strained that off . into a kIttle
An we thickened it with this
This clear jell anyhow it looks like cornstarch
Only they call it clear jell.
And you'd uh . fix that like a sauce an you'd pour that back over that
An serve it like that
An they thought it was fried apples most of time they didn't know the difference. [chuckles]
But it was good . I . it was really good.

Linda: I like any kind of squash. [49a:312 9/86]

After an initial reference to Linda's knowledge and to Linda, Sarah shifts to third-person narrative structuring which decontextualizes reference from the immediate speech event to the frame of a retelling[30] in which Sarah makes no interactive demands on the other interlocutors, although, hearing her, we have the choice of uptake. She grounds the narrative in objects in our common field of interaction, however, pointing to kettles and using gestures to show us how it was done in the basement of this very kitchen. In such a framing, the first- and second-person pronominal constructions, "we'd put brown sugar and butter" and "you'd uh, . fix" toward the end of the narrative foreground reportative and denotative functions. Deictic functions of "we" and "you" are not lost, however, as Sarah points to herself and to the rest of us through their use. These distancing devices remove the instructional sequence from what the kitchen workers are doing at the moment while including them in a past event. The narrative therefore assumes a timelessness characteristic of Ash Creek "stories" that is also protomythic as Bernie becomes a legendary someone who cooked squash close to perfection.

This instructional narrative therefore has the instrumental function of informing the other interlocutors about how Sarah would like yellow squash to be cooked without using direct and unambiguous control acts inherent in imperative usages co-occurring with "showin" actions. The other participants can learn from this story in a manner that does not impose upon or limit their own ways of cooking while implying they could do it better. At the same time, (7.14) includes all participants either through terms of address ("Linda"), turn-taking responses ("I like squash"), and presumed sharing of knowledge (all interlocutors have potential squash instructional narratives) as actual or potential participants in a socioeconomic activity (cooking squash for others). This merging of laborers into a small group of squash preparers through instructional narrative transposes individual productivity into culturally appropriate behavior without violation of coequality norms.[31]

The most developed "showin" communication appears in activities that residents refer to as "teachin someone" ("proper" register) or "learnin somebody" ("country" register). The reason for getting together is to instruct or be instructed, and the entire social interaction may indeed be little more than a "showin" communication. In these situations, traditionally[32] an older person, such as a grandmother or a retired person, "schools" or "learns" one or two children or younger adults in what regional folklorists have called "traditional" tasks (e.g., basket making, spinning, quilting, or crafting)[33] for which they have family or community recognition and reputation. In many cases these showing occasions become routinized events as participants develop an apprenticeship relationship with each other. These kinds of role relations create "claims" expectations, which then develop into forms of social bonding, in which, ideally, the "learner" enhances or promotes the reputation of the teacher through his or her skill.

These task-learning exchanges are often complex, multifunctional events. The intimacy created by close physical proximity, much eye contact, and generally warm, modulating voices adds an affective dimension to many of these occasions that transforms an otherwise matter-of-fact linguistic-socioeconomic process into a highly social act.[34] Verbal, material, gestural, and behavioral significations become laminated into a single composite but mutable whole. Individuals, things, and actions become reflexive extensions of each other. When coupled with the willing compliance that "showin" imperatives require, these instructional dyads or triads can create highly personalized socioeconomic relationships that transcend or dominate any potential commodity exchange or wage purpose. For this reason, these apprenticeships have tended to be restricted to close family members or to those in strong "belongin" relations with each other.

Older residents indicate that such apprenticeships were more common in the past and covered a greater range of tasks. Many younger residents in their late teens or early 20s also support these observations by not volunteering to learn them and avoiding situations in which they can be volunteered under "volunteerin" discourse contextual constraints. Although not disinterested, they do not see how knowing these things will help them "get by," and learning them takes "so much time." Such instructional patterns are therefore undergoing cultural transformations.

"Learnin somebody" communication, like all Ash Creek task-focused semiotic systems, is not bound strictly to specific tasks but to broader categories of tasks that reproduce specific types of relations among communicative components. So while spinning or herbal healing may be nearly lost arts in Ash Creek, "learnin somebody" communication is being transformed to accommodate other kinds of tasks in which basic, underlying cultural relationships are still being reproduced and others lost. These shifts manifest a major reconstitution of community socioeconomic patterns.

Segment (7.15) represents established "learnin somebody" structuring, although Bill is doing it in the same manner in which he instructs nonlocals who visit the Environmental Center:

(7.5) (*Setting: Woodcarving session with Bill who is accustomed to giving lessons and who has observed Environmental Center teaching staff teach over several decades. Except for me, the other three participants are local, an unusual situation for Bill at this time. The three visitors are Chuck, his wife Karen, and their eight-year-old son David. David is beginning to receive instructions on how to carve.*)

Bill: So

Ya see it's not wantin to carve tha that way.

When it gives ya trouble ya got to turn it around an ((go)) this way. [flips wood over]

An too . if ya cut yourself

You . you put your fist against ya here and you're carvin out like this [fist against chest so that knife strokes are away from the body]

So when the knife flips off ya see your hand hits first

So ya don't hit yourself with your knife . because it's . it's sort a automatic

Ya hold your arm real close to ya here [arm with knife held close to torso]

So *usually* . one side carves one way . and the other side carves the other

That's the way . the . grain . works.

So when you're carvin this way ya see ya don't see your mark here [When carving the back side, the penciled pattern doesn't show.]

But you carve down a little ways ya can always glance over to see [turns wood over to see the pattern]

Where your mark is.

Now when you make this curve [curve in the pattern]

You put your thumb down here now if you do everythin I show you you won't be cut

Put your thumb down there ya see an it sort a shaves down like that [puts thumb on wood to control knife stroke]

Just let that stay . an you shave down

((?1.0?)) like **an you go back this side** . an you you'll be forgItten a lot of this stuff an

I'll jIst keep showin ya

An you take that off careful like that ya see

Cause ya come down against this *too* hard you'll split it off an you wont cut your . cut your mark off

[Too heavy a stroke may cause the wood to splinter resulting in the loss of a pattern line.]

So when you're doin this ya see you're doin little sharp strokes

If ya gIt beyond your mark don't worry about it

We'll uh . there's a lot of people change styles with their butter knives

[chuckles from Bill and boy]

Now ya take *this* **off ya see** you you gonna use your thumb again for leverage

See there?

Your thumb's over—

David: Uh-huh

Bill: —here an your knife 'll come off

An if you have up there too high it'll come off when you can't ((?2.0?))

But you you make sure your thumb is down there

Below where your knife comes [off]

David: [uh-huh]

Bill: An you'll never gIt cut if you you always remember these tips. [8a:00 11/85]

The arrangement of participants on benches and old chairs during this exchange was much like a barn, shed, or back porch setting most consistent with older patterns of "whittlin" instruction. Residents commented on how Bill taught them "right." The task is a straightforward one: to make a wooden butterknife from a pattern based on a regional craft shop example using a three-bladed pocketknife, sandpaper, and vegetable oil. Bill has drawn a pattern with a pencil on a flat, rectangular piece of cedar. He is carving David's knife while David, a local child and distant kin, sits beside him watching attentively. Bill frequently looks at David especially when "makin a pAY:nt" such as "an you'll be forgIttin a lot of this stuff an I'll just keep showin ya." Unlike most nonlocals of similar ages whom Bill has instructed, David is essentially mute, listening and watching very carefully, backchanneling only when Bill signals by eye contact or intonation that it is needed. This norm of one interlocutor abdicating turn-taking rights in "learnin somebody" discourse clearly foregrounds the status disparity between the two participants: the right to talk literally belongs to Bill, who knows what he's doing. Deictics "this," "it," "here," and "that" referential phrases, such as "sharp strokes" that reference what Bill is actually doing at the time, and the shifter pronouns "you" and "your" that index the boy and his butterknife currently in Bill's hands create a pragmatically dominated text that reveals little semantico-referential discourse cohesion. Bill's physical activities with his knife clearly predominate in the hierarchy of signification modes in the communication.

In fact, the major cohesive device that does exist consists of the sequencing of manual actions linked through repetition of "you" in potential imperative constructions that can also be understood as indicatives.[35] This verbal repetition creates a weak parallelism, which encodes the status differential of the participants through the power of these types of clauses to evoke compliance.[36] Nevertheless, these visual and tactile modes of activity are indeed so effective that what Bill did cannot be effectively or efficiently "told" here as referential discourse; the activity must be shown. Yet, if the discourse sequence were abandoned, and some, especially men, prefer almost speechless instruction presumably to avoid marking the status asymmetries, instructional precision would have been lost and David might have hurt himself if Bill had not "showed" David what would happen if the knife were held improperly. With its linguistic ability to reference specific steps and actions, "learnin somebody" discourse is necessary to transmit the knowledge and skill necessary to complete a task, but it is ultimately subordinated to those nonverbal semiotic processes of simply doing it. This blending of meaningful human utterances to meaningful nonverbal actions creates, in turn, a composite communication, drawing on multiple modes of signification. No mode can be isolated from the others without altering the cultural significance of the entire activity; all modes, including language, are necessary for its success. The use of language, however, infuses the entire activity with its capacity to create relations of power and control. In this case, these relations are culturally acceptable.

This particular showing communication is also innovative in that Bill most commonly instructs individuals who visit the Environmental Center rather than members of his "belongin" network. In this sense, he is assuming the status of an unpaid teacher transmitting local knowledge to tourists or visitors who are merely sampling something of the mountain "culture." In this particular situation, David's parents deliberately brought their son to Bill, in part because they valued this man's competency as a person and as a teacher. Their role as chaperons is also innovative, and, given busy schedules, they were only able to bring him one time. Finally, Bill's "whittlin" is not a highly valued task in community ranking of male tasks and is not generally transmitted through fully developed "showin" communication. He has developed it as his contribution to the ongoing programs of the center, a formal, incorporated institution, not as a task central to the reproduction of Ash Creek socioeconomic patterns. Therefore, this type of "learnin somebody" communication reproduces certain core "claims," developing and enhancing processes that are not commoditized, but does so for a product whose value is diminuated in Ash Creek systems of valuation and in a setting in which transitory nonlocals learn very little about mastering the knowledge and skill necessary to perform the craft in a manner that would enhance Bill's "name" in the community.

Segment (7.16) is a less successful innovative application of "learnin somebody" communication, not entirely because Joan is young and I am impatient, but in large part because of difficulties she has in applying "learnin somebody" communication to the problem of filling out a form:

(7.16) (*Setting: Receptionist's area in the local medical clinic waiting room. Joan is giving me job instructions; for the next few months I will fill in for her when she is ill or taking time off. We have been talking for about 1.5 hours. Training is in progress.*)

[Joan uses her finger to point to different places on the various forms or actually holds small pieces of paper up in the air as she instructs me.]

Joan: Uh . but then
On the on the Kentucky Medical card
The way I do that
Ok.
Now this is *different* then these kind of cards [holds cards up]
See this is got one subscriber's name—

Anita: —Uh-huh—

Joan: This is got all of them in the family that's covered.

Anita: All right

Joan: Ok . who *ever* has come in to see Mill
You put their name . up here.
[points to proper place on form]

Anita: —Ok

Joan: **Then you put their number**

Anita: [I got] ya

Joan: [ok]

Now *I* always put KMC . with pareth . parentheses and then Medicaid

That way they'll know its from Kentucky

I don't even know if we're supposed to take a out of state ke uh [medical]

Anita: [medicaid]

Joan: card or not

But I do that jIst in case

You might wanna have a number

Uh I don't ful this . fill this—

Anita: Uh-huh

Joan: —out

[I] don't [fool with this] [points to box on form]

Anita: uh- [huh] [fill about that]

You have to do this [one]

Joan: **[jIst] start here at sex**

[points to box marked "sex"]

[Both chuckle.]

Joan: **An . an then go on with that . an then go on with that** [points to different boxes on form]

Anita: Ok. [10b:42 10/86]

This segment represents a portion of a 1.5-hour training session in which Joan attempted to train me to do her job on a fill-in basis. She has trained others who told me that the job is very complicated. Some trainees have resigned, saying the job is too difficult. I came away frustrated, feeling that I had absorbed little and had no grasp on what the job entailed. This segment exhibits part of the problem. First, basic participant relations are skewed with respect to culturally normative frameworks. Joan does have the "right" to instruct other women in her duties since "healin" is within women's domains and since reading and writing are women's activities. Yet she is also young, without a widely known name for herself in the community so that, in cultural terms, her "place" in her "belongin" networks is less defined and still very much open to negotiation. Therefore, her "place" to instruct is also uncertain, especially when the trainee is older than she and is a nonlocal outsider. Discourse segments not included here exhibit this problem as she giggles, apologizes, or uses other deference behavior not only to me but also to a number of trainees older than herself.

In addition, the task of filling out a section of a patient's encounter form that requires us to refer to an insurance card does not produce a final and new product, but new writing on a form. Seemingly amenable to "learnin somebody" discourse, this shifting from the manual labor of shaping or modifying material items to simply filling in blocks or sections of a form with a pen is a major one in terms of "learnin somebody" discourse functions. In the physical activity context in which "learnin somebody" discourse usually appears, each step in the process of completing a task acts as an indexical pointer to what step comes next. Here, however, an utterance cannot just gloss a co-occurring nonverbal physical activity. There is an intervening level of semiosis, that of reading first and then writing words and symbols on the paper. "Learnin somebody" discourse forms must first map onto reading activities and then to physical movements that result in marks on a piece of paper. Normative "learnin somebody" discourse is not structured for this conflation of semiotic systems.

In this case, the expected glossing, or referring, function of normative "showin" discourse is reproduced. Joan treats each medical card according to the configuration of print on it, setting each one apart from the other by its markings in a manner similar to appliqués or quilt pieces. Each item on the card receives attention, even though such careful examination has little to contribute to the knowledge needed to fill in the form.

The imperatives, such as "you put their name . up here," direct a task that is more appropriately considered as "marking" an ideograph, in Ong's (1982:86) sense of an image whose meaning is established by conventional association rather than by an alphabetic mapping (indexing) to a phonological representation. The referential meaning of the utterance refers to placing an image on a form rather than "writing" a text. Repeated use of the lexeme "put" rather than "write" or some other verb denoting a writing activity reinforces this ideographic sense. Each name is repeated, pattern style, in the box marked "name." Finally, the utterance "jIst start here at sex" directs me to begin marking at a particular place on the form where a configuration of print conforming to "sex" is located. I am to respond to this image as if it were a point on a pattern from which to begin a manual task. According to the referential meaning of the utterance, I should look for these same print marks when I fill out a new form and make a new mark. None of this discourse refers to *reading* these marks as words. None "tells about" the medical form itself or describes abstractly the kinds of information mediated through writing that are needed to complete it. With the further omission of an appropriate writing-on-forms lexicon such as "read," "write," "enter," "box," "code," or "line" as well, this discourse segment does not meet a basic function of Ash Creek instructional discourse to map speech as precisely as possible onto pertinent action within the immediate context. The speech does not use linguistic forms that accurately "gloss" the requisite literate actions required, nor does it "explain" the goals and purposes of the task at hand.

This discourse segment does, however, meet the structural requirements of Ash Creek "learnin somebody" discourse, including the use of some imperatives and a dependency on the sequence of motor activities. In this case, speech appropriate to the Ash Creek socioeconomic discourse repertoire becomes inappropriate as the activity itself does not meet the structural requirements of the discourse, nor does the discourse meet the needs of the activity.

Such meaning disjunctions are significant in terms of "place" indexical relations and the interactive power such relations create. At a basic level, the ineffective use of "learnin somebody" discourse makes creation of appropriate "place" indexicals unlikely. When the imperatives and other utterances do not gloss or direct a co-occurring activity, then the discourse cannot index an appropriate participant framework. The result is a failed instructional sequence in which power relations are not clear. This disjunction is interpreted by community trainees (always women) in terms of their ability to understand and do the job, even when literacy skills are not a factor. Yet this type of position is a prerequisite for most offices and critical for effective corporate organization, a very common type of position in most urban workplaces. This example is not an isolated one, encountered only with this particular clerk. In many situations involving women learning office tasks, I observed that similar discourse/activity disjunctions occur.[37]

Even though this segment reveals disparities between the nature of the procedures being instructed and the type of task-focused discourse used to instruct how to do them, it relies extensively on task-focused imperatives as directives to the learner. Although "you put" clauses in general can be interpreted as indicatives in which "you" functions as an indefinite pronoun, the segment "you put their name . up here, sex" has clearly a command function, marking the knowledge disparity between the two interlocutors. In misapplying an instance of "learnin somebody" communication to a set of literate-oriented procedures, Joan intensifies this disparity by obfuscating the purposes of the various job-related activities. This type of discontinuity between communicative practice and laborial activity does not occur merely when this receptionist is training a new person. Obviously this problem is not unique, occurring in many work settings in which the job requires manipulation of printed forms using reading and writing. As a number of local women who had "tried" office "work" said, "I'm just not smart enough for that kind of thing." The problem may be less in the cognitive disparities of the trainees and more in the kind of communicative structure readily available to use in such settings.

Segment (7.17) represents a widely spreading and innovative use of "learnin somebody" communication, one readily adaptable to a market economy and institutional settings that attach an actual or potential dollar value to "educational" demonstrations.

(7.17) (*Setting: Public demonstration of traditional mountain crafts at Environmental Center during summer 1985; Kaziah, a local woman in her seventies is demonstrating the spinning of wool at a large spinning wheel, a task for which she has been paid. She sheared a sheep using hand shears earlier in the day, so she had about 15 pounds of raw wool with her as well as the carded wool she was spinning. About 15 men, women, and children, all nonlocal visitors to the center as part of a special weekend activity, are gathered around, some sitting on the building porch floor, others standing. Four center teaching staff and I are also present.*)

Kaziah:	Well . I don't think I'll have to worry about wool.
	[Group chuckles.]
	I had that three hundred an fifty pound give to me.
Woman:	I heard about that.
Kaziah:	An, . I've even been makin quilts out a it . out it.
Man:	Making quilts out of wool?
Kaziah:	Yeah.
	You can uh
Man:	Maybe ((?3.0?))
Kaziah:	Yeah . have a big ol uh
	Haya . I mean cardin machine thing that I card by hand
	But . uh I make . make it in a big flat batch
	An . had it in quilt it on the machine
	An boy it really makes a warm quilt too when you think [about it]
Group:	[oo:h]
	[a few minutes later during the same demonstration]
Woman:	Is the end of that thing smooth
	Ur does it have a groove or what?
Kaziah:	No . it's just . just like a nail.
Woman:	Ok.
	[side comment from one participant to another participant (4.0)]
Kaziah:	The main art in spinnin is in holdin your thread lettin it run an come out the end
	See . see this end is what does your work
	It ((?trips?)) it over an over . an twistes it .
	[56a:232 & 295 7/85]

Clearly performative rather than participant-interactive, this segment exhibits a very different participant framework than does (7.15) or (7.16). No one in the audience is expected to actually comply with the instructions provided by Kaziah, the demonstrator, and the "learnin somebody" discourse structuring no longer has the goals functional effect of instructions. In fact, it assumes a textual structure as "you" becomes an indefinite pronoun, and intonational contours are indicative rather than imperative. The type of interactional bonding experienced by David with Bill and the expression of affect in making David's butter knife in (7.15) are not contextually created.

Instead, Kaziah and her demonstration are commodities that the group consumes before leaving. The group has certain expectations in terms of their tastes as well, which will be reflected in their informal evaluations of their center experience. She is expected to convey something of an "old-timey" nostalgia to the audience, a group of nonlocals, usually urbanites from regional cities in Ohio, Michigan, Illinois, Kentucky, or Indiana. This particular performer consciously states that she demonstrates both for money and for prestige among those interested in folklore, and she recognizes that such demonstrations have little impact on her family, Ash Creek, or on the visitors. She's marketing a service and the speech forms that accompany it in order to meet their expectations of Appalachian "ethnicity."[38] In meeting this need, she is conforming to Batteau's (1985:45) recognition that "the genius of capitalism is that it continually places new segments of human experience on the market and extracts surplus value out of them." Kaziah willingly engages in this process under a "motive of seduction" (Batteau 1985) in which she is, for a moment, the focus of attention and interest for those educated nonlocals who visit the center and is therefore temporarily included in their world and the things they buy.

However, as in all Ash Creek "showin" discourse contexts, Kaziah's demonstration would be ineffective without the "learnin somebody" discourse patterning that shapes its cultural implications and semiotic significations, and the "showin" discourse would become meaningless without the action that it references. Yet it is different in form, function, and meaning from segments (7.15) and (7.16). Kaziah is on stage, alone on the porch of one of the campus buildings, presenting herself in a bright "old-timey" dress in front of many observers rather than one or two co-participants. Most do not want to learn how to spin, but to enjoy the presentation for its entertainment and so-called educational value and to ask questions accordingly.[39] In addition, the first portion of this segment is dominated by "I" clauses, which describe how Kaziah got her wool and how she cards it rather than mapping reference onto what she is actually doing simultaneously. The two "you" forms cue the audience only to watch and listen. This portion does not contain directives. Yet the second portion of the segment does contain a normative "learnin somebody" discourse syntax at the end replete with attributive possessives ("The main art . . . is holdin your thread . . ."). But there is no one doing the spinning with her. This segment is one in which the "you" clauses must be interpreted as indicatives containing indefinite pronouns that function rhetorically, not as instructions. Kaziah's identity is extended only over the spinning wheel and the yarn, not to another person who is a co-participant in doing the spinning.

In watching Kaziah give such demonstrations on several occasions, I noticed that her discourse was somewhat scripted, offering similar content and structuring in each event. Under such public performative constraints, the communicative event acquires a task-boundedness and routinization that is further reinforced by the nonparticipatory role of a transient audience. The effect is the creation of socioeconomic commodity dominated by its exchange value in the regional market in which Kaziah and other folk craft demonstrators participate. Without the apprenticeship instructional frames characteristic of "learnin somebody" discourse, however, cultural knowledge to construct these communicative events becomes problematic. Younger demonstrators taught at the center or regionally are no longer available to continue the "showin" discourse communicative patterns Kaziah knows well. Instead, corporate, capitalistic enterprises at regional "heritage" centers, such as Dollywood, the Museum of Appalachia, and Berea College craft enterprises, assume responsibilities to "preserve our heritage" through public craft demonstrations that rarely employ "showin" discourse communication. A number of teenage, young adult, and parental-age Ash Creek residents occasionally participate in these preservation efforts, not as demonstrators or practitioners but as paying visitors to Dollywood, or occasionally, as Berea College students. Commoditization is complete.

Socioeconomic Significance of Task-Focused Imperative Discourse

Task-focused "helpin out" communication, in its various forms, is at the very core of Ash Creek socioeconomic relations because it reproduces a culturally appropriate division of labor within the task-oriented economy of Ash Creek and is instrumental in the reproduction of an ideology of labor communication. The Ash Creek epithet "helpin out" applies to a broad range of tasks performed by individuals in culturally sanctioned symmetrical-status participant frameworks who then use specific communicative forms to accomplish the task and reproduce these relations. "Helpin out" metapragmatic discourse provides the means for interpreting these symmetrical status work relations.

Most men describe their positions in a work group or company as "helpin [Personal Name] out," regardless of the amount of wages they are being paid or the corporate level of the organization employing them. As they prefer to work with family and kin with whom they can also have "belongin" relations and develop "claims" in the laboring context, men frequently conflate issues of wage-labor with issues related to "belongin" networks. As a result, local employers and work groups embedded within these conflations of labor patterns will tend to reproduce these task-focused communicative patterns as well.[40]

Appropriately used task-focused discourse is highly utilitarian in many situations because of its referential capacity to specify precisely what task activities are required and because of its pragmatic capacity to index actions and participant statuses. In task-focused discourse events, it assumes a lesser communicative value than nonverbal modes of communication, reproducing an ideology of communication that speaking practices "do" something in terms of effecting a perceived end or goal.

The discourse forms appropriate to such communicative patterns are also instrumental in generating new types of task-focused communicative situations or in blocking the incorporation of others. Through powerful indexical relations, pragmatic constraints restrain and constrain the types of tasks that can readily be accepted and the participant relations to accomplish them. Activities that diminuate physical labor and elevate literate activities, information gathering and manipulation, or long-term, coordinated activities are reframed into political events in which an authority who can "take care" of them is sought. In the case of educational instruction, tasks emphasizing literate activities are accepted when offered as action-oriented methods to "get things done" (e.g., to purchase goods from a catalogue or to keep accounts more efficiently) but are given lower priority or denied when presented as noetic processes that do not appear to produce an end product or service. Task communication that redefines indexes to task participant frameworks culturally valued as "male" or "female" are also incorporated slowly or denied access, as female miners or male childcare providers find themselves marginalized or ostracized from community life.[41]

Appropriate uses of imperatives are especially significant discourse structures within "helpin out" contexts because of their goals functional effect of evoking compliance and revealing control and authority relations. Speakers are allocated "rights" to direct others in culture-specific ways at disjunctures in the task system where there is an acknowledged disparity in knowledge or skill. In these "rights" is a culturally recognized and approved use of power, but of power to direct work or labor of which the speaker is a part, not to mitigate, alter, or direct the behavior of another for some purpose other than to cooperatively produce a product or piece of work. For these uses, "orders" are needed; task-focused imperatives are not culturally recognized "orders."

8 "DOIN FOR SOMEBODY": ORDERS AND IMPERATIVES

"You should a done this and you should a done that."

Shortly after I moved to Ash Creek (June 1985), I was riding in a car with two other women, one local and one a staff member at the Environmental Center. The local woman was discussing her marriage and how good her husband was as a spouse. She said several times, "He loves me, he does for me." I subsequently heard this trope many times, usually, but not always, from women. Men would of course change the pronoun to "She loves me, she does for me." [notes 6/85]

At an Environmental Center community event in the summer of 1986, I overheard two local men talking. One was talking about being married and his wife's merits. He said to the other, "She cooks the bacon, and I follow the bacon." [notes 7/86]

"ORDERS," OR UTTERANCES THAT SPEAKERS RECOGNIZE as verbal directives from one individual to control the behavior of another, are the most powerful speech acts in the Ash Creek repertoire in their effect on potential socioeconomic cohesion or disruption. When contextualized in ways residents interpret as appropriate, "orders" provide an unambiguous semiotic system for conjoining labor or work among individuals who belong to different gendered domains of political-economic control. Appropriate use of "orders" thereby reproduces or creates socioeconomic relations among those perceived as cultural unequals. When spoken appropriately within the "doin for somebody" contexts of Ash Creek socioeconomic activity, such normative imperative uses represent critical, core indexes of inclusion, affection, or "love," as defined by Ash Creek usage.[1]

"Orders," however, are not the only requesting discourse used in constructing "doin-for" communicative practices. All forms in the requesting discourse repertoire can enter into the ongoing daily "doin for" patterns as well. Spoken primarily among close "belongin" network members, these "doin for" discourse practices provide the linguistic-economic means for extending "claims" relations across gender categories and for creating or maintaining laborial, distributive, or consumptive activities among the full range of Ash Creek residents. Maintenance of these relations allows residents the linguistic privilege of using "orders" and reproduces a critical domain of the Ash Creek linguistic-economic system.

Properly used, "orders" assume presuppositional indexical meanings that signify strong, positive relations among participants and mitigate the goal functions of imperatives so that they are not classified as "person-centered control acts" (Ervin-Tripp, O'Connor, and Rosenberg, 1984), but as simply a way of "askin" for something. Improperly used, they become a means by which socioeconomic relations can be disrupted, broken, or terminated; improperly used, they can become one step in a continuum of negative socioeconomic acts from ostracism from "claims" reciprocity networks to hostile prestations labeled "messages" or "presents," and, finally, to violent harm to property or person.

Appropriate Use of "Orders"

No contexts exist in Ash Creek in which an adult man can appropriately "order" another adult man using imperative or other "order" constructions. In fact, no discourse structures exist outside of "helpin out" task contexts for one male interlocutor to directly and unambiguously request or direct another man's behavior. An adult man should know how to behave or has good reason for behaving as he does; he can't be "told" what to do,[2] and infringements upon others' "rights" or threats to their "name" cannot be addressed directly through discourse. When one man "wants" or "needs" to direct another's behavior, he does so in an extremely indirect manner. Within a system of such verbal indirection, "orders" given by men to men are not only inappropriate but highly abrasive as well. Consequently, the following discussion excludes any conceivable "order" discourse exchanges between adult men only.

Appropriate situations of use do exist, however, between men and women, older women and younger women, adults and young children, and preachers and saved Christian women. If fictive "belongin" relations are created, teachers (or educational professional staff) and medical practitioners can use "order" discourse with parents or clients. Participant interactions under such asymmetrical participant frameworks create contexts in which task-focused "helpin out" communication cannot apply but "doin for" communication can. Yet similar to task-oriented "helpin out" imperative discourse, appropriate "doin for" "order" uses also depend on the "rights," "place," and actual or potential "claims" of participants. Imperatives must demand something that the requestor has a "right" and "place" to demand. Furthermore, the requestor generally, but not always, has some type of "claim" over the requestee. Therefore, the indexical significations presupposed or created in these contexts are generally clear to interactants and usually have socioeconomic functions.[3]

Unlike "helpin out" imperatives-in-use discourse, however, even within contexts in which "rights," "place," and "claims" are culturally recognized, compliance may not be forthcoming by any addressee in a specific "doin for" communicative event. Many "doin for" imperatives are completely unacknowledged by addressees. Even when addressees do comply, many have difficulty recognizing them as explicit directives formally similar to "orders."

Whether an addressee complies is often predicated on recognition that a "doin for" relationship exists with a high level of "claims" on both participants. Compliance then becomes a highly social and volitional act in which the presuppositional indexes of interpersonal relations reproduced in communicative events assume primary functions over the propositional structure of the utterance. For example, following is a narrative Bill told me about his childhood with his grandmother, with whom he lived at the time:

(8.1) (*Setting: Maintenance building of the Environmental Center during woodcarving session. Participants: Bill and I.*)

One time Bill was out fishing down by the creek when his grandmother called "Come here" to get him to come to the house. He ran as quick as he could, dropping his pole. She said "Thread my needle" so she could continue sewing because her eyesight was limited. I asked if he minded dropping what he was doing and running in when she called "Come here" and if he minded being told to thread the needle. With a surprised look, he said, "No, not at all . because I loved her so much." [notes 8/85]

On the other hand, if fewer "claims" were recognized between the two of them, the grandmother may not have called or Bill could have ignored her call. The creek was approximately 150 feet from the house and, if asked to explain why he did not come, he could have easily asserted that he had not heard her or he could not stop what he was doing. That Bill complied with the imperative indexed the strength of the "doin for" relationship and reproduced a basic, highly valued cultural process of symbolic semiosis in the community. The grandmother's imperatives indexed such a relationship. The attributive possessive in the imperative clause indexed an item co-present and valued for the tasks in which she used it, and from which Bill benefited. It therefore bound their interpersonal relationship to the material world of goods as well. The relationship was trihedral; verbal, material, and interactional relations merged to form a single instantive expression of "love." A laborial form of Mauss's "spiritual bond" (1967:11), this willingness to comply, complicated by numerous reciprocal obligations to be available to continue to "do for" the speaker, motivates the kinship-based, "belongin" socioeconomic interactions of the community. Without it, no empirical means exist to maintain a cohesive, cooperative exchange of labor or services across status groups within extended family socioeconomic units (see figure 8.1).[4]

The intersections of presuppositional indexical relationships captured by figure 8.1 are routinely reaffirmed, expanded, or newly created in each instance of imperative use. They should be viewed not as static, reified concepts mechanically applied to a particular situation but as a dynamic choreography of indexical significations created by two individuals interacting affectively in a world of "things" and "needs."

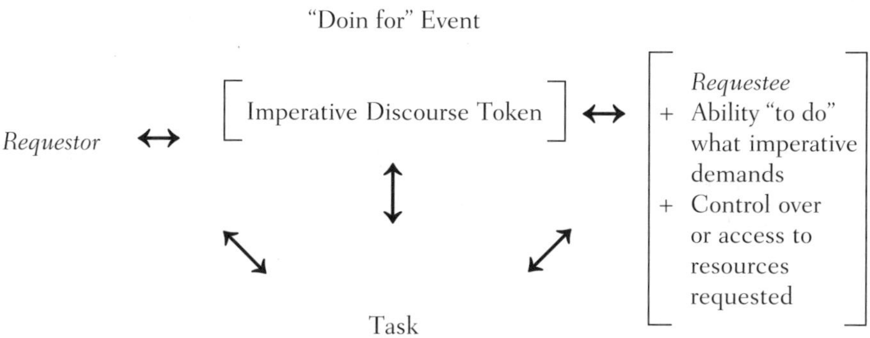

Figure 8.1. "Doin for" "order" relations

Ash Creek interlocutors develop idiosyncratic patterns of acceptable imperative usage between or among themselves which range from occasional to frequent use of them. All individuals will use appropriate "order" discourse within their culturally-normative "rights," "place" and "claims" domains; some will rely more on them than others:

(8.2)

(8.2.1) (*Setting: Local mom-and-pop grocery store; participants are Betty, two of her male grandchildren, approximate ages of two [Sammy] and four [Tommy], and I. No customers are present; I am attempting to repair a price label gun.*)

Betty: Are you goin to my house ur yours?

Sammy: Yours ((?2.0?))

Betty: **Go in . cause—**

Sammy: I don't wanna go in.

Betty: Well . you, ya . you got no ((?1.0?)) place to go fur you.
You'll learn that ((?schoolhouse?)) . like a
Wake him up
Now ya got my keys on ya
An don't lose ɛm
Cause I couldn't gIt in the house if ya do
Go with Im Tommy.

Tommy: I don't want to.
Can I take my toys?

Betty: Yeah . if Sammy goes with you.

Tommy: I'll take my toys with me,
He can—
[Two boys talk to each other (5.0).]

Betty: Can it do it's thing? [to me about the labeling gun]
Tommy: NO . NO [to Sammy]
Betty: Huh?
Go with him honey . he don—
Tommy: —I don't want to.
Betty: He don't go by himself.
You want me to go with you . Sammy?
Sammy: No . no:
Betty: I'll go with ya.
[Sammy shakes head no]
Well . if . if you don't go with him I'll have to go with you
An you'll have to go.
Sammy: No . I don't have to go.
Betty: **You do too.**
[further protestations from Sammy; Betty goes with him and takes him]
[44a:121 1/86]

(8.2.2) (*Setting: Homemakers' meeting at Environmental Center; only one child is present. He has just left the meeting room, wandering off.*)
Mother: Hey Thomas Edward.
Thomas.
GIt back in here. [3b:62 3/87]

(8.2.3) (*Setting: Waiting room of county hospital*)
Mother: Behave.
[smacks child's behind; child hides under chair, then continues running around; no correction from mother] [notes 6/87]

Segments (8.2.1)–(8.2.3) represent a common and frequent participant structure of adult women directing the behavior of their own children, grandchildren, or one of their sibling's children. In keeping with much adult-child discourse, they exemplify aspects of a socialization process by which young members, in this case, boys,[5] are incorporated into cultural semioses of the community.[6] Socioeconomic implications of each speech event are referentially opaque. The utterances, however, overtly index women's "right" to control, or attempt to control, children through their directive functions. An adult female family member is clearly directing or attempting to direct the behavior of a child into culturally normative channels. In each case, however, compliance is problematic. In (8.2.1) Betty, the grandmother, eventually volunteers to take Sammy, the younger child, to her house next door to play, away from the activity of the store. This "volunteerin" releases Tommy, the older grandson, from her previous command. In (8.2.2) the child eventually complies only when physically obligated to do so by the mother holding him, and in (8.2.3) the child ignores both the verbal directive and the nonverbal physical punishment, continuing his behavior without further sanctions.

This pattern of tolerance for noncompliance underscores the presuppositional indexes signified in "doin for" imperative discourse. Most residents assume that children will comply with adult "orders" as they learn to "love" or "do for" them in close "belongin" networks, not just because a parent uttered them. Thus, compliance with imperative constructions creates indexical significations predicated on a child's perceived willingness or "volunteerin" motivation. Compliance leads to a metapragmatic gloss of "a good child," one who "loves" the adult speaker and can therefore be expected to meet labor, services, or goods "needs" as a teenager or adult. These relations extend into adulthood and old age. They often equal or supersede the strength of "doin for" relations created through marriage. When directives from parents or other close natal kin conflict with directives from spouses, many residents will opt to comply with the parental demand at the expense of the spouse's.[7]

Socioeconomic implications become more transparent in the use of conventionalized or stylized imperatives between adult family members and children. Expressions such as "give me some sugar" (meaning a kiss or a hug) are frequently combined with clauses offering to perform a good or service:

(8.3)

(8.3.1) If you give me some sugar . I'll gIt you a pop. [mother to young son] [notes 7/86]

(8.3.2) Give papaw some sugar an he'll fix your bike fər ya [mother to young son] [notes 7/86]

(8.3.3) Here's your ice cream . now give me some sugar [mother to young daughter] [notes 10/85]

In such discourse, demands for affection are closely bound to "doin" activities with socioeconomic implications through syntactic orderings of clauses and the patterned use of attributive possessives: displays of affection are exchanged for labor or goods in an obvious expression of reciprocal equivalence.

Simultaneously, the "rights" of the adult to use imperative discourse assert authoritative relations in specific speech events in the form of unambiguous, direct commands. Whether the child chooses to comply or not, assertions of cultural inequality are reproduced in "doin for" imperatives to children, revealing a "doin for" discourse continuum (see figure 8.2). This continuum generally applies to those in "belongin" relations and who have or want to have "claims" over each other. It can, however, be extended to others under certain conditions. Within "belongin" contexts, authority, "rights" to control of resources, compliance, and complex levels of affect intersect and interact to construct a web of multifunctional meanings indexed by appropriate use of "doin for" imperatives. Within the semantic plane of reference, imperative discourse within conversational segments can also construct reciprocal socioeconomic activities by causing exchanges of labor or valued goods. Through actions of verbal utterance by the adult and nonverbal compliance by the child, socioeconomic processes are incorporated into

– ← "Doin for" Imperative Continuum → +

	←	Addressee Response	Addressor/Addressee Relation	Addressee Response	→		
Physical violence to person	Messages, "warnins" presents (dog poisoned, anonymous message sent in mail, uninvolved visitor delivers message)	Noncompliance	"Belongin" relation	Noncompliance	Reluctant compliance (excuses, hedges, multiple demands needed)	Self-justified compliance (meets personal want or need)	Willful compliance (love)
Physical violence to person	Messages, "warnins" presents (dog poisoned, anonymous message sent in mail, uninvolved visitor delivers message)	Noncompliance	Non-"Belongin" relation	Reluctant or willing compliance	Continued relationship with addressor	Fictive "belongin" status	Willful compliance (love)

Figure 8.2. "Doin for" imperative continuum

this multiplex matrix of meanings such that authority relations, socioeconomic "claims," and "love" are united into a common semiosis.

Within the pragmatic plane of discourse, appropriate adult "doin for" imperatives tend to become routinized and predictable because most residents' daily interactions are highly predictable. Both men and women commonly interact only with a small number of people, who constitute their core "belongin" networks. These highly patterned and expected interactions ensure that presuppositional indexical significations are strongly reinforced. Segment (8.4) reflects such routinization:

(8.4) (*Setting: Kaziah's home; taping session on items of mutual interest to her and me: crafts, haint (ghost) stories, old stories about Ash Creek settlers, and her life story. Her husband is in the bedroom napping. No other participants. I have been a regular visitor and we both feel comfortable with each other.*)

Kaziah: Come in here an sing a song, Dad . Dad.

Anita: Yeah . he might
If you don't tell Im
He might not know a song.

Kaziah: Come in here an sing Niter a song.

Anita: Come on
Ya gonna sleep all afternoon?

Kaziah: Come on.

[She begins singing a hymn and husband comes out from the bedroom. He eventually makes an attempt at singing a song.] [27a:13 8/85]

Control is not contested and compliance is eventually given. Segment (8.4) reflects well-developed "doin for" patterns among older residents. It is Kaziah's "right" to demand that her husband come to "her" kitchen. After more than 50 years of marriage, Kaziah has created "place" relations with him that allow her to call him from someplace else to "her kitchen" in order to visit with a guest, although she cannot to "make" him sing. She is trying to get him to "do" for her by demanding that he sing. He eventually tries. Her offering of a traditional hymn as a choice indicates willingness to construct a joint effort at sharing mountain religious songs with an outsider, thus potentially framing the event as a task-focused activity. It was also an effort to get her husband to join in a religiously connoted act, an activity he seldom embraces. The economic applications of this exchange lie within the "rights," "place," and "claims" relations the two of them have developed with each other. Kaziah can count on her husband to "do for" her when she demands it. And she will demand, at least most of the time, only when it is "right" and her "place" to do so. The imperatives will, in turn, index these relations.[8]

Segment (8.5) represents an embedded "doin for" imperative construction, retold by Tammy in narrative form as part of a semi-formal audiotaped interview by me:

(8.5) (*Setting: Open-ended interview with Tammy, a young woman office worker at the Environmental Center. Tammy has been talking about her family and their lives. No other participants. Current topic is her father's background.*)

Anita: Did he uh . gIt much education?
You said college courses at Berea. [Berea College]

Tammy: Yeah . he took some college courses at Berea
Most uh . his uh . high school . was through the home study.
So

Anita: He did it himself then

Tammy: Yeah . uh-huh.

Anita: How about your mother?

Tammy: My mother didn't finish her high school.
Her parents wouldn't let her.
So . she wanted to be a teacher
She went here at Hill House for a while [Environmental Center was a county school in the 1950s.]
And uh . she worked a lot with her teachers an she was student teaching at the same time she was trying to go to high school.

Anita: Uh-huh.

Tammy: And uh . what her parents said was
An ah . basically it was her father.
She had two other sisters
An she sa . an he said "Well . if they're not gonna go . **you can't go**."
An . so she tried to talk them into goin . but they said no we don't want to.
So they went ahead an they got married.
An my mother was . in . heard my father say "no . **you're not gonna go to school**."

Anita: Huh.
So:

Tammy: He didn't believe that women needed an education . ya know.
He said women are gonna gIt married an that's it.

[53a:173 3/85]

Both "doin for" and "helpin out" discourse domains are referenced in this example, revealing the dynamic interplay of both domains within Ash Creek cultural life. The father shifts individual authority rights to the arena of action where gender, knowledge, and skill egalitarianism apply: if the daughter can persuade her sisters to engage in the task of going to school, then he will approve. They do not "volunteer" to do so, so the command stands. If task egalitarianism within the central "belongin" unit of the family cannot be maintained, then the behavior of the daughter is not "right," and the father maintains his "rights" to exercise authority. Yet his authority is not contested, nor are his imperatives interpreted as "orders." In Ash Creek terms, he is not going against her wishes but is "doin for" her.

Residents account for individual variation in frequency and semantic extent of "doin for" imperative use by citing how some people are more "mean" than others, or by noting other personality traits such as taciturnity, suggesting a system dominated by politeness criteria.[9] From a socioeconomic perspective, such comments reflect speaker choice constrained by cultural limits placed on "rights" and "place" domains of control. When these constraints are violated, negative sanctions are likely to be forthcoming:

(8.6) (*Setting: Sarah, Linda, Cindy, and I "just talkin" in the Environmental Center kitchen one hot summer afternoon.*)

Sarah: Willie? Ol Willie?

Cindy: Yeah man

He had his thing

He had his thing on a butt one day

Last year when the ((?.5?)) didn't like the dance thing

An Anne tol him to quit an she came home an told me.

I come up here the next time to dance.

I went an I told Madeline . I said . I said . I said I . ya know I told her what Anne had said about Willie

I said "I just want ya to know

I'm gonna *gIt* him tonight."

An bu:ddy I did.

Caught him right downstairs at the community building.

Tom Jones was comin up

An I had Billy pinned right down there up against the wall an Tom Jones caught me

Guess he stopped him from bein hit.

I said "**Don't you *NEVER* do anythin like that to my girl again**."

An he said . **"Well, don't go away mad" he said "Let's shake on it."**

He stuck out his hand to shake an I just turned an walked off.

	He was just standin there . buddy
	If he hadn't been so old . oh *God* I'd hit Im
	I swear to God I would.
Linda:	**He's got it bad.**
Cindy:	He's got somethin bad.
	He's got to wantin women bad is his problem
	He thinks he's a lady killer an he's an old ((?1.0?))
Linda:	((?What is he . seventy??))
Cindy:	Lord . I don't know.
Linda:	He's too old to ((?cut the mustard?)) [laughs]
Cindy:	[cut the mustard]
Sarah:	Mary . he ain't too old to pat . though.
All:	[unclear overlap as agreement voiced]
Sarah:	**He'd pat on us.**
Cindy/Linda:	[unintelligible overlap ((4.0))]
Cindy:	I'll tell you what
	I'd give him a *million* dollars if he'd try me.
	That'd be his last.
	[further discussion of man's grandson's similar behavior and other harassment incidents]
Sarah:	She said "What's the matter with you?
	Don't you like men?"
	I said "**I like men**
	But I like em in their place" [all laugh]
	[108a:271 7/86]

Certainly violation of Ash Creek "doin for" communication applies in this narrative example in multiple ways. Willie was alleged to have sexually accosted Cindy's daughter, a teenage girl, which is a core violation of "rights." Willie was not Cindy's husband, nor had the two of them constructed any other "place" relations that could have made his behavior acceptable. At the community level, there were no acceptable "place" relations possible for this type of behavior. He was not "doin for" Cindy's daughter in any way. Cindy, a divorced mother, responds to this violation with actions that are more consistent with male protective "doin for" behavior for daughters and other close female relatives in a "belongin" relationship.[10] A woman can assume these protective roles when a husband cannot be present or does not exist. The imperative, "Don't you *NEVER* do anythin like that to my girl again," could be potential appropriate "doin for" "order" discourse.[11] Here, however, no "doin for" context can exist because the imperative's very use by a woman to a man creates a participant framework that violates these presuppositional indexes. Cindy inverts gender roles by using it, creating a participant structure of cultural unequals in which the man is in an inferior position. It becomes an unambiguous "order."

Yet Willie seems conciliatory with "Let's shake on it," a task-focused form commonly used among men as a positive gesture enhancing "claims" when "makin a deal." Willie contradicts his own co-equal discourse markers, however, with the imperative "don't go away mad," which is a common expression from a man to a woman in the "doin for" imperative repertoire. In essence, Willie counters her efforts at demeaning his social position with an imperative that demeans hers. Cindy ignores the conciliatory gesture; he maintains his "rights" as a man not to be "told" to comply with an imperative through his manipulation of indexes with counter-imperatives; Cindy continues to be angry, recognizing that he has not acknowledged *her* claim to authority. She is ready to address his violation of her "rights" and "place" with physical violence, overtly tempered only by his age.[12]

The women listening to the conversational narrative acknowledge her "rights" and "place" criteria, giving her positive feedback (e.g., "He's got it bad," and "He'd pat on us"). Sexual access improprieties are egregious "rights" and "place" violations for nearly all Ash Creek women and for those men who affirm the Christian morality preached in local churches. Among this audience, Willie is a man out of "place" and "wrong"; their metapragmatic discourse justifies Cindy in using "doin for" imperative discourse and in threatening to use coercion to gain compliance. It would have been better, however, if Cindy had her "own man" to confront the aggressor.

"Doin for" "order" discourse, appropriately or inappropriately used, regulates interpersonal access to or denial of valued goods, services, or labor when co-participants are unequal in access to these goods or services. Therefore, despite the significant affective component associated with "doin for" imperative uses, appropriate "order" uses within these "doin for" participant frameworks cannot be subsumed only under conditions of intimacy and familiarity and still capture the socioeconomic implications of them. Nor can the indexical relations created by their use be fully understood.[13] To argue that intimacy alone motivates the use of "doin for" imperatives is to distort the relationship to goods and services that motivates their use.

As an example of the socioeconomic force of these relations, certain central resource domains related to those physical entities *always* referenced by first-person attributive possessive constructions tend to be excluded from this appropriate "order" requesting discourse system. Human possessors of the items referenced by these constructions have the "right" to deny others access to them through "doin for" imperatives. These constructions reference not only body parts (as in "my arm") but also entities strongly associated with an individual's person (e.g., "my pipe" or "my pocketbook"). A requestor cannot use imperatives to gain compliance from the requestee to manipulate such entities even when "rights," "place," and "claims" relations are strongly developed between them. When a parent needs to examine a child's body for the extent of a minor injury, for example, many parents will use "volunteerin" or direct "askin" communicative systems alone, avoiding imperatives. While variation exists in this discourse practice among parents with children, "rights" to violate personal space and body proxemics are seldom given at any age:

(8.7) A six-year-old girl ran her hand over a rough wooden rail, obtaining a splinter. Her father, mother, and grandfather offered to remove it, using direct "askin" discourse constructions to obtain her compliance for the investigation and removal of the object. No one "told" her to stand still, put out her hand, or be quiet. [notes 3/86]

Local nurses and medical practitioners regularly report patient reluctance, primarily by adults of childrearing age or older, to have a physical examination and to being "told" to assume positions for examination by practitioners or family members. [notes 8–10/86]

A local man reported that no one, not even his wife when she was alive, could cut his hair but he, much less utter imperative constructions to position him in certain ways to perform the task. [notes Oct. 85]

These contexts in which "doin for" imperatives are excluded even among close "belongin" network members who have very strong "rights," "place," and "claims" relations with each other contrast with other contexts where imperatives are extended to anyone, including strangers. When the speaker is well within his or her "rights" and when gatekeeping greeting discourse is not required, compliance can become obligatory for *any* addressee who is a cultural unequal.[14] Under such conditions, nouns denoting or second-person pronouns indexing requestees are creative indexes, incorporating all listeners into the "doin for" event and extending "doin for" discourse beyond close "belongin" networks. Such usages therefore reveal a core set of linguistic-economic relations within the appropriate "doin for" "order" system that construct basic socioeconomic domains of control and power by those who can appropriately utter them.

Extensions of Appropriate "Doin for" "Order" Situations

While "doin for" "order" discourse itself may not be stylized, that is, constituting a set of nearly identical tokens, the domains of resources it references or indexes will be highly predictable for a given individual. Given the frequent and time-intensive interactions with core members of one's "belongin" network, residents often come to consensus about what entities these referential domains should encompass. As a result, residents of the same gender in the same "belongin" network often have similar inventories within specific resource domains. Each individual will have distinctive personal mannerisms and "ways of doin things," but overlap of entities that a man or woman is expected to have control over or use rights to will be extensive among such groups. Because of extensive overlap in "belongin" network membership among residents, these presumptions of resource domain inventory and use are shared by most Ash Creek residents. As a result, individual, subjective assertions of control areas become cultural ones as well. Corresponding to regularized attributive possessive domains of reference, these control foci center on key resource production areas for each gender. Metapragmatic functions of discursive genres that reference and express fundamental or Pentecostal interpretations of scripture and religious expression provide the linguistic resources necessary to legitimize and "naturalize" these human and valued resource relations.[15] Rarely are the "doin for" imperative events associated with these core control areas not extended to everyone, regardless of "rights," "place," or "claims" relationships. In fact, they become opportunities for asserting and developing "rights," "place," and "claims" both inside and outside "belongin" networks.

For example, a woman's basic productive "rights" of homemaking, cooking, and childbearing and childrearing constitute such central "rights,"[16] and women therefore expect compliance in response to imperatives spoken within these domains of socioeconomic control. Unless the host is young enough to have enculturated media and urban valuations of thinness,[17] a woman will utter an imperative directing a visitor of any status, from her own children to a visitor never before encountered to have a drink or eat some food. Failure to comply "hurts the feelins" of the host, precipitates negative talk about the visitor, and can conclude further "rights" to visit.

Bill's narrative in (8.8) reports an occasion in which the woman, distant kin to Bill with whom he has not developed any "claims," asserts her "place" through her "right" to demand compliance to a command to eat:

(8.8) (*Setting: Elicited retelling of a "story" from Bill by me during woodcarving session at the Environmental Center maintenance building. Participants: Bill and I.*)

Anita: We were talkin about . ya know we were just talkin about your hirin yourself out to do . plowin an such.

Bill: Yeah . this was uh back in . the 50's I think

I was workin on a farm

It was Sarie Smith .

An they sent me down there to plow for her

An uh . of course several other people.

This particular day I was plowin for her .

An uh . she wasn't expectin me

I didn't tell you this part

So she gIts all her grandkids out

An grabs a hoe an stuff like that to break the corn stalks off the field

Anita: [laughs]

Bill: So I had a lot a these

Disk plows ya know

Anita: Yeah

Bill: That . had a little dish plow that rolled.
An she said "Well honey . if you'll give us a little time
Then we'll rake ya up a start
An then we can keep ahead uv ya
((?Cause?)) a so many grandkids.
"Well you don't—
Anita: —Uh-[huh]
Bill: —[Have] to do that."
She said . "Well you can't plow through those cornstalks."
I said "Yeah . it wont make a bit a difference."
An uh it was kind a ((?worked her a diffrent way?)) cause she hadn't never seen anything plowed but with a mule.
Anita: Yeah
Bill: ((?1.0?)) Take the cornstalks an burn ɛm.
So I started plowin an it uh came . bout eleven thirty . ur quarter til twelve
An uh . a couple a the grandkids turned up out there where the tractor was
An come up by the side uv it an
I realized they was wantin somethin.
I stopped the tractor.
They said . "Well . uh . Granny's got dinner ready."
And uh . I said . "Well I . I brought my lunch with me.
An
They were all this . uh . all this ya got here fore the ((?crop?)) come."
So they went on back an I started my circle again
A five round circle
Made about one circle an *she* was standin there bout the same place the boys was
Next round I think.
She says uh . I stopped the tractor
An she says . "Now . I ain't" said
"I went to all that trouble to gettin dinner for ya an now you gonna *eat*."
An I said . "Well I . I brought my . dinner with me."
An uh . she said . **"Well you jus uh . jus not eat that dinner"**

An said **"I fixed dinner fur ya an you're gonna eat with us."**
[chuckles]
So . oh: man
She had the best meal ever was fixed . I'll tell ya.

Anita: Um:

Bill: Them ol people
Whew.
Unbelievable what they can throw together . in a short period a time.

Anita: Do you know what it was?

Bill: She had uh shucky beans . chicken n dumplings
Fried potatoes . fresh milk which was right from the cow . that mornin
And uh . I don't know what kind a meat it was
Whether it was pork ur a . well it must a been pork
Besides the chicken an dumplins
But she had some kind a . an it may uv been fixed from breakfast
But . people had a habit if . if they'd fried pork for breakfast
They'd set it up for dinner.

Anita: Uh-huh.

Bill: An it didn't look like it was fresh from frying
She had cor . cornbread a course
They all had cornbread.

Anita: Uh-huh

Bill: An uh . sometimes they had fresh biscuits I don't know if they had fresh biscuits ur not
But a lot a times when they fixed chicken an dumplins
They'd fix biscuits
With chicken an dumplins
Cause they always fixed gravy in it
I how . don't remember how they did that
But anyway they'd have this bowl of gravy
Plus the chicken an dumplins.
Chicken gravy.
My grandmother did that. [107b:059 4/86]

Bill's efforts to dissuade her and avoid compliance are denied as the imperative assumes a direct "order" construction (e.g., "I fixed dinner fur ya an you're gonna eat with us"). The preposing of a "need" justification clause before the imperative makes salient the labor value placed on food preparation and provides an explanation for why he must eat the meal. With this semantic emphasis on food preparation labor, both Bill and the woman can draw equivalencies between his labor and hers and develop "claims" relations created through reciprocity equivalents. Without such correlations, she would have been in his debt for plowing her garden and would have suffered an affront to self. Noncompliance from Bill would become an anti-social and anti-economic act.

Bill further recognizes the reciprocal laborial prestation referenced by "doin for" imperatives by praising the woman's quality, quantity, and diversity of menu. The lexical ordering of food items is conventional, with special items first (shucky beans and chicken and dumplings), then drink (always "fresh milk from the cow"), then routine vegetables, then the main meat, and type of bread. With this complete list of conventional items, however, praised with the stylized hyperbolic expression "the best meal ever was fixed," the value of the woman's productive labor assumes high culturally valued status as well. Its quality legitimates her "right" and "place" to demand compliance, to use "doin for" discourse by creative indexical extension, and to acquire symbolic capital through valued replication of core women's resources.

The humorous quality of segment (8.9)[18] reporting events that happened in a similar food productive context undercuts and devalues this core productive labor, while simultaneously denigrating commodity distribution for monetary exchange:

(8.9) (*Setting: Elicited retelling of a narrative by an older man in his basement workshop. This narrative occurred in an area close to but outside Ash Creek and was told to me by a colleague who teaches at the local community college. Participants: Man and I.*)

Man: Ok

This lady . who was a neighbor uv ours live across the holla . in another holla

Sh she was uh noted for makin moonshine

So I guess this was her means of uv support.

So the story goes

An I'm sure it's true

[clears throat]

One of the men went up . once . to buy some moonshine

Uh nothin uncommon about a pint or half pint

An course when he got there

She'd just had a run to come off

An uh she'd been . samplin her own moonshine

An uh at the same time she was killin the chicken

Killin the hen

[clears throat]

An uh . she was uh . she was makin dumplins an a course she had some feathers in the dumplins.

She asked this gentleman if he'd like to . stay an eat uh *dinner* with her.

He said "No . thank you"

Said "I . I . I never did care fur chicken n dumplins."

An she had an ol pistol layin on the table

An she got that *pistol* an put it in her hand an says

"Oh yes by God you'll stay."

He said "Yes . an matter a fact I like chicken n dumplins."

So uh apparently he thought he might make ((?up?)) with her.
[122a:95 1/90]

The content of the narrative, moonshine production and distribution by a woman, is unusual, disjoining appropriate indexes of valued, Christian tasks and calling into question her "rights" as a woman. Her consumption of it further devalues these "rights." The male visitor tries to simply buy some of her product as "tradin" event, but she attempts to reframe the exchange into a reciprocal "claims" event, similar to the one created in (8.8) through a prestation of a valued food item, replete with feathers. Unlike the woman in (8.8), however, this cook does not have any symbolic capital on which to draw, a condition reproduced in this event by the poor quality of the meal. The man chooses to foreground the commodity exchange function of the event, using politeness discourse involving "likes" to refuse the less than tempting pro-offering. The woman recognizes the devaluation of her "rights," responds with a "doin for" imperative, and reinforces the obligatory expectations of this command with a threat of coercion. These verbal and nonverbal actions force a reframing of the event into a culturally valued reciprocity exchange. Such coercion, however, did not result in a positive creation of "claims" relations, but merely provided closure to a satiric and somewhat slapstick anecdote reflecting negatively upon her "name," an anecdote that then achieved community status as a "tale."

This anecdote does, however, encapsulate one possible pattern in Ash Creek's "doin for" imperative discourse continuum (figure 8.2). First, it poses a direct "askin," then a rejection, followed by an imperative creatively indexing possible use of violence through discharge of a firearm, followed by verbal and physical compliance. In Ash Creek speaking practices, however, appropriate "doin for" imperative interactions extended to non-"belongin" networks frequently do not gloss possible use of violence. The potential violation of the powerful and complex indexes that imperatives create is sufficient to enforce compliance. Noncompliance by an addressee in these core "doin for" events constitutes a maximum abrasion or erosion of the speaker's cultural identity, a self embedded in task-focused domains of socioeconomic productive, distributive, or consumptive activities.

Of course, these "doin for" imperative indexical patterns of use extend to the broader and more expansive domains of control exercised by male speakers, which include more public settings than are usually frequented by women. Under "rights" criteria in general, adult men can extend "doin for" imperatives broadly, to a number of cultural domains, under scripturally sanctioned approbation. The authority and control functions of such extensions frequently dominate the socioeconomic components, creating obvious, transparent exercises of power. Unlike the primarily economic activities accompanied by control or authority demands frequently found in women's "doin for" imperative extensions with other adults, authoritative or controlling demands frequently subsume potential or actual socioeconomic functions in men's "doin for" imperative extensions. "Wants" may surface as more central self-focused (ego-oriented) justifications for uttering the imperative.

Segments (8.10) and (8.11) reflect this male construction of a hierarchy of imperative functions by demanding behavior modification with no or minimal task-directed implications. In (8.10) the man simply wishes the woman to change positions instead of himself for some personal "want"; no task is in progress:

(8.10) (*Setting: I am standing in lane leading to a woman's house, having taken her home; visiting male resident initiates exchange. Man is distant kin to woman.*)

Man: **Sherry . come back here a minute.**

Woman: Me?

Man: I wanna talk ta ya.

[She walks over to him.] [notes 6/87]

In (8.11), Bill is extending, somewhat hyperbolically, command discourse to a pet, which, with noun substitution, could occur in nuclear family contexts between fathers or grandfathers and young children:

(8.11) (*Setting: Woodcarving session at Environmental Center maintenance building; participants are Bill and I and our respective dogs.*)

Bill: Fido.

Fido . down

Down I'll beat ya.

Anita: [to her dog] Now sit, .

[I attempt to direct my dog to sit.]

Bill: [chuckles]

Anita: [My efforts continue.]

Bill: **Fido . sit [claps hands twice]**

Si:t.

All right.

Sit . sit.

Anita: There ya go.
Bill: Man . I'll spank ya.
Anita: I'm gonna gIt a little work done . Doggie.
Just a little.
Bill: Ya have to gIt *serious* with that dog.
Anita: Yeah. [Both chuckle.] [48b:008 5/86]

Compliance by both our dogs is minimal, like many children's behavior, and, despite threats, Bill took no punitive measures to coerce behavior modification.

Male speakers in both (8.10) and (8.11) are exercising control over highly valued resources that receive regularized attributive possessive grammatical marking;[19] transparent economic functions of exchange, distribution, or consumption are absent. Yet both reveal core "doin for" relations that affect linguistic-economic patterns through reproduction of "rights" and "place" relations. Exercise of these relations in other contexts often does have transparent socioeconomic impact. Generally men ask women in their "belongin" networks to do things for them or to provide information that results in an economic transaction, and dogs work in searching or retrieving game and provide a financial resource by breeding them.

Segments (8.12)–(8.14) represent complex "doin for" imperatives embedded within religious discourse. Religious performances like this one are extremely complex in the intertextual symbolic meanings the discourse creates and the metapragmatic and pragmatic indexical meanings the entire event presupposes or creates. They also reveal the metapragmatic functions of imperatives from which appropriate "doin for" imperatives emanate into the quotidian social plane of Ash Creek interactions.[20]

The embedded ("entextualized") imperatives in (8.12) are quotes from King James scripture and therefore assume reported speech functions in addition to interactional and interfacial ones created in the immediate speech event:[21]

(8.12) (*Setting: Adult Sunday school at a community holiness church in the Pentecostal tradition. Participants are about 12 church members, a few visitors including me, and the preacher, Robert. This discussion occurs late in the service, as the preacher is explaining the lesson.*)

Preacher: *Jesus* said "I will build my church"
Talkin to the disciples.
An then he said
He would give Peter the keys to the kingdom
An he says "Whatsoever ye shall *find* on earth shall be found in heaven. Whatsoever ye shall lose on earth shall be lose in heaven."
Showin . that the church *does* have . a certain amount of authority . to discipline its ((?fellowship?)).

> When the body of Christ . which is the church . is in tune with God and in *line* with God as
>
> As his word an as he would have
>
> Then it is God's active force upon this earth
>
> They do have that authority.
>
> In . in the absence of Christ . while Christ was here
>
> He was ((?the one?)) ruler
>
> He was the one . that was in authority.
>
> Now . since he went away . he gave authority
>
> To the church.
>
> You know the last commission was **"Go ye therefore an teach all nations an baptize them in my name."**
>
> He said ***teach* them to observe or practice all things** I've committed you ya see Christ *gave* them authority.
>
> He *gave* them authority to do these things.
>
> And the church *does* have a certain amount of authority . to deal
>
> With unruly members.
>
> Not tha . not that we're sayin that all rule ((?1.0?))
>
> And every effort should be made to keep members from goin astray. [20a:338 7/86]

The preacher is not only reporting what Jesus said, but is assuming the stance of someone acting as his mouthpiece, as the authority who has the "right" to say them for Jesus.[22] Quotations from such an unquestioned sacred source assure authoritative legitimacy of the male supreme deity; Jesus's "right" to utter imperative commands is literally unquestioned.

Critical to Ash Creek "doin for" interpretive structures, however, is recognition that these imperatives also represent "doin for" discourse tokens when considered as speech uttered by the preacher to the congregation. Members "in tune with God and in line with God" will willingly comply to these directives because they "love" Christ so much. They may be mediated through the preacher and transcend textual embeddings and reportative functions created by written scriptural rhetorical structure, but they are, in this interpretative framework, literally God's voice to the listener, talking personally to each church member.[23] In this sense, the imperatives are immediate and interactive, didactic, and deontic in their dominant purposive functions and positively affective in their indexical functions. They are also extremely strong presuppositional indexes of idealized asymmetrical relationships involving male authority. The preacher becomes the intermediary interlocutor to make salient these relations through his performance of sermonic discourse.

He continues this catalyst role in (8.13) by demanding the membership to "think for a minute" about the question of "order":

(8.13) (*Setting: Later in the same Sunday school meeting as in* [*8.12*]; *same participants, same lesson*.)

Preacher: Ya know if there was no order
If there was no government
See God provided government in the church
Now government in the church is *not* gonna ((?struck ya?))
It's in the church for protection.
An the same way in . in our national government here
If it . is carried out like it should be
Now I know we can all point a finger an say "Well, this is dirty"
An in some places I guess it is.
But if we *had* no order . here in America
If it was just a free for all . a give an take
A . a: . a six-shooter is your law an order
What would happen to this country?
Now *think* for a minute
Wouldn't that be chaotic?
Wouldn't that be? [20a:485 7/86]

As a preacher, "called by God to 'do' for Him," in Ash Creek verbal expression, he has the "right" to demand compliance from church members in matters of continued, willing expressions of spiritual "love." Failing to comply is not a sign of faith, and, in "doin for" discourse, violates indexes of "love" presupposed by such imperatives. The stylized imperative ("Now think for a minute") closing (8.13) indexes these rights as well.

The text of (8.14) exemplifies another aspect of "doin for" imperative discourse through the verbal genre of "prayin":

(8.14) (*Setting: Adult Sunday school meeting in community holiness church, Pentecostal tradition. Participants: members, a few visitors including me, and preacher, for a total of about 20. Preacher is beginning the meeting with prayer.*)

Preacher: **Let's ask the lord to help us out a little bit**
A big class
[clears throat]
Uhm
That's good

We're here to learn somethin about the Lord's business in heaven.

Bless us father to come . to this . class this mornin Lord

An hear thy word so that we might learn . dear God

Somethin . fundamental to help us

In turn make us willin to learn an help us to ((?deal?)) with life's journey.

Thank you for each one of us here . oh Lord . an for those who couldn't be here.

Those . Lord . who would love to be here but's not able.

O:h God . we thank thee

You who have work .worked and brought us to safety

And refuge at a time of ((?broken hope?)).

Lord, just bless these ((?lone?)) chilren today

An bless our classes throughout this buildin

An not only here

But . father, throughout this land today

Because it's throughout the nation and throughout the world that ((?you counsel?))

***Let* us learn**

That we might be a help to others for truth we are brothers and sisters.

Lo:rd . we thank you (?.5?) that great day that coming

((?When you end?)) that separation.

Lord . we pray thy . creation ((?1.0?))

Prai:se the lord.

Sit down . or stand. [to congregation] [21a:000 7/86]

The prayer prologue begins with a task-framing "let's" construction, indexing the event as a group activity. The use of the first-person plural pronoun is maintained throughout the prayer, merging the congregation with the preacher as petitioners. Those present therefore become included in ritualized discourse as both speakers and as listeners who responded to the preacher's "prayin" with nodding heads or raised hands. In longer prayers, they might inject an "amen" as an acknowledgment of agreement. The targeted addressee of the prayer is therefore dual, to the divinity by denotation, but to the congregation by deixis and by presupposing indexes.[24] Once again, a textualized discursive form merges the interlocutors of a highly contextualized event into an entextualized frame of reference that is, in this case, cosmic in scope and mythic in dimension.

The prayer closes with another, "praise the Lord," more fully expressed as the trope "let us praise the Lord," a highly conventional and frequent religious conversational topic change marker. The prayer itself begins with a stylized imperative, "Bless us Father," which is followed later by "just bless these ((?lone?)) chilren an bless our classes," and "let us learn," all of which are directly addressed to the divinity. In Ash Creek "doin for" discourse, these imperatives are not subjunctives (e.g., a reformulation of "may you bless us") nor direct "askins" (e.g., "we ask you to bless us"), but imperatives with the directive force of "orders." As a "called," chosen member of the saved and as someone who is assumed to be in a particularly strong relationship of faith with the divinity, the preacher's "right" to using "doin for" imperatives with the church membership also grants him the "right" to direct God. Similar to a child in strong "doin for" relations with a parent, a Christian strong in the faith can make demands of God and expect compliance. If the relationship is "in line," then the "doin for" relationship will be binding, and God *will* comply with the imperative. Residents indicate that this kind of relationship between preachers, or others whose faith is strong, and God gives them enormous power.

This "doin for" participant structuring is both generative and typological. The dynamic metapragmatic interconnections among sacred written texts, conventional religious speaking genres and practices, and "doin for" pragmatic and metapragmatic relations between human and divine agents produce interactive and complex significations that are metaphorically extended or directly reapplied to secular interactions between cultural unequals.

Furthermore, the core "doin for" relations asserted in these meaningful religious discursive events become types,[25] or what Silverstein designates as "interpretive schemes" (1998), which legitimate and justify male authoritative and political-economic behavior to women and to others in asymmetrical participant frameworks. The reapplication of these types to quotidian contexts reproduces discursive patternings that residents interpret as comparable to (or deviant from) the discursive forms and functions constructed in ritualized language. Practicing Christians in Ash Creek, or those affirming these patterns of discursive legitimization of authority, assert authoritative relations with women, children, or other cultural unequals under these metapragmatic processes of indexical reapplication: the "doin for" authoritative indexical relations between Jesus and Christians referenced in scripture and interpreted in church apply to men's relations to others.

The socioeconomic impact of these written and oral intersections within "doin for" discourse is encompassing and sometimes forceful. Men's "rights" to exercise authority intersect with simple control over socioeconomic domains. The father's demand that his daughter not attend college without her sisters, for example, in (8.5) directed the woman's adult behavior into a conventional role of nonprofessional mother and wife, rather than a schoolteacher. For her to have defied this imperative through noncompliance would have indexed her breaking of "doin for" relations, and, in Ash Creek usage, the love for her father and sisters that such indexes symbolize. The father, from a typological perspective, was recreating religiously sanctioned "place" relations by such actions, as justified by numerous scriptural passages.

Contestative Gendered Domains of Appropriate "Doin for" Order Situations

When male appropriate "doin for" imperative contexts intersect with women's, contestation can result when "rights" to authority encounter "rights" to control resources. In these structurally disjunctive areas, individuals assess and reassess the strength of the "doin for" bonds and the "claims" each has on the other through routinized relations of compliance at one end of a continuum, highly strategic creations of competitive "rights" to imperative use at the other end, or positions in between. It is important to note that avoidance of imperatives by discussing each individual's "wants" or "needs" and coming to a compromise or conciliation rarely happens in these types of discourse events. The power of "rights" indexes in the use of "doin for" imperatives, as derived from church doctrine, supersedes recognition of a rational self who can adjust behavior on the basis of mutual decision making or negotiation:[26]

(8.15)

(8.15.1) *Competitive frame:* The male "right" to demand a close woman relative, usually his wife, to prepare a meal for him versus her control over cooked food production. The imperative form from the man is routinely "Fix me some dinner/supper."

Solution 1: Husband's commands are fully honored. In one instance, wife left a medical clinic setting in town, 25 miles away, after six hours of waiting to be examined for a significant complaint, in order to have her husband's supper ready. Noncompliance by the wife was likely to result in physical abuse [notes 9/86].

Solution 2: Husband's commands are met creatively by ensuring a meal is available in the refrigerator as leftovers or something simply needing warming whenever she cannot prepare one, when church, work, illness, or family "doin for" obligations do not permit. Husband agrees to arrangement. [notes 85–87]

Solution 3: Disabled husband prepares supper on evenings wife works; she prepares meals on other days, stocks the larder, and assumes food preparation tasks for large meals, picnics, reunions, or extended family get-togethers. Husband says he likes to cook. [notes 85–86]

Solution 4: Newly married couple eat supper at her mother's house frequently or in town on Friday or Saturday night. Wife states that she's not sure of her cooking yet. Husband accepting arrangement for the time being. [notes fall/86]

(8.15.2) *Competitive frame:* The male "right" to make decisions involving money and the degree of women's freedom outside the home as they relate to women's "right" to oversee childcare and medical care of children. Imperatives are creative, but frequently assume the form "Don't you take him/her there," "Stay at home, your place is here at home," or "No . I wont allow it."

Solution 1: Wife and other women in close "belongin" network take responsibility for taking care of others' children when one is working, shopping, or doing focused labor around the house at no monetary charge to each other. These same women assume decision-making responsibility in regard to medical care and in transporting children to clinics, doctors, or hospitals except in cases of extreme emergency. Husband or wife's father pays the bills. [notes 85–87]

Solution 2: Husband must approve any visits to a doctor or clinic, even in emergency situations. He may examine the child before deciding if a visit is necessary and gives wife the cash to pay the bills when due. Wife's sister frequently prays with wife for healing, and two of them will also decide if husband should be asked for permission. Wife leaves children with biological or church sister with whom she has "claims" when she performs occasional wage-labor, or takes them with her. Payment of services to church sisters is from her labor and is sporadic. [notes fall 86–spring 87]

Solution 3: Wife (a registered nurse) makes decisions about medical care, takes children to medical facility, has medical insurance from her employer to pay medical bills. Pays for childcare provided by a woman of husband's family from her salary. [notes 85–87]

These summations are typical of husband and wife negotiations over valued resources. They reveal the extent of pragmatic constraints on strategic action indexically and denotatively referenced through "doin for" discourse, especially as encoded in imperative forms. These constraints have clear political-economic ramifications. They determine both the scope and direction of compromise or accommodation by spouses. In all cases, the man maintains control over male core economic resources and the woman maintains at least productive control over female resources. The man does not "tell" the woman what to cook or how, nor does he deny the woman "rights" to direct or oversee the rearing or care of the child. Likewise, the woman does not assume control over money resources and adjusts the scope of her control over resources to the man's desired levels of decision making.

Solution 3 in (8.15.2), however, is an anomalous case as the woman assumes economic control over monetary resources as well as childrearing activities, violating core indexes of Ash Creek "doin for" discourse. She is "fotched on" (or "fetched in") from another state as the wife of a local resident and has a bachelor's degree. He has lived away from the area, has been unable to find "good work" in Ash Creek, and has begun college. She has achieved these levels of control under contestation and conditions of financial need. Although their residence in the community is accepted by others because he meets Ash Creek "belongin" criteria, both are removed from the centers of Ash Creek community life and neither is active in local churches. The pragmatic system of "doin for" indexicality is not immutable. Appropriate reproduction of it is, however, a significant, constitutive factor in participating in Ash Creek cultural life and its socioeconomic processes.

Wage-Labor "Doin for" "Order" Practices

When residents must adjust "doin for" order practices to wage-labor situations, particularly in the frequent cases when some or all co-workers are known kin or within their "belongin" networks, they attempt, if at all possible, to extend "doin for" patterns to this new situation just as they do with "helpin out" wage-labor frames with cultural equals. Such workplace practices recreate "belongin" network relations similar to those in family or homeplace events. Among other configurations, waitresses and customers reproduce family food consumptive relations, car mechanics recreate all-male family groupings in which the men "do for" the clients as they do for "belongin" network women, and female medical practitioners are placed into the traditional role of healer, using contemporary prescriptions and medical equipment to provide services inside and outside of the home setting.

Segment (8.16), a service encounter, contains two imperatives within a conversational exchange that constructs a take-out order. Neither speaker has close "claims" on the other, although each meets the basic "belongin" criteria of Ash Creek should they wish to begin them, and each is aware of the other's "rights" to do so:

(8.16) (*Setting: Local diner during midday; interlocutors are Susie, her mother Debbie [patrons], Darlene, who is the only waitress, and I. "Jane" is Susie's niece. Darlene is presumed kin to women, but links are uncertain.*)

Susie: [to Debbie] She should fix Jane one so we can take it home.

[to Darlene] **Dar . fix Jane a plain hamburger and fries an when we gIt ready**

We'll take it with us.

Darlene: **Tell me when you want me to start it.**

Susie: All right. [32b:96 7/86]

This participant framework constructs an event in which "doin for" imperatives *can* be appropriately used and the imperative reflexively indexes this appropriate framework.

Extensions of "doin for" imperatives require that core socioeconomic domains of control be extended from nonwage labor, familial, or kinship settings into workplace situations so that imperative indexical meanings can continue to replicate or reproduce these core domains. In this example, Darlene is extending a woman's domain of cooked food production to a clientele of customers, both male and female, adult and child, as women do in home kitchens. Susie's use of the imperative "Dar . fix Jane a hamburger" recognizes this extension and assumes a discourse iconicity with imperatives used by children to a mother at home. It also marks

Susie's status as a mother who "loves" her child and "does" for her, further binding the waitress to comply.

Darlene's response, "Tell me when you want me to start it," also reproduces "doin for" claims in her willingness to perform the task in accord with the customer's "wants" rather than her own. This shift is signified by the direction of decision making referenced by pronominals: "(*you* tell *me*"). The insertion of a time factor through the semantics of the clause ("when you want me to start it") postpones preparation until the customer is ready. Darlene's acquiescence to Susie's wishes foregrounds the service function of the event as a potentially transitory encounter in which an exchange of money is expected. This utterance results in a slight variation from similar domestic imperative utterances in which the cook may announce when the meal is ready in response to the kinds of negotiated relations presented in (8.15). This variation is minor, however, and sufficient iconicity with Darlene's home "doin for" imperatives remains to extend "doin for" imperative discourse to wage-labor situations without violation of the indexicals they create in "belongin" network contexts. Socioeconomic processes are both transformed and reproduced through multifunctional form/meaning covariation in routine, frequent, and core discursive structures.

As a public interaction, however, this type of restaurant setting presents a number of "doin for" contradictions over the full range of women's typical daily discourse events. First, the basic participant frameworks that form the semiotic foundations of the "doin for" system are questioned by the restaurant situation itself. The public setting creates strong expectation of cash payment for both service and food. This expectation of payment gives employer, employee, and customer "rights" to control action different from those in a home or "belongin" group occasion. The locus of exchange value is shifted from affective reciprocity bonds, or "claims," to capitalistic monetary loci of meaning. The intersections of these two different semiotic systems within a common communicative context promotes contestative relations that frequently end in the sale or closing of the business after relatively short periods of operation. In this case, complaints were that the employer did not pay the waitresses enough; the employee did not collect payment properly or wrongfully gave food away to family members or community preachers; the "wrong kind" of customers patronized the establishment, so other groups of community residents avoided the establishment for fear of moral defilement; and too few paying customers patronized the business, so food spoiled. This restaurant was in business for about one year.

Furthermore, as waitresses, customers, and occasionally the employer gave priority to the replication or reproduction of "doin for" indexes, the capitalistic demands placed on customers' behavior to pay money for food are ignored or significantly redefined without being discarded. Working for wages and waiting on strangers with whom no "claims" exist or can potentially exist create situations in which extensions of these "doin for" indexes and the interpretive schemes that they construct can become highly problematic. For this establishment, one patron used the restaurant as a place to sell Amway products; older children "hung out," killing the day and buying little except perhaps a soda pop or eating some item given to them by the waitress; Bible study became a regular event; and, for a brief period, men who were "on the make" were patrons. Similarly, some waitresses used the phone for long personal calls or conversed at length with family members, other kin, or strangers who were patrons. These interactions maintained or created "claims" relations in the process. In addition, the waitresses sometimes brought dishes made from their own kitchen resources to add to the menu without recouping the food preparation costs.

These extensions of family "doin for" events broaden the scope of appropriate imperative uses and can create the kinds of contestative areas between male authority domains and women's control of resources found in domestic settings. Women become out of "place." Husbands, fathers, brothers, preachers, and other male kin in close "belongin" relations with the women laborers begin asserting authority, "tellin" women either to quit, to modify their at-work behavior (work fewer hours, behave more modestly, or dress differently), or "do" for them at home rather than for the customers. In terms of "doin for" discourse, women are expected to reassume the reproduction of appropriate indexicals rather than transforming them. In brief, men often reassert their control over women's "place" relations. With some exceptions, women attempting to work in Ash Creek generally comply by resigning, often under severe financial hardship, or, in other cases, never seek this type of wage-labor situation.

Segment (8.17) is another example of a service encounter in which a woman extends "doin for" imperatives to a wage-labor context. Although similar to (8.16) in service-focus, this instance represents a more task-bounded situation in which "doin for" extensions are highly restricted to post office–related activities, and where routine monitoring of finances and service is performed by a for-profit federal agency:

(8.16) (*Setting: Local post office in the morning right after mail has been delivered. Man's conversation is with female postal clerk. "Wage card" is a term this individual uses for a mining disability check. The problem is over the man's belief that there is an incorrect name on the envelope so that the check was perhaps sent to the wrong person.*)

Man:	Here's another one a them wage cards.
	Next one comes **let it ((?do a?)) favor for me.**
Postmaster:	What?
Man:	Them wage cards ya know.
Postmaster:	Oh . ((?1.0?))
Man:	No . no .
	That wage card [shows her his card]
Postmaster:	Oh ((?1.0?))
Man:	Yeah.
	That way they show that ((?writin?)) on it.
	My name is William B. Smith.

Postmaster: **Well . if they do**
You just tell me an I'll
I'll probly—
Man: —Mine was laid up for six months.
Them bunch a ((?crooks?)).
[He continues with a commentary on company's alleged incompetence.]
[63a:60 12/85]

It is difficult for this clerk to violate community "place" relations in this setting when she is restricted to standing behind a counter and to handling mail. Despite the workplace setting, "doin for" discourse still occurs in this segment. The clerk responds to the man's direct "askin" ("let it ((?do a?)) favor for me.") by offering to route his check to the right post office box if it comes under a different name. This offering extends a woman's domain of literate labor to the work context. So appropriate is her use of imperatives that the man does not acknowledge the offer verbally or gesturally but continues speaking, overlapping her description of what she would do. In doing so, he violates a rigorously enforced conversational turn-taking norm not to interrupt regardless of gender. The offer has been made, however, and if he complies with the imperative, she will route the mail to the proper location.

The encounter also reproduces one aspect of a significant domain of "doin for" discourse, that of literate activities. A clear division of literate labor exists in Ash Creek in which women perform reading and writing tasks for men under "doin for" constraints. As in this example, these tasks are instrumental or utilitarian, even when reading scripture. This example reproduces this important cultural system, a major source of women's prestige and identity,[27] through "doin for" discourse, marked by the use of an imperative, which indexes an appropriate participant structure of women who perform the literate labor and men who benefit from it.

Nonlocal professional women and men who engage in Ash Creek communicative events invariably use imperatives appropriate to formal institutional hierarchies of professional roles to various degrees,[28] frequently violating "doin for" imperative indexes. They then discuss residents' apparent inability to take advice or follow directions. Those who are able to participate for extended periods in Ash Creek develop an intuitive or conscious awareness of the power of imperative discourse, learning to avoid it:

(8.18) (*Setting: Local medical clinic during open hours. Millie, a nurse practitioner, is in charge of the clinic and is returning the phone call of a mother about her young son who has received a head injury. As one side of a conversation, there are disjunctions in the text as Millie listens to Mary's remarks. I have deleted early responses that contain brief greeting remarks and back-channeling "ok" and "uh-huh" as Mary narrates her son's condition.*)

Millie: Hi Mary?
[deletion—about 1.5 minutes]
Did it knock Im out though?
Yeah
How long did it *take*?
He wouldn't *talk*?
So he'd say that.
Ok
Right
Ok . no headache or anything
Ok
You might just watch Im . ya know
Uh . if he gIt . ya know . start vomiting . ur gIt real *drowsy* ur anythin like that.
Sometimes after they gIt hurt they will ur want a take a nap
An . ya
Right
An . yeah . yeah
An if he wants to this evenin I'd let Im
But I'd wake im up in about an hour an see if he wakes up easy
Yeah . you might want to tonight too every couple a hours
Does he wake up easy usually?
Or is he hard to wake up?
Ok.
Well **just see if he's about like usual . ya know.**
All right?
O:k . Uh-hum. Ok . all righty.
Uhm bye [hangs up]. [61a:377 5/86]

Millie has developed fictive "claims" with this caller and with many residents through church membership and "place" relations as a "sister" in the church. Nevertheless, she cannot develop "doin for" "claims" with residents in her role as a medical practitioner because no clear domain of socioeconomic control exists for women medical professionals in Ash Creek except as their activities overlap with women's healing and nurturing domains.[29] As a woman, she can therefore draw on the domain of healer, for which a "doin for" discourse exists and whose imperative construction repertoire is potentially available for replication or transformation. She does this in (8.18).

Female healers control activities and resources related to the tasks of curing. In constructing a "place" in a "belongin" network, a healer's task-oriented imperatives to instruct or direct curing techniques, including routines in taking medicine, changing bandages, or cleaning a wound, receive positive acknowledgment and are not considered "orders." Conversely, participant frameworks such as the one presented in (8.18), in which Millie's professional skills and expertise are foregrounded to diagnose an illness, require nonimperative requesting forms. Imperative uses would be interpreted as "orders." In this instance, direct imperatives are modified with the modal "might" ("You might just watch Im" and "you might want to tonight"), mitigating "order" status. The verb phrase "might want" within an embedded imperative is uncharacteristic of Ash Creek usage, as it addresses a volitional state to perform a task. Given the instructional force of the clause to perform an activity, "might need" would have been more appropriate. The use of first-person forms in "I'd let Im, but I'd wake im up in about an hour" also avoid construction of "order" discourse, relying instead on common narrative instructional practices. The use of a clear imperative at the end of the discourse segment constitutes an insertion of a formulaic usage common to Millie's medical discourse ("just see if he's about like usual"), followed by a formulaic topic closing ("ya know") and a topic-closing question characteristic of Millie's speech.[30]

A result, however, of these nonimperative uses is that the decision-making professional skill and abilities of the practitioner must become unmarked, refocused as topics appropriate to the nonimperative requesting discourse system of "doin for" pragmatics in the community. To obtain compliance or a voice within these interfacing events, the professional must engage in developing "doin for" relations in particpant frameworks where "claims" can be developed, however unconsciously achieved. In this case, Millie has extended her Christian sister role fully, creating task-focused and "doin for" relations through church identification and participation. As a result, many residents, especially women active in their church, also "do for" Millie by following her "askins" and other forms of nonimperative requesting discourse, talking about the clinic's personnel and clients as a "family."[31]

The examples in (8.16) through (8.18) represent routine, frequent communicative events that reproduce or reconstruct core "doin for" relations. "Doin for" discourse and the imperatives at its center construct socioeconomic relations that work against or possibly in syncretic relations with capital accumulation. These socioeconomic relations favor women rather than men in most literate activities and dismiss or redirect professional decision-making knowledge and skills into resource control domains compatible with Ash Creek gender-based divisions of labor. These are powerful boundary maintenance processes, rooted in the semiotic power of language to create highly meaningful indexes involving constructions of self, domains of socioeconomic control, authority, and "love."

The implications of such structurings are highly significant for socioeconomic articulation with other, more formal and commodity-focused forms of wage-labor marginal to or outside of community life. Functioning as linguistic-economic gatekeeping encounters, these "doin for" wage-labor patterns exclude most outsiders from all but the most transient service transactions because they have service expectations that may not be met in local businesses. Outsider patrons usually come from different linguistic-economic systems in which imperatives that demand labor or services do not index "doin for" participant frameworks. Nor are they familiar with the metapragmatic discursive practices which constitute interpretive schemes for these frameworks. They therefore find themselves complaining about "doing business" locally: prices for them are at or above the going market rate in regional cities while they hear others "get a deal;" the speed of service can be slower because those locals within the "doin for" wage-labor system are given a higher priority; or the service may be less accommodating than that given some valued local customers. Newly arrived professionals find that their skills appear to be unwelcome, that their patronage is low, or that they have difficulty "talking" to locals about change.

Similarly, community residents practiced in such linguistic-economic patterns often encounter service exclusion or personal frustration when they engage in capitalistic commodity-based or sales-oriented interactions with outsiders in local institutions, such as a medical clinic or school, or when traveling to regional cities to "trade" or "do business" with a government office such as those related to welfare, Social Security, or the Internal Revenue Service. Expecting those forms appropriate for "doin for" discourse, they may meet instead professional clinical discourse, educational institutional discourse patterns, formal interview structurings, or other forms of imperative-permitting requesting utterances that demand compliance on the basis of professional status criteria rather than personalized relations rooted in reciprocal labor expectations.[32] Local outlets of regional or national organizations or corporations often participate in a type of syncretism in order to participate in local businesses or services.[33]

Ash Creek residents, especially older ones, frequently choose to avoid any situation in which such interactions are possible, even if it means avoiding the local medical clinic when a certain doctor is present; putting their children in another school, usually private and Christian; or not doing business with a particular store. Outsiders often find themselves leaving the area, often citing residents' inability to use their professional skills or services properly or adequately.[34]

Exceptions to these avoidance practices include "tradin" at mass market chain or fast-food stores in town where service encounters are highly routinized and usually quite brief and where clerks' interactive discourse is usually stylized according to company policy or framed in nonimperative requesting discourse forms of a "volunteerin" type such as "Can I help you?" or "What else do you need?" When such discourse is coupled with electronic bar code scanners, interaction is indeed minimal unless the patron already knows the clerk, which is less common for Ash Creek residents than with those living in or closer to town. Some parents and most younger residents view such places to trade as affordable and yet mainstream (and therefore prestigious). Such linguistic-economic situations circumvent professional imperative discourse and the negative indexical relations of these perceived "orders." Purchasing at these discount stores and restaurants is readily assimilated into Ash Creek cultural life because the basic "doin for" imperative system is not threatened or significantly transformed: the cultural order need not be substantially altered.

Inappropriate "Order" Uses

When discourse conforming to "order" formal features is spoken between two or more interlocutors in neither a "doin for" nor a "helpin out" relationship, or when it is used in contexts in which an appropriate relationship is impossible to create or reproduce (e.g., between two unrelated adult men), Ash Creek residents assign it to the metapragmatic system of "orders." In various ways they designate such speakers as out of "place" and "wrong." "Orders" call into question the existing cultural order, negating, denying, or threatening those very positively valued symbolic meanings associated with appropriate uses and the hierarchy of metapragmatic discursive processes that constitute an ideology of "order" communication. Through violation of the presupposed indexical significations associated with the utterance of them, improper usages also show how these very indexical relations contextualize participant relations, socioeconomic behavior, and the circulation of valued entities. An examination of culturally inappropriate "orders" and order discourse reveals both the junctions and disjunctions in the "order" system, providing a window into those semiotic processes that perpetuate Ash Creek linguistic-economic patterns.

"Orders" or "orderin" is talked about more than observed in Ash Creek daily discourse. Avoidance patterns are so strong and "doin for" relations sufficiently expansive that, unless a resident assumes a "proper" or "puttin on airs" status characteristic of outsiders and those acting as professionals in a formal institutional setting, inappropriate uses rarely occur. When incidences do arise, their ramifications are significant:[35]

(8.19)

(8.19.1) A foreman of the Environmental Center maintenance crew very rarely used any form but task-focused imperatives with his crew, in keeping with cultural rules of imperative uses. Once in midsummer, however, a worker indicated a "need" to take the weekend off and not cut grass, his job, because of an irritating skin ailment. The foreman suggested a solution involving wearing a different type of clothing and long sleeves; the worker indicated it was too hot. The foreman used a bald imperative construction: "You've got to work this weekend or I'll have to let you go." The worker resigned on the spot and was later reported by some to have harassed the foreman and sabotaged some equipment [notes 7/85].[36]

(8.19.2) A local man reported that an outsider visiting the Environmental Center had wanted locals to put their land into a wildlife preserve; he used imperative constructions in making his views known to other men. Residents thought he was "orderin" them to give up their control over the use of their land; the outsider was talked to ("warned") by a neutral party, but felt that he was "right" and continued to talk about the project. His car was made inoperable, and he left the area soon after that. [notes 8/85]

In each of these examples, the participant framework included a requestor whom the requestee perceived as demanding compliance on the basis of the speaker's role as foreman or trained environmental activist. Neither of these roles is one of the Ash Creek choices for "doin for" participant relations. Therefore, neither requestor was recognized by Ash Creek requestees as being "right," in his "place," and as having "claims" over them. Nor *could* "doin for" "rights" and "claims" criteria ever apply because both requestors are of the same gender and relative age as the targeted requestees. Nor was a cooperative task framework established so that "helpin out" task-focused imperatives could be used. Without a culturally appropriate relationship indexed in "order" situations of use, there was no compliance. Instead, destruction to valued "property" resulted.

When Ash Creek residents are left without a pertinent and relevant interpretive scheme within which to frame the "order" as appropriate, they create one, saying that these "orders" embarrass them, "shame" them, hurt their "pride," or make them feel like children. They often conclude with "and I ain't gonna take it." Culturally-inappropriate "order" discourse creates major, significant problems when local residents and professionals from formal, corporate institutions interact and should be examined as a major cause for mobility and labor relations problems. As a constitutive element in creating language socioeconomic relations, its power to create interfactional misfires and nonverbal recriminations characteristic of the far end of the requesting communication continuum (figure 8.2) is encompassing.

"Messages" and "Presents"

Without a means to directly and politely communicate a desire or "need" to modify another's behavior, an insensitive outsider can continue highly resented behavior for long periods with no indication from residents that disapprobation is rampant among members of a "belongin" network or the community at large. Being "nice," or meeting well-developed face-to-face politeness criteria, "don't count for nothin."[37] Ash Creek men and women respond to abrasive and contestative relations from both "belongin" network members and others in a number of ways.

For problematic areas related to moral matters with "belongin" network members, women (occasionally men) will pray over a church member either in the course of a service or in very private settings; if a remonstrance is considered appropriate, a preacher or church member will "give a talkin to" a member of the congregation while "preachin" during a service or in private. These events frequently exhibit socioeconomic implications through the metapragmatic functions of the religious discourse. The ritualized genres of "prayin" and "preachin" provide idealized interpretive schemes for personal behavior that practicing Christians must acknowledge as correct. Not to conform runs the risk of being "out of line" with God and with other Christians and of being rejected from the socioeconomic community ("belongin" network) that church membership represents.

To address more secular, routine problematic relations, the most common communicative patterns used are indirect, metaphorical, and suggestive discourse. It is often presented through quotations from scripture worked into "just talkin," by narrative exempla or parables that address relevant themes or behavior. Speakers may also use first- or third-person narratives about their own behavior or someone else's. For example, one mother needs to somehow tell her sister-in-law that she feels her niece's dating behavior is dangerous or immoral. She narrates a story to her sister-in-law about how she got her own daughter to come home early at night by embarrassing her in front of other family members. Or a man watching another perform a task tells a story about how someone he knows has done that same task, but did it differently.[38] Outsiders frequently fail to recognize these oblique directives, while residents seldom fail to uptake on one.

Though often effective, such indirect means may fail when an individual feels he or she is within her "rights" or "place" to continue a behavior, when "claims" relations are weak or nonexistent among participants, or under idiosyncratic reasons (such as personally acclaimed divine sanction). Under such conditions, other residents may resort to avoidance techniques by moving or changing their daily patterns. For example, a woman begins attending another church, or a man buys his gas at another store. On the other hand, a resident may engage in oblique threats or actual personal violence. Very rarely, and only if the one feeling victimized has strong "takin care of" political relations with the county official, a resident may resort to legal action, a choice that requires an amount of money most residents either do not have or feel would be wasted because of political patronage structures.

An infrequent response to inappropriate "order" discourse, but one preferred over physical violence in Ash Creek, is a set of apparently agentless verbal or material communications that convey opaque, ambiguous, but highly negative affective meanings. Potentially or actually economic in their ramifications, such "messages" or "presents"[39] have a negative sanctioning role as their dominant function, making very clear to the recipient that some action or set of behaviors is intolerable by at least one other resident. They occur in highly problematic areas in which core resource domains are severely threatened or critical cultural relations indexed by appropriate uses of requesting discourse are being severed.

"Messages" may be verbal or nonverbal. Verbal "messages" functioning as warnings are more common than nonverbal. They come into play when someone who is in a belonging relation with other residents is engaged in an action considered potentially harmful or dangerous to him or her, such as when a married woman talks too freely to a man of questionable name. Christians may first bring the matter up indirectly at a prayer meeting, but any resident may also use direct "askin" discourse to request an uninvolved third party to deliver a verbal "message," or an uninvolved party may volunteer to deliver one. This messenger will know the offender and will be in some type of appropriate "rights" and "place" relationship with him or her. Often structured as indirect discourse, these communications suggest that "people are talkin" about something or that "someone is doin" something so that the addressee is clearly informed that given behavior is not acceptable without being accused directly. Both the indirectness and the distance of the speaker from the action obfuscate the actual agency and source of the "message."[40] The burden is then placed on the listener to modify or cease this activity.

Should this not happen, a direct and perhaps violent confrontation is likely between those directly involved.

Nonverbal "messages" are extremely rare, have direct economic ramifications, and are often more negative and dramatic than verbal ones. Addressing core areas of a given individual's personal, gendered domains of activity,[41] these actions are also seemingly agentless, as great care is taken to ensure anonymity. For men, hunting dogs may be poisoned, trucks made dysfunctional or burned, or guns stolen or damaged; for women, negative gossip (a verbal exception with respect to other actions) about their fidelity or other aspects of their reputation may circulate, affecting their marriage or potential for marriage; something personal may be stolen; or a home may be damaged or burned. Nonverbal, action-oriented "messages" are clearly hostile. Without the referential capacity of verbal messages to communicate some level of specificity or without the primitive function of voice to index the identity of the speaker, the nature of the behavior prompting the material "message" is often unclear, as well as the identity of the agent. Talk becomes rampant as residents discuss the why and who involved in such actions. Victims may decide to retaliate against some possible but not necessarily known perpetrator, often at a later time and place. "Grudges" created by "messages" result in highly fractured "belongin" networks in the community until the matter is considered dormant and face-building actions reconstruct "claims" relations among all but the core members involved. If the recipient of such negative sanctions can assign an identity to the perpetrator, accurately or inaccurately, relations can be broken for long periods of up to 20 or 30 years, if not permanently. Should encounters between them happen, or should the shame be considered of irreconcilable proportions, physical violence to persons can result. Sending nonverbal "messages" is highly risky requesting communication.

Still another mode of agentless requesting occurs when residents invert the positive gift-giving structures signifying "claims" (chapter 3) to send an anonymous and negative "present" to an individual to suggest that a specific behavior be altered. These may include, but are in no way limited to, entities traditionally associated with witchcraft such as rotting meat, skin, or bones from lesser valued hunted animals (e.g., raccoon, opossum, or rat). The deeply symbolic significations associated with these forms can be extended to apply to a wide range of putrefying or scatological items, such as rotted garbage or dead wasps, or some purchased product signifying negative personal hygiene, such as soap or deodorant. These items are usually placed on a porch, in a mailbox or newspaper box, or they may be actually mailed. Highly effective, such requesting communication has a potent message of demanding the recipient to reconsider his or her behavior, to abstain from visiting a given setting, or to leave the community.

"Presents" are not typical of Ash Creek interaction and should not be interpreted as such. Rather, they are marked, highly salient communicative modes for directing behavior without committing a resident to the indexicality of self-recognition through face-to-face encounters or to be committed to the complex pragmatic relations of "rights," "place," or "claims." Given the well-developed ability of residents to decode or decipher subtexts within indirect and suggestive discourse, to recognize complex and indirect "volunteerins" in the process of conversation, and to apply conversational metaphors, parables, and narratives to their own behavior, such blatant or hostile nonverbal directives assume a stark, visceral, affective component that calls into question the receiver's integrity and "place" in Ash Creek society at the most primitive level. This basic, primal questioning of self is a conclusion recipients of such "presents" are very aware of as they frame and construct responses to the community "talk" that will always result, regardless of efforts at privacy. Both "messages" and "presents" fracture relations in Ash Creek; when they become rampant, the social order is in serious jeopardy of disfunction or maladaptation.

That portion of an ideology of lingustic-economic communication constituted through use of "doin for" discourse maintains a conjoined and cooperative socioeconomic order through frequent, conventional, and pervasive use of highly interactive, dynamic, and sociocentric speech events. At its focal center is appropriate use of imperatives. These imperatives are fully semiotic events in which referentiality is only one aspect and often a minor component of meaning. The pragmatic and metapragmatic meanings they create or reproduce as constituents of a linguistic-economic communication embed the grammaticality of the utterance in a mesh of socially constructed functions. Many of these functions directly affect the ebb and flow of basic goods and services in the community and organize or disjoin a division of labor. If the pragmatic functions of these discourse forms are significantly redefined to index different political-economic resource domains, then the existing cultural order will be seriously threatened. The existing processes for organizing labor, for acquiring, producing, distributing, and consuming commodities, goods, and labor will be altered, and intersecting domains of personal and gender identity, and extremely basic emotive and affective relations with others, will also be called into question. When Ash Creek residents utter the well-known trope, "Ain't nobody tellin me what to do," they are reinitializing a complex set of pragmatic and metapragmatic interconnections among all levels of linguistic-economic communication from the most contextualized to the most ritualized. In this sense, a person's use of the trope is not personal; it is culturally encompassing, constituting a local system of language and socioeconomic relations.

9 CONCLUSION

"The way we do things is different."

When a female family member suffered a personal crisis, women in her "belongin" network who were also church members got together with her to pray. Afterwards, in talking about the positive outcome from this "prayin," Susie said, "Yeah, buddy, we got a lot of power." [notes 8/88]

One day in 1997 a local woman and I were talking about changes in the community. The acquisition of a volunteer fire department in 1994 was one topic. The local woman related a narrative about a "takin care of" problem between the Ash Creek volunteer fire department personnel and a county politician. She ended by saying, with frustration, "Everythin's political." [notes 8/97]

THIS BOOK BEGAN WITH ANECDOTES about contestative labor interactions in Ash Creek. I suggested that these highly negative responses from laborers were located not in the pathology of the person but in the meanings of the communication constructing the socioeconomic interaction. I can now claim that a significant cause of the conflict lay in the ways in which the imperatives contextualized the various communicative events for the different participants. Ash Creek residents understood the imperatives as "orders" and responded to them in a manner consistent with the Ash Creek patterns of responding to "orders." The effects of the misunderstandings were personal, deeply personal. But the source of the problem was in the different ways the interlocutors interpreted what they heard, not because of abnormal personalities. These processes of interpretation are constructed in the daily interactions of residents in relation to the material world. As a result of this social construction of meanings, they are complex, socially constituted signs and therefore within the cultural realm.

This book argues further that when Ash Creek residents make requests or demands on others within the "needs" system of requests, they are *constructing* the local socioeconomy. This perspective differs from more dominant views about the relationship of language to economics. One dominant view is that language assigns semantic meaning to an exchange, a purchase, or an act of labor in terms of its economic worth (for example, a lamp is worth "$40" or a portrait is a "family heirloom"). Another is that language provides ideological interpretations as a vessel for expressing superstructure (e.g., a state of the Union address may legitimate certain economic policies and reproduce dominant hegemonies). Bourdieu's (1977a) interpretation of language as constructing symbolic value in "linguistic markets" and Rossi-Landi's (1983) interpretation of language as circulating entities in markets where it can have economic value were groundbreaking theoretical attempts to get past these sharply defined dichotomies between language and material realms of economics. Coulmas's (1992) thorough overview also critiques these dichotomies, and sociolinguistic work indebted to Labov (e.g., 1966, 1972) seriously undercuts conceptions of political economic language as only ideological. As Friedrich (1989), Gal (1989), Silverstein (1984), and, especially, Irvine (1989) argued, however, these insights still maintain that relations to materiality are analogous or homologous rather than similtudinous and are rooted in a presumed immutable duality between the verbal and the material. These works directly critiqued the premises on which these dualities are formed and called for more complex formulations of how speech-in-use at the micro-level of actual social interaction constitutes relations to materiality.[1] This book responds to these calls from an ethnographic approach to requests-in-use to show that how Ash Creek residents ask (or do not ask) for things and the meanings these requesting events construct are critical components to the maintenance, reproduction, and alteration in the local socioeconomy. This approach to requests-in-use reveals that they are patterned and systematic. Therefore, the relationship between speech and material socioeconomic entities is more encompassing and complex in its functions than these dominant interpretations have heretofore held.

I adopted an ethnography of discourse approach to how Ash Creek residents ask for *some thing*. This approach shifts the locus of the basic analytical unit from the properties of the utterance or set of utterances alone to that of a communicative event in which speech is one of many possible communicative modes and is "directly governed by rules or norms for the use of [communication]" (Hymes 1972:56). Communicative events become the focus of analysis, and the ethnographic approach permits consideration of them as they interrelate with other communicative events in the community. Interconnections and interrelationships among various instances of linguistic-economic communication become available when the ethnographic approach is fully applied to the speech of a community or, in this case, primarily among members of "belongin" networks who interact with each other regularly.

This ethnographic approach is successful because corporate and formal institutional organizations have little representation in Ash Creek. The Environmental Center is the only formal organizational presence. It is minimally corporate and has developed syncretic work relations with its local staff over its 80-year history. The school system is consolidated, so the nearest grade school is eight miles from Ash Creek and has little direct impact as an institution on most residents' daily lives. As noted in chapter 7, most residents do not work in formal institutional settings; only one works for a corporation in which he is separated from the "belongin" network processes dominant in the community. The kinds of clear and distinct separations between "workplace" and "private life" that lead to methodological problems in anthropological ethnographical research are absent in Ash Creek (see Batteau 1996 for a thorough analysis of these problems).

Furthermore, I am exploring speech in a variety of my native language with which I have familiarity and with many individuals who are accustomed to having nonlocals ask them about how they talk and how they "do things." I will not dispute claims of some cultural anthropological arguments of researcher projections of elitist hegemonies or infusion of subjective interpretations.[2] Indeed, I avoided focusing my research on the most textualized genres of poetic and ritualized language exactly for these reasons.[3] At the more contextualized levels of requesting communication, however, where I can rely on the metalingual and metacommunicative properties of language to clarify, gloss, refer to, and interpret events often through less poetic and more referential language functions, the ethnographic approach is a strength. I make my claims on the basis of it.

Because of the richness of these methods, I have also shown that speech and material communications are often in paradigmatic substitution with each other or are in rule-governed sequences in the taking of turns within a socioeconomic communicative event. In events where requesting verbal communication is most contextualized, if it is present at all, verbal communication is less valued than is nonverbal communication. The significations each creates invert the generally presumed hierarchy of semiotic value given to speech. In these types of events, meaning features of both verbal and nonverbal significations conflate. The boundaries between material and verbal modes of communication blur so that clear distinctions between verbal and material realms do not hold.

Verbal requesting patterns also contextualize the requesting communication through presupposing and creative indexical relations or through denotative reference. In doing so, requesting communication becomes tightly anchored to the social and socioeconomic frameworks in which it occurs, reflexively guiding and shaping how these frameworks unfold and emerge in the ongoing processes of socioeconomic interaction. Who can make a request of whom for what purpose and for what kinds of goods or services is constrained and constituted by the pragmatic and metapragmatic meanings of the communication appropriate to requesting events.

Requesting communication constructs participant frameworks that organize the division of labor in the community. This division of labor is further constrained by delimitations of privileged networks within which an appropriate participant framework *can* be constructed. The most encompassing and richly developed networks are "belongin" ones constructed through uses of attributive possessives in conversational discourse. Requesting communication appropriate to these "belongin" networks usually transforms any commodities or commoditized services into other systems of valuation, especially ones created by attributive possessive constructions.

Requesting Practices and the Flow of Commodities

Requesting communication within "belongin" networks must index certain core relationships among participants and valued entities. These relationships cannot be isolated as independent variables but are deeply interpenetrating valuations of interpersonal, socially focused identities. Residents' assessment of these valuations does, however, define three polarities: "rights," "place," and "claims." "Rights" usually apply to the rectitude of a given request by a specific requestor to a requestee as ultimately legitimated by scriptural authority and as mediated by religious discursive practices. "Place" relations imply the negotiated position of the requestor with respect to others in his or her "belongin" network and with respect to the requestee in a specific requesting event. The strength of the interpersonal reciprocity relationship as it is instantiated in a specific requesting event asserts the status of "claims" relationships. The constant, often daily reassessment of the strength and scope of "rights," "place," and "claims" relations among members of a "belongin" network provides Ash Creek residents with their most basic means of assessing personal identity. It is, however, an identity in constant flux and determined by one's socioeconomic relationship with others and with the valued entities indexed by the communicative form(s) co-present in a requesting event.

The Ash Creek local economy cannot survive by "belongin" network requesting practices alone, however. These practices rarely produce commodities, do not construct the purchase of commodities or maintain commodity market activities, nor do they usually interface directly with county and regional political power networks. Yet many of the goods and services that these practices circulate are obtained in capitalistic markets as commodities or as payment for wage-labor. Ash Creek therefore depends on other patterns of organizing requesting practices within the socioeconomic communicative repertoire.

Residents designate two other major patterns: "takin care of" and "tradin." When embedded in utterances within routine conversational discourse, "takin care of" becomes a metapragmatic designator interpreting interactions in which someone having access to resources, such as capital, commodities, jobs, and professional positions, provides access to these resources for those who do not. "Tradin," on the other hand, designates socioeconomic activities in which each participant exchanges commodities usually through the use of money as an exchange medium.

"Takin care of" relations are the major means by which the highest valued commodities nearly always enter or leave Ash Creek. Exceptions involve the sale of natural resources such as natural gas to a corporation by a local landowner. Even then, the sale goes through county courts where "takin care of" patterns can intervene and affect the sale. County control of valued resources by politically known benefactors ensures that any new capital initiative, whether by corporations, government, or private foundation, will be redirected to local residents through them.

Efforts by nonlocals to circumvent these "takin care of" relations in order to transform these power relations, such as was attempted by the lobbyist in segment (7.10), result in residents' reassigning "takin care of" interpretations to the underlying control issues expressed by the discourse. Or, if those benefactors exercising "takin care of" relations presume that an attempt to transform power from nonlocals or locals is an actual threat, they may engage in seemingly agentless "messages" or "presents" behavior (chapter 8).[4] In either case, local residents are likely to interpret the requesting patterns organizing such efforts as "orders" and respond accordingly.

Those benefactees receiving benefits from "takin care of" benefactors are in turn obligated to provide loyalty through "helpin out" services to these benefactors, sometimes at great personal sacrifice, leading to the frustration of the local woman mentioned in the anecdote beginning this chapter. These acts of fidelity and the requesting events at their core construct specific types of "rights," "place," and "claims" relations. "Rights" may be contested according to the way power is exercised but rarely rejected as long as the benefactor continues to control valued resources. "Place" relations are constructed in terms of these power and control dimensions. They may be minimally asymmetrical, as in the kinds of "takin care of" behaviors found at local mom-and-pop stores, or they may be markedly disparate in, for example, political patronage controlling certain county jobs. "Claims" are *created* through the patronage/client relations that "takin care of" requesting communications construct. "Claims" are not presupposed as a necessary component of a participant framework, as they are in "belongin" network requesting interaction. Common exceptions exist, however, when the interactants can draw on preexisting "belongin" relations to conflate obligations and reconstruct them under "takin care of" constraints. Attributive possessive constructions seldom apply to these "takin care of" relations as they do in "belongin" networks. Constructions such as "my county executive" or "her grocery store clerk" are not appropriate. "Claims" are therefore always risky and precarious. When "takin care of" relations are recognized and relatively developed, however, residents will say so-and-so "owes me" [*predicate referencing what is owed*] or, occasionally, "I owe [person's name] [*predicate referencing what is owed*]."

The relationship between "takin care of" constituencies and "belongin" networks often overlap in Ash Creek and the county at large in part because the population density is relatively low. "Takin care of" benefactors have extended "belongin" networks that intersect with their "takin care of" domains, and benefactees often have "belongin" network members who control valued commodities or capital. Any given requesting event may involve extensive shifts in how residents reconstruct participant frames to strategically manipulate the various relationships appropriate to each. Consequently, "takin care of" constituencies are often very similar to the benefactor's "belongin" networks. With the limited number of county residents having even a minimal mastery over the literate skills necessary to obtain and circulate many types of commodities and capital, many benefactors control several resource domains as well. The requesting practices that constitute the local socioeconomy assume extremely complex presuppositional indexical significations under these convoluted and overlapping socioeconomic and political economic interactions. Some residents find them so confining, in fact, that they welcome opportunities to move elsewhere to avoid them. Others find them supportive and sustaining. None can avoid them.

"Tradin," on the other hand, represents requesting events in which both "belongin" and "takin care of" networks and the "place" and "claims" relations within them are either insignificant or inapplicable. Approximating barter forms of exchange, market commodities change hands in flea markets, local or regional business establishments, or roadside stands. Noncommodities become commodities in dyadic "tradins" of guns, knives, alcohol, or other valued goods in back lots, roadside yard sales, church rummage sales, or under-the-counter exchanges. Cash is usually involved, but not always, and nonbusiness "trades" can involve haggling. As with "takin care of" and "belongin" networks, however, local "tradin" relations often construct participant frameworks that can be reconstructed throughout the exchange to reframe the exchange into a "belongin" or "takin care of" relationship. For example, a local church rummage sale in which items are ostensibly on display for "trade" becomes reframed into a "belongin" "claims" exchange when the vendor's sister takes a garment in exchange for more or significantly less than the marked price. Similarly, the proprietor of a local mom-and-pop store waives the cost of a small item or extends credit to "belongin" network members, transforming "tradin" exchanges to "doin for" ones at the expense of making a profit. Finally, a business in town may discount items to below cost or give them away to those county benefactors in powerful political positions. Or they exercise a two-pricing system—one for commodities sold to those not in the proprietor's "belongin" or "takin care of" networks and a lower price for those who are.

In addition, among men, "tradin" can become interpersonal negotiations often directed by "wants" for the exchange of valuable commodities through "makin a deal" requesting practices. As with straightforward "tradin," "makin deals" can occur within "takin care of" and "belongin" networks.

Constitution of an Ideology of Socioeconomic Communication

Ash Creek requesting discourse constructs pragmatic and metapragmatic interconnections among the full range of verbal and nonverbal communicative practices and genres in the Ash Creek communicative repertoire. How these connections are constructed shapes the organization of labor and the acquisition, distribution, consumption, and deterioration of valued entities in the local socioeconomy. They do much more, however. These communicative processes accumulate in the reflexive, ongoing interactions of residents with each other under an interrelated hierarchical arrangement of indexical meanings. This arrangement of meanings constitutes how residents interpret relationships among material entities and themselves as socially constructed beings. An ideology of socioeconomic communication emerges in how residents reconstitute this hierarchy through nonverbal and verbal interaction. This ideology is actually an amalgamation of numerous personal ideologies that emerge from interpersonal consensus in how similar respresentations of linguistic-economic communication should be interpreted. They guide how residents initiate and respond to macro-level processes of power and political economy.

The hierarchy of indexical significations are of course embedded in communicative forms and practices, and the interrelationship of these forms and practices is constructed by these indexical significations. Briggs (1988:223), Silverstein (1996a), and Urban (1989:43), for example, organize these interrelationships as continua from highly contextualized forms in which the meanings of verbal representations are deeply embedded into surrounding nonverbal situational features to highly textual (or "entextualized") forms in which intratextual relations dominate the construction of meanings. Figure 9.1 continues this linear approach by illustrating a continuum of socioeconomic communicative practices from those most closely aligned with material or laborial productive, consumptive, or distributive acts and to those most removed from them.

Nevertheless, interconnections between various levels of abstraction occur as reflexive presuppostional and creative indexical relations, denotative reference, and retextualization of discursive forms from one level to another. For example, a resident "testifies" in church about how God intervened in a specific daily life activity in well-formed "testifyin" narrative structuring. He narrates what happened using expressions that describe how he almost struck a man because he "ordered" him to do something at work, but "God helped me out" or "God took care of me that day,"so he did not. Meanwhile, while at work, he may pray with others at a break.[5] The verbal practices making up the continuum enfold on themselves in such complexly reflexive ways that the ideology of socioeconomic communication they constitute permeates every facet of Ash Creek life. Residents interpret it as natural, immutable, and, most centrally, God-given.

Political Economy, Power, and Requesting Practices

Those quotidian requesting practices that constitute the local Ash Creek socioeconomy reproduce and create interpersonal and intrafamily expressions of power and control of local resources through "helpin out" and, especially, "doin for" requesting patterns within "belongin" networks. These authority or control relations are often constructed, however, in conventional and routine communicative patterns. Residents frequently do not recognize the requesting communication as willful strategic manipulations of a "wantin," ego-focused self and therefore do not assign them value as constructions of power, although their effects certainly reproduce symmetries or asymmetries in access and control of local resources.[6] Rather, residents recognize that expressions of power reside in more (en)textualized, less contextualized linguistic genres to which they may or may not have access.

The verbal repertoire of Ash Creek includes religious genres of ritualized discourse captured in figure 9.1 to which all residents have access if they are saved Christians. None is recognized as having more power than that of group "prayin." Ash Creek residents frequently pray together as small or large groups generally in church or at home, but also in stores, parking lots, hilltops, graveyards, and any

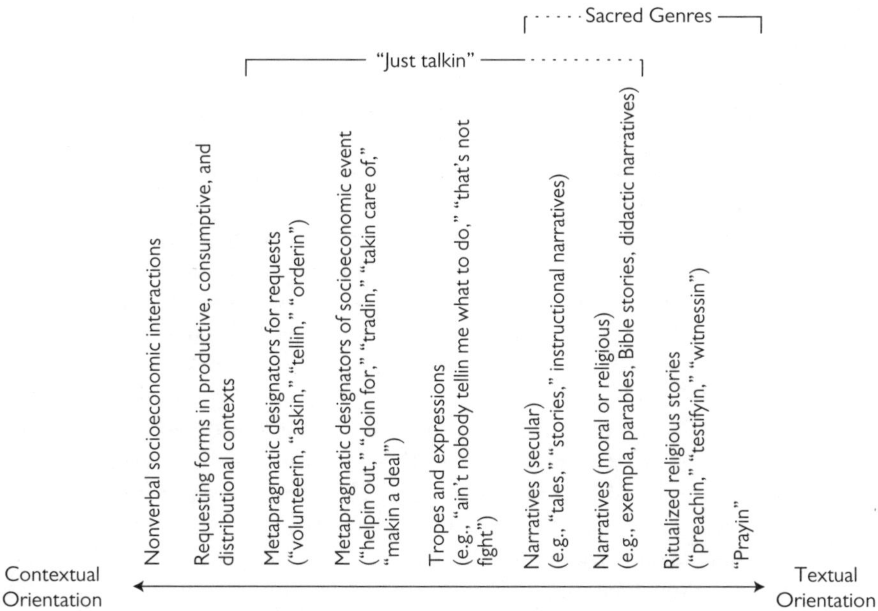

Figure 9.1. Continuum of socioeconomic communicative practices

other local setting, in a performative stance and style consistent with fundamentalist or Pentecostal Protestant traditions.[7] All individuals involved pray simultaneously, each constructing his or her own prayer. This collective act creates a blending of voices under stylized intonation and prosody structures that are diagnostic of the genre. Each prayer makes its own unique contribution to constructing empowering relationships with God.

The referential content of "prayin" is frequently structured as direct requests to God for some divine intervention in human social or socioeconomic life. No verbal genre is more valued, none presumed to be more powerful. None regulates Ash Creek requesting patterns more directly both through providing an idealized template for how requesting participant frameworks should function and through access to divine power, which can provide the entities requested.[8]

Yet the political economic sectors regulating Ash Creek's access to commodities and capital rely on different linguistic genres of power, some literate-based and others requiring mastery of "proper" English and its grammatical variations from Ash Creek speech. Those who have political control over "takin care of" resources are most likely to profess such access accurately or with some exaggeration. These individuals tend to live "in town." None lives in Ash Creek. With the exception of a few former directors of the Environmental Center who were nonlocal but from the region, no one in Ash Creek has access to or mastery of these genres of power and to the requisite participant frameworks they index. Local schoolteachers such as Sally (segment 2.13), and nurse practitioners, such as Millie, may have college degrees, but they are women and they are trained in fields that provide means for syncretic assimilation into the local Ash Creek socioeconomy (teachers and healers) rather than in opposition to it.

At the same time, Ash Creek residents' ideologies of socioeconomic communication (and the more encompassing ideologies of political-economic language) exclude admission of these communicative practices into the local linguistic-economic repertoire. When various professionals representing different fields and disciplines interact with Ash Creek residents, the verbal repertoire they draw on to construct participant frameworks is assigned value and interpreted according to the pragmatic and metapragmatic patterns discussed throughout this book. These professionals commonly find that ways of talking that empower them elsewhere are trivialized and dismissed by residents; the "doin for" "order" continuum may be activated. Residents use these experiences to evaluate those who use similar repertoires of political economic language. Commonly, residents dismiss them, make them the brunt of humorous narratives or insensitive jokes, or use their behaviors as examples of how not to behave.[9] They resort to their own verbal resources of power to disclaim them. But the loci of political economic power and the capital that sustains them do not reside in Ash Creek. The ideologies of political economic language that legitimate them are not only absent from the Ash Creek socioeconomy, they are excluded from it.

Yet the patterns of requesting discourse that construct linguistic-economic events that, in turn, constitute an Ash Creek ideology of socioeconomic communication, are not anti-captialistic. All residents are extremely aware of the power of money, "want" it, "need" it, and consider labor as the major way of obtaining it either through wages or by producing a product (such as garden produce) that is "traded." Many embrace the Protestant work ethic fully, working long hours and at physically trying tasks, although not necessarily for wages.

The irresolvable tensions lie in the constitution of ideologies of powerful language. It is not that Ash Creek residents rely on "prayin" for power or that those from whom "takin care of" benefactors obtain capital and power rely on secular expressions of power such as legal documents, speeches, marketing prospecti, and scientific research. Rather, "prayin" is a member of a complex set of requesting practices that interconnect pragmatically and metapragmatically to constitute ideologies of political economic communication that, in turn, constitute residents' social identities with each other with the material entities they value. At this level it may be appropriate to discuss these irreconcilable differences as cultural differences.

Ideologies of Socioeconomic Communication and Socioeconomic Theory

Concepts, approaches, and arguments by social and socioeconomic theorists rarely appear in this book even when they may seem most applicable. Such omissions are intentional. A more primitive "need" (in its Ash Creek sense) is to explore *how* residents construct language and socioeconomic relations through their use of socioeconomic communication. I assert the linguistic anthropological position that learning how residents construct these relations is rooted in understanding how language-in-use constitutes the material and social life that gives meaning to these constructions (see especially Gal 1998; Silverstein 1998; Woolard 1998 for theoretical statements of this position). In doing so, I agree with Nash's stance that "[m]ost important, [ethnographic acounts] must include the actors' interpretations of the processes in which they are participating, rather than making (as many of them do) preemptive statements purporting to be the authentic etic account" (1992:291). By "actors' interpretations," however, we must consider verbal and nonverbal communications as their own empirical modes of constructing these interpretations, not as interactionally neutral vessels that simply transport constellations of meaning from one mind to another once minimal levels of grammar have been mastered. From this orientation, probing how the indexical "facts" expressed in socioeconomic interaction *systematically* construct relations among social beings, valued economic entities, and language has a more basic value than does manipulation of ethnographic observations and data to support or reject certain socioeconomic models. For by understanding the construction of these processes of systematic interconnectivity, we can develop informed and culturally sensitive theories of the interrelationships between micro-levels of communicative interaction and the macro-levels of political economic ideologies.

This formulation demands an empirical basis. According to Silverstein, "The analytic moment of understanding the 'ideological' grows vividly out of the data of language" (1998:138). Before theoretical concepts can apply, there must first be an understanding of how the "data of language" has significance to those who utter it and how uses of it among a community of speakers construct a hierarchy of interrelated indexical meanings.

Consequently, I minimize application of socioeconomic theoretical concepts to avoid possible applications of the dominant hegemonies[10] expressed in the very constructions of them. My goal is to present residents' own constructions of their ideologies of socioeconomic communication through my writing about them (or "us," for I view myself as a community member) while maintaining a stance that affirms the noetic functions of academic research. This orientation makes clear that Ash Creek residents do not view a distinct, rational separation of the "productive" from the "ideological," nor do they clearly distinguish in many cases between labor for goods and labor for commodities. Nor is Ash Creek fully capitalistic in the sense of separating economic activities from other sectors of social life: "In capitalist society, production becomes a sphere that has a life of its own, one that is cut apart from areas of our experience (work versus play, job versus home, occupation versus religion, etc.)" (Briggs 1988:366). In Ash Creek, production is integrated into nearly all activities through residents' task-focused orientations toward daily life.

But the linguistic-anthropological orientation I assume yields more than these distinctions, which are implied in much of the historical and socioeconomic literature about rural coalfield Appalachian communties (e.g., Banks 1980; Dunaway 1996; Eller 1982; Gaventa 1980; Halperin 1990; Lewis, Johnson, and Askins 1978; Pudup, Billings, and Waller 1995; Whisnant 1981). It yields information about those linguistic-economic processes that continue these interpretive schemes, those constructions of socioeconomic and gendered selves who engage in reproducing or transforming the Ash Creek linguistic-economic ideologies of communication, and their relationships to the constitution of language-material relations. It incorporates a dynamic, emergent, and constructed perspective on the processes of linguistic-economic relations without negating the empirical reality of forms that function to presuppose or create meaning. It allows the merging of linguistic and material modes of communication under a common investigative framework. In this sense, this approach to language-in-use as sets of pragmatic and metapragmatic arrangements of hierarchies of indexical signs closely addresses Voloshinov's axiomatic claims about the "problem of the relationship between sign and existence":

> 1. *Ideology may not be divorced from the material reality of sign* (i.e., by locating it in the 'consciousness' or other vague and elusive regions);
> 2. *The sign may not be divorced from the concrete forms of social intercourse* (seeing that the sign is part of organized social intercourse and cannot exist, as such, outside it, reverting to a mere physical artifact);
> 3. *Communication and the forms of communication may not be divorced from the material basis*. (1973[1930]:21; italics in original)

This book uses this linguistic anthropological orientation to compose a partial account of these relationships. My fundamental purpose is to examine how metapragmatic designators (expressions, tropes, and phrases interpreting socioeconomic activity) organize the requesting communication in Ash Creek for its residents and how this requesting communication constructs the local socioeconomy. It entextualizes these relationships within a continuum (fig. 9.1), a hierarchy of Ash Creek linguistic-economic discursive practices from the most contextualized pole to most textualized pole. This focus, however, requires that each pole of the continuum be neglected for careful analysis of how linguistic-economic practices establishes indexical interconnections across the full range of communicative practices. Therefore, the book steps between the rich and copious scholarship on requests, speech acts, and conversational analysis at the contextualized pole of communicative practices and the extremely complex research on textually developed and ritually valuated verbal genres at the more textualized pole.[11]

These omissions must be addressed more fully to construct a more complete understanding of how not only Appalachian but all ideologies of political economic communication are constituted and how they construct social, political, and economic praxes of power. This is a daunting task but one that must be attempted. Only then will ideologies of political economic language *inform* rather than be made to *conform* to socioeconomic theory, linguistic anthropological theory, and a common theory of culture.

APPENDIX A

PARTICIPANTS

Each interlocutor whose speech is transcribed or who is referenced in transcriptions more than once in this volume are, except for me, assigned a unique pseudonym. This rhetorical device, recommended by DuBois et al. (1993), aids in reading the texts and provides some continuity in recognizing speakers across texts. Following are biographical sketches about each speaker based on 1986 information:

Abe	Young adult man in late twenties who is not from Ash Creek. Married Bill's daughter, Heather, and lives up a holler away from the geographical center of Ash Creek social life. Has two young children. Travels two hours each way to Kingsport, Tennessee, daily for work as an electronics salesman. Family moved from Ash Creek about 1989.
Anne	Nonlocal grade school teacher who moved to Ash Creek as a "back to lander" who wanted to escape the pressures of city life. Taught in county grade school and taught community college extension classes at the Environmental Center. Shared house with Cindy and her children. No longer lives in Ash Creek.
Bernie	Older man born in Ash Creek who is a trained United Brethren minister. Oversees mission on Ash Creek; former Environmental Center director. Has a wife and two grown daughters and one son. Married daughter and family live next to him on family land; son is also a minister who lives at the mission. Bernie passed away in the early 1990s.
Betty	Older, widowed woman born in Ash Creek who ran a local mom and pop store. Store was closed in 1989.
Bill	Older widower in midfifties who works for the Environmental Center as a night watchman. Born in Ash Creek and has strong

"belongin" relations from both parents and his deceased wife's kin. Teaches "whittlin," or woodcarving, for no money to interested outsiders who visit the Environmental Center and some locals. He has two grown children, one male (Jeremiah) and one female (Heather). Both married. He lives on campus. Semi-retired in 1995; woodcarving sessions are now for community residents and are taught in the center's woodshop for free.

Billy	Susie's husband, truck driver from Ash Creek who is often gone during the week on overnight hauls.
Carol	Middle-aged native Ash Creek woman (about 50) who has very well-developed "belongin" relationships through her natal and her husband's family. Husband is a truck driver; has two children, one male, one female. Daughter graduated from high school, was going to college. Carol is a part-time cook at the Environmental Center.
Chuck	Non–Ash Creek man in his late thirties who was an underground coal miner. His wife, Karen, is from Ash Creek and is Carol's sister. Chuck and Karen moved to Ash Creek to live on family land after Chuck became physically unable to work in the mines. Chuck was briefly maintenance foreman at the center. They have one son. They no longer live in Ash Creek.
Cindy	Non–Ash Creek widow in her midthirties from an adjoining county. Has six children, five boys and one girl, all under sixteen. Lives with a grade school teacher, Anne, who is not from the region. Worked temporarily at the center as a maintenance worker. No longer lives in Ash Creek.
David	Karen's son about nine.
Debbie	Non–Ash Creek middle-aged woman (about 47) from another area of the county who married an Ash Creek man. Now lives on husband's family land. Husband, a former heavy equipment operator, receives disability payments. Has five grown children, four grandchildren, all living in Ash Creek area. Two married daughters live adjacent to the house. Carol and her husband live next door. Debbie is a full-time cook at the Environmental Center.
Devon	Non-local teaching staff member of the Environmental Center. Has a master's degree, wife, and two children. Left after one year.
Dillon	Ash Creek resident by birth who is in his midfifties and is married to Sarah. Has worked at the Environmental Center for at least 30 years as its farmer. Two married children who do not live in Kentucky.
Doris	Grade school teacher in her thirties from Ash Creek. Married a local man and has two preteen children.

Dorothy	Ash Creek resident from birth, middle-aged widow (about 52). Husband was a coal miner. Dorothy reupholsters furniture and works part-time as a cook at the Environmental Center. Has three children, two married daughters and a young adult son who lives with her. Lives on husband's family land. Chuck and Karen live next door.
Edward	Nonlocal resident in his seventies. Retired Environmental Center director. Has a valued "name" in the community for his educational efforts over a forty-year period. College educated. Two sons, married and living elsewhere. Married to Elizabeth. Lives in center campus housing.
Elizabeth	Nonlocal resident in her seventies. Retired Environmental Center assistant director who also teaches environmental classes to outsider students for free. Also has a valued "name" in the community. Married to Edward. Elizabeth passed on in 1992.
Heather	Bill's daughter in her twenties. Married to a nonlocal man with two children. Took some community college classes at the main campus. Moved from Ash Creek in 1989.
Joan	Young married woman in her early twenties. High school graduate who lives in an area adjoining Ash Creek. She and her husband left Ash Creek for Florida. They lived there for about one year and returned. No children during fieldwork period.
Karen	Locally born woman in her thirties. Married to Chuck and has one son, David. Environmental Center office staff worker for about three years. No longer lives in Ash Creek.
Kaziah	Older woman born locally. Makes and sells crafts and has participated in center activities as a paid demonstrator for two decades. Husband retired from government forestry position. Kaziah died in 1991. Her husband died soon after.
Linda	Locally born woman in her fifties. One of the full-time cooks at the Environmental Center. Divorced with two grown daughters who are married with children. Has worked as a cook in major national tourism locale. Moved from Ash Creek in the early 1990s to live close to her daughter in an adjoining county.
Madeline	Assistant director of the Environmental Center while I was living there. From out of state. Moved after two years.
Mable	Locally born woman in her forties. Two adult daughters, one teenage son. Married a local man who drives a truck. Took community college extension classes. One daughter a college graduate.
Mary	Locally born woman in her late seventies married to Tom. Gardens and has four or five middle-aged married children. Mary passed on in the early 1990s.

Millie	Trained nurse practitioner from out of state. Managed local clinic on Environmental Center grounds from 1983–1994 when clinic closed. She moved to an adjoining county to work at another clinic.
Rebecca	Mable's younger sister. Locally born, married nonlocal man who drives a truck. Has six children. Has taken community college extension classes. Currently works for the Environmental Center in community programs.
Robert	Locally born man in his late forties. Preacher for local church. Married a local woman. Has three adult children. Drives a truck.
Sally	Locally born woman in her early thirties. Elementary school teacher. Divorced, no children, living with her parents. Married in 1991.
Sandy	Locally born woman in her early sixties. Married with four adult children. Two live out of state. Married a local man who is retired/disabled. Lived and worked in Ohio for several years. Full-time cook for the Environmental Center.
Sarah	Locally born woman in her early fifties. Married a local man and has two adult children who are married and live out of state. She is the head cook at the Environmental Center.
Susie	Locally born woman in her late twenties. One of Debbie's daughters. Married a local man who drives a truck on long hauls. Has three young children. Does temporary part-time labor in Ash Creek.
Sam	Bill's son in his early twenties. Married with one child from a previous marriage. Worked at the Environmental Center for several months as a maintenance worker. No longer lives in Ash Creek.
Tammy	Locally born woman in her early twenties. Graduated from regional college. Single, worked for the Environmental Center for about one year. Moved from Ash Creek for work shortly after I arrived.
Terri	Locally born woman in her early fifties. Married, two adult children who are married and live out of state. Husband is retired heavy equipment operator who now enjoys traveling to flea markets to obtain collectibles. Has a large garden and engages in limited cash cropping of vegetables.
Tom	Non–locally born man in his seventies who sells his garden produce for income. Married a local woman and has four or five middle-aged children who are also married. Linda is his daughter. Tom died in early 1990s.

APPENDIX B

SUMMARY OF DAILY ACTIVITIES

Routine Activities for Men

Age +40 (grandfathers)—Disabled (*N* = 3)

Daily

Travel by truck to:
- Hunt/be in woods
- Talk "politics" with known political officials or kin
- Obtain alcohol
- "Make deals" or "trade" or talk to businessmen about deals

Garden/outside projects around house

Hang around house/local stores or garage, talking

Visiting with other family members

Watch television/videos at home at night

Weekends

Same as weekdays except more expansive family get-togethers and visits

Occasional

"Help out" a male neighbor/kin in a project

Travel to some regional town or city for "tradin," medical care, or to confirm a "business" deal

Attendance at local public or school meetings having political implications (for example, water meeting, road meeting)

Attendance/participation at marriages/funerals

Age +40 (grandfathers)—Working for Wages (*N* = 4)

Daily

Wage-labor, co-workers usually kin, in coal truck company supervisory or maintenance work (3 men)

"Helpin out" at family mom-and-pop store (retired coal truck company owner) (1 man)

Outside or repair chores at household

Visit with children/other family members

Watch television/videos at home after work

Weekends

Sporadic attendance at church services

Larger, more formal family supper or visiting

Travel to town for necessary food and other supplies on Saturday

Outside or repair chores at household

Occasional

Travel to "trade" for truck or other expensive item (all men)

Trips away from community area with other male kin to fish, do "business," or attend church conferences (2 men)

Attend or participate in funerals or marriages (all men)

Provide labor for family emergencies (trips to regional hospitals, grave preparation, protect a young person at an event, etc. (all men)

Age 18–40 (married) (*N* = 15)

Daily

Work (wage-labor) (mining, truck driving, maintenance work) (12 men)

Not working full-time/permanent (3 men): looking for work or engaging in temporary jobs (for example, carpentry, temporary truck hauling, seasonal work at environmental center)

Outside or home repair chores

Visiting with buddies who are of similar age and kin or with close male family members

Nonworkers: travel to town to discuss deals or trade

Engage in cash activities (for example, bootlegging, cockfighting, marijuana growing); more frequent among unemployed

Weekends

Church-related activities (1)

Outside chores and repairs (especially for those working)

Extended visiting with family members

Travel to town to eat out/"trade" with wife or family

"Party" (2 men)

Hunt/fish/be in woods (especially for those working)

Occasional

Attend/participate in marriages or funerals

"Vacation" trips with wife or family to King's Island Amusement Park (Ohio), Dollywood (Tennessee), county fairs, fall festivals, or a lake

"Help out" a male family member or "neighbor" (distant kin or church member) in a complex construction or repair project

Attend school basketball or football game

Age 16–25 (Single) (N = 2)

Note: Most single men of this age group leave the community temporarily or permanently to find work or, in one case, to go to Berea College; this sample represents one young man living at home with his mother, father deceased, and another who has left the community and then returned and who was frequently gone to visit other male kin living elsewhere.

Daily

Attend community college classes (1 man)

Scout for temporary or permanent wage-labor or cash work (1 man)

Visit or travel with other male family members

Do outside chores and repairs for mother (1 man)

Ride four-wheeler with passenger or alone (1man)

Visit with current girlfriend when possible (both men)

Run errands for mother in town or in community (1 man)

Homework (1 man)

Weekends

Travel to an event (e.g., high school sporting event, gospel sing, fair, country-western performance at a festival) (1 man)

Going out on a "date" involving travel to town for a meal, cruising around, drinking (1 man), attending church functions (1 man), going to town for videos and watching them at home, or attending an event

Homework (1 man)

Occasional

Cash labor in temporary work (e.g., driving a truck (1 man) or mowing grass (1 man)

Attend or participate in marriages or funerals

Travel with mother to deliver products of her home business or to perform some family business (1man)

Routine Activities for Women

Age +40 (grandmothers) (N = 7)

Note: Two women in this age category earn cash through cottage industries. Dorothy (a widow) reupholsters furniture in a shed on her property; the other (Kaziah) makes and sells crafts such as corn shuck dolls, flowers, knitted products. These two women, who frequently travel to market or deliver their goods are not included in the following summary.

Daily

Household activities (cooking, cleaning, washing, stoking heating stove or stoker [one has oil heat], if chickens are present, feeding them or collecting eggs)

Usually some childrearing activities with grandchildren from babysitting to cooking for them to going to used clothing center at local church to look for clothes or making clothes

Gardening/canning (For older women, gardening begins in February and ends in late November or even December)

Visiting with daughters or other women in family

Telephone conversations with women kin (2 exceptions)

Wage labor (3 women) in women's tasks (cooking, cleaning, health care)

Prayer meetings and Bible study (once or twice weekly, visitations to sick church members for prayer, faith healing)

Watch television or videos at night/listen to radio during day

Weekends

Church activities

Extended and more formal visits with family, often involving a Sunday dinner

Watch television or videos

Clean house after family visits and dinner

Occasional

Activities with husband (if alive) such as fishing, picnicking, travel to town for "tradin"

Gospel sings or revivals

Church conferences in Frankfort, Kentucky, or Cleveland, Tennessee (2 women)

Travel to craft events (1 woman)

Travel to shop, attend festivals/events (e.g., Dollywood, outlet stores in Pigeon Forge, Tennessee, flea markets) (Husband must accompany if alive, but widows will go with sisters or other women family members [2 exceptions])

Attend or participate in marriages/funerals (Women always prepare food for these events unless they are among the bereaved)

Travel to town with other women to "trade" for groceries, clothing, or household items (uncommon, about once per month, unless in company of husband)

Age 17–40 (married with children) (*N* = 9)

Note: This group is the most diverse in terms of daily activities, as several are entering the wage-labor market under severe economic stress within the family.

Daily

Home maintenance and cleaning

All activities related to food preparation and serving

Visiting with mother (if local) or mother-in-law (if alive)

Childcare and childrearing activities (including school activities, medical care)

Church activities (prayer meetings and Bible study; faith healing of ill church members)

Gardening (2 women) (Note: Most of these women obtain garden produce from their mothers or mothers-in-law)

Home product sales (Amway/Avon/Blair), paid babysitting, or temporary/part time wage labor in seasonal activities, temporary government-funded projects at Environmental Center, or at local diner/post office/store

Wage-labor full time at gender appropriate jobs (6 women) (e.g., teacher's aid at gradeschool, secretary at mining company, grade school teacher, nurse's aid)

Weekends

Church activities

Extended and more formal visiting with family members, often including Sunday dinner at "Mom's"

Occasional

Activities with husband: fishing, trips to accepted regional events (Dollywood, King's Island, etc.), target practice, picnicking.

Attendance or participation at marriages/funerals (Women always cook food for these events unless they are among the bereaved.)

Summer church camp teachers or participants if their children attend

Attend revivals/gospel sings

Travel to town to "trade" for groceries, clothing, household items (Visits vary: two women travel 2–3 times weekly; others usually once a week or once every two weeks, unless with husband on weekends)

Age 18–30 (single) (N = 2)

Note: Unmarried women in this age group do not stay unmarried in Ash Creek very long after high school graduation. Those who do not marry are either in college (University of Kentucky [1 woman]; Alice Lloyd College [1 woman]; local community college [1 woman]; Berea College [1 woman], or have finished college and moved to a more urban area for employment [1 woman]; the two women reported below live with parents. One is divorced, the other is saving money by living with her widowed mother.

Daily

Work as gradeschool teacher or bookkeeper in town

Do household chores

Attend community college classes or perform projects such as craft activities

Involved in county educational activities, attends various meetings (1 woman)

Visit extensively with women friends and family of same age (Friends were generally met in college, through marriage, or through work-related contexts)

Weekends

Date, socialize with women friends, attend craft events or other regional events including country music performances; shop at regional cities; eat dinner out; visit tanning salons, hairdressers in town

Most frequently, shop and visit with women friends in community

Occasional

Attend regional meetings related to work; take weekend trips

NOTES

Chapter 1

1. The literature on these interpretive processes as they apply to coalfield Appalachia appears in all disciplines and in fiction. I suggest, as particularly helpful for this discussion, Corbin (1981), Davis (1984), Ury (1982), and Whisnant (1983).

2. For those familiar with this region, further description of the topography, local businesses and institutions, and of the residents themselves in other sections of the book will dissolve any anonymity this pseudonym may convey. Nevertheless, I felt it necessary to conform to both federal guidelines regarding the use of human subjects and the American Anthropological Association's Statement on Ethics (1990) by introducing at least some element of anonymity to protect residents from potentially harmful interests. Similarly, all names of residents are fictitious as are any references to place or business names. In discussing this book, some residents indicated they would like to have their real names used; others did not. Use of real names for some and not others would have allowed readers familiar with the area to infer the identity of those fictionalized. I therefore chose to use aliases in all cases.

3. By "peripheral" I do not mean "marginal" in the sense of extraneous or expendable, but "exporters of agricultural and extractive products . . . forming the 'periphery'" (Hopkins 1982:19), which are necessary to maintain "core" economic areas that export manufactured goods. This usage is in keeping with Wallerstein (1974), whose model of global economics has been applied to the history of Appalachian land ownership and use patterns in intriguing ways by Dunaway (1996).

4. One significant difference between Roadville and Ash Creek is in reading and writing. Many residents of Ash Creek do not read or do not read well or often. One young mother in her twenties reported that she used to read but found that she "uses" it so seldom now that she has just about forgotten how. This devaluation of reading among many families means that the interactive patterns described by Heath (1983) do not apply. For those families who do read and write often, reading patterns with their young children conform to Heath's findings.

5. Social historical and cultural anthropological works which have addressed these presuppositions in various ways include Anglin (1992, 1993, 1998), Eller (1982), Fisher (1993a, 1993b), and Whisnant (1981). See also other articles in Fisher (1993c).

6. I am using "heteroglossic" to capture the multichanneled and polysemous meaning of *possibilities* that Bakhtin (1981) captured in his coining of this term, a distinction Duranti (1994) developed fully in his analysis of Samoan language and political economic relations.

7. By "utterance," I mean a unit of speech that is a spoken analogue to a "sentence" (Levinson 1983:18). Irvine (1996) discusses the importance of "utterance events" as distinct from "speech events" because of their ability to index specific participant roles, roles that may change over the course of a speech event.

8. In Halliday and Hassan's (1976) sense of abbreviated syntactic units.

9. As an "index" to what is becoming a voluminous bibliography of sources, allow me to suggest Hanks (1996b), Lee (1997), Mertz and Parmentier (1985), Parmentier (1994), Silverstein and Urban (1996a), Urban (1991, 1996b), and most centrally, Silverstein (1976, 1979, 1981, 1985, 1993, 1996a, 1998).

10. Certain sociolinguistic studies modeled after methods and theoretical frames developed by Labov (1966, 1972) have made contributions to the understanding of class, gender, and educational achievement issues in coalfield Appalachia (e.g., Blanton 1985, 1989; Christian 1978; Christian, Wolfram, and Dube 1988; Wolfram, 1977; Wolfram and Christian, 1975, 1976; Wolfram and Fasold, 1974, and Wolfram and Schilling-Estes, 1998). These studies assume these straightforward definitions of index in which a particular component of the speech string indexes some presumed sociological or socioeconomic variable such as class, gender, or educational level.

11. Gumperz (1982, 1992, 1996) discusses how prosodic features, among others, are critical in disambiguating affect and intent. Lutz and Abu-Lughod's edited volume (1990) marked recognition of the political dimensions of affect and emotions as expressed in indexical signs (see also Urban 1996b). Haviland's (1996a, 1996b) focus on gesture is also groundbreaking, showing how affect is culturally constituted through indexical signs.

12. I take this geological metaphor from Duranti (1997), Graham (1996), Silverstein (1998), and Urban (1996b). Its connotations of encrusting discursive forms with immutable or nearly immutable particles is apt for Ash Creek usages.

13. This example is an adaptation of Silverstein's (1996a) reanalysis of Brown and Gilman's (1960) and Ervin-Tripp's (1972) pioneering analysis of how variation in terms of address indexes different social roles and statuses in context. Hanks (1992, 1996a) and Irvine (1998) also apply concepts related to creative indexicality in their reconsiderations of honorifics and the constructions of participant roles.

14. Gal's (1989) overview of the literature began this explosion, but the articles in Schieffelin, Woolard, and Kroskrity (1998) capture more systematic applications of these theoretical developments, reflecting the power of this integration of disparate methods, approaches, and models in linguistics, linguistic anthropology, semiotics, social theory, and political economic theory.

15. Woolard's review (1998) is outstanding in its grasp of the issues, its scope, and its clarity. See Woolard and Schieffelin (1994) as well.

16. Subsequent linguistic anthropological critiques of Searle's speech acts develop the implications of Rosaldo's observation thoroughly and from philosophical perspectives. See Hanks (1996b) and Lee (1997).

17. For example, Drew and Heritage (1992), Ervin-Tripp (1976, 1981, 1996), Ervin-Tripp et al. (1987), and Weigel and Weigel (1985).

18. Economic anthropologists have made a distinction between economy and political economy from the outset (e.g., Herskovits 1952; Polyani, Arensberg, and Pearson 1957; and Sahlins 1972). Economic anthropology has tended to focus on material rela-

tions to production, distribution, and consumption (Halperin 1994; Ortiz 1983). I use the prefix socio: to emphasize the relationship of economic patterns to social relationships, in keeping with recent theoretically diverse works on the construction of cultural meaning of economic items through their relations to social relations (e.g., Appadurai 1986; Gregory 1982; 1997; Gudeman 1986; Halperin 1994; Munn 1992; and Weiner 1992).

19. I use "symbolically" in a Peircian sense of "'general signs,' that is, signs which have the identity they have . . . independently of any concrete speech events or contexual application" (Parmentier 1994:7). Symbols also grounded in "conventional associations" which are not context dependent (Parmentier 1994:27).

20. The social and psychological dualities and conflicts these contradictory valuations can have on personal identity have been aptly and poignantly portrayed in Jennings (1998).

21. I am deliberately vague in some details about Ash Creek in order to give some modicum of anonymity to it and its residents. What I call the Environmental Center has a long and nationally recognized reputation. Citing certain details would immediately tell many regional readers exactly where I was.

22. In keeping with linguistic anthropological norms, I use Appalachian English words for local topographical features. I do not gloss them if they appear in a standard American English dictionary, as "holler" does.

23. As hubs of county activity, Eastern Kentucky coalfield towns (greater than 2,000 populations) are multiethnic. Doctors are often foreign-born; coal-company personnel, chain-store managers, and state-agency personnel are often nonlocal, if not from out of state. With very few exceptions, political power, however, is vested in locally born white families.

24. Appalachian reckoning of kinship through highly developed discursive practices organizes most residents' activities and social interactions. Cultural anthropological discussions consistent with the types of interactions I found in Ash Creek can be found in Batteau (1983a, 1983b), Beaver (1986), Bryant (1983), and Hicks (1976). These ethnographic accounts detail the strength of the gender-based reciprocity relations facilitated by "kinship structures," their contribution to the replication of patronage-oriented political structures in which males negotiate votes for power, their primary role in shaping religious expressive practices, and their central place in organizing community interactions. Batteau's (1983b) insight that "privacy" begins at the foot of a holler rather than at the front yard is helpful in understanding Ash Creek residents' organization of land. Those living along the sides of the creek are making a statement of being more "public" and accessible than those living up Jones Holler. My claim, however, is that these kinship relations are constituted through communicative systems, not given *a priori* by virtue of certain objectively recognized blood relations (chapter 2).

25. Kentucky health laws regarding food preparation were not violated.

26. McCauley's (1995) seminal work on what she calls Appalachian Mountain religion is comprehensive in its discussion of the historical, social, and religious significance of this concept in coalfield Appalachian churches. She argues that the "community of saints" is not deviant from Protestant Christian practices, but in a direct line from the seventeenth-century Pietist traditions of protestant Scotland.

27. Among the most comprehensive treatments of this period in terms of its impact on Appalachia are Blackside (1995) and Bowler (1985).

28. For discussions of this pattern from an historical perspective, see Beaver (1986) and Eller (1982).

29. Figure 1.1 is a close approximation of Ash Creek. Digitalized topographic data from the United States Geological Survey were used to create it. I have, however, changed the arrangement of some architectural features for purposes of anonymity.

30. Beaver's (1986:52–53) discussion of changes in three western North Carolina communities can apply here, although the shift to a view in which the area is "a series of roads flowing vaguely from one intersection to the next" is not yet total in Ash Creek.

31. Coal mining was still a major industry generating jobs in the mid-1980s. It is no longer. Logging has become a major extractive resource activity in the last few years.

32. Many Ash Creek young adults leave Ash Creek for work in regional cities where most are employed in various heavy equipment or construction industries. Some join the military. How they adjust their requesting patterns to these new situations is a matter for comparative research.

33. Accepted discussions of coalfield Appalachian settlement history are currently under significant scrutiny. The dominant pattern has been that Scots-Irish, German, Welsh, northern English, and a small percentage of Swiss settled the region from about 1720–1820 on small, independently owned homesteads (Beaver 1986; Eller 1982; Fischer 1989; Mitchell 1991). Dunaway (1996), however, calls these settlement patterns into question through detailed analysis of absentee landholding patterns during the period.

34. On several occasions, I found myself being "preached at" during religious services as preachers condemned the kinds of behavioral pitfalls education can lead one into. I found that much of their commentary had merit, especially in terms of reconstituting the kinds of ideologies of linguistics-economics this book touches on.

35. The kinds of "back to lander" situations described by Beaver (1986), where urban professionals settle in rural Appalachian areas to get away from urban problems and to experience "nature" more directly, have not occurred in Ash Creek, presumably because its infrastructure is problematic and it is too close to surface coal mining activities to be attractive.

Chapter 2

1. This claim should be interpreted not as a reassertion of the concept of "private property" as being fundamental to political economic theory but as an encouragement of thought about some possible relationships between the possessive relations discussed in this chapter and the legacy of Puritan political economic constructions of self via Locke. McCauley's (1995) arguments regarding Appalachian Protestant religious traditions make clear the choice involved in maintaining Calvinist and Pietist sixteenth-century religious encodings of a "willed" self in relation to a diety. MacPherson's (1962) discussion of how Puritan conceptions of individual possession and property were reflexively expressed in sixteenth-century English political philosophy may also apply.

2. For example, studies of Melanesian exchange systems have delimited how personal biographies are infused into the life histories of exchange items. The meanings of highly valued exchange items are intrinsically related to both the spheres of circulation into which they pass and qualities of character publicly known by those who possess them. See Damon (1990), Gregory (1997), Munn (1992), and Weiner (1992) for elaborations of this point. For a pertinent and related discussion, see Appadurai (1986) and Hoskins (1998).

3. Foremost among this scholarship is the work by Mertz and Parmentier (1985) and Parmentier (1985, 1994). This shift in focus has opened up explorations of cultural constructions of self in relation to nonselves through different forms and levels of

semiosis constructed through, in Bakhtin's (1981) words, "the dialogic" nature of human communication.

4. By "conversation analysis," I mean the methods and theories initiated by Garfinkel (1967), Schegloff (1972), Sacks, Schegloff, and Jefferson (1974) and related to an ethnographic study of discourse in Moerman (1988) and in Hopper 1990–1991). "Turn-taking" and "adjacency pairs" are basic concepts in this tradition. "Turn-taking" is the patterned exchange of conversational contributions by cooperative interactants. "Adjacency pairs" are routinized expectations about how a particular type of turn should be structured. An example is that of a telephone greeeting: "hello" is followed by an identification of some type from the caller. Advocacy of conversation analysis in ethnography of discourse scholarship has been discussed by Sherzer (1987a) and prefigured in the work of Hymes (1981).

5. The accepted point of view on possessives has been to view them as a type of locative in which the possessive construction indicates where the referenced possessed noun is. See Lyons (1977:722–723).

6. See Fox (1981), Heine (1997), and Taylor (1996) for comprehensive discussions of this reassessment.

7. The saliency of tropes about culturally constructed forms of possession permeates scholarship on the region along the dimensions of personal items, extended family control of resources, and usufruct of land. The early nonfictional literature was particularly emphatic in its discussions of these domains. See, for example, Campbell (1921) and Kephart (1922).

8. To not misrepresent Parmentier, he does go on to say that this typology should not be taken too seriously because of its overgeneralities (1994:109). For a critiques of this simplistic quality, see Hill and Irvine (1992).

9. Discussion of the ways these popular images have been created is provocatively captured first by Shapiro (1978) and later by Batteau (1990).

10. I am indebted to this perspective on land tenure disputes to Duranti (1990). See also Besnier (1990) and Hoskins (1998).

11. The full range of English possessive constructions as expressed by Ash Creek discourse is open to further exploration. Studies such as Heine (1997), Lyons (1977), Taylor (1996), among others, distinguish between attributive possession of the type "John's cow" in English and predicative constructions of the form "John has a cow" in English. Predicative constructions using "have" are rare in Ash Creek, however. Strongly preferred are "got" constructions of the form "John got him a cow" or "Jill got her a husband." Furthermore, "of" possessive constructions of the type "child of mine" are also problematic because of the habitual function of certain "of" constructions as in "He takes a walk of an evenin" where "of" expresses a habitual, expected sense of doing this activity every evening. These grammatical variations from standard written American English constructions suggest different meanings and functions of possessives as well.

12. For a discussion of these personal pronominal variants, see Blanton (1989), Shopen and Williams (1980), C. Williams (1992), Wolfram and Christian (1976) and Wolfram and Schilling-Estes (1998).

13. This type of argument for a relation between grammatical categories and thought as a mediator for cultural categories can be traced to Whorf (1956 [1939]) and Sapir (1921, 1966) under the rubric of "linguistic relativity." I am, however, making this assertion in light of recent reassessments of this area. As Gumperz and Levinson (1996:9–10) have stated, "the issue of linguistic relativity shifts significantly. From an 'inner circle' of links between grammar, categories, and culture as internalized by the individual, the

focus shifts to include an 'outer circle' of communication and its relation on the one hand to interaction in social settings and on the other hand to individual patterns of cognition which are partly contextually attuned."

14. See Hawkins (1981), Heine (1997), Quirk et al. (1972, 1985), and Taylor (1989, 1996) for semantic discussions of types of possessive constructions in English and Deane (1987) for a discussion of animacy hierarchies in English possessives. This study focuses less on the types of possessives possible in Ash Creek discourse as on those language and culture processes that constrain the use of those common constructions that intersect with socioeconomic domains.

15. Framing, as used here, is indebted to Goffman's reformulation of Bateson's (1972) coinage of the term. Goffman (1974:10–11) assumes "that definitions of a situation are built up in accordance with principles of organization which govern events—at least social ones—and our subjective involvement in them; frame is the word I use to refer to such of these basic elements as I am able to identify."

16. Ericson and Schultz (1981) applied the metaphor of "gatekeeping" to job interviews in order to show how lack of knowledge about and mastery of interactional frames and conversational structures can become very real barriers in gaining access to professional positions for which an individual may otherwise be qualified.

17. Conversations often include an evaluation of a local or county professional in terms that rarely mention the person's professional credentials but often mention his or her "same as anybody" criteria. One doctor in town, for example, was discussed as a man who ran a backhoe, hunted, and fixed up his place "like the rest of us." He was considered a very good doctor. One common indicator of at least marginal "belongin" status is verbal in the form of various tropes such as "She talks just like we do" or "He don't talk like he's above us." I obtained a type of "belongin" status by entering the community by living at the Environmental Center for a year and by teaching county community college extension courses at the center. Once the center director introduced me to center maintenance staff and I got to know them, some, in turn, would introduce me to others in the community as either a teacher for the college or as a person living at the center. As I got to know and talk more with local residents, a ripple effect occurred. I would be introduced as Debbie's friend at the center or Anne's friend, the teacher, or just Linda's friend (or buddy). In large part due to the long history of the center's policy of having student teachers, interns, and temporary teachers, this teacher role was well recognized by Ash Creek residents and one they could experientially relate to. My speech varied from academic American English to urban southern Ohio patterns, which overlapped in many ways with local women's conversational patterns. I was able to fool some out-of-state visitors, but not Ash Creek residents.

18. While statistical analyses of such possessives would provide an indirect measure of the distribution of possessives in the kinds of grammatical environments in which they occur, such analyses would not consider the speech event and discourse structure elements critical to the meanings of possessives being developed here. Considered interesting but tangential, statistical distributions of "belongin" possessives have been reserved for a later discussion.

19. "Triple handed" is not a transcriptional error. I assume Linda is referring to the practice of playing three spoons as a percussion instrument rather than the usual two. "Playing spoons" is an old musical tradition and consists of putting two spoons back to back in one hand and then smacking them against the other hand and a thigh to create a rhythm.

20. I am using "goal function" in Urban's (1993:241) formulation. He notes that goal functions are "the ways in which speech, as a form of social action, is used to accomplish particular ends that the speaker has." Goal functions contrast with "signaling functions," which "have to do with the contributions of a given stretch of discourse to the communication of which it is a part." His formulation is prefigured in Silverstein (1976, 1979). His formulation is appropriate here because it avoids the inherent problems of assigning only speaker or hearer intent, as Searle's (1976) "illocutionary force" and "perlocutionary force" does.

21. In a randomly selected corpus of 15 tapes, 66 of 73, or 95%, of $[+\text{human N}]_{NP}$ were kinship terms; the other seven possessed noun tokens included proto-kinship terms ("her little boyfriend" and "his bride"), labor relationships ("his staff," "her workers," and "our server"), and recognized nonkin status terms ("my neighbors" and "her doctor").

22. Indeed, much of the Appalachian scholarship assumes that kinship as revealed in extended family networking is the major social organizational unit (e.g., Beaver 1986, Bryant 1983; Hicks 1976).

23. Ash Creek kinship terminology is consistent with American English terminology, with only two notable deviations. Residents talk about marriages in which two brothers would marry two sisters. Children of each marriage are said to be "double first cousins" with each other, a recognized kin term in Ash Creek. In addition, residents tend to bifurcate grandparent terms so that matrilateral grandparents are "mamaw" and "papaw," while patrilateral grandparents are "grandma" and "grandpa." Based on information from surrounding counties, this bifurcation occurs but is variable in its terms of reference. Other speakers in the area report that "mamaw" and "papaw" or "grandma" and "grandpa" could apply to either set of grandparents. "Grandma" and "grandpa" tend to be more formal uses.

24. I am using this phrase in a manner consistent with Bourdieu (1984) but with the understanding that this capital represents a counterhegemonic representation to the symbolic capital of class as Bourdieu conceived. Those with high symbolic capital in Ash Creek may not also have acquired high symbolic capital as recognized by working or middle-class white Americans whom they encounter when visiting regional cities or on television.

25. Sociolinguists working in urban areas frequently discuss a person's "network" as that group to which an individual orients his or her speech patterns rather than members of a "speech community" (Hymes 1984 [1968]) and then presume that these networks exist a priori (e.g., see Milroy 1980). I am suggesting here that there is a language-based system for constructing such communities.

26. Appadurai (1986) and Kopytoff (1986) make two points of direct relevance here. First is that a sharp distinction between a commodity and another type of exchange item is false within a global economy. "Things" can move in and out of a commodity state. Second is Appadurai's construction of "regimes of value" rather than "spheres of exchange." The former, he argues, captures value variability from situation to situation. The latter suggests a complete sharing of cultural assumptions regarding value. Certainly these two points apply to the assignment of value among Ash Creek entities.

27. In a randomly selected sample of 15 audiotapes, only 10 (6%) of 158 tokens were trisyllabic; none were tetrasyllabic or higher. Of these, all represented style (or possibly code) shifts or incorporation of specialized jargon of a particular workplace:

> our hamburgers (2 tokens) (compound lexeme, meets AE mono and disyllabic stress pattern as first syllable is also a free morpheme)

supervisor's office
their property (versus AE "their land")
our population
my suspicions
my vacation
her kidney infection
your salary (versus AE "your wages" or "your pay")
my /mae•neyz/ (loss of middle unstressed syllable to conform to AE disyllabic patterns very common to the point of being rule-governed)

28. This discussion is not intended to suggest in any manner that the form of Appalachian English spoken by many Ash Creek residents is in some sense "deficient." Rather, the purpose of this discussion is to suggest some grammatical constraints on lexeme selection in possessive construction, which functions in part to distinguish this speech from, for example, network television speech, and to suggest that these differences have cultural implications in terms of socioeconomic intersections.

29. That these constructions are constrained by discourse rules of use becomes even clearer when contrasted with preferences of non–Appalachian English speakers in Ash Creek or the immediate locale. When five nonlocal individuals were presented with these examples, alternative nonpossessive constructions were preferred except for the token "your five dollar bill" (which elicited acceptable responses as well as alternatives such as "Did you get a dime back out of the five?"). The Ash Creek usages were considered unusual.

30. In a randomly selected sample of 15 audiotapes, 85 (54%) of 158 [–human N] possessive tokens were of this task-oriented type; 44 (28%) were body parts (e.g., "my head") or other self-directed inalienable constructions (e.g., "his name"); and 29 (18%) were other types including pet terms (which could also be task-oriented in other clause structures) such as "his dog," and other items having potential use value (e.g., "their property"). Abstract constructions and inanimate possessor nouns also fall into this category (e.g., "your problem," "Bill's trouble," and "last year's taxes").

31. This claim is supported by the data described in note 30 and by my understanding of grammatical preference. I told my Ash Creek friends that I was interested in mountain speech as it actually occurred so I could get it "right." This led to them being more open in correcting me and in talking openly about their speech preferences. I could both ask about and practice my use of possessive constructions.

32. In actuality, most women's "cars" are titled to their husband or father. This genderization of cars is nearly obligatory—if a woman drives a truck, or owns one, there must be a special reason. I know of only one woman, Dorothy, who owns and drives a truck regularly. She is an older widow and residents acknowledge that she has a "need" for a truck and must drive it because the only man in the household is her young adult son who is often in town and is taking courses at the community college.

33. A woman may be called a kin term such as "Sissy" as a nickname or familiar term of address, but most go by her first or, and very commonly, middle name. Men, on the other hand, regularly go by nicknames so often that an outsider can be seriously misled about individual male identities.

34. Both Hanks (1990) and Parmentier (1994) develop this distinction from grammatical and semiotic perspectives. See also Lee and Urban (1989) for a series of linguistic discussions of the role of self in a social world, especially Urban's (1989) reconsidera-

tion of Benveniste's (1971) discussion of personal pronouns as deictics. See also Greenburg (1986) and Silverstein (1977, 1993).

35. After Geertz (1973) who makes a distinction between discourse that is straightforward and denotationally obvious ("thin") versus communicative representations that are polysemous, highly multifunctional, and richly symbolic ("thick").

36. I make this claim on the basis of overhearing a significant number of male-only work talk exchanges. I was either in the room next to where they were working, inside a house when they were working on the outside of it, or working in the same room on another task. Women can easily eavesdrop on men who are engaged in talk with others if the woman is in an appropriate setting and doing an appropriate task.

37. I use the term "story," like Heath's (1982, 1983) usage for Roadville, South Carolina, working-class whites. A "story" in Roadville is an oral discursive narrative that references past events assumed to be "true," meaning they occurred in a manner consistent with what events actually transpired. I also use the term as in Bauman's (1986 [1991]:51–52) discussion of South Texas white narrative performance styles and structurings in which the events are "independent and antecedent to the narratives" but "in a general sense the compound knowledge gained by *both* doing and telling helps give shape to each new [narrative]."

38. I am drawing on the well-developed body of scholarship on how Bakhtin's (1981, 1986) approach to "voicing" and "reported speech" impacts the contextual and cultural significance of narratives. See Bauman and Briggs (1990) and, especially, the articles in Lucy (1993c).

39. Making and distributing moonshine is, of course, still done in this part of Kentucky, but much less frequently and in smaller quantities than in the past (before 1980), at least as reported to me.

40. Both hypothetical (elicited) examples and actual discourse-in-use examples are included here to make clear the contrast sets involved. A * (asterisk) indicates cultural unacceptability rather than the more standard ungrammaticality.

41. I am drawing on the thorough discussion of this process of transforming quotidian discursive utterances and their indexical significations into mythic narratives in Urban (1991).

Chapter 3

1. The term "requests" has its own scholarly literature as well as various folk, popular, and professional linguistic ideologies of what constitutes a request utterance, sequence, event, or function. Much of the scholarly literature has used English as its language of reference (e.g., Austin 1962; Ervin-Tripp 1976; Ervin-Tripp et al. 1987; Levinson 1983; Schegloff 1979; and Searle 1975, 1976, 1991). The spoken English variety used by most Ash Creek residents is likely to support models and theoretical orientations of this scholarship, with certain adjustments for "dialect," such as the absence of "please" and a preference for "got" rather than "have" constructions. I am, however, using "request" and "requesting discourse" in a broad sense to include utterance and discursive events that residents would assign the metapragmatic designator of "askin" or "tellin" or "orderin." In focusing on the different metapragmatic schemes of these speakers for purposes of their relations to the constitution of a local ideology socioeconomic language, I approach issues of what constitutes "requests" differently than more commonly acknowledged approaches suggested by the sources I cited. A careful examination of how Ash Creek requests conform or do not conform to this scholarship is left for subsequent attention.

2. These observations conform in general to the findings of request formal patterns for English as have been reported by, for example, Brown and Levinson (1987 [1978]), Ervin-Tripp (1976, 1996), Ervin-Tripp, O'Connor, and Rosenberg (1984), and Levinson (1983).

3. I am using "participant framework" in a manner consistent with Goffman (1981:3): "When a word is spoken, all those who happen to be in perceptual range of the event will have some sort of participation status relative to it. The codification of these various positions and the normative specification of appropriate conduct within each provide an essential background for interaction analysis." For a modification of this definition to "participation framework" to accommodate shifting recontextualizations of roles by discourse as a conversation unfolds, see Schiffrin (1987) and M. Goodwin (1990). For a broader contextualization, including such factors as spacial arrangements and gesture, see Hanks (1993, 1996a).

4. Since Brown and Gilman's (1960) ground-breaking work, the study of how pronominal shifts construct power relations has led to interesting analyses of how personal pronouns shift function in requests. Brown and Levinson (1987 [1978]), Ervin-Tripp (1976, 1982, 1996), Ervin-Tripp, O'Connor, and Rosenberg (1984); Gordon and Ervin-Tripp (1984), and articles in Cole and Morgan (1975) have contributed significantly to our understanding of how the relationship between pronoun shifts, terms of address, and request form function to index authority, status, and formality.

5. I am referring specifically to works by Friedrich (1979 [1966]), Leaf (1989), Singer (1989), and Urban (1989) in which the construction of "self" is related to philosophical discussions of "self" as cultural representations expressed in linguistic forms of personal pronouns, particularly first-person pronouns.

6. I am drawing specifically on Jakobson's (1971) recognition of the multifunctionality of pronouns so that they can both index various participant roles in speech events and also function as clausal subjects and Benveniste's discussion of the instantiation of "I" in discourse so that "*I* can only be identified by the instance of discourse that contains it and by that alone" (1971:218). Urban's (1989) analysis of five types of "I" that construct five types of selves captures the complexity of how personal pronouns can bond context to an utterance and vice versa.

7. These pronominal uses to include or remove participants from requesting events conform to requests in general and are thoroughly discussed in the speech act literature. See, for example, Brown and Levinson (1987 [1978]); Ervin-Tripp (1980, 1981, 1982) Ervin-Tripp, O'Connor, and Rosenberg (1984); Gordon and Ervin-Tripp (1984); Levinson (1983); and Searle (1996).

8. In addition to the sources mentioned in note 5, see also Irvine (1979) and Lee (1997:202–221). I should note that there are specific differences in how these different personal pronominal uses are grammatically structured, especially in requests.

9. Ethnographic accounts, biographies, case studies, and other studies incorporating participant observation of communities or families have passing discussions of this material covered in this section. Hicks (1976), for example, discusses indirectness among men in making suggestions about how to perform a task; Batteau (1983b, 1985) discusses sociopolitical relations and their effect on local economy; Beaver (1986) mentions nonverbal patterns in family life; and Stephenson (1968) discusses problematic work relations. None assumes a linguistic stance, however, and I mention them as support for this argument from different theoretical and disciplinary orientations.

10. Formulaic expressions such as "who does he think he is talkin to us like that" or "it's not her place to ask for that" gloss conversational discourse about assertions of

individual selves in social interaction. Exploring these domains led me to ask whether certain expressions such as "I'm tellin you to study on it" in hypothetical contexts were acceptable or not. Residents were commonly able to evaluate such expressions, often with additional commentary.

11. Gordon and Ervin-Tripp (1984) discuss "want" and "need" request forms as "conventional types" (1984:307) and later discuss "wants" as a type of instrumental goal with respect to children's mastery of request social and situational goals. Here, however, I am capturing how many Ash Creek residents assign metapragmatic meaning to request tokens. Using discursive forms to assign "wants" and "needs" interpretations to requesting behavior constitutes another of the dichotomization preferences mentioned in chapter 1. Residents have a well-developed repertoire of speaking practices for discussing each.

12. Appadurai (1986) asserts that all economic exchanges are political and involve acts of control. Gal (1989) and Irvine (1989) note that language and political economic relations also must involve issues of power and control. See also Bloch (1975) and Myers and Brenneis (1984) for cultural anthropological approaches to the issue of power in the relationship between language and socioeconomy.

13. The practical function of much socioeconomic activity to meet subsistence or biologically dominated levels of daily life is very well developed in Ash Creek community life and mitigates conscious or negotiated perceptions of "power" as strategic goals in exchanges. Although issues related to control or status negotiation are inherent in requesting events, to focus on how given individuals strategically manipulate the requesting repertoire in order to demonstrate these social and political implications, without first considering the cultural norms that generate and motivate choice in requesting discourse selection processes, would be to distort those interpretive structures at the center of Ash Creek economic processes. When a woman requests a cooking item from her daughter by saying "let me borrer your mixer," as she has requested many times before, status or control relations are being reproduced rather than asserted, negotiated, or manipulated. Therefore, the following discussion focuses on describing these patterns at a typological level. I did not conduct a microanalysis of a few specific instances of use, though recognizing that such studies would be a welcome addition to the basic patterns presented here. See Hanks (1990) for a thorough discussion of these processes of nonstrategic manipulations of routinized and indexical utterances.

14. Early literary accounts of "mountain" speech have particularly emphasized how expressions, metaphor, analogy, and metonymy enliven the conversational speech of many Appalachian residents. Local color writers were especially interested in creating an ethos of "color," often with little regard for accuracy. For discussions, see Shapiro (1978) and C. Williams (1992). For a list of the many sources on expressions, see McMillan and Montgomery (1989).

15. I am using this term to capture the functions of "sayins" in a composite of all discursive practices that can incorporate "sayins" in situations of use. This formulation, after Silverstein (1998), is different from Geertz's (1973) use of "interpretive structures." "Structures" suggests something more permanent and bounded in terms of formal features, functions, and meanings than is intended here.

16. A number of researchers have discussed "rights" as a significant variable in making requests. Gordon and Ervin-Tripp, for example, note that "[r]ights and obligations are often related to specific social roles" (1984:300), capturing in a general sense what I am arguing here. Their usage is, however, in keeping with dictionary denotative meanings and, I presume, legal uses of the term. I am using "rights" as it is defined by

residents and as it is used in the full range of discursive practices in the community. The word assumes slightly different sense relations under these constraints.

17. "Kinds of people" is a polysemic phrase used to classify others than oneself into ranked categories of human types such as Catholics, African Americans, sinners, and educated researchers. I have reduced the semantic features of this phrase to the most primitive level here, that of gender, age, and whether someone is a "called" preacher or a saved soul versus a sinner who does not affirm church teachings and practices.

18. A few residents, primarily men, frequently link "rights" to constitutional guarantees, especially as iterated in the Bill of Rights. Most, however, legitimate community uses of "rights" to quotations from biblical scripture or church dogma.

19. Basically, Ash Creek residents distinguish between two socially ranked groups, themselves and those who are "not one of us." The latter are commonly labeled as "proper," or "above their raisin" (see Hicks 1976; Puckett 1992). Because of my focus on how local residents construct a meaningful community-level socioeconomic system, this discussion excludes events when members of the "not one of us" ranking may be present. Interfacing communicative events in relation to power and authority dimensions in the entire political economy are extremely complex, frequently involving residents from town, from the region, and from other parts of the state, exceeding the focus of this book.

20. In Ash Creek, all preachers are men. In some Pentecostal Holiness churches in nearby communities and in the Church of God of Prophecy, which has an Ash Creek congregation, female preachers are permitted. Ash Creek residents are well aware of this Pentecostal tradition and appropriate churches would recognize female preachers if one were called to a particular church.

21. Ash Creek preachers conform to Appalachian and Southern rural preferences for "called" rather than seminary-trained religious practitioners, a cultural norm that is also linked to valuation of different religious discourse genres than found in denominational, professionally accredited Christian churches. MacCauley (1995) gives a thorough discussion of the history of this religious tradition, but see also Dorgan (1987), Jones (1998), Patterson (1995) and Titon (1988). Two Ash Creek preachers have received some religious instruction. One attended a Bible college sanctioned by the denomination; the other received instruction as part of maintaining affiliation with the Church of God of Prophecy.

22. M. Rodman (1992) has discussed these issues and their importance to anthropology extremely well in arguing that place plays an agentive role in empowering cultural voices (see also Allen and Schlereth 1990 and Feld and Basso 1996 for a discussion about region and place in U.S. communities). Stewart's (1996a, 1996b) discussion of place in West Virginia, coal camps focuses more on the level of interpretive schemes in narrative from a postmodern theoretical perspective. The discussion offered here focuses on the semantic, pragmatic, and metapragmatic meanings constructed through requesting and other quotidian discourse.

23. See in particular Allen (1990); Batteau (1982, 1983a, 1983b); and Bryant (1981).

24. "Homeplace" as a symbol of cultural organization and personal identity permeates the fiction, historical accounts, and folklore of the region. Giardina (1987), M. Williams (1995:165–169), and Long's (1994) fictional, folkloric, and musical treatments have merit here.

25. I make this claim on the basis of casual conversation I had with residents who live in the coal towns and former coal camps of the county, while I was visiting town and teaching extension classes for the county community college throughout a two-county area from 1987–1993, and on Stewart (1988).

26. Extensions of the geographical meaning of "place" include seating arrangements at family events such as a formal meal, riding in a truck or car, or when breaking beans on a porch or canning garden produce in a kitchen. These physical placements of "belongin" networks members reveal clearly the second, interactional meaning of "place" as access or control of resources with respect to others.

27. "Close" family members include natal and affinal nuclear family kin, or fictive kin having nuclear family status (parents, spouses, children). Much tension exists, however, as to priorities of "claims" within this group, and each family negotiates its unique configuration of priorities and inclusion. Conflicts revolve primarily around "rights" of natal kin, especially mothers, and "rights" of spouses, both husbands and wives. In one family, for example, a newly married woman asserted her natal "claims" by spending the day after the wedding at her mother's, leaving her new husband to visit with whom he wished or do whatever he wanted. He visited his parents. In another case, a wife lived virilocally, relinquishing her rights to visit her own family in another county to be with her husband and his parents, as he "wanted." She counted on her mother-in-law to "keep him in line" (to be responsible to his wife and children), so that he would honor her "claims" over him.

28. One such example appeared in a woodcarving session with Bill. I had discovered that a male Ash Creek resident was a kinsman of his. I commented on this man being kin; Bill said "Yes," looked away, and further commented on how he didn't "claim him." I didn't ask why, but observation of this man's behavior and other residents' stories about him made clear that his behavior was not "right." Later that evening Bill volunteered some stories about this man's actions. Some women would volunteer such stories as conversational topics, without any cue from me.

29. Divorce is, of course, a case in which legal dissolution of the "claims" relations associated with marriage can apply. I know of no divorce in the generation older than 25, although a few couples under 25 divorced while I was there. Even then, "claims" tend to continue among the various affinal family members, especially when complicated systems of obligation and exchange as "rights" are also continued. The "rights" and "claims" disputes invariably involve grandparents, if they are living, and frequently include siblings of both sides. A person's "belongin" network is usually affected by a ripple effect through the interlocking and reckoned kinship ties so that much of the community becomes involved.

30. Use of these terms is commonly followed by the given first name of the referenced or addressed individual so that the most common formulation would be "Sister [first name]" or "Brother [first name]." Nicknames are rarely used. Informal and casual usages are not uncommon, such as "sis" or use of the kinship term without a first name.

31. In encounters with non–Ash Creek residents in this and adjacent counties, I observed "placin" patterns similar to those in Ash Creek. The ways in which a nonlocal could negotiate fictive "place" relations, however, varied somewhat with respect to professional status. In the small towns in the area (e.g., Cumberland, Harlan, Hyden, and Middlesboro) other types of health care professionals, civil and mining engineers, and managers of national retail establishments could all have a basis for establishing "place." In most cases, however, these individuals were also part of "belongin" networks and had kin in the area.

Chapter 4

1. This statement is made on the basis of comparing Ash Creek requesting patterns to contextually sensitive scholarship on requests in business or corporate workplace

settings such as Drew and Heritage (1992), Ervin-Tripp (1976, 1996), Firth (1994), Gumperz (1982, 1996), Linde (1988, 1993), and Weigel and Weigel (1985).

2. Of course, under modern legally enforced funeral practices, some funeral needs are necessarily not local and must be formally requested. In Ash Creek, however, many funerals still conform as much as possible to the more time-honored home or church burial in which many "needs" were handled in a seemingly spontaneous and unplanned manner, all under well-developed "rights," "place," and "claims" relations.

3. Do not assume, however, that a well-developed and binding relationship is necessarily positive for both parties, particularly in terms of male/female relations. Frequently they are highly positive, but not uncommonly one party may find the control elements inherent in such relations confining or limiting, if not oppressive.

4. Sarah was in her late forties or early fifties at the time this leave-taking was spoken. Her use of "girls" as a term of address represents a form common among women in workplaces in the post–World War II era when she first began working.

5. Puckett (1995). Gordon and Ervin-Tripp (1984:297) explore manipulations of expected indexicals as "instrumental moves," noting that "requests often confirm existing social relations" and that speakers can use requests to signal changes in relations. The formulation of this point in terms of "claims" problems here is indebted to their observations and simply builds on them by considering the problem from an ethnographic approach to discursive pragmatic and metapragmatic relations.

6. Voloshinov (1973 [1930]: 115) defined reported speech as "speech within speech, utterance within utterance, and at the same time also *speech about speech, utterance about utterance*." Lucy (1993b:95) distinguishes between reported speech functions that "characterize," that is, "predicate about," the metapragmatic meanings of particular utterances and functions which "(re-)present the reported utterance." Here, Edna "characterizes" Sandy's original utterance as an imperative rather than "presenting" it as it was actually spoken and with the same presuppositional indexical meanings it would have had. In approximating rather than repeating the original utterance ("characterizing" it), she neutralizes any "order" status of Sandy's original utterance. See Bakhtin's (1981) masterful formulation of the role of reported speech in construction of socially constituted, contextually based dialogic interactions among interlocutors, Jakobson (1971 [1957]), and Lucy's (1993c) edited volume on recent theoretical investigations into this interesting area of discourse.

7. Uptake, in Austin's (1962) usage, means that a listener acknowledges or ratifies the conditions stated by the speaker's speech act by some additional utterance. Here, I am using the term in a similar manner but am also specifying that the response be a statement or narrative of a problem, or "need."

8. A transparent example of this shift to the respondent occurs in telephone discourse. The normative local pattern for phone calls is for the caller to recognize the voice of the respondent, offer a minimal greeting or none at all, and begin the message portion of the call. Should the voice of the respondent be unfamiliar, the caller will make a direct request by saying, "Who's this?" A reply of a name is the minimum expected, with "belongin" greeting behavior desired (for example, "Ann Jones, Mary's daughter-in-law," with Mary as the usual respondent). Nonlocal women routinely find the pattern difficult to adjust to, for fear of losing their anonymity. Ash Creek patterns, however, require that the respondent of a request, even an indirect request of self-identification through voice recognition in a phone call, must provide the necessary information, goods, labor, or services whether asked directly or through extremely indirect means.

9. See Drew and Heritage (1992), Ervin-Tripp (1976), Linde (1988), and Weigel and Weigel (1985).

10. When I began teaching classes at the community college campus, I noticed that this pattern was normative for many of the students enrolled and for other visitors from the county. Staff from the area responded in the "volunteerin" manner I observed in Ash Creek.

11. The term "volunteerin" as used here parallels Searle's (1976) "commissive" speech acts in which the speaker is committed to some future course of action. The obligatory implications of "volunteerin," however, have similarities to Searle's "directives," utterances in which the speaker tries to compel the listener to do something. The two speech act categories conflate in Ash Creek usage. Contextual pragmatic meanings (indexical functions) also constrain or reconfigure functions of the propositional structure of Searle's commissives and directives.

12. This example is taken from my notes rather than from audio-recordings. I could remember short sections of discourse in a relatively accurate manner but found that I did not trust my memory for long narratives. Therefore, I have not attempted to present the narrative portion of this exchange as text.

13. This term is in Schriffrin's (1987) usage of replies that mark a stage in the conversation.

14. For those who are not in one's "belongin" networks, vague or nonexisting "claims" relationships will extend to most contexts and most needs. For those in the requestor's "belongin" network, this condition would apply to unusual or previously undeveloped contexts. One such possibility would be for a wife to create a "volunteerin" discourse pattern to ask her husband for use of his truck.

15. Narratives from visitors and nonlocals about confusion over the meaning of this clause are common. I often used these narratives as a means for opening up conversation about other perceived differences these nonlocals had observed or encountered. Such information was often useful in exploring other cultural or linguistic differences. I should make clear, however, that intonation and nonverbal communicative cues are consistent with English statements of compliance and that "I don't care to" indicates willingness to perform a task.

16. In general, this discussion conforms to Levinson's thorough presentation of "pre-requests" (1983:356–364). His four-turn sequencing (after Merritt 1976) differs from the Ash Creek six-stage pattern, but his insight—that the sequencing of these patterns "allows the producer to check out whether a request is likely to succeed, and if not to avoid one in order to avoid the subsequent dispreferred response, namely a rejection" (1983:357)—is directly relevant. Nevertheless, "volunteerin" sequencing in the Ash Creek requesting repertoire is so conventionalized that noncompliance is rare once a requestor has framed a "volunteerin" context. I use the term "stages" rather than "sequences," a term central to conversational analytic theory (Sacks, Schegloff, and Jefferson 1974) because each stage can involve its own set of sequences, or conversational "turns."

17. Levinson argues that "let me" constructions are imperatives (1983:266). The permission sense of "let," however, shifts the focus of these potential imperatives to the addressee, or what Hanks (1992:68) calls "altercentric"participant domains. Furthermore, Davies (1986) argues convincingly for treating "let" constructions as an "imperative of a rather special kind, which complements the ordinary imperative in allowing the specification of types of subject which can not occur in other imperatives." He further argues that /let/ "constitutes the presentation of a proposition as a potentiality" (1986:250). Ash Creek residents do not classify "let me" or "let's" constructions as "orders."

18. See Brown and Levinson (1987 [1978]) for a rigorous discussion of politeness as a model for social interaction. It is in their sense of the "principles out of which social relationships, in their interactional aspect, are constructed: dimensions by which individuals manage to relate to others in particular ways" (1987:55) that I am using the term.

19. This type of construction is well-studied and, although critiqued (e.g., Brower, Gerritsen, and de Haan 1979), is attributed to middle-class, urban women's speech (e.g., Brown and Levinson 1987 [1978]; Coates 1986, 1996; Lakoff 1977a, 1977b; Tanz 1987). Sarah has worked with nonlocal women extensively at the Environmental Center for over 30 years. I assume, pending contradictory data, that this construction represents a borrowing from the speech of these nonlocal women.

20. The distribution of double modals in Southern Mountain Speech, or what some scholars label Appalachian English, is well documented and is diagnostic of this speech variety (Christian 1978; Mishoe and Montgomery 1994; Shopen and Williams 1980; C. Williams (1992); Wolfram and Christian 1976; Wolfram and Schilling-Estes 1998).

21. "By "stylized" I mean the use of what Gumperz calls "formulaic expressions" (1992:231). See also Urban (1988).

22. Austin (1962) argued for a class of "performative" verbs including such words as "promise," "apologies," "ask," and "warn," which, when predicated in first-person pronominal declaratives (e.g., "I promise I will attend."), accomplish some function other than describing a state of affairs. The use of "promise" in such constructions, for example, effects a state of having committed a speaker to a future action. In Ash Creek embedded "volunteerins" such as exemplified here, stating that the person referenced using a third-person form (e.g., "Joe") will "volunteer" a tool conforms neither to Austin's formulation of performative effect or to Ash Creek residents' metapragmatic system for interpreting "let" constructions.

23. See Ervin-Tripp, O'Connor, and Rosenberg's (1984) discussion of person-centered control acts versus task-centered control acts. See Myers-Scotton (1993) for her description of "statusful" control acts in which recognition of a fixed status in a given interaction can index a speaker's authority for committing to future acts. Direct "askins" in Ash Creek conform to the kinds of asymmetrical relations each of these articles develops with respect to the control of valued resources.

24. "Contexts" as used here accords with Duranti and Goodwin's (1992a) rich discussion. It also is very similar to Ervin-Tripp (1976, 1996) and Gordon and Ervin-Tripp's (1984) use of "situation," with the added dimension of indexical significations to "rights," "place," and "claims" relations.

25. These indexical relationships of "place" are so regularized and patterned that they are deeply sedimented (presupposing) indexical signs amenable to the kinds of analyses applied to terms of address (e.g., Ervin-Tripp 1972) and are certainly a central construct in discursive practices which constitute ideologies of political economic language.

26. Outsiders, particularly those trained and working in medical areas, often find the flat, declarative intonation pattern of these requests, often given without politeness markers such as "please," to be intrusive and abrasive. Several conversational disjunctions involving these usages were reported to me in the course of fieldwork, each ending in both participants being very upset. Two medical practitioners reported these problems as one significant reason for leaving the area.

27. Certain professional positions, such as that of medical doctor, are, however, assumed to imply personal wealth through money. But having money is not synonymous with having power or control over valued resources such as land or votes until other "place" criteria are also established.

28. This use of direct "askin" requests would seem to contradict Levinson's (1987:250) discussion of how power asymmetries affect the use of politeness criteria where low power corresponds to high levels of politeness. As discussed here, direct "askins" would be less polite, more "bald on record," than "volunteerin" patterns. Yet Levinson (1987:25) notes that "in Tamil . . . some direct requests (specifically those of low R [rank]) may occur from subordinates to superordinates, providing that such requests are mitigated with he appropriate honorifics." Similar conditions apply in Ash Creek. Exaggerated praise about how someone is performing his or her job or the prestation of gifts (in political arenas, these "gifts" may be promises of blocks of votes from "belongin" network members) will predate a direct "askin." Furthermore, many professionals develop "takin care of" relations with residents (chapter 5) that provide ongoing opportunities for residents to "claim" the services of professionals. Nevertheless, professionals cannot use their professional credentials as self-evident presuppositional indexes to use direct "askins" with those they serve. These credentials have negative value among most Ash Creek residents as indexes of false superiority or probable exploitation. Professionals must reconstruct their "footing" in Goffman's (1979; 1981) sense of positioning of self when speaking to configure an appropriate "participation status," or relationship to what he or she is saying in a given utterance event, so they do not evoke these negative indexical meanings and the metapragmatic relations they entail.

29. A curious representation of the problematic presuppositional indexical relations in use of these "if you don't care to" forms arose in data analysis. As audiotaping of informants required permission and therefore certain levels of trust in the researcher, events recorded tended to be in contexts in which "belongin" relations applied or in which claims relations had been fairly or strongly developed. Consequently, taped examples were weakly represented in the discourse corpus, and I relied on notes to provide examples of this widely talked about, highly salient "askin" discourse form.

30. Of the four mom-and-pop stores in Ash Creek at the time I lived there, one prepared sandwiches for customers; the other three did not. Two had kitchen facilities where the proprietor could fix meals for close "belongin" network members, usually children or grandchildren.

31. Note that "if you don't care to" constructions do not carry the same semantic meaning in more standard, urban American English discourse. They imply compliance rather than unwillingness. Outsiders find this salient marker of semantic differences between Ash Creek and more standard, broadcasters' American English an unsettling factor in relating to Ash Creek residents, particularly since it is used so frequently. Note as well that "please" is not used in Ash Creek except as a marked variation, often indexing the "proper" speech of educated outsiders. "Please" can have negative value. "If you don't care to" is an approximate, but not synonymous, substitution because of its presuppositional indexical meanings.

32. As used here, these "culturally validated conditions" are not the same as Austin's (1962) "felicity conditions." Austin was concerned with creating a typology of conditions that performative utterances must meet if they are to succeed. Indexical relations to context or metapragmatic functions are not part of his theoretical argument. Here, the presumption is that direct "askin" requests must index certain contextual meanings presuppositionally or creatively to effect compliance. They must also entail metapragmatic discourse regarding the interpretations given to "place," "rights," and "claims" in interpersonal relations. In the Ash Creek requesting discourse system, "place" relations supersede formal institutional or professional valuation of a person's skills or authority, often calling into question these valuation systems.

33. By "ritualized speech," I mean oral discursive forms that are relatively stable "types" or "genres" in which "thematic content, style, and compositional structure" exhibit certain formal and predictable structuring (Bakhtin 1986:60). Ritualized speech includes supernatural or cosmological forces or divinities as interlocutors and exhibits "heightened" uses of the semiotic capacities of language to create densely woven intersections of all possible Peircian signs (see Briggs 1988:328–330 for elaboration of this description).

Chapter 5

1. This approach to an analysis of speaking practices recognizes fluidity and creativity in form, function, and meaning relations as actual speakers interact with one another. This stance is in keeping with Goffman's (1981) "forms of talk," which emphasize the interactional component of quotidian speech. I am also indebted to subsequent scholarship on social interaction that has focused on the complexities of interrelationships among discursive "contexts" and situational ones such as Duranti and Goodwin (1992b), Brown and Levinson (1987 [1978]) and Sacks (1992).

2. Very few residents engage in producing goods for market exchange. Tom and Mary and one other couple grow vegetable produce for sale, but they market it directly in town at a locally owned grocery store. A few women have made crafts for sale at the Environmental Center, but sales were slow and the women stopped producing them. Dorothy occasionally does reupholstering of furniture in the immediate region as a paid service. Bill never markets his woodworking product. Kaziah is one exception. She markets her crafts through regional craft shows, avoiding the entrenched "takin care of" system of marketing goods. She does, however, draw upon "claims" relationships for rides to these craft shows. Her production of crafts, however, has little local currency or value except by some staff at the Environmental Center. She does have a regional "name" as an outstanding example of a folk artist. Regardless, with no local appreciation for her commodities, she cannot develop "takin care of" relations.

3. The focus of this work is on socioeconomic relations; the political economy and language issues raised by "takin care of" discourse are, however, extremely significant to the construction of power in Ash Creek, the county, and the Kentucky area, with implications for much of rural Appalachia. Batteau's (1983b:145) treatment of these relations from a cultural anthropological perspective has applications to Ash Creek as well:

> Articulated by kinship, friendship, and patronage, these [political dependencies] form a lattice-work extending downward from state politicians to courthouse officials to family patriarchs, and finally down to the individual voters. Through the control of patronage jobs and development resources, this system absorbs the very opportunities for survival and economic improvement in eastern Kentucky.

A thorough linguistic anthropological treatment of them is needed by someone who has greater access to settings where political power is asserted or negotiated than I. My role as a female researcher working among families and, primarily, women's networks excluded me from many, but not all, of these settings. I encountered "takin care of" as a trope far more frequently when I assumed a professional role as a community college faculty member when I was in greater contact with those exercising political economic power. One function of "takin care of" political relations is to obtain political jobs for one's constituency. Batteau (1983b:146) comments that "it is perhaps one of the most typical of the rituals of dependence in the region, and it creates some of the most durable and far-reaching ties of dependence; yet because it is so private, I was unable to observe it." I came to dread hearing people utter "we'll take care of ya" to me because of its presuppositional indices of reciprocal obligation and loyalty.

4. Briggs's (1996b) edited volume is ground-breaking in its constitutive approach to the use of narrative to foster conflict and inequality in social life. His summation (1996b:235–237) has particular relevance to these types of Ash Creek contestations because of its sensitivity to how verbal conflicts with discursive authority "shape discursive and social relations and inequalities." This typical Ash Creek pattern of conflict emotes verbal representations that undercut the dominant patterns of authority in the region while supporting alternative patterns of noncapitalistic patronage. See also Gal (1991) and Haviland (1977).

5. Anglin (1992, 1993, 1998), and Kingsolver (1992, 1998a) describe how workplaces develop a type of syncretism in which both local interpersonal work expectations and corporate for-profit functions are reconstituted. Anglin (1998) also reveals how such relations can quickly become contestative and reframed as labor resistance.

6. A very common lung disorder, black lung, or silicosis, is a carbonization of the lungs due to prolonged inhalation of coal dust. Smoking of tobacco may hasten the deterioration or increase its severity. It regularly affects a person's ability to work and frequently is a cause of death. Most men in Ash Creek have worked as underground coal miners at some point in their lives. I entered Ash Creek at a time when most new claims to coal companies or unions for this type of workman's compensation were denied because funds for such benefits no longer exist. Instead, individuals file for Medicaid, Medicare (if old enough), or Social Security Supplemental Income.

7. For a presentation of how these fast-food chains train eastern Kentucky fast-food employees to use these scripted requesting sequences, see Johnson (1991).

8. One proprietor of a very small grocery store indicated a loss of over $5,000 in one tax year due to unpaid debts. Collecting on such debts is unthinkable, as disruption of "claims" relationships can drive away other patrons or, potentially, cause negative sanctions such as burning of the store. Problems with food stamp cash exchanges can also occur under these enormous pressures from residents to make sure proprietors "act right" by them. Proprietors regularly express such losses as doing "right by the community" or as a service "for the good of the community," and not ostensibly to make a profit. One local store minimizes these losses by setting credit limits. Those who cannot or do not comply trade elsewhere. The local car repair garage also engaged in barter of parts and used vehicles as an adjustment to these "takin care of" practices.

9. At the same time, recent investigations of eastern Kentucky school districts by the State Board of Education under new reform legislation has noted frequent so-called misuse of state funds as school district personnel "take care of" those in their fictive claims network. Such practices are well within the norm of "takin care of" patterns familiar to Ash Creek residents but run counter to authorized use of funds under formal institutional corporate guidelines.

10. The use of "help" instead of "hɛp" or "hlp" indexes this speaker as someone who is speaking more formally, or "proper." She is a young woman in her early twenties who eventually moved to Florida with her husband (and then returned after a year).

11. When interlocutors are speaking face-to-face, as Susie and the vendor were here, "doin for" imperatives generally involve direct eye contact and often involve use of hand gestures as the speaker points or gestures in the direction of what is needed. Direct eye contact is a highly significant communication in Ash Creek. Most interactions avoid eye contact unless making a point. The preferred seating pattern is to sit in rows or so

that all are watching or doing something so they are not looking at each other while talking. Older residents have especially well-developed systems of eye contact communication. Making what they consider to be unnecessary eye contact is a highly unsocial act and disrupts social interaction.

12. This household is the most removed from public interaction in Ash Creek. Members rarely visit local stores and do not attend local churches or grade school events. It has no electricity or no running water and relies extensively on garden produce and hunting for food stuffs.

13. These relations are not, however, directly similar to the kind of "spiritual" or metaphysical gift-like bonding suggested by Mauss (1967) but are rather systems of obligation, more consistent with those described by Sahlins (1972) or Strathern (1971).

14. "Makin a deal" discourse is a well-developed and often highly political speaking practice, involving negotiations, compromises, and careful attention to saving face, and often appears as a distinct speech act within "takin care of" speaking practices as well as within transparent exchange activities. As a primarily male form of frequently secret negotiation, it is not easily available for audiotaping.

15. Bauman (1986 [1981]) is directly relevant here. His discussion of "lying" in narrative as a necessary verbal skill in Canton, Texas, dog trading applies to Ash Creek. His observation that dog trading merges two important American figures, the hunter and the trader, also has relevance.

16. By investment activities, I mean any activity in which capital (or "money") is used to make more money: for example, retirement funds, stocks, bonds, mutual funds, or real estate. Several residents have interest-bearing savings accounts, certificates of deposit, or perhaps even an Independent Retirement Account (IRA) at a bank. Many older residents keep cash in a "safe" place at home.

17. Younger residents will code switch to Standard American English "shop" or "buy," especially in the presence of an outsider. Some teenagers say they prefer to use "buy," as "trade" is an old-fashioned word or simply not the correct word, imbuing /trade/ with less prestige value than /buy/.

18. Local towns where Ash Creek residents usually "trade" do not have a wide variety of regional or national chain businesses. Except for a small outlet of one regional clothing/department store specializing in urban clientele with professional-level positions, these towns offer fast food restaurants, discount stores, and local outlets of national car and heavy equipment dealerships (e.g., Ford, Chevrolet, and John Deere). These businesses constitute the kinds of national chains or outlet businesses residents frequent and know about.

19. Local merchants are acutely aware of these changing patterns, as greater percentages of the limited cash incomes of most county residents are spent at these national or regional chains. When systems of shopping preference by older residents based on "claims" and "belongin" network criteria are also considered, merchants find that their potential set of buyers is reduced further. As many Ash Creek women and some men also buy only at stores owned or operated by professed Christians, the competition in small markets becomes daunting. With the state's efforts at improving "good" (paved) roads to federal and interstate highways, travel to other regional towns such as Corbin and cities such as Lexington is increasing, further draining the pool of potential customers from the local towns' businesses. The result is a local marketplace with lower and lower inventories of fewer and fewer goods, as the roles of businesses to influence or determine economic "needs" are being abrogated to chain stores and restaurants. For a presentation of quantitative data documenting this process, see Eller (1994).

20. Bauman (1986:13) notes that flea markets are primarily women's events in Canton, Texas. Both genders of Ash Creek residents visit flea markets, usually in families. Groups of women may travel together; men rarely go without women. Women use flea markets for obtaining dishes, glassware, or clothing, especially socks, underwear, and men's work clothes. Men often "trade" for old farm or mining tools, hand tools or replacement parts such as drill bits and ax handles, or hats. Children get toys, baseball cards, dolls, and other inexpensive children's items. Plants, small decorative items, vehicle decals and specialty plates, memorabilia, and potential collectors' items are often sought as well.

21. Home shopping networks on cable television are not available in Ash Creek. Ash Creek residents had extremely limited access to channels when I was living there. The hills surrounding homes along the Ash Creek valley and the branching hollers restrict reception of radio and television signals. Those able to buy and successfully place satellite dishes could receive a broad range of channels, but these were few in Ash Creek. I counted three in 1987. The Environmental Center and homes near it received four channels from a local cable hookup; further down Ash Creek, eight. None of these was a home shopping channel. The situation has not improved significantly. Post-1990 visits have not focused on counting additional satellite dishes or direct television outlets.

22. Being "above your raisin" (or "being above your raising" in standard orthography) is a widely used trope that has complex implications. In general, it encompasses any behavior that suggests a person is evaluating himself or herself as superior to family and close kin in the community. Speaking "proper," getting advanced education, or exhibiting presumptive displays of wealth are some behaviors commonly associated with "gettin above your raisin." The deontic force of this trope should not be confused with "gettin ahead," where a person acquires economic stability without engaging in behaviors that assign relatives to a lower status (or perceived lower status). "Gettin above your raisin" has enormous moral force in Ash Creek. The social and political economic ramifications of the discursive incorporation of this trope in speech reconstruct and reconfirm the dualistic system of social ranking into "one of us" or "those that think themselves better than we are." Once labeled "above your raisin," a person has enormous difficulty participating in Ash Creek socioeconomic life and the "belongin" networks that direct the ebb and flow of socioeconomic activity. A full discussion of this trope should receive its own scholarly space.

23. C. Martin (1987) discusses eastern Kentucky Appalachian material culture as receiving similar diminution. For example, he notes that, regardless of how much time, effort, and creativity a woman puts into creating a quilt, she always talks about it as "only a quilt" when complimented on her creativity.

24. Irvine (1989:251) notes that this reduction and simplification of speech in task contexts may be a function of the work at hand and does not require the full semiotic potential of speech.

25. Bauman (1986[1981]) discusses how dog trading enhances identity and reproduces gender roles through narratives. I should note that dog trading, apparently a well-developed exchange event in Canton, Texas, would also be highly unusual at flea markets visited by Ash Creek residents. Instead, dogs are traded locally, usually on the owner's property.

26. "Honey" is not a term of intimacy or informality in Ash Creek or the immediate three county region. "Honey" is a term of address generally, but not always, used toward women. It is contrasted with "buddy," which is generally used as a term of address for men. Both terms are frequently reduced to one syllable: "hon" and "bud." They con-

stitute what Brown and Levinson (1987 [1978]:90) recognize as "speaker and addressee" honorifics. They mark the status of the interacting participants as socially ranked only in gender and function as creative indexes to both the discursive and situational context, cueing listeners into how to interpret the verbal exchange (as male-male speech, male-female speech, female-male speech, or female-female speech and all semiotic meanings these participant dyadic relations entail). See Irvine (1998) for insightful discussions about how relationships between honorific and social forms are best understood through cultural ideologies of language. She notes that this approach suggests a connection to how power relations are constructed in a social order.

27. Occasionally a widow or single woman may appropriate male "makin a deal" discourse norms and engage in some type of "makin a deal" discourse. These are, however, unusual situations and must be justified in terms of not having a man available to do them for her. Occasionally, Dorothy would "make deals" in town that pertained to her home furniture reupholstering business. I encountered no instance in Ash Creek in which a woman engaged in political "makin a deal" discourse. The Ash Creek county judge executive at the time, however, was a woman. Presumably she "made deals" in this political capacity. Her unique position in the political hierarchy of the county was outside the scope of this study, but it suggests some interesting restructurings and reframings of "makin a deal" discourse (as well as "takin care of" practices).

28. Gender was something of an issue in gaining access to listening to such discourse, but the larger restrictive issue was one of the political nature of most deals. Many fully developed "deals" are made quietly, in private, and often in more isolated or less frequented settings. Some, such as marijuana sales, may be constructed in a code. A fuller understanding of the discursive properties of this speaking practice would certainly be useful to help one comprehend the nature of power, control, and political enfranchisement in this area.

29. Quotatives in Ash Creek conversational narratives are often "presentational" (Hanks 1992) and, according to audiotape examples, are remarkable facsimiles of the original utterance in syntax, phonology, and prosody. I save discussion of the narrative structuring and dialogic "voicing" of these recorded examples for another volume.

30. Subsequent experiences living and working in locales and counties outside of Ash Creek but within the region allow me to make this claim. Furthermore, Ash Creek's county political structure relies on "takin care of" and "makin a deal" practices for county residents according to non–Ash Creek reports to me and my own experiences out of Ash Creek.

Chapter 6

1. Imperative intonation generally conforms to those intonation contours reported for English commands (Bolinger 1989; Pike 1945), although other phrasal prosodic structures characteristic of Appalachian English (C. Williams 1992) are frequently superimposed upon this basic pattern.

2. These examples represent a set of possible imperative constructions characteristic of Lyons (1977:748) "jussives," which are sentences that characteristically issue mands. "Mands" refer to commands, demands, requests, entreaties, and so on (745). They need not be only imperatives, but in general, conform to them either by syntax, prosody, or contextualization processes characteristic of imperative uses. These imperatives are also cultural in the sense that residents assign a metapragmatic designator, "orders," on the basis of their presuppositional indexical functions recreated under particular participant frameworks and in specific communicative contexts. Because of these functions, they also have language and political ideological ramifications.

3. For discussions of English imperatives, see Beukema and Coopmans (1988), Davies (1986), Huddleston (1984), Lyons (1977), Quirk and Greenbaum (1975), Quirk et al. (1972, 1985).

4. These examples are characteristic of Ervin-Tripp's (1976) extensive study of imperatives in American English; their omission in the Ash Creek requesting repertoire suggests that the inventory of Ash Creek imperatives varies from those reported for other varieties of American English. The implications of such variations are many, but one applicable to this study is that the pragmatic meanings created by use of Ash Creek imperative forms constructs a different linguistic-economic system than that sampled by Ervin-Tripp and others working in more urban settings and with speakers of other English varieties.

5. I use "stylized" to conform with Urban's (1991) usage and to distinguish these conventional forms from Ong's (1982) use of "formulaic" discourse. Ong"s usage conveys a negative connotation, suggesting a mnemonic or primitive function(s) for such forms, aiding an interpretation that they assist a finite memory or limited intelligence in so-called "oral" cultures. Urban (1991:25), on the other hand, drawing upon Hymes (1972), notes that style "consists in a recognizable set of features. . . . They are . . . such non-Saussurean forms as intonation contours, voice qualities, and participant role alterations."

6. Ong's (1982) assertion that formulaic discourse in oral societies functions mnemonically, as triggers to memory or recall devices, is inapplicable to this category of imperative uses in Ash Creek. Although Ash Creek can be considered a predominantly oral community, these forms are clearly framing structures, marking a transformation or change in conversational or other discourse function.

7. Compliance by the addressee to imperatives presented in segments (6.4.1–6.4.4) is absolutely obligatory; failure to comply will result in termination of relationship in many households. Any relaxation in a speaker's expectations of compliance to these forms signifies that the speaker has lived elsewhere or has been strongly influenced by others who have.

8. This observation is based on common understandings of the role of "openings" in conversational analysis. For discussions, see Sacks, Schegloff, and Jefferson (1974) and Schegloff and Sacks (1984 [1973]).

9. Leave-takings such as "come to supper" or "spend the night with us" therefore perform two oppositional functions: they end the current interaction and signal the possibility of a future one. In this sense, they resonate with Darnell's (1985:69) findings that Cree speakers avoid indications of interactional closure in order to emphasize the continuity of the relationship.

10. See Gumperz (1982) for a discussion of how an interpretation of these conventional phrases applies to conversational analysis as approached in this study. For related discussions, see Brown and Yule (1983), Goodwin and Heritage (1990), and Levinson (1983). For discussions of expressions in Appalachian English, and there are many, see McMillan and Montgomery (1989). In particular, see Miller (1985) and C. Williams (1992).

11. These relationships correspond to what Brown and Yule (1983:192–93) classified as endophoric co-referential relationships in which the interpretation of the forms lies within the text.

12. Benveniste (1971), Greenburg (1986), and Urban (1989) discuss situations in which the polysemous and multivocal properties of second-person pronouns within discourse are simultaneously deicticly and denotatively referential, as is the case here.

13. I infer from this metapragmatic discursive act that the staff will comply with the director because they have no choice; jobs are too hard to find in this area and most of the staff are middle-aged with few assets and a locally valued but less literate repertoire of skills. Others present may have interpreted this conversational turn differently.

14. Sacks, Schegloff, and Jefferson (1974) first recognized "turn-taking" as a basic and universal pattern in conversational exchanges. I am using the turn in this sense of ways of organizing talk. See also Goodwin and Heritage (1990).

15. Puckett (1993). See also Heath (1983:218–220) for a discussion of Roadville reading and writing cultural patterns.

16. Outsiders are unknowns in this sense, since no one has "learned" them. Consequently, their behaviors are subject to misinterpretation and confusion. When sociolinguistic problems compound the confusion, the outsider is even more at a disadvantage.

17. In such instances, "sayins" cease to be merely clichés or hackneyed phrases, but rather deeply sedimented presuppositional indexes functioning metapragmatically.

Chapter 7

1. The use of the singular here may suggest a monolithic set of interpretations toward labor by residents, an invalid assertion. Rather, multiple perspectives toward what constitutes "doin something" are revealed in "just talkin." I use the singular "ideology" here to capture the significant overlap of certain central features common to most residents' ideologies of task communication.

2. This perspective toward wage-labor supports an interpretation of Ash Creek's socioeconomy as one that does not conform to post-Lockean separations of "the economic" from the rest of cultural activity. Certainly the metapragmatic interconnections among discursive forms in the creation of a local ideology of socioeconomic communication supports this more holistic and integrated view.

3. Published recountings of these types of Appalachian narratives as "products," meaning examples of a verbal genre that can be extracted from context and appreciated for their own merits, are common, often by private publication for the author's family or community. For example, see Jones and Wheeler (1987) and C. Williams (1992). Stewart (1996b) does not take the "product" approach but does present conversational narratives she remembers as texts similar in rhetorical structure and thematic content to Ash Creek patterns I heard.

4. "Helpin out" is not the same thing as "doin for" someone. The former applies to cooperative task situations in which knowledge of the task and the labor involved in producing the product is shared, perhaps differentially but nevertheless distributed over the participants; the latter applies to situations in which one individual is performing a task or activity for another under conditions in which the recipient is not also participating in the labor. This is a critical distinction in Ash Creek socioeconomic life.

5. By "cultural equals" and "cultural unequals," I mean the assignment of co-participants into one of two rankings on the basis of the participant framework that reflexively indexes appropriate task-focused communication and, in turn, is indexed by it. I am indebted to Hanks's (1992:68) formulation of Common ground (Sociocentric), Speaker (Egocentric) and Addressee (Altercentric) participant domains. He describes Common ground domain as "pragmatically symmetric" because it joins the Speaker and Addressee into relatively equal footing relative to the referent. Speaker and Addressee participant domains are asymmetric because "they split the Speaker from the Addressee." "Helpin out" communication is symmetrical in his development of the term.

6. I prefer to use the word "classification" for this type of metapragmatic function for this productive grammatical system because of its taxonomic implications (see Agar 1975, Gossen 1974, and Stross 1976 for further discussions of the sense relations of this term when applied to speech).

7. As used here, "face" is both Goffman's (1967:5) usage as "an image of self delineated in terms of approved social attributes" and Brown and Levinson's (1987 [1978]: 61) definition as "something that is emotionally invested, and that can be lost, maintained, or enhanced, and must be constantly attended to in interactions."

8. This finding differs from Ervin-Tripp's (1976:24) that first-person plural pronouns are used in a downward direction by authorities. Supervisors, foremen, and managers of a task-oriented work task commonly use "we" in some requesting token in a manner that could be analyzed to conform to her observation. At the same time, so do all other workers performing a "job" or task. Furthermore, the use of "we" as a false plural (the so-called "royal we") does not occur in Ash Creek. If the "we" subject forms in appropriate Ash Creek task-focused requests do encode power relations, they are not recognized as such by Ash Creek residents.

9. These failures are not the same as Austin's felicity conditions. He bases failures of a given utterance containing a performative verb on the basis of nonconformity to surrounding features so that "something *goes* wrong" (1962:14). Here, I am making claims about the failure of a semiotic indexical sign function reflexively created by features of the utterance and by the participant frameworks they index. The former is a failure of co-occurring variables to be in accord; the latter, a failure of an index to signify what interlocutors presume it should.

10. In Bourdieu's (1984:291) sense of amassing images "of respectability and honourability that are easily converted into political positions as a local or national *notable.*" If Joan is to continue to live and "belong" in Ash Creek, she will not use any symbolic capital she accumulates for overt political position, but she can use it to influence others in the community who value and participate in medical health care. These will be mostly women and their pre-adult children.

11. Once formed, these committees failed to function successfully. As argued here, these failures occurred in large part because of the inability of members to use cooperative task-focused discourse appropriately, both in terms of acceptable semantic structuring and in terms of appropriate participant frameworks that are needed to create culturally recognized "rights" and "place" relations in order to authenticate the use of such forms.

12. Ervin-Tripp, O'Connor, and Rosenberg's (1984) classification of such uses as "task-centered control acts" is relevant here to the extent that they have isolated a utilitarian usage of directive (including imperative) constructions within communicative contexts. However, their formulation relies on a strategic model in which the speaker desires that a task be performed. In Ash Creek usages, such a speaker-oriented categorization is only one aspect of many task-focused uses and can be misleading. For a discussion of nonstrategic uses of interactive discourse, see Duranti (1988).

13. I do not pursue the implications of this statement further in large part because some type of visual image is needed to capture the complexities of these exchanges. Groundbreaking linguistic anthropological research into the conflation of these semiotic systems can be found in Hanks (1990) and Haviland (1996a, 1996b).

14. In contrast to Weigel and Weigel's (1985) study of migrant workers, I observed no example of imperatives being used by a foreman or boss to direct laborers in performing a task. One example formed the basis for the firing/quitting event presented at the beginning of chapter 1. This, however, was a strategic use on the part of the foreman. He used imperatives deliberately to cause the worker to resign. In situations where cooperation is needed, task-directing imperatives exist only as facilitators for accomplishing a given action, whether lifting, placing, moving, cutting, or any other culturally valued action.

15. See Gal (1991) on the role of silence in constructing power relations.

16. The stereotype of the taciturn mountain man can be directly attributed to cultural elaboration of this task-oriented hierarchy of communicative modes. Women generally perform tasks alone or as independent activities done communally, such as quilting or bean breaking. Consequently, situations in which norms of taciturnity would apply are less frequent for women's work, and communal activities, when they occur, are dominated by other forms of talk such as "just takin," "gossipin," and personal narratives about how they do a particular task.

17. See Ervin-Tripp (1976:32) for a slightly different formulation of these types of imperatives. She couches their use on the basis of "normative" (as is common at the dinner table) or in response to physical distance between the interlocutors. The closer the addresser is to the addressee, the more likely an unmitigated imperative.

18. Studies of politeness lead by Brown and Levinson (1987 [1978]) are certainly appropriate and possible in this situation. A number of studies have noted that "turn-taking" can be nonverbal. For example, see Atkinson and Heritage (1984), Blum-Kulka, House, and Kasper (1989b), Drew and Heritage (1992), Ervin-Tripp (1976), Goffman (1967), Goodwin and Heritage (1990); for linguistic anthropological applications, see also Duranti (1997:245–279), Gal (1991), and Ochs (1988). Here, however, I am making the argument that the immediate situation of moving goods and the physical location of them constrains and directs what moving discourse can occur.

19. I make this claim on the basis of multiple conversations with company supervisors or owners, older adult workers who were students in the community college where I taught, and through workshops in Ash Creek and adjacent counties in which I focused on workplace communication.

20. Such constraints are significantly different from those described by Weigel and Weigel (1985) for migrant farm workers. The pragmatic constraints operative in Ash Creek for directions require that the imperative speaker have the "right" to direct a task that each is complying to accomplish; such constraints do not apply to those described by Weigel and Weigel, who are workers conscious of working under an authoritative supervisor as wage-laborers.

21. A few individuals do not consider all wage-labor situations as "helpin someone out." Generally, however, they are among the set of men who have worked for large corporations or grew up elsewhere, for example, two men who have mined for Shamrock Coal Corporation in West Virginia or in Wyoming, one who worked the production lines for General Motors "up North," one young woman who works for a heavy equipment company in town, or a few young adults who have clerked at Kmart or bagged groceries at Kroger's.

22. I contributed to the organization of the event behind the scenes because of multiple complaints about the diminishing quality of well water; a local preacher introduced the organizer and I assumed the role of interested listener. Local water quality issues intersected with anger over the role of a coal company, which was extending its underground mining into Ash Creek substructures. Some residents argued that the extension of shafts past their legal boundaries was polluting their wells with particulates. When a segment of Ash Creek collapsed, draining underground rather than in the creek bed, one local resident took the company to court and won. I did not want to appear as if I were taking sides in this issue; therefore, I withdrew into the background during this meeting.

23. See Batteau (1981, 1982, 1983b) for a discussion of this type of political figure, who acts as a broker between local, community interests and county officials who

control resources. Such a position requires a lot of free time to visit the courthouse and talk to other politically involved men in the county or legislative district.

24. An obvious exception to this strong, highly valued linguistic-economic system occurs when residents enter the military. The mountain region, and Ash Creek notwithstanding, is noted for particularly high enlistment rates. Residents discuss the "order" format of the military as a necessary evil, focusing instead on their own prowess with arms or equipment or on the camaraderie and friendship formed with other noncommissioned "buddies." It should be noted that Ash Creek men discuss enlistment primarily as a source of income and a secure retirement.

25. For related discussions of the significance of "orders," see Hicks (1976) and Ray (1983).

26. The pronominal shifts in this conversational segment are significant in terms of Ash Creek first- and third-person pronominal usages. The rhetorical, indefinite, denotative "you" that begins this segment contextualizes the discourse into the sociocentric domain of Ash Creek social life by designating an all-inclusive, generic "you." Shifts to "I" redirect the focus to an egocentric domain of the speaker's own experience, and the third-person forms that conclude the unit reflect Bill's own experiences as a "teacher," a position he valued highly. This shift from the "out there," social world of cultural life to the highly subjective and personal world of individual experience is a very common, expected, and core discourse process in the full range of speaking practices in Ash Creek; the pronominal expression of them here is merely a hint at a complex linguistic encoding of Ash Creek's cultural expression of the self in a social world (for a discussion of the sociocentric versus egocentric dimensions in social life on which I base these comments, see Hanks 1990, 1992; Lee and Urban 1989; for pronominal shifts, see Hanks 1990 and Silverstein 1985).

27. This linguistic norm for the use of instructional discourse is of course highly significant in understanding the functions of literacy and literate practices in Ash Creek, for much literate knowledge depends heavily on written instructions and processes of telling about how something works or its possible causes. For most Ash Creek residents, such practices are not normative and can be said to violate their patterns and schema of how knowledge should be acquired. For educators who advocate the current slogan "learning by doing," Ash Creek patterns do not readily include literate forms and are therefore not synonymous with the kinds of models being developed and applied in various classrooms (see Heath 1983; Puckett 1992).

28. I discuss the implications of these constraints more fully in my 1995 and 1998 articles. The implications of showing rather than telling for educational achievement are also significant. Heath (1983) notes that rural white populations in her South Carolina study area of Roadville fell behind more professional, urban students around the fifth grade. She focused on storytelling contextual norms to discuss this disparity; I would suggest as an additional hypothesis that instructional norms shift in the upper grades from a more hands-on showing of an activity to more abstract verbal instructional patterns that contradict "showin" instructional discourse norms. My discussions with high school teachers and community college faculty in Ash Creek's county supports this hypothesis, especially in subjects such as math in which verbal instructions become the major means of communicating manipulations of abstract symbolic notations.

29. This claim requires some clarification. As of 1996, Bill's woodcarving sessions became a community event involving some women. Held in the woodshop of the Environmental Center, as many as 15 local men and women of various ages gather to whittle and talk. These sessions vary in their frequency, averaging once every six weeks or so. The one I visited in August 1997 was organized in response to my visit. All of these indi-

viduals have some connection to the center. Most have worked there as staff and most were also grade school students there when it was a county school. Held at the center, these sessions evoke interactive patterns reminiscent of these residents' school days and the mixed-gender patterns created during school activities and events. A similar type of mixed gender interaction occurs at the end of the year when the center puts on its annual Christmas play, an event performed entirely by local residents. I did not find these patterns to be well developed in other community or family gatherings, activities, and events away from the center.

30. For discussions on shifts to narrative to decontextualize a speaker's observations, see Bauman and Briggs (1990), Briggs (1993a); M. Goodwin (1982); Lucy (1993a); Silverstein (1985).

31. It is this normative process of narrative task-referencing that has proven to be successful in the widely imitated Foxfire educational movement, begun by Eliot Wigginton (Wigginton 1972). Drawing on these narrative speaking practices, his approach requires students to write them as "stories." Arguments are then made by educators and community leaders that such students are "preserving their cultural heritage," thereby developing a discourse function into an ideology of literacy that has implications for regional efforts at "preserving our heritage."

32. I use the word "tradition" in the sense of observed or reported procedures for doing some physical activity or task that transcends at least three generations. For example, Kaziah's manner of knitting sweaters is reportedly very similar to the way her grandmother made them.

33. "Crafting," as used by Ash Creek residents, refers to any hand-created item whose function is subsumed under its display or decorative purpose. Most crafts are either modifications of homemade children's playthings or are produced from kits purchased from mail order catalogues. Crafts include, but are not limited to, such items as corn shuck dolls, quilt squares to be used as wall decorations, stuffed dolls, clothespin necklaces, sunbonnets, decorative aprons, and whittled spoons or scoops. What I call "craftin" does not conform to what C. Martin (1987) calls Appalachia's "art of the useful" in which aesthetic elaboration has to also have instrumental functions useful to survival. Nearly all Ash Creek residents conform to his observation in their valuation of artistic elaboration of material things. Kaziah and a few other women, however, now engage in "craftin" for home decoration or as a cottage industry to augment household income. Kaziah has been successful in making her "crafting" a vocation. Her crafts are commodities.

34. A microanalysis of one of these communicative events would require a multichanneled recording method, such as a videocassette recording, as well as a competent computerized method of analyzing such a recording. Using such recording methods was not a choice at the time of data collection. Collecting such data in Ash Creek would be extremely difficult, given residents' perceptions of outsiders' use of pictures of them, and undesired in this study as well, as it would necessarily risk a violation of confidentiality as settings and participants would be revealed.

35. These "you" clauses, as in "ya got to turn it around an (go) this way," can also be analyzed as indicative clauses describing action in which "you" is generic, rhetorical, and an indefinite pronoun rather than a deictic. It is this ambiguity that mitigates the potential "order" status of such clauses and the metapragmatic signfications that orders create.

36. If David fails to comply when he performs the same task, he will be corrected, the "you" utterance reuttered in the same or similar form until he does. Failure to comply consistently will result in a termination of the teaching activity. Individual "teachers" vary in their "patience" with their learners; Bill is noted for being especially patient.

37. In the course of living and teaching in the area for an extended period, requiring that I engage in encounters with local medical facilities, businesses, educational institutions, churches, and other institutions, examples of workplace instruction were readily and frequently observed. In efforts to comply with federal and professional guidelines regarding consent in audio-recording, I recorded few of these encounters.

38. Kaziah consciously shaped her "demonstrations" to conform to what nonlocals told her they wanted or expected in a "true" Appalachian woman. She had a costume she wore and certain props, including a large spinning wheel that she never used as a girl (she, like most other mountain women in the area, used a smaller wheel so that the spinner could sit and spin instead of walking back and forth for hours.) She is, in this sense, conforming to Castile's observation about Native Americans: "[T]hey are still inextricably linked to the ebb and flow of the dominant society and its markets and are subject to the rules of its regulators" (1996:747).

39. Kaziah's demonstrations at the center appear to be prototypical representations of Parmentier's (1994:134–142) analysis of Colonial Williamsburg, Virginia. He notes that these unfolding sequences of signs are particularly powerful because they do not evoke explicit, entextualized metasemiotic forms like those encoded in creation myths or ritual. Interpretation by the visitors, the tourists, is left open. Building on Barthes (1986 [1967]), he adds that a "historiticizing sign" (read: museum piece) validates the reality of the event. Finally, his thesis is that "Colonial Williamsburg's overt educational and recreational functions mask a powerful covert function of reproducing and legitimizing a system of social distinctions in contemporary American society" (Parmentier 1986:136). Kaziah's demonstrations in the setting of the center with its old log buildings creates an image that reproduces images of the rustic, simple mountaineer woman. Because she is a living representation of this past, she presents a semiotic event that the audience can generalize to contemporary Appalachian residents. Her demonstrations perpetuate the image of the mountaineer as "our contemporary ancestors" (Frost 1899) and the contemporary socioeconomic order, which elevates "middle-classness" and its educational and technological amenities (Shapiro 1978).

40. Anglin (1992, 1993, 1998) also recognizes the importance of the reconstitution of industrial work relations for women in her cultural anthropological analyses of women's roles in the mica factories of North Carolina. Her analyses suggest that women develop what I call "doin for" relations with bosses and "helpin out" relations with other female workers to reconstruct factory settings as extensions of family ones.

41. An interesting reformulation of these indexes is currently occurring as younger community men talk about or, in one case, embrace nursing as a career. Men are establishing new gender indexes in task-oriented discourse that includes activities appropriate to nursing because they see nursing as stable, marketable, and relatively high-paying. In talking about this field, most of these men clearly articulate their reasons as financial, revolving around an adequate paycheck, rather than nurturing the ill. Acquiring money, a traditionally male domain, is clearly a major motivating interpretive structure encouraging the transformation. I know of no Ash Creek men, however, who have actually pursued a registered nursing educational program.

Chapter 8

1. When asked if ____ "loves" ____, residents reply, almost invariably, with a trope similar to the following:

a. I love ____, he/she does for me.

b. She lo:ves ____, he does for her.

c. He loves ____, she does for him.

2. Hicks (1976) discusses these constraints from a cultural anthropological perspective. He notes that third-person narratives presumably about someone else in a similar circumstance assume directive functions in situations when a man needs or wants to direct the behavior of another. Batteau (1983b) and Stephenson (1968) also noted the "sensitivity" of men to directives in the Appalachian communities they observed. I found that these typological narratives could also direct the behavior of women, particularly when I was in the position of community college teacher in a county adjacent to Ash Creek's.

3. "Doin for" orders often convey a sense of intimacy or familiarity as well and could be reinterpreted under approaches addressing these affective relations (see, for example, Besnier 1990; Irvine 1979; and Lutz and Abu-Lughod 1990). It would limit the full range of their cultural significance, however, if their socioeconomic functions were omitted from discussion.

4. The influx and community acceptance of government transfer payments and return of migrants who worked in urban corporate wage-labor relations in the last 20 years has had significant impact on the reproduction of this form of linguistic-economic relationship. A number of younger individuals now view these "doin for" imperative-permitting relationships as too binding or time-demanding, keeping them from consumer-oriented activities such as shopping or making them perform tasks such as gardening or canning, which they view as no longer necessary. They consider these tasks as too labor-intensive, especially when they prefer to grocery shop in town. None, however, can reject this semiotic system entirely and still remain in Ash Creek.

5. Similar noncompliance behavior is frequent for young girls but is less tolerated. See Looff (1971) for a discussion of these differences in parental permissiveness among Appalachian children (see also Keefe 1988 for discussions of related issues).

6. The importance of these processes of "language socialization" (Ochs and Schieffelin 1984) to becoming a community member through language is not a focus here. Masterful studies on this process are Ochs (1988), Ochs and Schieffelin (1979, 1983), Schieffelin (1990), and Schieffelin and Ochs (1986). For the development of requesting strategies and practices, see, for example, Bock and Hornsby (1981); Ervin-Tripp and Mitchell-Kernan (1977); Gordon and Ervin-Tripp (1984). A major contribution of these studies that influenced these Ash Creek observations has been to refocus studies of children's mastery of language to the plane of the contextualization of language in social interaction. See also Heath (1983).

7. Residents tend to reside close to the parents of one of the spouses. Married children with parents next door or nearby will commonly spend much of their free time at the parents' homeplace, with or without their spouse. Newlyweds will frequently spend much of their honeymoon at the "folks' place." In one case, the bride was at her mom's the day after the wedding and the husband was at his mother's. In this case, both sets of parents resided in Ash Creek.

8. In order to get to know as many residents of Ash Creek as I could, I volunteered to run errands and do common household tasks for older people in the community in return for conversation, food, or audiotaping. This was the case here. I did attempt to paint Kaziah's bedroom ceiling but appreciated the help of her visiting grandson who actually knew how to paint well. When my voluntary housekeeping became known to the cooks in the Environmental Center kitchen, I became the brunt of some teasing. From these efforts, I did, however, earn a reputation, or "name," among some for "not being afraid to work."

9. Certainly the model of politeness as a means of organizing cooperative social interaction formulated by Brown and Levinson (1987 [1978]) is relevant here and could yield a rich understanding of Ash Creek social interaction. Discussion of the events under politeness criteria, however complexly understood, would distort the reciprocal socioeconomic implications of "doin for" violations and the ways in which they contribute to the constitution of an ideology of socioeconomic language.

10. Women generally have scope over children's upbringing and well-being, but men's domains include physical protection of children in their belonging network. An example of this behavior occurred one summer evening at the Environmental Center playground where local teenagers were playing unsupervised. A teenage boy was angry with a local girl and pushed her around and shouted obscenities at her. Cindy and I were talking some distance away. Cindy called the girl's home. Within only a few minutes, two carloads of men arrived at the center to accost the young man, ready to assault him. No fighting or injuries occurred, but there was some shouting and many "doin for" imperative tokens uttered. The young man left quickly.

11. A readily conceived context would be like that described in note 10 in which a parent was reprimanding another's child for behavior toward his or her "own."

12. Cindy is a physically strong woman who regularly performs at male levels of physical strength. I knew of no occasions when she actually attacked someone, but she certainly had the ability to do so. Reports were that she had engaged in fights in the past.

13. For pertinent theoretical discussions of the limits of formality and informality, see Irvine (1979, 1982, 1985); see also Brown and Levinson (1987 [1978]) and Goffman (1967, 1974) for its relevance to face-to-face interaction; Labov (1972) approaches variations in levels of informality and intimacy in terms of style shifts. I am arguing that other considerations apply that are encoded in such linguistic features as attributive possessives.

14. As in regularized possessive constructions, the constitution of "cultural unequals" in Ash Creek is accomplished by routine, highly presupposed indexical relations created by the repetitive utterance of similar imperative tokens in similar situations.

15. By "naturalize," I mean the ongoing processes of ritualized genres and other discursive forms to effect specific interpretations of human and resource relationships. These processes result in relationships that assume a "naturalness," a sense of timeless permanence and priority that makes changing their configuration "unnatural." I am indebted to Silverstein and Urban (1996b:16), who view the "texts" resulting from such processes as a "series of prior entextualizations/texts which lie discursively behind [a specific text], and a complex diachrony of social interactions out of which it was produced and continues to reanimated." Also relevant is Parmentier's argument that

> individuals within a system have a tendency to regard conventions as naturally motivated, that is, as being *objective* rather than socially constituted, *invariant* rather than malleable, *autonomous* rather than dependent, *eternal* rather than historical, *universal* rather than relative, and *necessary* rather than contingent (1994:176).

16. These core or central "rights" are grammatically encoded in obligatory possessive constructions, as discussed in chapter 2. If a noun phrase requires that the speaker use a possessive construction within the Ash Creek socioeconomic system, then the speaker generally has the "right" to demand compliance from others when using imperative discourse, which references such a phrase as the direct object (e.g., "gIt me my gun")

or to demand compliance from those to whom such phrases apply (e.g., "gIt me my gun" from father to daughter).

17. I encountered only one woman for whom conformity to thinness issues affected these imperative uses. This woman substituted a sugarless drink such as Diet Coke instead of the obligatory sugared drink or food. The overwhelming majority of Ash Creek residents of all ages do not conform to urban, professional class norms of acceptable weight. Most, however, are not obese.

18. The narrative offered in (8.9) is one version of a folk narrative that I heard many times in Ash Creek and surrounding communities. This segment represents a non–Ash Creek resident's allegedly true version, which he allowed me to audiotape and use. Ash Creek taping constraints excluded taping of allegedly true "tales" of dubious acts by residents. I am including this narrative for its relevance to this discussion about "doin for" extension patterns. Its form, content, and context of utterance are consistent with Ash Creek norms.

19. Bill's failure to assign a possessive marker in his utterance "you're goin have to gIt serious with **that dog**" is therefore significant in terms of this discussion. "My" dog was a stray that had wandered onto the Environmental Center campus, where it became a campus dog of sorts. I had been feeding it, however, and attempting to domesticate it. Bill was acknowledging its lack of identification with a particular person. He is also using a pattern of deictic distancing here. When residents are commenting on an action, moving it from the egocentric domain of self activities, they will use the relative pronoun "that." For example, one day, after narrating a past activity in which she exercised decision-making independence, Karen said about herself, "It's untellin about that one," decentering the narrative from herself and recentering it into a third-person plane of Ash Creek "doins."

20. Urban (1985:313) is directly relevant here. In detailing the multifunctional relationship between two formal, ritualized speech styles and their quotidian analogs in Shokleng, he writes: "These various aspects of multifunctionality [of linguistic utterances] combine to yield a crucial property of speech styles: because linguistic features of a given style may occur elsewhere, the social context indexed by a speech style can be related to other contexts and meanings."

21. I am drawing upon Bakhtin (1986) and, especially, subsequent theoretical elaborations of his discussion on the construction of voice in reported speech. See particularly the articles in Lucy (1993b, 1993c) and Urban (1993). For a theoretical discussion of "entextualization" as a process that reconstructs and therefore revalidates sacred texts and valued narratives, see Bauman and Briggs (1990) and Silverstein and Urban's introduction (1996b).

22. Kuipers (1990) analysis of Weyewa ritual speech performances is directly relevant here. His careful analysis of the entextualization (Bauman and Briggs 1990) of Weyewa "words of the ancestors" by a performer in performance resonates well with Ash Creek preachers' embodiment of Christ's "words" in preaching. Titon (1988) captures some of this merging of self with divinity as well. The question of a preacher's "rightness" is open for further analysis but is linked to a personal iconicity with Christ as manifested in the performance of "preachin" and its entextualized, "decentered" forms in quotidian discourse. Urban's (1993) delineation of "imperative coordination" in Shokleng reported speech in mythic narrative is also important here for its complex multifunctional structuring within mythic performative contexts and reapplications (entextualizations) in quotidian exchanges. He notes that these collective social purposes are "cultural functions."

23. The nature and cultural construction of the Appalachian preacher's identity through speech and oral scriptural traditions has only begun to be studied. Patterson's

(1995) description of preaching with singing in Primitive Baptist churches, Titon's (1988) analysis of preaching as cohesive force in community construction, and McCauley's (1995) descriptions of the historical context surrounding different transcribed narratives are tangential to a substantive analysis just on the kinds of identities created by Appalachian preaching. The preacher represented in these segments presents himself as an interpreter and role model of Jesus' words and life. Other preachers I have observed become an embodiment of scripture and scriptural knowledge in human form when they preach.

24. See Duranti and Brenneis (1986) for richer and more theoretical discussions of how the "audience" can author performances. See also Borker (1986).

25. As used here, "type" refers to the metaphoric process by which a secular narrative, event, or set of actions is presumed to be structurally iconic with a scriptural or religious narrative or set of actions, thereby giving divine credence to the secular event. This analogic form of reasoning was, of course, a dominant raison d'etre of the rise and success of American Puritanism, a religious orientation dominant in Appalachian spiritual expression (see, for example, McCauley [1995] and Titon [1988]).

26. As audiotaping of intrafamily verbal interactions was generally not granted, these examples represent summations of exchanges heard in the course of fieldwork, exchanges that included imperatives.

27. Puckett (1992) discusses these issues in greater detail; other writers, however, have also noted the clear division of labor in who performs reading and writing tasks in the region (for example, Hicks [1976] and Weller [1965]). Heath (1983) offers relevant analyses of reading activities for Roadville, a white South Carolina Piedmont community.

28. See, for example, Ervin-Tripp (1976, 1982), Ochs (1988), Ochs and Schieffelin (1979, 1983), Schieffelin (1990), and Schieffelin and Ochs (1986) for discussion of requests and women's roles.

29. I noted six women and two men, including me, who acknowledged Millie's status as a professional nurse practitioner through their discourse. All of them were nonlocals; two were married to local men but had lived in cities for extended periods.

30. Tag questions rarely appear in Ash Creek women's conversational discourse and, if they do, are a clear index of an assimilation of more of the kinds of professional or middle-class uses reported by Coates (1986, 1996), Kramarae, Schulz, and O'Barr (1984), and Lakoff (1975).

31. The clinic Millie administered closed in 1994. The "doin for" relations she created have continued, however. Several women residents now travel 40 miles to the clinic where she now works. The strength of these "doin for" claims is also manifested as "trust": these women comment frequently on how good she is and that they know she will give them informed medical advice.

32. For related discussions, see Briggs (1986), DiPietro (1982), Ervin-Tripp et al. (1987), Gumperz (1982), and Heath (1983).

33. Anglin (1992, 1993, 1998) discusses these syncretic patterns for mica factory women in rural western North Carolina from a cultural anthropological theoretical perspective. Formal institutions such as the community college serving the Ash Creek population adjust to these boundary maintenance problems in very complex and highly diversified ways. Invariably, however, residents from the area who have acquired at least minimal credentials to meet state requirements have the most success in the organization, as their ability to use Ash Creek "doin for" and task-focused discourse in culturally appropriate ways is high. Such institutions also replicate "belongin" networks, as most employees have close family or kin also working at the institution. Interfacing functions with urban or state professionals engender discourse practices that participate in dual

interpretive structuring. The same discourse patterns can communicate one constellation of meanings to outsiders and another constellation to local residents based on pragmatic rather than semantic planes of signification.

34. From 1985 to 1991, I encountered three medical practitioners, one social worker, four primary or secondary educators, and seven community college faculty who had resigned because of job-related frustrations with "locals" or local sociopolitical structures.

35. No inappropriate uses were actually recorded, although a few discourse segments commenting on them were. The examples given represent notes or transcriptions of these commentaries.

36. Details of these occurrences are deliberately presented in general or vague terms in order to protect the names of the individuals who were involved. As inappropriate "order" occurrences frequently result in conflict or tension between the participants, such generalization is necessary.

37. At one point, I encountered a temporary problem regarding a local woman who thought I was spending too much time with her husband when he was working at the Environmental Center. Bill performed the role of messenger and discussed the problem with me. I said that this man's wife had been very nice to me. He retorted very quickly, "That don't mean *nothin*." I ceased observing all-male work crews.

38. See C. Martin (1987), Hicks (1976), and Ray (1983) for in passing discussions of how men use these narrative patterns with other men.

39. The terms used to refer to these agent-denying processes of socioeconomic communication are derived from expressions or lexemes used by residents in conversation.

40. Specific examples are deliberately omitted from this discussion because of their highly inflammatory and private nature. To discuss them or transcribe the conversational discourse pertaining to them would violate confidentiality at a basic level.

41. As discussed in chapter 2, these core areas are expressed grammatically through regularized use of attributive possessive constructions. For those core resources that are culturally sanctioned, such as guns, dogs, vehicles, spouses, and children, these uses of nonverbal messages attack not only an individual's personal identity, expressed as his or her "name," but his or her community identity as well. Some nonverbal messages address idiosyncratic domains of personal identity expressed in regularized possessives in discourse about that particular individual. A man's bee gums (hives), which are routinely referenced as [+poss /gums/] may be destroyed, for example.

Chapter 9

1. These 1989 works have of course been elaborated upon by other theoretical scholarship, particularly in terms of recent formulations of linguistic ideologies, as discussed in the Introduction (see Schieffelin, Woolard, and Kroskrity 1998). Their basic claims, however, remain the cornerstones of this new way of viewing language and material relations.

2. I am responding to articles in Clifford and Marcus (1986) in making this statement, and, in particular, to Marcus (1986) and Asad (1986). I am also indebted to Nash's (1992:275) observation that "textual interpretation is useful only when employed along with traditional methods of participant observation and the eliciting of informants' own interpretations."

3. See Bauman and Briggs (1990), Briggs (1988, 1993a), and Silverstein (1993) for discussions of how more textualized and performative genres are less presupposingly indexical and more creatively indexical. The process of entailment that creative indexes effects is constructed of very complex symbolic significations in the mythic plane of

meaning. For someone who is unfamiliar with the socially constructed norms of use for these textualized performances, the possibility of interpretation outside the range of users' own is wide even over long periods of time. When preexisting negative valuations of the genres already exist in fieldworkers' own ideologies of religious discourse, as they were for me, the problems of merging my own interpretations with practitioners were significant. To use an Ash Creek expression, "You won't gɛt it right."

4. Also allowing me to make this claim are other instances involving nonlocal Environmental Center administrative staff who attempted to transform the mission and purpose of the center as well as various experiences I had when teaching for the county community college. It would remove anonymity to specifically discuss these instances, but I can say that alleged results of such efforts were that the center staff was excluded from the lower prices given to locals in good standing at certain town businesses, from the best interest rates at at least one local bank, and from having publicity for center events published in a local newspaper.

5. I should clarify that most Ash Creek men are not regular churchgoers and many are not "saved." Nevertheless, this scenario is based on observed behavior.

6. Briggs and Bauman (1992), Gal (1989), Irvine (1989), and Woolard (1998) argue for the "political" or power dimension of all language having economic functions. Here, I am claiming the residents superimpose interpretations on these inherent power relations to disclaim them as exercises of it.

7. For historical, sociological, and cultural anthropological discussions of this practice in Appalachia, see Dorgan (1987), Kimbrough (1995), McCauley (1995), Patterson (1995), and Titon (1988).

8. Tape-recording group "prayin" is not only difficult to do because of the multiplicity of voices speaking simultaneously, it is also a violation of privacy to attempt it. "Prayin" participant frameworks are sacred arrangements of individuals. Engaging in activities such as audio-recording that deny the highly subjective and deeply personal interaction with others and God are literally defiling acts. They also can break the requesting connection with God through loss of concentration and perceived inauthenticity of the message so that the content of the "prayin" is not valid.

9. These processes resonate with Basso's (1979) descriptions of Western Apache depictions of "the Whiteman." Here, however, the processes of "making sense" out of the behavior of those having political economic power is not ethnic, but moral. Most Ash Creek residents deny any ethnic or racial differences with other "whites" and strongly defend their moral rights of equality under either constitutional or scriptural grounds.

10. In Gramsci's (1992 [1975]) sense of the extension of dominant ideologies of control into all sectors of society. R. Williams (1977) provides a rich elaboration of Gramsci that has applicability to Ash Creek in terms of his recognition of the pervasive, permeable infusion of dominant hegemonic symbols into the daily lives of subordinate classes.

11. Most linguistic anthropological scholarship clusters toward analyses of more textualized genres. Those within the language and political economic dimension that have had direct impact on the approach taken in this book are, to note only a few, Briggs (1988), Gal (1979), Kuipers (1990), and Woolard (1989).

REFERENCES

Agar, Michael. 1975. Cognition and Events. In *Sociocultural Dimensions of Language Use*, ed. Ben Blount and Mary Sanches, pp. 41–56. New York: Academic Press.

Allen, Barbara. 1990. The Genealogical Landscape of the Southern Sense of Place. In *Sense of Place: American Regional Cultures*, ed. Barbara Allen and Thomas Schlereth, pp. 152–163. Lexington: University Press of Kentucky.

Allen, Barbara, and Thomas Schlereth, eds. 1990. *Sense of Place: American Regional Cultures.* Lexington: University of Kentucky Press.

American Anthropological Association. 1990. *Statement on Ethics.* Arlington: American Anthropological Association.

Anglin, Mary. 1992. A Question of Loyalty: National and Regional Identity in Narratives of Appalachia. *Anthropological Quarterly* 65(3): 105–116.

———. 1993. Engendering the Struggle: Women's Labor and Traditions of Resistance in Rural Southern Appalachia. In *Fighting Back in Appalachia: Traditions of Resistance and Change*, ed. Stephen L. Fisher, pp. 263–281. Philadelphia: Temple University Press.

———. 1998. Looking Beyond the Factory: Regional Culture and Practices of Dissent. In *More Than Class: Studying Power in U.S. Workplaces*, ed. Ann Kingsolver, pp. 53–72. Buffalo: SUNY Press.

Appadurai, Arjun, ed. 1986. *The Social Life of Things: Commodities in Cultural Perspective.* New York: Cambridge University Press.

Appalachian Regional Commission. 1996. *General Economic Indicators: Appalachia and United States 1965–Latest Data Available*. Washington, DC: Appalachian Regional Commission.

Asad, Talal. 1986. The Concept of Cultural Translation in British Social Anthropology. In *Writing Culture: The Poetics and Politics of Ethnography,* ed. James Clifford and George E. Marcus, pp. 141–164. Berkeley: University of California Press.

Atkinson, J. Maxwell, and John Heritage, eds. 1984. *Structures of Social Action*. New York: Cambridge University Press.

Austin, John L. 1962. *How To Do Things with Words*, 2nd ed., eds. J. O. Urmson and Marina Sbisà. Cambridge: Harvard University Press.

Bakhtin, Mikhail. 1981. *The Dialogic Imagination: Four Essays*. Ed. Michael Holquist, trans. Caryl Emerson and Michael Holquist. Austin: University of Texas Press.
———. 1986. *Speech Genres & Other Late Essays*. Ed. Michael Holquist, trans. Caryl Emerson and Michael Holquist. Austin: University of Texas Press.
Banks, Alan. 1980. *Labor and the Development of Industrial Capitalism in Eastern Kentucky*, 1870–1930. PhD dissertation, McMaster University, Toronto.
Barthes, Roland. 1986 [1967]. The Discourse of History. In *The Rustle of Language*, pp. 127–140. Trans. Richard Howard. New York: Hill and Wang.
Basso, Keith. 1979. *Portraits of "The Whiteman": Linguistic Play and Cultural Symbols among the Western Apache*. New York: Cambridge University Press.
Bateson, Gregory P. 1972. *Steps to an Ecology of Mind*. New York: Ballantine Books.
Batteau, Allen. 1981. Appalachia as a Metropolitan Problem. *Social Analysis* 7: 3–23.
———. 1982. Mosbys and Broomsedge: The Semantics of Class in an Appalachian Kinship System. *American Ethnologist* 9: 445–466.
———, ed. 1983a. *Appalachia and America: Autonomy and Regional Dependence*. Lexington: University Press of Kentucky.
———. 1983b. Rituals of Dependence in Appalachian Kentucky. In *Appalachia and America: Autonomy and Regional Dependence*, pp. 142–167. Lexington: University Press of Kentucky.
———. 1985. A Contribution to the Critique of Political Economy. In *The Many Faces of Appalachia*, ed. Sam Gray, pp. 41–46. Proceedings of the 7th Annual Appalachian Studies Conference. Boone: Appalachian Consortium Press.
———. 1990. *The Invention of Appalachia*. Tucson: University of Arizona Press.
———. 1996. There Is No Such Thing as an Organizational Subculture. Unpublished manuscript.
Bauman, Richard. 1986 [1981]. *Story, Performance, and Event: Contextual Studies of Oral Narrative*. New York: Cambridge University Press.
Bauman, Richard, and Charles L. Briggs. 1990. Poetics and Performance as Critical Perspectives on Language and Social Life. *Annual Review of Anthropology* 19: 59–282.
Bauman, Richard, and Joel Sherzer, eds. 1989 [1974]. *Explorations in the Ethnography of Speaking*. 2nd ed. New York: Cambridge University Press.
Beaver, Patricia. 1986. *Rural Community in the Appalachian South*. Lexington: University Press of Kentucky.
Benveniste, Emile. 1971. *Problems in General Linguistics*. Coral Gables: University of Miami Press.
Besnier, Niko. 1990. Language and Affect. *Annual Review of Anthropology* 19: 419–451.
Beukema, Frits, and Peter Coopmans. 1988. A Government-Binding Perpective on the Imperative in English. *Linguistics* 25: 417–436.
Blackside, Inc., producers. 1995. *America's War on Poverty* [video-recording]. Alexandria: PBS.
Blanton, Linda. 1985. Southern Appalachia: Social Considerations of Speech. In *Toward a Social History of American English*, ed. J. L. Dillard, pp. 79–90. The Hague: Mouton.
———. 1989. Mountain English. In *Encyclopedia of Southern Culture*, eds. William Ferris and Charles Wilson, p. 777. Chapel Hill: University of North Carolina Press.
Bloch, Maurice. 1975. *Political Language and Oratory in Traditional Society*. New York: Academic.

Blum-Kulka, Shoshana, Julian House, and Gabriele Kasper, eds. 1989a. *Cross-Cultural Pragmatics: Requests and Apologies.* Advances in Discourse Processes 31. Norwood, NJ: Ablex.

———. 1989b. Investigating Cross-Cultural Pragmatics: An Introductory Overview. In *Cross-Cultural Pragmatics: Requests and Apologies*, ed. Shoshana Blum-Kulka, Juliane House, and Gabriele Kasper, pp. 1–34. Advances in Discourse Processes 31. Norwood, NJ: Ablex Publishing.

Bock, J. K. and N. E. Hornsby. 1981. The Development of Directives: How Children Ask and Tell. *Journal of Child Language* 8: 151–164.

Bolinger, Dwight. 1989. *Intonation and Its Uses.* Stanford: Stanford University Press.

Borker, Ruth. 1986. "Moved by the Spirit": Constructing Meaning in a Brethren Breaking of Bread Service. *Text* 6: 317–337.

Bourdieu, Pierre. 1977a. The Economics of Linguistic Exchanges. *Social Science Information* 16(6): 645–668.

———. 1984. *Distinction: A Social Critique of the Judgement of Taste.* Trans. Richard Nice. Cambridge: Harvard University Press.

Bowler, Betty. 1985. "That Ribbon of Social Neglect": Appalachia and the Media in 1964. *Appalachian Journal* 12: 239–247.

Briggs, Charles. 1986. *Learning How to Ask: A Sociolinguistic Appraisal of the Role of the Interview in Social Science Research.* New York: Cambridge University Press.

———. 1988. *Competence in Performance: The Creativity of Tradition in Mexicano Verbal Art.* Philadelphia: University of Pennsylvania Press.

———. 1993a. Generic versus Metapragmatic Dimensions of Warao Narratives: Who Regiments Performance? In *Reflecive Language: Reported Speech and Metapragmatics*, ed. John Lucy, pp. 179–212. New York: Cambridge University Press.

———. 1996a. Conflict, Language Ideologies, and Privileged Arenas of Discursive Authority in Warao Dispute Mediations. In *Disorderly Discourse: Narrative, Conflict, and Inequality*, ed. Charles Briggs, pp. 204–242. New York: Oxford University Press.

———, ed. 1996b. *Disorderly Discourse: Narrative, Conflict, and Inequality.* New York: Oxford University Press.

Briggs, Charles L., and Richard Bauman. 1992. Genre, Intertextuality, and Social Power. *Journal of Linguistic Anthropology* 2: 131–172.

Brower, Dede, Marinel Gerritsen, and Dorian de Haan. 1979. Speech Differences between Women and Men: On the Wrong Track? *Language in Society* 8: 33–50.

Brown, Gillian, and George Yule. 1983. *Discourse Analysis.* Cambridge Textbooks in Linguistics. New York: Cambridge University Press.

Brown, Penelope, and Stephen Levinson. 1987 [1978]. *Politeness: Some Universals in Language Usage.* 2nd edition. New York: Cambridge University Press.

Brown, Roger, and A. Gilman. 1960. The Pronouns of Power and Solidarity. In *Style in Language*, ed. Thomas Sebeok, pp. 253–276. Cambridge: Cambridge University Press.

Bryant, F. Carlene. 1983. Family Group Organization in a Cumberland Mountain Neighborhood. In *Appalachia and America: Autonomy and Regional Dependence,* ed. Allen Batteau. pp. 27–47. Lexington: University Press of Kentucky.

Campbell, John C. 1921. *The Southern Highlander and His Homeland.* New York: Russell Sage Foundation.

Carver, Craig. 1987. *American Regional Dialects: A Word Geography.* Ann Arbor: University of Michigan Press.

Castile, George. 1996. The Commodification of Indian Identity. *American Anthropologist* 98: 743–749.

Christian, Donna. 1978. *Aspects of Verb Usage in Appalachian Speech*. PhD dissertation, Georgetown University.

Christian, Donna, Walt Wolfram, and Najo Dube. 1988. *Variation and Change in Geographically Isolated Communities: Appalachian English and Ozark English*. Tuscaloosa: University of Alabama Press.

Clifford, James, and George Marcus, eds. 1986. *Writing Culture: The Poetics and Politics of Ethnography*. Berkeley: University of California Press.

Coates, Jennifer. 1986. *Women, Men and Language: A Sociolinguistic Account of Sex Differences in Language*. New York: Longman.

———. 1996. *Women Talk: Conversation Between Women Friends*. Malden, MA: Blackwell.

Cole, Peter, and Jerry Morgan. 1975. *Syntax and Semantics 3: Speech Acts*. New York: Academic Press.

Corbin, David. 1981. *Life, Work, and Rebellion in the Coal Fields: The Southern West Virginia Miners, 1880–1822*. Urbana: University of Illinois Press.

Coulmas, Florian. 1992. *Language and Economy*. Cambridge, MA: Blackwell.

Damon, Fred. 1990. *From Muyuw to the Trobriands: Transformations along the Northern Side of the Kula Ring*. Tucson: University of Arizona Press.

Darnell, Regna. 1985. The Language of Power in Cree Interethnic Communication. In *Language of Inequality*, ed. N. Wolfson and J. Manes, pp. 61–72. The Hague: Mouton.

Davis, Dee Alvin. 1984. *Strangers and Kin*. [video-recording] Whitesburg, KY: Appalshop.

Davies, Eirlys. 1986. *The English Imperative*. London: Croom Helm.

Deane, Paul. 1987. English Possessives, Topicality, and the Silverstein Hierarchy. *Proceedings of the 13th Annual Meeting of the Berkeley Linguistics Society*, pp. 65–76. General Session. Berkeley: Berkeley Linguistics Society.

DiPietro, Robert J., ed. 1982. *Linguistics and the Professions*. Norwood: Ablex.

Dorgan, Howard. 1987. *Giving Glory to God in Appalachia: Worship Practices of Six Baptist Subdenominations*. Knoxville: University of Tennessee Press.

Drew, Paul, and John Heritage, eds. 1992. *Talk at Work: Interaction in Institutional Settings*. New York: Cambridge University Press.

Du Bois, John, et al. 1993. Outline of Discourse Transcription. In *Talking Data: Transcription and Coding in Discourse Research*, eds. Jane Edwards and Martin Lampert, pp. 45–89. Hillsdale, NJ: Lawrence Erlbaum.

Dunaway, Wilma. 1996. *The First American Frontier: Transition to Capitalism in Southern Appalachia, 1700–1860*. Chapel Hill: University of North Carolina Press.

Duranti, Alessandro. 1988. Intentions, Language, and Social Action in a Samoan Context. *Journal of Pragmatics* 12: 13–33.

———. 1990. Doing Things with Words: Conflict, Understanding and Change in a Samoan Fono. In *Disentangling: Conflict Discourse in Pacific Societies*, eds. K. Watson-Gegeo and G. White, pp. 459–489. Stanford: Stanford University Press.

———. 1992. Intentions, Self and Responsibility. In *Responsibility and Evidence in Oral Discourse*, ed. Jane Hill and Judith Irvine, pp. 24–47. Cambridge: Cambridge University Press.

———. 1994. *From Grammar to Politics: Linguistic Anthropology in a Western Samoan Village*. Berkeley: University of California Press.

———. 1997. *Linguistic Anthropology*. New York: Cambridge University Press. Duranti, Alessandro, and Donald Brenneis, eds. 1986. The Audience as Co-Author. Special issue of *Text* 6: 239–347.

Duranti, Alessandro, and Charles Goodwin. 1992a. Rethinking Context: An Introduction. In *Rethinking Context: Language as an Interactive Phenomenon*, eds. Alessandro Duranti and Charles Goodwin, pp. 1–42. New York: Cambridge University Press.

———, eds. 1992b. *Rethinking Context: Language as an Interactive Phenomenon*. New York: Cambridge University Press.

Duranti, Alessandro, and Elinor Ochs. 1996. Use and Acquisition of Genetive Constructions in Samoan. In *Social Interaction, Social Context, and Language: Essays in Honor of Susan Ervin-Tripp*, ed. Dan Slobin, et al., pp. 174–189. Mahway, NJ: Lawrence Erlbaum.

Eller, Ronald. 1982. *Miners, Millhands, and Mountaineers: Industrialization of the Appalachian South, 1880–1930*. Knoxville: University of Tennessee Press.

———. 1994. *Kentucky's Distressed Communities: A Report on Poverty in Appalachian Kentucky*. Lexington: Appalachian Center, University of Kentucky.

Erickson, Frederick, and Jeffrey Shultz. 1981. *The Counselor as Gatekeeper: Social Interaction in Interviews*. New York: Academic.

Ervin-Tripp, Susan. 1972. On Sociolinguistic Rules: Alternation and Co-Occurrence. In *Directions in Sociolinguistics: The Ethnography of Communication*, ed. John J. Gumperz and Dell Hymes, pp. 213–250. New York: Holt Reinhart and Winston.

———. 1973 [1964]. *Language Acquisition and Communicative Choice*. Stanford: Stanford University Press.

———. 1976. Is Sybil There? The Structure of Some American English Directives. *Language in Society* 5: 25–66.

———.1980. Speech Acts, Social Meaning, and Social Learning. In *Language: Social Psychological Perspectives*, ed. H. Giles, W. P. Robinson, and P. M. Smith, pp. 389–396. New York: Pergamon.

———1981. How to Make and Understand a Request. In *Possibilities and Limitations of Pragmatics*, ed. H. Perret, M. Sbisa, and J. Verschueren, pp. 195–209. Amsterdam: John Benjamins.

———. 1982. Structures of Control. In *Communicating in the Classroom.*, ed. L. C. Wilkinson, pp. 27–47. New York: Academic.

———.1996. Context in Language. In *Social Interaction, Social Context, and Language: Essays in Honor of Susan Ervin-Tripp*, ed. Dan Slobin, et al. pp. 21–36. Mahweh, NJ: Lawrence Erlbaum.

Ervin-Tripp, Susan, and C. Mitchell-Kernan, eds. 1977. *Child Discourse*. New York: Academic.

Ervin-Tripp, Susan, Mary C. O'Connor, and Jarrett Rosenberg. 1984. Language and Power in the Family. In *Language and Power*, ed. Cheris Kramarae, Muriel Schulz, and William O'Barr, pp. 116–135. Beverly Hills: Sage Publications.

Ervin-Tripp, Susan, et al. 1987. Understanding Requests. *Linguistics* 25: 107–143.

Feld, Steven, and Keith Basso, eds. 1996. *Senses of Place*. Santa Fe: School of American Research Press.

Fine, Elizabeth. 1999. Ventriloquizing the Voiceless: A Critical Assessment of the New Ethnography. In *The Voice of the Voiceless: Proceedings of the XVI International Colloquium on Communication*, ed. Edith Slembek. St. Ingbert, Germany: Roehrig-Universitaetsverlag.

Firth, Alan. 1994. *The Discourse of Negotiation: Studies of Language in the Workplace*. New York: Elsevier Science.

Fischer, David Hackett. 1989. *Albion's Seed: Four British Folkways in America*. New York: Oxford University Press.

Fisher, Stephen L. 1993a. Conclusion: New Populist Theory and the Study of Dissent in Appalachia. In *Fighting Back in Appalachia: Traditions of Resistance and Change*, ed. Stephen L. Fisher, pp. 317–336. Philadelphia: Temple University Press.

———. 1993b. Introduction. In *Fighting Back in Appalachia: Traditions of Resistance and Change*, ed. Stephen L. Fisher, pp. 1–14. Philadelphia: Temple University Press.

———, ed. 1993c. *Fighting Back in Appalachia: Traditions of Resistance and Change*. Philadelphia: Temple University Press.

Fox, Barbara. 1981. Body Part Syntax: Towards a Universal Characterization. *Studies in Language* 5: 323–342.

Frake, Charles. 1972. "Struck by Speech": The Yakan Concept of Litigation. In *Directions in Sociolinguistics: The Ethnography of Communication*, ed. John Gumperz and Dell Hymes, pp. 106–129. New York: Holt, Reinhart, and Winston.

Friedrich, Paul. 1979 [1966]. Structural Implications of Russian Pronominal Usage. *In Language, Context, and the Imagination: Essays by Paul Friedrich*. Stanford: Stanford University Press.

———. 1989. Language, Ideology, and Political Economy. *American Anthropologist* 91: 295–312.

Frost, William G. 1899. Our Contemporary Ancestors in the Southern Mountains. *Atlantic Monthly* 83: 311–319.

Gal, Susan. 1979. *Language Shift: Social Determinants of Linguistic Change in Bilingual Austria*. New York: Academic Press.

———. 1989. Language and Political Economy. *Annual Review of Anthropology* 18: 345–367.

———. 1991. Between Speech and Silence: The Problematics of Research on Language and Gender. In *Gender at the Crossroads of Knowledge: Feminist Anthropology in the Postmodern Era*, ed. M. di Leonardo, pp. 175–203. Berkeley: University of California Press.

———. 1998. Multiplicity and Contention among Language Ideologies: A Commentary. In *Language Ideologies: Practice and Theory*, ed. Bambi B. Schieffelin, Kathyn Woolard, and Paul Kroskrity, pp. 317–331. New York: Oxford University Press.

Gal, Susan, and Judith Irvine. 1995. The Boundaries of Languages and Disciplines: How Ideologies Construct Difference. *Social Research* 62: 967–1001.

Garfinkel, Harold. 1967. *Studies in Ethnomethodology*. Englewood Cliffs, NJ: Prentice-Hall.

Gaventa, John. 1980. *Power and Powerlessness: Quiescence and Rebellion in Appalachian Valley*. Urbana: University of Illinois Press.

Geertz, Clifford. 1973. *The Interpretation of Cultures*. New York: Basic Books.

———. 1988. *Works and Lives: The Anthropologist as Author*. Stanford: Stanford University Press.

Giardina, Denise. 1987. *Storming Heaven: A Novel*. New York: Ivy Books.

Goffman, Erving. 1967. *Interaction Ritual: Essays on Face-to-Face Behavior*. Garden City, NJ: Doubleday.

———. 1974. *Frame Analysis*. New York: Harper & Row.

———. 1979. Footing. *Semiotica* 25: 1–29.

———. 1981. *Forms of Talk*. Philadelphia: University of Pennsylvania Press.

Goodwin, Charles, and John Heritage. 1990. Conversation Analysis. *Annual Review of Anthropology* 19: 283–308.

Goodwin, Margorie. 1982. "Instigating": Storytelling as a Social Process. *American Ethnologist* 9: 799–819.

———. 1990. *He-Said-She-Said: Talk as Social Organization among Black Children*. Bloomington: Indiana University Press.

Gordon, D., and Susan Ervin-Tripp. 1984. The Development of Requests. In *The Acquisition of Communicative Competence*. ed. R. Schiefelbusch and J. Pickar, pp. 295–322. Baltimore: University Park Press.

Gossen, Gary. 1974. *Chamulas in the World of the Sun: Time and Space in a Maya Oral Tradition*. Cambridge: Harvard University Press.

Graham, Laura. 1996. *Performing Dreams: Discourses of Immortality among the Xavante of Central Brazil*. Austin: University of Texas Press.

Gramsci, Antonio. 1992 [1975]. *Prison Notebooks*, ed. Joseph A. Buttigieg, trans. Joseph A. Buttigieg and Antonio Callari. New York: Columbia University Press.

Greenburg, Joseph. 1986. Introduction: Some Reflections on Pronominal Systems. In *Pronominal Systems*, ed. Ursula Wiesemann, pp. 1–6. Tubinger: Gunter Nar Verlag.

Gregory, C. A. 1982. *Gifts and Commodities*. New York: Academic Press.

———. 1997. *Savage Money: The Anthropology and Politics of Commodity Exchange*. Amsterdam: Harwood Academic Publishers.

Gudeman, Stephen. 1986. *Economics as Culture: Models and Metaphors of Livelihood*. London: Routledge and Kegan Paul.

Gumperz, John. 1982. *Discourse Strategies*. New York: Cambridge University Press.

———. 1992. Contextualization and Understanding. In *Rethinking Context: Language as an Interactive Phenomenon*, ed. Alessandro Duranti and Charles Goodwin, pp. 229–252. New York: Cambridge University Press.

———. 1996. The Linguistic and Cultural Relativity of Inference. In *Rethinking Linguistic Relativity*, ed. John Gumperz and Stephen Levinson, pp. 374–406. New York: Cambridge University Press.

Gumperz, John, and Dell Hymes, eds. 1972. *Directions in Sociolinguistics: The Ethnography of Communication*. New York: Harcourt, Brace, and World.

Gumperz, John, and Stephen Levinson, eds. 1996. *Rethinking Linguistic Relativity*. New York: Cambridge University Press.

Halliday, Michael A. K., and Ruqaiya Hassen. 1976. *Cohesion in English*. London: Longman.

Halperin, Rhoda. 1990. *The Livelihood of Kin: Making Ends Meet "The Kentucky Way."* Austin: University of Texas Press.

———. 1994. *Cultural Economies: Past and Present*. Austin: University of Texas Press.

Hanks, William. 1990. *Referential Practice: Language and Lived Space among the Maya*. Chicago: University of Chicago Press.

———. 1992. The Indexical Ground of Deictic Reference. In *Rethinking Context: Language as an Interactive Phenomenon*, eds. Alessandro Duranti and Charles Goodwin, pp. 43–76. New York: Cambridge University Press.

———. 1993. Metalanguage and Pragmatics of Deixis. In *Reflexive Language: Reported Speech and Metapragmatics*, ed. John A. Lucy, pp. 127–157. Cambridge: Cambridge University Press.

———. 1996a. Exorcism and the Description of Participant Roles. In *Natural Histories of Discourse*, eds. Michael Silverstein and Greg Urban, pp. 160–193. Chicago: University of Chicago Press.

———. 1996b. *Language and Communicative Practices*. Boulder: Westview Press.

Harney, William Wallace. 1995 [1873]. A Strange Land and a Peculiar People. In *Appalachian Images in Folk and Popular Culture*, 2nd ed., ed. William. K. McNeil, pp. 45–58. Knoxville: University of Tennessee Press.

Haviland, John. 1977. *Gossip, Reputation, and Knowledge in Zinacantan*. Chicago: University of Chicago Press.

———. 1996a. Projections, Transpositions, and Relativity. In *Rethinking Linguistic Relativity*, ed. John Gumperz and Stephen Levinson, pp. 271–323. New York: Cambridge University Press.

———. 1996b. Text from Talk in Tzotzil. In *Natural Histories of Discourse*, ed. Michael Silverstein and Greg Urban, pp. 45–78. Chicago: University of Chicago Press.

Hawkins, R. 1981. Towards an Account of the Possessive Constructions: NP's N and the N of NP. *Journal of Linguistics* 17: 247–269.

Heath, Shirley Brice. 1982. What No Bedtime Story Means: Narrative Skills at Home and School. *Language in Society* 1: 49–76.

———. 1983. *Ways with Words: Language, Life, and Work in Communities and Classrooms*. New York: Cambridge University Press.

Heine, Bernd. 1997. *Possession: Cognitive Sources, Forces, and Grammaticalization*. New York: Cambridge University Press.

Herskovits, Melville. 1952. *Economic Anthropology: A Study of Comparative Economics*. New York: Knopf.

Hicks, George. 1976. *Appalachian Valley*. New York: Holt, Rinehart and Winston.

Hill, Jane. 1995. Junk Spanish, Covert Racism and the (Leaky) Boundary between Public and Private Spheres. *Pragmatics* 5: 197–212.

———. 1998. Today There Is No "Respect": Nostalgia, "Respect," and Oppositional Discourse in Mexicano (Nahuatl) Language Ideology. In *Language Ideologies: Practice and Theory*, eds. Bambi Schieffelin, Kathryn Woolard, and Paul Kroskrity, pp. 68–86. New York: Oxford University Press.

Hill, Jane, and Kenneth Hill. 1986. *Speaking Mexicano: Dynamics of Syncretic Languages in Central Mexico*. Tucson: University of Arizona Press.

Hill, Jane H., and Judith T. Irvine, eds. 1992. *Responsibility and Evidence in Oral Discourse*. Cambridge: Cambridge University Press.

Hopkins, Terence K. 1982. The Study of the Capitalist World-Economy: Some Introductory Considerations. In *World-System Analysis, Theory and Methodology*, ed. Terence Hopkins, Immanuel Wallerstein et al., pp. 9–38. Beverly Hills: Sage.

Hopper, Robert, ed. 1990–1991. Special Section: Ethnography and Conversation Analysis after *Talking Culture. Research and Social Interaction* 24: 161–387.

Hoskins, Janet. 1998. *Biographical Objects: How Things Tell the Stories of People's Lives*. New York: Routledge.

Huddleston, Rodney. 1984. *Introduction to the Grammar of English*. Cambridge Textbooks in Linguistics. New York: Cambridge University Press.

Hymes, Dell. 1964. Introduction: Toward Ethnographies of Communication. *American Anthropologist* 66(pt. 2): 1–34.

———. 1972. Models of the Interaction of Language and Social Life. *Directions in Sociolinguistics: The Ethnography of Communication*, ed. John Gumperz and Dell Hymes, pp. 35–71. New York: Holt, Rinehart and Winston.

———. 1974a. *Foundations in Sociolinguistics*. Philadelphia: University of Pennsylvania Press.

———.1974b. Ways of Speaking. In *Explorations in the Ethnography of Speaking*, eds. Richard Bauman and Joel Sherzer, pp. 433–451. New York: Cambridge University Press.

———. 1981. *In Vain I Tried to Tell You*. Philadelphia: University of Pennsylvania Press.

———. 1984 [1968]. Linguistic Problems in Defining the Concept of "Tribe." In *Lan-*

guage in Use: Readings in Sociolinguistics, ed. John Baugh and Joel Sherzer, pp. 7–27. Englewood Cliffs, NJ: Prentice-Hall.

Irvine, Judith. 1979. Formality and Informality in Communicative Events. *American Anthropologist* 81: 773–789.

———. 1980. How Not to Ask a Favor in Wolof. *International Journal of Human Communication* 13(1): 3–49.

———. 1982. Language and Affect: Some Cross-Cultural Issues. In *Contemporary Perceptions of Language: Interdisciplinary Dimensions*, ed. H. Byrnes, pp. 31–47. Washington, DC: Georgetown University Press

———. 1985. Status and Style in Language. *Annual Review of Anthropology* 14: 557–581.

———. 1989. When Talk Isn't Cheap: Language and Political Economy. *American Ethnologist* 16: 248–267.

———. 1990. Registering Affect: Heteroglossia in the Linguistic Expression of Emotion. In *Language and the Politics of Emotion*. ed. C. Lutz and L. Abu-Lughod, pp. 126–161. New York: Cambridge University Press.

———. 1996. Shadow Conversations: The Indeterminancy of Participant Roles. In *Natural Histories of Discourse*, ed. Michael Silverstein and Greg Urban, pp. 131–159. Chicago: University of Chicago Press.

———1998. Ideologies of Honorific Language. In *Language Ideologies: Practice and Theory*, ed. Bambi Schieffelin, Kathryn Woolard, and Paul Kroskrity, pp. 51–67. New York: Oxford University Press.

Isserman, Andrew. 1996. *Socio-Economic Review of Appalachia: The Evolving Appalachian Economy*. Report for the Appalachian Regional Commission. Washington, DC: Appalachian Regional Commission.

Jakobson, Roman. 1960. Concluding Statement: Linguistics and Poetics. In *Style in Language*, ed. Thomas Sebeok, pp. 350–373. Cambridge, MA: MIT Press.

———. 1971 [1957]. Shifters, Verbal Categories, and the Russian Verb. In *Selected Writings II*, pp. 130–147. The Hague-Paris: Mouton.

Jennings, Kathy. 1998. White Like Me: A Confession on Race, Region, and Class. *Appalachian Journal* 25(2): 150–174.

Johnson, Anne. 1991. *Fast Food Women* [video-recording]. Whitesburg, KY: Appalshop.

Jones, Loyal. 1984. Appalachian Religion. In *Encyclopedia of Religion in the South*, ed. Samuel S. Hill, pp. 38–42. Macon, GA: Mercer University Press.

———. 1999. *Faith & Meaning in the Southern Uplands*. Urbana: University of Illinois Press.

Jones, Loyal, and Billy Wheeler. 1987. *Laughter in Appalachia: A Festival of Southern Mountain Humor*. Little Rock: August House.

Keefe, Susan. 1988. *Appalachian Mental Health*. Lexington: University Press of Kentucky.

Kephart, Horace. 1922. *Our Southern Highlanders: A Narrative of Adventure in the Southern Appalachians and a Study of Life Among the Mountaineers*. New York: Macmillan.

Kimbrough, David L. 1995. *Taking Up Serpents: Snake Handlers of Eastern Kentucky*. Chapel Hill: University of North Carolina Press.

Kingsolver, Ann E. 1992. Contested Livelihoods: "Placing" One Another in "Cedar," Kentucky. *Anthropological Quarterly* 65: 128–136.

———. 1998a. Introduction. In *More Than Class: Studying Power in U.S. Workplaces*, ed. Ann Kingsolver, pp. 1–20. Buffalo: SUNY Press.

———, ed. 1998b. *More Than Class: Studying Power in U.S. Workplaces*. Buffalo: SUNY Press.

Kopytoff, Igor. 1986. The Cultural Biography of Things: Commoditization as Process. In *The Social Life of Things: Commodities in Cultural Perspective*, ed. Arjun Appadurai, pp. 64–91. New York: Cambridge University Press.

Kramerae, Cheris, Muriel Schulz, and William O'Barr, eds. 1984. *Language and Power*. Beverly Hills: Sage.

Kuipers, Joel. 1990. *Power in Performance: The Creation of Textual Authority in Weyewa Ritual Speech*. Philadelphia: University of Pennsylvania Press.

Labov, William. 1966. *The Social Stratification of English in New York City*. Washington, DC: Center for Applied Linguistics.

———. 1972. *Sociolinguistic Patterns*. Philadelphia: University of Pennsylvania Press.

Lakoff, Robin. 1977a. Politeness, Pragmatics, and Performatives. In *Proceedings of the Texas Conference on Performatives, Presuppositions, and Implicature*, ed. Andy Rogers, Bob Wall, and John P. Murphy, pp. 79–106. Washington, DC: Center for Applied Linguistics.

———. 1977b. Women's Language. *Language and Style: An International Journal* 10: 222–247.

Leaf, Murray. 1989. Singer, Kant, and the Semiotic Self. In *Semiotics, Self, and Society*, ed. Benjamin Lee and Greg Urban, pp. 171–192. New York: Mouton de Gruyter.

Lee, Benjamin. 1997. *Talking Heads: Language, Metalanguage, and the Semiotics of Subjectivity*. Durham: Duke University Press.

Lee, Benjamin, and Greg Urban, eds. 1989. *Semiotics, Self, and Society*. New York: Mouton de Gruyter.

Levinson, Stephen. 1983. *Pragmatics*. Cambridge Textbooks in Linguistics. New York: Cambridge University Press.

Lewis, Helen, Linda Johnson, and Donald Askins, eds. 1978. *Colonialism in Modern American: The Appalachian Case*. Boone, NC: Appalachian Consortium Press.

Linde, Charlotte. 1988. The Quantitative Study of Communicative Success: Politeness and Accidents in Aviation Discourse. *Language and Society* 17: 375–399.

———. 1993. *Life Stories: The Creation of Coherence*. New York: Oxford University Press.

Looff, David. 1971. *Appalachia's Children: The Challenge of Mental Health*. Lexington: University Press of Kentucky.

Long, Kate. 1994. *Pieces from the Heart*. [audio-recording] Charleston, WV: Kate Long.

Lucy, John. 1993a. Metapragmatic Presentationals: Reporting Speech with Quotatives in Yucatec Maya. In *Reflexive Language: Reported Speech and Metapragmatics*, ed. John Lucy, pp. 91–125. New York: Cambridge University Press.

———. 1993b. Reflexive Language and the Human Disciplines. In *Reflexive Language: Reported Speech and Metapragmatics*, ed. John Lucy, pp. 9–32. Cambridge: Cambridge University Press.

———, ed. 1993c. *Reflexive Language: Reported Speech and Metapragmatics*. New York: Cambridge University Press.

Lutz, Catherine, and Lila Abu-Lughod, eds. 1990. *Language and the Politics of Emotion*. New York: Cambridge University Press.

Lyons, John. 1977. *Semantics*. 2 vols. New York: Cambridge University Press.

MacPherson, Crawford. 1962. *The Political Theory of Possessive Individualism*. Oxford: Oxford University Press.

Marcus, George E. 1986. Contemporary Problems of Ethnography in the Modern World System. In *Writing Culture: The Poetics and Politics of Ethnography*, eds. James Clifford and George E. Marcus, pp. 165–193. Berkeley: University of California Press.

Martin, Charles. 1987. Appalachia's Art of the Useful. *Natural History* 96: 50–59.

Mauss, Marcel. 1967. *The Gift: Forms and Functions of Exchange in Archaic Societies*. New York: W. W. Norton.

McCauley, Deborah. 1991. Grace in the Heart of Appalachian Religion. In *Appalachia: Social Context Past and Present*, 3rd. ed. eds., Bruce Ergood and Bruce E. Kuhre, pp. 355–362. Dubuque, IA: Kendall/Hunt.

———. 1995. *Appalachian Mountain Religion: A History*. Urbana: University of Illinois Press.

McMillan, James B. and Michael Montgomery. 1989. *Annotated Bibliography of Southern American English*. Tuscaloosa: University of Alabama Press.

Merritt, Marilyn. 1976. On Questions Following Questions in Service Encounters. *Language in Society* 5: 315–357.

Mertz, Elizabeth. 1998. Linguistic Ideology and Praxis in U.S. Law School Classrooms. In *Language Ideologies: Practice and Theory*, eds. Bambi Schieffelin, Kathryn Woolard, and Paul Kroskrity, pp. 149–162. New York: Oxford University Press.

Mertz, Elizabeth, and Richard Parmentier, eds. 1985. *Semiotic Mediation: Sociocultural and Psychological Perspectives*. New York: Academic Press.

Miller, Jim Wayne. 1985. Beaucoons of Words. *New York Times Magazine*, Jan. 13, pp. 9–10.

Milroy, Lesley. 1980. *Language and Social Networks*. Oxford: Blackwell.

Mishoe, Margaret, and Michael Montgomery. 1994. The Pragmatics of Multiple Modal Variation in North and South Carolina. *American Speech* 69: 3–29.

Mitchell, Robert, ed. 1991. *Appalachian Frontiers: Settlement, Society, & Development in the Preindustrial Era*. Lexington: University Press of Kentucky.

Moerman, Michael. 1988. *Talking Culture: Ethnography and Conversation Analysis*. Philadelphia: University of Pennsylvania Press.

Munn, Nancy. 1992. *The Fame of Gawa: A Symbolic Study of Value Transformation in a Massim (Papua New Guinea) Society*. Durham: Duke University Press.

Murfree, Mary Noailles. 1884. *In the Tennessee Mountains*. Boston: Houghton Mifflin.

Myers, Fred, and Donald Brenneis, eds. 1984. *Dangerous Words: Language and Politics in the Pacific*. New York: New York University Press.

Myers-Scotton, Carol. 1993. *Social Motivations for Codeswitching: Evidence from Africa*. New York: Oxford University Press.

Narayen, Kirin. 1993. How Native is a "Native" Anthropologist? *American Anthropologist* 95(3): 671–686.

Nash, June. 1992. Interpreting Social Movements: Bolivian Resistance to Economic Conditions Imposed by the International Monetary Fund. *American Ethnologist* 19(2): 275–293.

Ochs, Elinor. 1988. *Culture and Language Development: Language Acquisition and Language Socialization in a Samoan Village*. New York: Cambridge University Press.

———. Indexing Gender. 1992. In *Rethinking Context: Language as an Interactive Phenomenon*, ed. Alessandro Duranti and Charles Goodwin, pp. 335–358. New York: Cambridge University Press.

Ochs, Elinor K., and Bambi B. Schieffelin, eds. 1979. *Developmental Pragmatics*. New York: Academic Press.

———. 1983. *Acquiring Conversational Competence*. Boston: Routledge and Kegan Paul.

———. 1984. Language Acquisition and Socialization: Three Developmental Stories. In

Culture Theory: Essays in Mind, Self, and Emotion, ed. R. Schweder and R. LeVine, pp. 276–320. Cambridge: Cambridge University Press.

Ong, Walter J. 1982. *Orality and Literacy: The Technologizing of the Word*. New York: Methuen.

Ortiz, Sutti, ed. 1983. *Economic Anthropology: Topics and Theories*. Monographs in Economic Anthropology, No. 1. New York: University Press of America.

Parmentier, Richard. 1985. Times of the Signs: Modalities of History and Levels of Social Structure in Belau. In *Semiotic Mediation: Sociocultural and Psychological Perspectives*, ed. Elizabeth Mertz and Richard Parmentier, pp. 131–154. New York: Academic Press.

———. 1994. *Signs in Society: Studies in Semiotic Anthropology*. Bloomington: Indiana University Press.

Patterson, Beverly. 1995. *The Sound of the Dove: Singing in Appalachian Primitive Baptist Churches*. Urbana: University of Illinois Press.

Philips, Susan. 1993. Evidentiary Standards for American Trials: Just the Facts. In *Responsibility and Evidence in Oral Discourse*, ed. Jane H. Hill and Judith T. Irvine, pp. 248–259. New York: Cambridge University Press.

Philips, Susan, U. Susan Steele, and Christine Tanz, eds. 1987. *Language, Gender & Sex in Comparative Perspective*. New York: Cambridge University Press.

Pike, Kenneth. 1945. *The Intonation of American English*. Ann Arbor: University of Michigan Press.

Polyani, Karl, C. W. Arensberg, and H. W. Pearson, eds. 1957. *Trade and Market in the Early Empire*. Glencoe, IL: The Free Press.

Preston, Dennis R. 1985. The Li'l Abner Syndrome: Written Representations of Speech. *American Speech* 60: 328–336.

———. 1996. Where the Worst English Is Spoken. In *Focus on the USA*, ed. Edgar W. Schneider, pp. 297–360. Philadelphia: John Benjamins.

Puckett, Anita. 1992. Let the Girls Do the Spelling and Dan Will Do the Shooting: Literacy, the Division of Labor, and Identity in a Rural Appalachian Community. *Anthropological Quarterly* 65(3): 137–147.

———. 1993. *Seldom Ask, Never Tell: Speech Acts and Socioeconomic Relationships in a Rural Eastern Kentucky Community*. PhD dissertation, University of Texas at Austin, Austin, Texas.

———. 1995. Speech Acts and Cultural Resistance in a Rural Eastern Kentucky Community. *Journal of the Appalachian Studies Association* 7: 111–120.

———. 1998. Rights, Place, Orders, and Imperatives in Rural Eastern Kentucky Task-Focused Discourse. In *More Than Class: Studying Power in U.S. Workplaces*, ed. Ann Kingsolver, pp. 96–123. Buffalo: SUNY Press.

Pudup, Mary Beth, Dwight Billings, and Altina Waller, eds. 1995. *Appalachia in the Making: The Mountain South in the Nineteenth Century*. Chapel Hill, NC: The University of North Carolina Press.

Quirk, Randolph, and Sidney Greenbaum. 1975. *A Concise Grammar of Contemporary English*. New York: Harcourt Brace Jovanovich.

Quirk, Randolph, et al. 1972. *A Grammar of Contemporary English*. London: Longman.

———. 1985. *A Comprehensive Grammar of the English Language*. London: Longman.

Raitz, Karl B., and Richard Ulack. 1984. *Appalachia: A Regional Geography: Land, People, and Development*. Boulder: Westview Press.

Ray, George. 1983. *An Ethnography of Speaking in an Appalachian Community*. PhD dissertation, University of Washington. Seattle.

Rodman, Margaret. 1992. Empowering Place: Multilocality and Multivocality. *American Anthropologist* 94: 640–656.

Rodman, William. 1991. When Questions Are Answers. *American Anthropologist* 93: 421–434.

Rosaldo, Michelle. 1982. The Things We Do with Words: Ilongot Speech Acts and Speech Act Theory in Philosophy. *Language in Society* 11: 203–237.

Rossi-Landi, Ferruccio. 1983. *Language as Work & Trade: A Semiotic Homology for Linguistics & Economics*, trans. Martha Adams et al. South Hadley, MA: Bergin and Garvey.

Sacks, Harvey. 1992. *Lectures on Conversation*. 2 vols. Cambridge, MA: Blackwell.

Sacks, Harvey, Emmanual Shegloff, and Gail Jefferson. 1974. A Simplest Systematics for the Organization of Turn-Taking in Conversation. *Language* 50: 696–735.

Sahlins, Marshall. 1972. *Stone-Age Economics*. Chicago: Aldine.

Sapir, Edward. 1921. *Language: An Introduction to the Study of Speech*. New York: Harcourt Brace Jovanovich.

———. 1966. *Culture, Language and Personality: Selected Essays*, ed. David Mandelbaum. Berkeley: University of California Press.

Schegloff, Emanuel. 1972. Sequencing in Conversational Openings. In *Directions in Sociolinguistics: The Ethnography of Communication*, ed. John Gumperz and Dell Hymes, pp. 346–380. New York: Holt, Rinehart and Winston.

———. 1979. Identification and Recognition in Telephone Openings. In *Everyday Language*, ed. George Psathas, pp. 23–78. New York: Lawrence Erlbaum.

———. 1992. In Another Context. In *Rethinking Context: Language as an Interactive Phenomenon*, ed. Alessandro Duranti and Charles Goodwin, pp. 191–227. New York: Cambridge University Press.

Schegloff, Emanuel, and Harvey Sacks. 1984 [1973]. Opening Up Closings. In *Language in Use: Readings in Sociolinguistics*, ed. John Baugh and Joel Sherzer, pp. 69–99. Englewood Cliffs, NJ: Prentice-Hall.

Schieffelin, Bambi. 1990. *The Give and Take of Everyday Life: Language Socialization of Kaluli Children*. New York: Cambridge University Press.

Schieffelin, Bambi, and Elinor Ochs. 1986. *Language Socialization Across Cultures*. New York: Cambridge University Press.

Schieffelin, Bambi, Kathryn Woolard, and Paul Kroskrity, eds. 1998. *Language Ideologies: Practice and Theory*. New York: Oxford University Press.

Schiffrin, Deborah. 1987. *Discourse Markers*. New York: Cambridge University Press.

Searle, John. 1969. *Speech Acts: An Essay in the Philosophy of Language*. Cambridge: Cambridge University Press.

———. 1975. A Taxonomy of Illocutionary Acts. In *Language, Mind, and Knowledge: Minnesota Studies in the Philosophy of Science*, ed. K. Gunderson, pp. 344–369. Minneapolis: University of Minnesota Press.

———. 1976. The Classification of Illocutionary Acts. *Language in Society* 5: 1–24.

———. 1991. "Indirect Speech Acts." In *Pragmatics: A Reader*, ed. Steven Davis, pp. 265–277. New York: Oxford University Press.

Shapiro, Henry. 1978. *Appalachia on Our Mind: The Southern Mountains and Mountaineers in the American Consciousness, 1870–1920*. Chapel Hill: University of North Carolina Press.

Sherzer, Joel. 1983. *Kuna Ways of Speaking: An Ethnographic Perspective*. Austin: University of Texas Press.

———. 1987a. A Discourse-Centered Approach to Language and Culture. *American Anthropologist* 89: 295–309.

———. 1987b. Poetic Structuring of Kuna Discourse: The Line. In *Native American Discourse: Poetics and Rhetoric*, ed. Joel Sherzer and Anthony C. Woodbury, pp. 103–139. New York: Cambridge University Press.
Shopen, Timothy, and Joseph Williams. 1980. Some Grammatical Characteristics of Appalachian English. In *Standards and Dialects in English,* ed. Timothy Shopen and Joseph Williams, pp. 205–209. Cambridge: Winthrop.
Silverstein, Michael. 1976. Shifters, Linguistic Categories, and Cultural Description. In *Meaning in Anthropology*, ed. Keith Basso and Henry Selby, pp. 11–55. Albuquerque: University of New Mexico Press.
———. 1977. Cultural Prerequisites for Grammatical Analysis. In *Linguistics and Anthropology*, ed. M. Saville-Troike, pp. 139–151. Georgetown University Roundtable. Washington, DC: Georgetown University Press.
———. 1979. Language Structure and Linguistic Ideology. In *The Elements: A Parasession on Linguistic Units and Levels*, eds. P. R. Clyne, William Hanks, and C. Hofbauer, pp. 193–247. Chicago: Chicago Linguistic Society.
———. 1981. The Limits of Awareness. Working Papers in *Sociolinguistics* 84. Austin: Southwest Educational Development Laboratory.
———. 1984. The "Value" of Objectual Language. Paper delivered at a symposium of the 83rd American Anthropology Association Meetings, Denver, CO.
———. 1985. Language and the Culture of Gender: At the Intersection of Structure, Usage and Ideology. In *Semiotic Mediation*, eds. Elizabeth Mertz and Richard J. Parmentier, pp. 219–259. Orlando: Academic Press.
———. 1993. Metapragmatic Discourse and Metapragmatic Function. In *Reflexive Language: Reported Speech and Metapragmatics*, ed. John Lucy, pp. 33–58. Cambridge: Cambridge University Press.
———. 1996a. Indexical Order and the Dialectics of Sociolinguistic Life. In *Symposium about Language and Society-Austin* III: (Proceedings of the Third Annual Symposium about Laqnguage and Society), ed. Risako Ide, Rebecca Parker, and Yukako Sunaoshi, pp. 266–295. Austin: Texas Linguistic Forum.
———. 1996b. The Secret Life of Texts. In *Natural Histories of Discourse*, eds. Michael Silverstein and Greg Urban, pp. 81–105. Chicago: University of Chigago Press.
———1998. The Use and Utility of Ideology: A Commentary. In *Language Ideologies: Practice and Theory*, ed. Bambi Schieffelin, Kathryn Woolard, and Paul Kroskrity, pp. 123–145. New York: Oxford University Press.
Silverstein, Michael, and Greg Urban, eds. 1996a. *Natural Histories of Discourse*. Chicago: University of Chicago Press.
———. 1996b. The Natural History of Discourse. In *Natural Histories of Discourse*, ed. Michael Silverstein and Greg Urban, pp. 1–17. Chicago: University of Chicago Press.
Singer, Milton. 1989. Pronouns, Persons, and the Semiotic Self. In *Semiotics, Self, and Society*, ed. Benjamin Lee and Greg Urban, pp. 229–296. New York: Mouton de Gruyter.
Stephenson, John. 1968. *Shiloh: Case Study of a Mountain Community*. Lexington: University of Kentucky Press.
Stewart, Kathleen. 1988. Nostalgia—A Polemic. *Cultural Anthropology* 3: 227–241.
———. 1996a. An Occupied Place. In *Senses of Place*, ed. Steve Feld and Keith Basso, pp. 137–165. Santa Fe: School of American Research.
———. 1996b. *A Space on the Side of the Road: Cutlural Poetics in an "Other" America*. Princeton: Princeton University Press.
Strathern, Andrew. 1971. *The Rope of Moka: Big-Men and Ceremonial Exchange in Mount Hagen, New Guinea*. New York: Cambridge University Press.

Stross, Brian. 1976. Speaking of Speaking: Tenejapa Tzeltal Metalinguistics. In *Explorations in the Ethnography of Speaking*, ed. Richard Bauman and Joel Sherzer, pp. 213–239. New York: Cambridge University Press.

Tanz, Christine. 1987. Introduction Part II. In *Language, Gender & Sex in Comparative Perspective,* ed. Susan U. Philips, Susan Steele, and Christine Tanz, pp. 163–177. New York: Cambridge University Press.

Taylor, John R. 1989. Possessive Genitives in English. *Linguistics* 27: 663–686.

———. 1996. *Possessives in English: An Exploration in Cognitive Grammar*. Oxford: Clarendon.

Titon, Jeff Todd. 1988. *Powerhouse for God: Speech, Chant, and Song in an Appalachian Baptist Church*. Austin: University of Texas Press.

Toynbee, Arnold J. 1935. *A Study of History*, Vol. 2. Oxford: Oxford University Press.

Urban, Greg. 1985. The Semiotics of Two Speech Styles in Shokleng. In *Semiotic Mediation*, ed. E. Mertz and R. Parmentier, pp. 311–329. New York: Academic Press.

———. 1988. Ritual Wailing in Amerindian Brazil. *American Anthropologist* 90: 385–400.

———. 1989. The "I" of Discourse. In *Semiotics, Self, and Society*, ed. Benjamin Lee and Greg Urban, pp. 27–52. New York: Mouton de Gruyter.

———. 1991. *A Discourse-Centered Approach to Culture: Native South American Myths and Rituals*. Austin: University of Texas Press.

———. 1993. The Represented Functions of Speech in Shokleng Myth. In *Reflexive Language: Reported Speech and Metapragmatics*, ed. John A. Lucy, pp. 241–286. Austin: University of Texas Press.

———. 1996a. Entextualization, Replication, and Power. In *Natural Histories of Discourse*, ed. Michael Silverstein and Greg Urban, pp. 21–44. Chicago: University of Chicago Press.

———. 1996b. *Metaphysical Community: The Interplay of the Senses and the Intellect*. Austin: University of Texas Press.

Urban, Greg, and Benjamin Lee. 1989. Introduction. In *Semiotics, Self, and Society*, ed. Benjamin Lee and Greg Urban, pp. 1–14. New York: Mouton de Gruyter.

Ury, William. 1982. *Talk Out or Walk Out: The Role and Control of Conflict in a Kentucky Coal Mine*. PhD dissertation, Harvard University.

Voloshinov, Vladimir. 1973 [1930]. *Marxism and the Philosophy of Language*. Trans. Ladislav Matejka and I. R. Titunik. New York: Seminar Press.

Wallerstein, Immanuel. 1974. *The Modern World System*. 3 vols. New York: Academic.

Weigel, M. Margaret, and Ronald Weigel. 1985. Directive Use in a Migrant Agricultural Community: A Test of Ervin-Tripp's Hypotheses. *Language in Society* 14: 63–80.

Weiner, Annette. 1992. *Inalienable Possessions*. Berkeley: University of California Press.

Weller, Jack. 1965. *Yesterday's People: Life in Contemporary Appalachia*. Lexington: University Press of Kentucky.

Whisnant, David. 1981. *Modernizing the Mountaineer: People, Power, and Planning in Appalachia*. Boone: Appalachian Consortium Press.

———. 1983. *All That Is Native and Fine: The Politics of Culture in an American Region*. Chapel Hill: University of North Carolina Press.

Whorf, Benjamin Lee. 1956 [1939]. *Language, Thought, and Reality: Selected Writings of Benjamin Lee Whorf*, ed. J. B. Carroll. Cambridge, MA: MIT Press.

Wigginton, Elliot, ed. 1972. *The Foxfire Book*. New York: Doubleday.

Williams, Cratis. 1992. *Southern Mountain Speech*. Berea, KY: Berea College Press.

Williams, Michael Ann. 1995. *Great Smoky Mountains Folklife*. Jackson: University Press of Mississippi.
Williams, Raymond. 1977. *Marxism and Literature*. Oxford: Oxford University Press.
Wolfram, Walt. 1977. On the Linguistic Study of Appalachian Speech. *Appalachian Journal* 5: 92–102.
Wolfram, Walt, and Donna Christian. 1975. *Sociolinguistic Variables in Appalachian Dialects*. Final Report No. NIE-G-74–0026. Washington, DC: National Institute of Education.
———. 1976. *Appalachian Speech*. Arlington: Center for Applied Linguistics.
Wolfram, Walt, and Ralph Fasold. 1974. *The Study of Social Dialects in American English*. Englewood Cliffs: Prentice-Hall.
Wolfram, Walt, and Natalie Schilling-Estes. 1998. *American English: Dialects and Variation*. Malden, MA: Blackwell.
Woodbury, Anthony C. 1987. Rhetorical Structure in a Central Alaskan Yupik Eskimo Traditional Narrative. In *Native American Discourse: Poetics and Rhetoric*, ed. Joel Sherzer and Anthony C. Woodbury, pp. 176–239. New York: Cambridge University Press.
Woolard, Kathryn. 1989. *Double Talk: Bilingualism and the Politics of Ethnicity in Catalonia*. Stanford: Stanford University Press.
———. 1998. Introduction: Language Ideology as a Field of Inquiry. In *Language Ideologies: Practice and Theory*, ed. Bambi Schieffelin, Kathryn Woolard, and Paul Kroskrity, pp. 3–47. New York: Oxford University Press.
Woolard, Kathryn A., and Bambi B. Schieffelin. 1994. Language Ideology. *Annual Review of Anthropology* 23: 55–82.

INDEX